WAY OF THE TRADE

Since 1996, Bloomberg Press has published books for financial professionals on investing, economics, and policy affecting investors. Titles are written by leading practitioners and authorities, and have been translated into more than 20 languages.

The Bloomberg Financial Series provides both core reference knowledge and actionable information for financial professionals. The books are written by experts familiar with the work flows, challenges, and demands of investment professionals who trade the markets, manage money, and analyze investments in their capacity of growing and protecting wealth, hedging risk, and generating revenue.

For a list of available titles, please visit our website at www.wiley.com/go/bloombergpress.

WAY OF THE TRADE

Tactical Applications of Underground Trading Methods for Traders and Investors

Jea Yu

BLOOMBERG PRESS
An Imprint of
WILEY

Cover images: katana © iStockphoto.com/Rick Sargeant; dramatic sunset © iStockphoto.com/Godmode; charts courtesy of Jea Yu
Cover design: C. Wallace

Published by John Wiley & Sons, Inc., Hoboken, New Jersey.
Published simultaneously in Canada.

For general information on our other products and services or for technical support, please contact our Customer Care Department within the United States at (800) 762-2974, outside the United States at (317) 572-3993 or fax (317) 572-4002.

Wiley publishes in a variety of print and electronic formats and by print-on-demand. Some material included with standard print versions of this book may not be included in e-books or in print-on-demand. If this book refers to media such as a CD or DVD that is not included in the version you purchased, you may download this material at http://booksupport.wiley.com. For more information about Wiley products, visit www.wiley.com.

Library of Congress Cataloging-in-Publication Data:

Yu, Jea.
Way of the trade : tactical applications of underground trading methods for traders and investors / Jea Yu.
pages cm.—(Bloomberg financial series)
Includes index.
ISBN 978-1-118-59068-3 (cloth); ISBN 978-1-118-66279-3 (ebk);
ISBN 978-1-118-66273-1 (ebk)
1. Electronic trading of securities. I. Title.
HG4515.95Y938 2013
332.64'202854678–dc23

2013007473

Printed in the United States of America.
10 9 8 7 6 5 4 3 2 1

Discovery consists of seeing what everybody has seen and thinking what nobody has thought.

—Albert von Szent-Gyorgyi

Contents

Preface

Way of the Trade covers the hands-on tactical applications of the UndergroundTrader trading methods in the new computerized algorithm-driven market place with an optimized market-tested hybrid approach for intraday, swing, and portfolio traders. The book addresses market realities in all their facets, not just concepts, through a first-hand point of view perspective complete with illustrations, analysis, lessons, case studies, insights, and stories. The delivery is multilayered and lateral to purposely challenge the conventional (shortchanged) mindset to stimulate, entertain, and ultimately enlighten the reader in the ways of the trade. The Way implies truth. Simplicity is an end goal that appeals to the masses. In the markets, the outcome of any trade will be green or red, profit or loss, simplicity in only two possible outcomes, but that's linear hindsight mentality.

Pure simplicity is a product of the relentless effort to meticulously improve efficiency while concurrently streamlining the process, often derived from a need to fill a void or fend off counterparties/competition. Technology embraces this same essence with faster, smaller, and cheaper. Moore's Law has been consistent for over 50 years, as it observes that chips will double the number of transistors and performance every two years as size, cost, and density decrease. The nature of efficient trading seeks to capitalize on the highest quality of price movement to maximize probability and profits while minimizing risk. The markets do provide these pockets of high quality price movements shuffled between mind-numbing headfakes, wiggles, and chop.

Reality reveals that the deck is very much stacked against the retail trader tangled in the false notion that markets are an even playing field. These same thunder and tumbleweeds markets are ruled by the algorithms and high-frequency programs that kidnap liquidity and extort it for ransom at the highest costs to participants. They conjure thunderous volume-backed movement in specific 15- to 30-minute cycles that suck in retail traders, only to rug-pull it out at the point of max pain, leaving nothing more than tumbleweeds afterward. Textbook breakout patterns rise just enough to trigger "confirmations" to suck in the most participants on the wrong side of the trade to twist the knife until panic ensues, forcing retail traders to bail out, only to bounce afterward.

Welcome to the "new" market landscape in the same minus sum game of trading. One that has "evolved" with the speed of technology-driven computer algorithms, high-frequency trading programs that can front run/hijack/kidnap liquidity in milliseconds, stuffing 20,000 bid/ask quotes at such blazing speeds that the rest of the market stands still as they pull their orders faster than the blink of an eye. These robots have access to the "invisible" liquidity occupying over 34 different dark pools that splice spreads into four-decimal-place increments untouchable and invisible to the retail trader. The only thing even about this playing field is that the algorithm (algo) and high-frequency trading (HFT) programs don't discriminate; every participant is prey, man or machine. Therein lies the clue to gaming the algos. The cliché "my enemy's enemy is my friend" comes to mind.

Add to that the rapid race with the media outlets to instantly produce the most market-jarring news/ rumors (same thing) from unnamed sources highlighting game-changing events or the rise of worldwide central banks with their artificial interventions topped off with back-tracked readjusted economic reports. Never have traders/investors been so overwhelmed, misled, and abandoned to fend for themselves. The landscape has unequivocally changed . . . whispering a very familiar quote, "'Necessity is the mother of invention." Thus *Way of the Trade* was written out of the necessity to address the application of the trading methods to the new algorithm-dominated thunder and tumbleweeds landscape.

Active evolution is not just growth, maturity, or experience—all of which occur passively with little or no effort (as long as you are still breathing). Active evolution often requires catastrophic trauma to shed the dead skin and stimulate a rebirth. Active enduring effort must perpetually be applied efficiently to nurture improvement beyond the prior thresholds to surpass prior limitations to develop a more refined template. Rinse and repeat. This is the essence of active evolution.

Not everyone can or is willing to go through that process (most may not even realize there is a process). Fortunately, that process is not required of all participants. The journey is one that most participants will identify with and hopefully learn from. Ultimate simplicity leads to purity. To attain simplicity comes from constant refinement of the process. This has been my journey.

Figure I.1 illustrates a wiggle-free trend move that can be tracked and played as you get acclimated to the application of the Katana.

FIGURE I.1 Wiggle-free trend move.

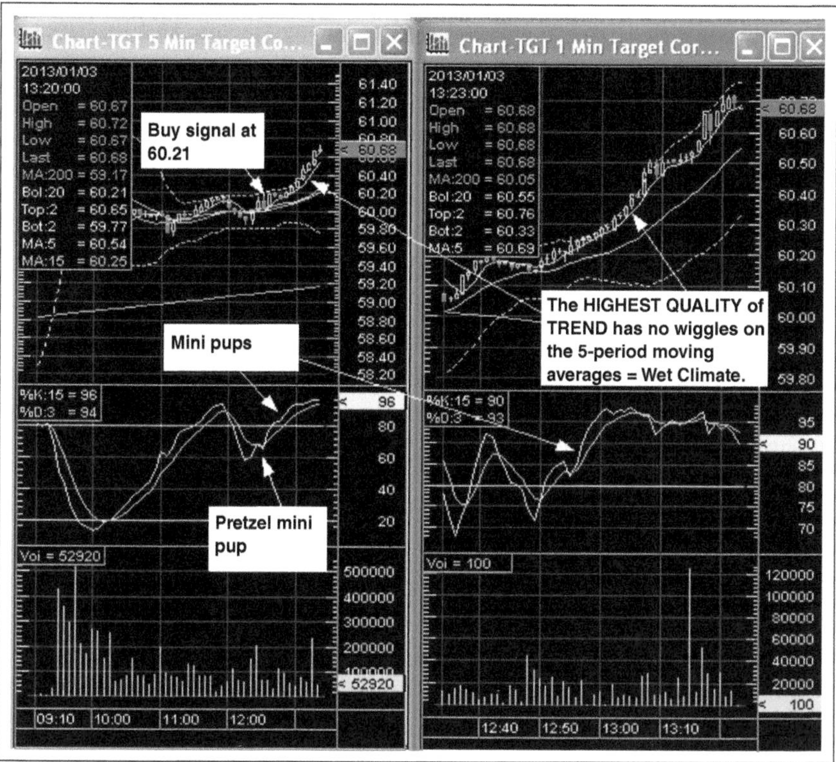

The purpose of this book is to clearly define the landscapes, the proper application, and the management of the methods while introducing new skillsets to further evolve readers in their journey to efficiently generate the desired outcome: to achieve consistent and compounding profits in all market landscapes or at least optimize the ones they are best accustomed to. Less is more. This is efficiency's manifesto. The high-quality price movements occur less than 20 percent of the time while noise takes up the other 80 percent. Most traders have to shuffle, trade, and struggle through the 80 percent in order to capture part of the 20 percent. With my refined methods, I go into very specific details on making that 20 percent portion your playing field while avoiding the 80 percent junk. This is efficiency. Constantly venturing through the 80 percent of the market noise is not only damaging to your capital, but erosive mentally, physically, and spiritually.

While the prior UndergroundTrader book series addressed a niche market catering exclusively to active traders, this book, with the distribution muscle of John Wiley & Sons and Bloomberg Press, will be inclusive to ALL retail market participants aka humanoids, including current/former (unemployed) daytraders, part-time/casual traders, swing traders, and investors. I address my own evolution of expanding services at UndergroundTrader.com with UndergroundSwingTrades.com and Benzinga Morning Profit Maker, out of necessity. I detail the collaborative evolution of styles that created the hybrid method that merges skill sets of the daytrader and investor.

The top daytraders of yesteryear have mostly disappeared, but the ones who are thriving now have evolved. They haven't learned to trade faster or more often; the computers would eat them alive. Conventional rebate, opening orders, pairs, and spread trading have lost their edges. Traders that manually practiced these strategies have tombstones that read DEATH BY ALGO. The evolution comes in the form of hybrid trading. While algorithms evolve in their speed, execution, and optimized coding, humanoids need to take a hybrid approach with the inclusion of portfolio trading.

The fertile active trading periods exist in spurt cycles and diminish quickly. A decade ago, I would shake my head at holding a position more than a few minutes or watching beyond the 3- and 1-minute charts. Now, I hold portfolio positions that fade the market for weeks to months at a time. This isn't the traditional form of buy and hold investing, but a market-calibrated portfolio management system that combines the precision execution, technical analysis, risk averseness, and timing of a daytrader merged with the voracious fundamental teardown scrutiny and analytics of an activist investor.

Over 70 percent of the trading volume on the U.S. exchanges is generated by computer program trades, which last on average 11 seconds. Over 70 percent of total volume is now done off-exchanges on over 34 dark pool exchanges. The liquidity can dry up so quickly that what appears to be a simple price wiggle can turn into a collapsing breakdown in a matter of seconds. What does this mean? It means the algos have the big guns and unlimited ammo.

They say you can't bring a knife to a gunfight. Considering the retail trader is only equipped with the equivalent of a knife, that conventional line of thinking is pretty depressing. Here's a lateral approach.

You CAN bring a knife to a gunfight . . . as long as there are other participants in the free for all. The more targets/participants there are, the more your odds of survival increase. Elements such as landscape, terrain, and climate will have a direct impact on the outcome. In fact, the elements alone can determine the outcome regardless of weapons. What good is a gun if you are butt-naked in subzero temperatures lost in the mountains? Would you rather be butt-naked and armed with a gun or fully clothed in insulated mountain apparel and a dull knife? With the latter, you could just let the elements play their role as the naked dude freezes nearly to death armed with his gun, while you stay warm, out of the line of fire until the coast is clear to score the kill. People fall victim to the elements in the markets just as they do in life. Speaking of knives, who needs a knife when you can wield a masterfully crafted Katana?

This Is the Way of the Trade

The applications, principles, methods, strategies, and philosophies in this book have been painstakingly manifested, handcrafted, and meticulously developed to flow as naturally and seamlessly as possible.

How Do You Take 1 from 19 and Get 20?

This book seeks to cover all the nuances within the trading system as if they were efficiently applied to the new market landscapes, climates, and terrain. I will also go into the most comprehensive details on every variation; stage, type, outcome, and game play on the proprietary perfect storm price pattern with tons of color examples. The overlooked, missing, and misunderstood components are fully addressed, for instance: how to use the algorithm and high-frequency programs to magnify your own profits. The hybrid portfolio trading skillset is covered in full detail. All the nuances of the application of the refined methods will be covered exhaustively and in depth.

In a nutshell, the flow starts with a descriptive narrative of how the markets have changed, mutated, to get to this point. The view from the turret is laid out. The evolution of the participants and the skillsets that have survived with each style are addressed in detail because they are the components of the new cross-bred player. Exhaustive attention is placed on the core trading system and methods. Most importantly, the application of the system is thoroughly detailed with real examples. The research process is categorized and labeled with step-by-step routines as never before, covered in depth. Stock selection is half the battle, which is the reason for covering all aspects, from finding candidates to trade, to how much time to allocate on the layers of research contingent on the type of trade, to determining targets and risk ahead of time. No matter how seasoned you are, that first trade of the day is like diving into cold water. The encounter covers all aspects of execution from entry to exit. The most significant by-product is the formation of a new style, portfolio trading, which is addressed meticulously: seamlessly shift gears to adapt to the market landscape, conditions, and terrain with deadly precision and skill.

The content is meticulously laid out to flow logically and seamlessly transition to further depths. Take your time and let it sink in. *Trading Full Circle* filled the gaps. *Way of the Trade* applies the skillsets, focusing on manifesting that by-product called consistent profits through the masterful application of the Katana seamlessly adapted to each market terrain.

Simplicity leads to purity. Purity is the truth, the essence of the WAY. In order to achieve this, three questions must always be answered: when, where, and how? To elaborate, this means when (to engage), where (to trade; stock selection in context of macro market conditions), and how (to execute and manage the trading system for optimum efficiency). At the outset, it appears simple. Underneath is where the complexity abounds, as factors come into play that render parts of the system ineffective at times. It is this below-the-surface complexity that frustrates, confuses, and ultimately extinguishes the fires for most people. I've witnessed this firsthand in real time through my services. The heartbreak of the decline of daytraders on my membership at UndergroundTrader.com ultimately led to the realization that not all people want to sit in front of the computer nine hours a day taking pieces out of the market (or getting taken by the market), nor do they have the ability to perform consistently through long periods. Some people were excellent executioners in the mornings only to be chopped away paper-cut-style all day long. Some people were just too busy and didn't have the time to participate in the momentum periods and foolishly pushed during tumbleweed periods to compensate only to dig deeper into the hole. Some people simply had a higher tolerance for pullbacks and wanted to focus on longer-term management ineffectively during downturns. The different templates go on and on. This forced me to adjust my mindset to accept and adapt to other styles beyond the intraday scalping methodology and art. I'll go over the timeline of landscape changes from an insider's perspective. The naked eye of the average retail trader would notice the effect maybe six months down the road, and the media perhaps 10 months, and the regulatory agencies at least 12 to15 months. In mid-2009, a very good friend of mine who led a team of proprietary traders was in shock. His guys, who were the most talented group of naturally gifted intuitive traders on the street, were getting massacred. These guys were heavy liquidity traders taking upwards of 50 to 100k positions playing market maker at times without the advantage of order flow. They were normally pulling 5 to 15k daily gains with drawdowns around 50 percent of that amount. Each one of these guys was generating 5 to 10 million shares in monthly volume. To me, they were the survivors of the daytrading era; despite decimalization and bull and bear markets, they had captured a niche magnificently. Yet things had changed drastically in a matter of months. His guys were getting picked off at every liquidity inflection point. Mind you, these guys thrived during the whole 2008 market meltdown each having been through the SOES bandit era, Internet bubble, recession, and housing boom, evolving from momentum to technical to a hybridized infusion of godly sensitivity meshed with inhumanly gifted intuitive reflexes. These were the highest caliber of natural intraday grinders I had ever known. In moments of capitulation where the masses panicked, they would covertly buy in, knowing intimately the slingshot reversal would kick in as it had done thousands of times and vice versa on spikes. However, instead of getting filled, the liquidity was being absorbed in thousands of pennies ahead of them on scale-ins and scale-outs, essentially trapping them and then savagely reversing the momentum and twisting the knife by magnifying the reversal of the reversal three to five to seven deviations to stop them out before reversion back to the mean—unreal and unprecedented. If it were a few instances or a few days, it could be written off as fluke. Instead, this happened routinely every single trading day getting worse and more extreme. This element left nothing on the table as it ravaged insatiably all the liquidity while spoofing bid/asks to manipulate the very essence of perception. The more tolerance they built up, the more the extremes would get stretched. Eventually, they were obliterated in a matter of months. A tree falls in the woods and no one hears it, right? To the naked eye of a retail investor, they had absolutely no clue. The first transparent evidence of the damage and residual effects of these new participants would be loudly illustrated by the Flash Crash of 2010.

A new phenomenon had injected itself into the very mechanics of the markets right at the point of execution. This element was methodically swiping liquidity, squeezing margins, and magnifying the extremes as outlier movements became the norm. Welcome to the rise of the HFTs, high-frequency trading programs. These programs were bid stuffing 20,000 quotes in milliseconds only to knee-jerk reactions under the guise of liquidity and demand. A simple 1,000 share order would evaporate many levels of bids the second it was put into the queue. All of a sudden, the playing field wasn't even the real playing field. Dark pools grew with access only to the institutional members. The penny spreads were split into thousandths of a penny. Spikes and drops came out of nowhere only to knee-jerk buyers to pay the highest price and panic out at the lowest price, rinse and repeat. This was the dawn of a new mutation not visible to the public until the Flash Crash of 2010. The HFT programs didn't cause the Flash Crash by shorting the markets. They were accomplices by pumping up the markets and then pulling out when the need for liquidity was abandoned. The public is pacified and kept at ease with rising equity markets. However, when the rise is artificially manipulated by leapfrogging HFT programs that create a hollow core, the inevitable collapse is magnified to extremes as illustrated by the 1,000-point Flash Crash on May 6, 2010.

I use these methods every single trading day with my services and trades. This is my baby that has grown painstakingly through the years as paradigms shift and landscapes alter. I've learned that there is always an invisible factor that requires more lateral thinking beyond the conventional ways. The markets will never be an even playing field. This is a foregone conclusion. The retail traders and investors will always be at the short end of the stick—misled, misinformed, and ultimately led to accept the belief that the market is always right. The markets are a man-made computerized monstrosity that feeds itself by cannibalizing its weakest participants. They say you can shear a sheep many times but only skin him once. The flagrant arrogance of the HFT infestation crossed that line by skinning the retail investor one too many times, causing a mass exodus and outflow of funds while ironically zombie markets continue to climb higher. Our own Fed, led by Ben Bernanke, has punished the savers into pushing toward risk instruments by implementing a zero interest rate policy (ZIRP) to very little avail. Compounding the effects of the Internet bubble, real estate bubble, decimalization, and the influx of HFT programs have done the most damage to investor confidence.

Before we set course, I have a simple riddle that personifies the essence of linear versus lateral. I like to call it layered thinking and the necessary mindset. Riddle me this: How do you take 1 from 19 and get 20?

If you know the answer, likely it's because you've already heard the riddle and the answer. It's not cheating. It's familiarity. The goal of the riddle is to stump those who have not heard it before as they strive to linearly curve fit a correct answer. The difference between knowing the answer and not is obvious. It's the haves and have-nots based solely on familiarity. That exemplifies my purpose: to provide familiarity through my eyes and my tactical daily application of the methods on a multilevel playing field through all landscapes and skillsets, so that you are familiar with what's in front of you. The wherewithal to react is in your hands. This is THE WAY OF THE TRADE.

Oh by the way, regarding the riddle, convert to Roman numerals. Figure it out from there!

Once figured out, the reaction may be that it's not fair and it's a trick question and so forth. This pretty much parallels the outcries of the retail trader/investor in these markets. All linear reactions are fostered through conventional (non)wisdom. The purpose is not to interpret, but to game the layered reactions of the other participants based on their interpretations.

Acknowledgments

I dedicate this manifesto to my fascinating daughter, Katana, whose unconditional love is only matched by her beauty, wit, determination, curiosity, warm daily hugs, and macro awesomeness; and my wonderful loving wife, Benita, for smacking me when no one else could and embracing me when no one else would, for being my inspiration and childhood soulmate. Special thanks to John Boyer for being my sentinel and extraordinary friend all these years, whose inspiration, brilliance, and foresight can only be matched by his unflinching loyalty, integrity, sincerity, and humility. Thanks to Bill and Linda Hughes, Murphy, and Trapper for awakening me to the nurturing effect that family can have on one's spirit and the nourishing effect the crockpot has on one's appetite. To Joe and Benita Villari Sr. and Dad for always looking out from beyond the clouds. To my momma, Duck Yu, for giving birth to me, instilling the template of determination, and proving yourself always right in the end, even when you think you're wrong. To Juliay Tippett-Yu, who married a marvelous and talented soulmate in Dr. Jesse, for giving birth to two amazing kids, Kiera and Broden, while still being my baby sister. To Frank Villari, for being an amazing brother-in-law, who is the embodiment of old-school suave, class, and swag wrapped in humility and respect, and favorite uncle to my daughter. To Phil Meade for over a decade of protection, guidance, and unconditional support even after the luster wore off, who has been by my side through the whole rollercoaster ride, who picked me up, brushed me off and inspired me to believe in myself to continue grinding forward. To Steve Schmidt for your faith and support. To my brother in arms, Danny Nourdin, thank you for always looking out for my best interests and guarding my family, for being a true Sentinel. To Wilson Chang, my closest friend, for two decades of unconditional friendship and brotherhood. To Kyle and Kenny for being the embodiments of relentless perseverance and innovation. Thanks to Suri Duddella for his appendix contribution to the manifesto. And to karma for a breathtaking roller coaster ride from the depths of the gutter to heaven . . . and back to the gutter and heaven (on a daily basis), rinse and repeat.

CHAPTER 1

The Mutation

The term *underground* suggests something hidden from the masses, be it a tangible product, information, a service, a movement, or a philosophy. It implies something special due to its rarity. As anything gets surfaced, becomes widespread, conventional, and mainstream, the urge for replenishing the depth transpires. That urge becomes a necessity.

It was that necessity that sparked the birth of UndergroundTrader.com in 1998. There was the craving to dig, discover, deliver, and share a deeper understanding of the markets and to find ways to capitalize from the knowledge. When someone quips, "Wow, that is deep . . .," that's the acknowledgement of depth, and UndergroundTrader.com is all about soaking, eating, drinking, sleeping, and swimming in depth. We are full of it! Depth, that is.

The deeper you dig, the more you grow to appreciate depth. This is how you develop a passion for it. The true students and aficionados of any endeavor share a deep passion for the depth of knowledge, be it Italian wines, haute cuisine, fashion, antiques, baseball cards, architecture, scrap booking, quantum physics, astrology, knitting, engineering, trading and so forth. The deeper you delve into any endeavor, the more passionate you become. This is organic and feeds the natural inclination for growth. *Not to work from the ground up, but from the surface DOWN.* The best way to trigger that innate hunger is to reveal the simplistic purity of what lies beneath. The surface is a footnote at best. My hope is that this book opens your mind, fuels your spirit, and purposefully directs your efforts on refining the A + B process, which will produce the by-product of C.

This is the essence of underground. It is way beneath the surface, and the only way to get there is by digging your way by shovel (or credit card). The passion for depth and the comfort of sharing that with a community of like-minded humanoids is the house of UndergroundTrader.

In my book *Trading Full Circle*, I said the journey is the reward. Here, in *Way of the Trade*, I'm saying the journey produces a by-product prize. The deeper one digs reaching more depth, the more of this heavenly prize one attains. What is this prize you ask? Knowledge? Close, but not quite. The prize is Enlightenment.

When very specific, much sought after, deprived knowledge is acquired it bridges the gaps and fills the voids allowing the current to flow uninterrupted to the light bulb! The synapses get overloaded with a power surge of depth that triggers a euphoric chemical reaction from the stimulation of dopamine production. Enlightenment is a drug. Enlightenment is nourishment for the soul. That makes UndergroundTrader.com the temple, or pharmacy, for those hungering for this heavenly prize. *Way of the Trade* is a pill that you should swallow at your own pace to let the enlightenment manifest itself and flow warmly and continuously.

The Phantom Menace

I thought *Trading Full Circle* (2010) would be the last book, wrapping up the UndergroundTrader legacy series (*Guide*, *Secrets*, and *Full Circle*). I assumed that the self-calibrating methods that I painstakingly and slowly developed were efficient enough to handle all market conditions. The methods can be adapted as a complete system or taken piecemeal to add-on and complement existing systems. Even though all the tools, methods, plays, and setups were carefully laid out, it became apparent that the proper application of the system needed to be clarified in more depth. This was amplified by the invisible infestation of a game-changing force that would permanently alter the DNA of market landscapes in unprecedented form.

These new elements are algorithmic and high-frequency trading programs. The monstrous volatility they created has churned through two generations of retail traders and arrogantly broken the cardinal philosophy of the ax. You can shear a sheep limitless times but can only skin it once. The aftermath of 2010 to 2011 resulted in the skinning of retail investors as fund outflows hit record highs. Zombie markets have risen controlled by the strings of the computers. This element has permanently augmented the nature of the landscape, which in turn requires adjustments to the application of the methods.

Let's go through a timeline of market landscapes and how the trading was during those periods in what I call *A Stroll Down Memory Lane: 1996 to 2012.*

1996 to 1997: Pacific Rim Crisis; Scourge of the Specialist, Rise of Daytrading

This era of Small-Order Execution System (SOES) bandits gained transparency as it became more mainstream. Online brokers were getting started. Datek created an electronic communications network (ECN) called ISLAND that provided direct fills between retail participants and even arbitrage opportunities against market makers. ARCA was developed shortly after. Instinet was an institutional-only accessible ECN that impacted momentum dramatically. INCA on level 2 was the precursor to the dark pools that emerged over a decade later where access was only to institutional professionals. Level 2 screen data became more popular as the ax market maker dominated the action in Nasdaq stocks. Specialists were cheating everyone with their front running guised under the notion of providing an orderly market. They had full monopoly control on order flow. I hated how these rats favored institutional clients and completely defrauded retail traders with their slow fills at garbage prices. I seriously hated trading NYSE stocks and stuck exclusively to trading Nasdaq stocks, where there were more market makers and competition among the participants. Prices were posted in fractions making for healthy profits on scalps.

The Pacific Rim crisis triggered a 554-point plunge on October 27, 1997, on the Dow Jones Industrial Average or 7.2 percent as the NYSE halted trading twice ending the session on a halt (wussies!). Nasdaq kept trading. Markets started to plunge the next morning again until Lou Gerstner, CEO of IBM, came out and announced that IBM was implementing a billion-dollar stock buyback in the open market! Since IBM was a Dow Jones component stock, this pulled up the Dow from –186 to close +137 on the day. Gerstner saved the markets! Alan Greenspan, chairman of the Federal Open Market Committee (FOMC), started his series of 11 rate cuts, which boosted equities markets. Some of these surprise rate cuts came in the middle of the day, which shocked the bears into sheer terror and a short-covering frenzy as markets were launched to the moon (with bears cuffed to the rocket).

1998 to 2000: Rise of the Daytrader: Internet Bubble, Irrational Exuberance

These were the mythical glory days of daytrading. A dinky record company called K-Tel released news that it was implementing an e-commerce website. No big deal, right? Wrong. The stock shot up from $7 to $70! This kicked off the Internet mania in technology stocks. Stocks like YHOO rose from $12 to $500 (pre-splits)! Countless stocks went from single digits to triple digits in a matter of days! Anything that had to do with the Internet soared to the stratosphere. Stock splits would spike stocks into and after the splits regularly. I remember a company called Netbank soaring from $20s to $150 in days. Daytraders piled into anything that had a head of steam, and market makers propped up tech stocks like there was no tomorrow. Everyone and his cousins were daytrading; making up to five figures a day was normal. A company called Zitel exploited the Y2K bug fears and sent its stock soaring from $4s to $200! No joke! Genome stocks like ENMD gapped from $5s to $70s on a press release. Fuel cell stocks like BLDP and FCEL were trading at over $100 a share! It was commonplace on any day to see stocks going from $10 to $40. Mark Cuban sold his Internet telecasting company Broadcast.com to Yahoo! for over a billion dollars in YHOO stock while it was trading above $300. The IPO market was ridiculous, as stocks priced at $30s would regularly open over $100. PALM was priced somewhere between $30 and $40 and opened up to $120! Overnight Internet millionaires and billionaires were being created daily. It was crazy! Stocks like BRCM and JDSU traded in the $200s and moved in a 20- to 30-point daily range. JDSU bought out fiber company SDLI for more than $400 a share! Switch and router makers like ESRX and QLGC were trading upper $100s. CSCO traded over $90, MSFT $100, EBAY in the $300s, QCOM split so many times as it literally brushed up to $1,000, and the Nasdaq Index rose to 5,000! The Dow Jones broke 10,000.

My T1 line with a whopping 1 mps download speed cost me $1,600 a month, but safe to say, that was a drop in the bucket with the piles of money the market was throwing around. I had 15 CRT monitors that provided enough heat and radiation to feel like summertime in the dead of winter and the pits of hell in summer.

Greenspan created a monster, and implemented a tightening policy by raising rates (six more times) to cool things down. He started to inject the term *irrational exuberance* into the FOMC statements. That's like setting the house on fire and then pointing it out to the fire truck. Which leads us to . . . oh, the horror . . .

2000 to 2003: Death of Daytrading; Internet Bubble Burst, Nasdaq Collapse, Bear Market Armageddon

All those rate cut eventually hit the equity markets in March 2000 as the technology-heavy Nasdaq peaked at an intraday all-time high of 5,132 before starting its death drop to an intraday low of 1,108 on October 10, 2002! Numerous Internet companies went bust during this period. YHOO tanked from over $220 to $13 a share, PMCS and AMCC went from the $100s to under $10, JDSU and CIEN went from the $100s to under $20, PALM collapsed under $10, and the list goes on and on. Daytraders got driven out of the markets by margin calls and heavy losses. IPO millionaires who didn't sell stock got decimated for capital gains taxes when they exercised options. For example, a company called Intraware traded up to $140 after its IPO. The stock collapsed to $55. The CEO's stockbroker advised him to exercise his options to take advantage of the cheap shares because it was eventually going back to triple digits. He exercised his options to buy shares under $1 when the stock was trading in the $50s, but he didn't sell any shares. The stock collapsed under $4 a share. To his horror, he found out that he owes over $3 million in capital gains taxes since exercising options is considered a capital gain even if you don't sell the shares. This same tragedy hit numerous IPO executives and insiders who exercised options and didn't liquidate their stock during the bubble. Mark Cuban was astute enough to collar his 14.6 million shares of YHOO stock trading in the split-adjusted $200s as it collapsed to $13s and to walk away with over a billion dollars from his sale of Broadcast.com.

The SEC implemented the pattern daytrader (PDT) rule to "protect" the little guy, and the exchanges approved decimalization. This one-two punch along with the bear market plunge pretty much wiped out the casual daytraders, along with most of the market makers on the Nasdaq. It may have also inadvertently sparked the birth of high-frequency trading programs that would ultimately exploit the spreads in thousandths of a penny. The 9/11 terrorist attacks on the World Trade Center further halted the exchanges and pummeled equity markets lower. The United States entered a recession and bear market until President Bush invaded Iraq in 2003. This put a bottom in the markets as the SPY bounced off a low in the mid $70s. Greenspan killed the equities markets with his drastic rate hikes after his drastic rate cuts. After the 9/11 attacks, he implemented a series of rate cuts again taking rates down to 1 percent by 2004. This caused the dollar to tank, while commodities and real estate skyrocketed. Thank you Mr. Greenspan for bubble number two!

2004 to 2007: Rise of the Bull Market and Housing Bubble

Markets started their recovery. Daytrading was still stifled due to PDT rules and the horrible decimalization squeezing profits. Level 2 lost its luster as chart reading played a bigger role. Housing stocks went into hyperdrive with home prices and financials. Credit was available to everyone. Investment banks generated record profits, unloading tons and tons of exotic derivative products that were linked to real estate, and funny paper spread like wildfire among the hedge funds and institutions. Goldman Sachs took over the world. The public went from flipping stocks to flipping houses. Everyone owned a mortgage company. The words *bad* and *credit* didn't exist in the same sentence. Countrywide Financial made a killing bilking everyone on subprime loans as CEO Angelo Mozilo dumped $139 million's worth of stock while assuring the public and shareholders there was no real estate bubble (and maintaining his year-long permatan). Program trading activity rose. Greenspan split for the private sector. Dow Jones peaked out at 14,164 in October 2007, all was good . . . and then . . . oh no . . . not again . . .

2008 to 2010: Real Estate Bubble Collapse, Global Financial Crisis, Stock Market Plunge

Yes, it happened again. The real estate and housing collapse took down the overleveraged institutions and financials that loaded up on the toxic paper. Bear Stearns and Lehman Brothers collapsed. The financials heavy Dow Jones Industrial Average collapsed to 6,600s by March 2009, where it finally bottomed out. Fears of a global collapse in the financial system prompted the Fed to issue the Troubled Asset Relief Program (TARP) to buy into the biggest U.S. banks thereby injecting cash and liquidity that would flow down to the consumers. Instead, banks turned to more profitable applications of the money by loading up on debt in emerging markets and more derivatives. The Fed implemented quantitative easing, literally printing money and killing off the USD, which worked to prop up equities markets and asset prices. The Dow Jones recovered back to 12,000s as banks and financials reinflated after the deleveraging. Retail investors and traders were driven out of the marketplace as participation and volume collapsed. High-volume prop rebate traders were still killing it with the volatility. Oddly, equities markets continued to rise despite mutual fund outflows. What was causing this?

2010 to 2012: Market Recovery, European Crisis, Rise of the Algos, and Dark Pools

Equity markets continued to float higher, but volatility rose even as overall market volume continued to drop. The market tended to have periods of extreme volatility, and then it evaporated. The last 30 minutes tended to get a crazy spike, driving up the markets into the close. The European debt crisis struck fears of global contagion as the paranoia of 2008 resurfaced. The algos and high-frequency trading (HFT) programs ran rampant as they received mass media attention after the 1,000-point intraday Flash Crash. HFTs and algos continued to run wild in 2011 as volatility went through the roof as the Dow Jones chopped in a 3,000-point range: 20 to 30 point S&P 500 futures gaps became commonplace. Prop traders got flushed hard by a phantom menace that purposely perverted the reversion methods past crazy standard deviation levels to trip everyone's stops long or short. What seemed like fat-fingered flukes continued to turn into a regular occurrence as out of control quote stuffing was so fast it delayed quotes for minutes at a time all the while tripping stops. This was serious because the most skilled prop shop gunslingers were getting smoked and vaporized at alarming rates. The algos/HFT machines wiped out prop traders as they emerged from the shadows and out of the dark pools, which also got media attention.

The Fed and Bernanke implemented more quantitative easing programs, driving up risk assets and further killing the U.S. dollar (USD). Bonds and fixed-income assets entered a bubble. Equities markets floated their way back on unprecedented central bank interventions from the European Central Bank (ECB), Federal Opening Market Committee (FOMC), Bank of Japan (BOJ), and so on. The SPY collapsed to $108s before bottoming and climbing back toward $140s by year-end 2012. The Mayan calendar was wrong.

Phew. I may be off on exact numbers and obviously left a lot out, but that's the general gist of what I remember from the past 15 years off the top of my head. Let me get a little more detailed about the high-frequency trading programs.

2009 to 2012: Rise of the Algorithm (Algos), High-Frequency Trading (HFT) Programs, Dark Pools and the Infamous Kill Switch

This was when the HFTs were most prominent and hit the point of maximum, almost blatant, transparency. We're talking pornographic. There was a type of HFT program called a *disrupter* that when switched on would literally scramble the futures in volatile shakes as it controlled the market by stuffing thousands of bids and asks to panic and nudging through knee-jerk reactions by participants in all directions. The typical HFT program would stuff a ton of bids at all levels to generate the appearance of hungry bidders, but if you tried to hit the bid to sell, they could pull their top bids in milliseconds (thousandths of a second) so fast they would never get hit and obligated to buy. This is called *spoofing*. If you were a willing buyer and put your order to buy on the bid, they could come in .0001 higher and swoop in ahead of you to take the shares. In other words, they distorted the "true" market prices with their ability to manipulate the perception of supply and demand. When you are able to place thousands of orders in milliseconds, it's like being able to hold time still. When you are able to stuff the order queue with thousands of bid/asks at millisecond speeds, it overflows the electronic exchange buffers to literally stall out all the data as long as you want. In 2011, there was a point where the HFTs would quote stuff the open and close of the markets so hard that it would take 20 minutes to even get quotes to match up correctly on the open and the close was impossible to trade in the dark. The HFTs exploited this advantage to literally jam up the exchanges to leave orders out there for the picking while the participants are left in the dark as their quotes are stalled out. *As it turns out, the exchanges were providing co-location deals to many of these HFT shops, giving them even quicker access to data and order fills! The exchanges would benefit from all the volume they generated, but as it turns out, at the expense of retail participation as overall market volume had been sliding.*

Typical HFT Sheep Skinning Cycle in 2009 to 2012

To put this in perspective, this is a typical situation of how the HFTs killed off retail traders up to early 2012. Let's assume you took 2,000 shares of XYZ at 19.05 on a nice spike up as inside market is 19.35 × 19.36. You have your order cued up to take the scalp with a 19.30 limit price and hit the execute button, and then your quotes freeze up as your order sits there. You assume it's been filled as you wait for confirmation as your quotes lock up making it impossible to cancel or place new orders. By the time the quotes catch up, the stock is at 19.05 where you entered, but you are waiting on confirmation of the fill, which is delayed, and as you panic, you decide to try to sell again, getting a fill confirmation at 18.90 turning a profit into a loss on the delayed quotes (–$300 loss versus +$500 profit), then it spikes back up to 19.20, which deeply vexes you until you get the late confirmation that you were partially filled for 500 shares out at 19.30, which means you did sell 500 shares for a profit of +.25 each for a +$125 profit, which brings a little relief as it cuts the loss to –$175 until you realize that means you over sold 500 shares giving you a net short position of –500 shares from 18.90! You check the stock and to your horror, it has jammed back up to 19.40. You try to cover in a panic and figure you will use a market order this time to assure yourself a fill. You place your order to sell 500 shares at market as your quotes are stalling out again. To your shock the confirmation comes back at 19.65 on the buy to cover for another –.75 loss on 500 shares (–$375) as the stock pops to 19.80, but when quotes come back to normal, the price is back to 19.19 × 19.20 on the inside. You realize with three different quote feeds, you are getting three different sets of quotes as the latency is off on each one. M##$@%#!! *This triggers right fist launching into monitor (again).*

The HFTs methodically exploited the KILL SWITCH ability to lock up the quotes and delay true market pricing by *spoofing thousands of orders in milliseconds* to cherry pick their fills while the public was left staring at locked up or late price data *turning your $500 profit into a –$550 loss!!* They purposely jammed up the exchange queue systems to stall out quotes while cherry picking the limit/market and stop orders while the public was left in the dark! Let's not even mention how they had access to more than 30 different dark pools to arbitrage pricing at .0001 increment price improvements while the public was frozen in time. Brokers would blame the exchanges and the exchanges would blame it on a fast market while racking up blood money for co-location fees from the HFTs who were working their kill switches with abandon! This left the retail traders and the public with the tab in the form of losses. The lopsided advantage was so blatantly obvious at this point, at least for those at the pulse of the bull. It took the public and the regulators forever to figure this out.

This is how HFTs killed off so many retail traders toward the end of 2011, until volume disappeared after November as the market just floated on super-low volume into 2012. The SEC cracked down on the spoofing, but it's still there, just not as arrogantly obvious these days. You can shear a sheep many times, but you can only skin him once!

Algo/HFTs in 2012 and Beyond

There has been much debate and controversy about the negative effects of high-frequency trading programs (HFTs). The arguments range from stealing market liquidity, price manipulation, and unnecessary volatility to being responsible for the Flash Crash. Since the SEC reined in the spoofing and the exchanges increased their latency and beefed up the capacity of their quote systems, much of the illegal advantages of the HFTs has been stripped away, thankfully!

This was the single most destructive advantage that the HFTs exploited, the kill switch. They literally had a *kill switch* to lock up the exchange quote system, leaving the public in the dark with locked up or delayed pricing while their orders were left in space waiting to be raptured at will, with no ability to cancel them. Finally, this exploit was exposed and neutralized. The law of transparency set in as they were catching more heat from the public and the regulators. HFT activity declined, and oddly during the summer and fall months of 2012 there was very little noticeable activity, which accounted for a deep drop in market volume and volatility. Remember, this is my view coming from the pulse, which tends to get transparency months and sometimes years down the road. That's why we're underground. We are the first to feel the tremors before they are felt at the surface.

The HFTs started to show back up toward the end of 2012, which actually was a relief as the thin volatility made for long boring flat afternoon sessions. Be careful what you wish for is an adage that rings true. Personally, I like the new kinder, gentler, and defanged HFTs. These days, they are just kidnappers and extortionists, unlike the suicide bombers of yesteryear blowing up quote queues and retail accounts.

While there are many negatives to these programs, many are misguided as to the effects they still have on the market. These days equity HFT programs tend to lift markets not collapse them, albeit in an artificial manner. Artificially propping up prices results in a hollow core that produces more violent crashes like sell-offs. We saw lots of this last year. In fact, HFT activity was rampant last year, but the volatility was just too much of a shock to the system. The media and government scrutiny have diminished much of the activity. While the masses may think this is good for the markets, for traders, it's a bane. HFTs and traders feed on two things, volume and volatility. Fewer participants mean less liquidity. Thin liquidity works both ways as market drops are faster with fewer willing bidders, but markets can float higher just as well with fewer sellers to step in the way. This is why markets continue to float higher as the algos/HFTs come in at the end of the day to prop up prices.

This is a market where mechanics override fundamentals, just as liquidity overrides price and machines override humanoids. Volatility has actually dropped dramatically since the beginning of this year, yet we are still scarred by the effects of the 30-point S&P futures gaps up and down that we saw all through the months from last June to October. Just as human participants have dropped, so have the computer participants. Last year's crazy volatility took a toll not just on humanoids but also on the machines, which is the real reason for the lack of volume all year long, the lowest in five years!

These programs were running amok, causing retail traders to pay the highest prices for positions and then pulling the rug out from investors when they wanted to sell. This crazy volatility has burnt untold scores of retail investors and traders as they left the markets all together. The damage was done severely last year. Mutual fund outflows continue to rise even as markets seem to float higher while the economy seems to be barely chugging along with little to no improvement. Market volumes are at five-year lows, and yet equity markets are trading near their five-year highs! It's not the retail guy causing this, but the algo programs. They prop up the market at inflection points to knee jerk the institutions to buy and then back off. If they do their job right, that hollow core will get filled out with institutional bids that get lifted. Rinse and repeat . . . bam yearly highs! The same thing happened from October to December last year as the SPY floated from 117 to 132 on tumbleweed daily volume. The same thing is happening now. HFTs have been tamed a bit and know their role.

While there are numerous types of trading algorithms in the markets, I'm just focusing on the specific HFTs that provide the coiled spring–like price movement. I'm only addressing the resulting price movement. One thing that HFT's provide for sure is price movement while liquidity, hopefully, is provided by the participants.

If successfully executed, HFTs can generate hours and even days' worth of gains in minutes. The first 90 minutes of the day and last 45 minutes of the day are when the HFTs are most prevalent. They are most prevalent in the highest-volume movers, which include big 10 gappers and dumpers of the day as well as the top tier of the S&P 100 stocks. If there is one word to describe the effects of HFTs, it's *magnify*. They magnify the price movements in concentrated spurts of activity during specific periods of time.

The best way to game the HFTs is to go where they roam. HFTs leave a lot of victims along the way, so you better have a strong trading method/system in place. The key is to buy early and sell into the momentum. You have to have a method or system to play these effectively. Most importantly, you have to take your money and walk away. The more you tangle with HFTs, the more chances are you will give money back. This is why it's important to hit and run before the tumbleweeds set in. This is called the *liquidity trap*. There is nothing worse than a flat, light-volume, tight-ranged, choppy, limp market.

HFTs can magnify a .15 scalp profit to .30–.50–.70 or more if timed correctly. We are talking hours' worth of price movement generated in a concentrated 10- to 20-minute time period.

There are certain patterns that capture these magnified moves, which can be found in the first 30 minutes of trading. These patterns I've discovered are called mini pups and pups (pup = Power Uptik). These are market-tested tension patterns used with a combination of stochastics and moving averages that gives an edge for stepping into nominal gains but magnified gains when HFTs step in. HFTs step in during multiple pup setups known as perfect storms.

Figure 1.1 is an example of the power of concentrated HFT action on GMCR on September 10, 2012. GMCR had no news and opened at 27.70. The market was overall flat as the SPY traded in a .30 range for the open. However, GMCR got jammed from the 27.70s to the 29.50s in the first 30 minutes as the HFTs leapfrogged each other pumping bids to panic the shorts and triggering buyers to come in off the fence.

Notice the spike in volume in Figure 1.2 as shorts get squeezed and panic buyers come in at the highest point in the 29.50s at 10 A.M. as they jam it

FIGURE 1.1 The nature of HFTs as they purposely push bids beyond the nominal range to trap bears and bulls into chasing liquidity at the highest prices.

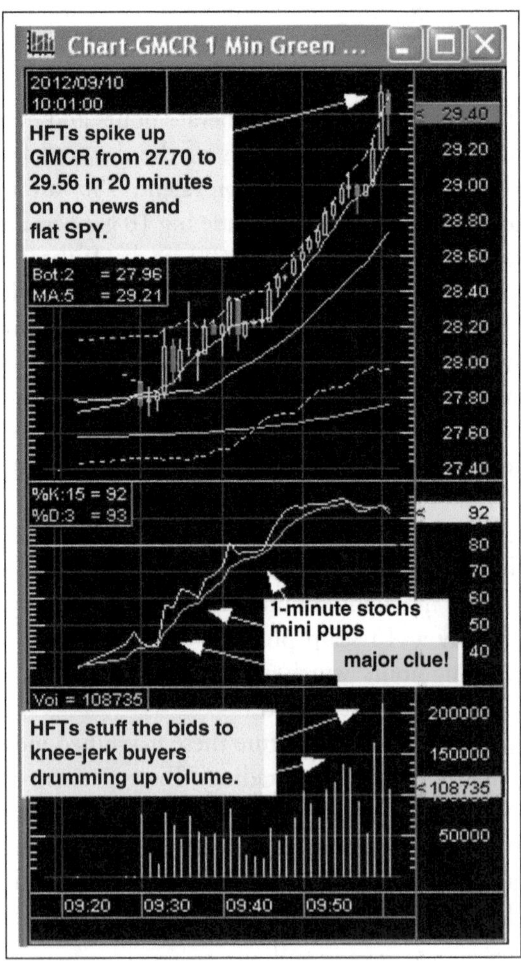

up +1.80 on no news or macro market movement. The HFTs back off the bids at 10:01 A.M. GMCR collapses -.60 to 29.20s to 28.90s as volume comes back down as HFTs walk away. The latecomers in the 29s pretty much got the rug pulled into the HFT riptide. This is what frustrates traders. Shorts got squeezed and late trend players got the rug pulled. So what is good about HFTs you might ask? How do you game the HFTs?

Figure 1.3 shows how we played GMCR's perfect storm breakout. We were able to scale out into tremendous liquidity at higher prices all due to the magnifying impact of the HFTs.

We took GMCR long at 28.10 on 9:36 A.M. and trimmed the spikes at 28.30, out +.20, at 28.50, out +.40 and locked 28.80, out +.70 as it spiked up through its daily upper Bollinger bands at 28.68. This is hours' worth of price movements compressed into less than 20 minutes after the market open! The

FIGURE 1.2 GMCR liquidity trap.

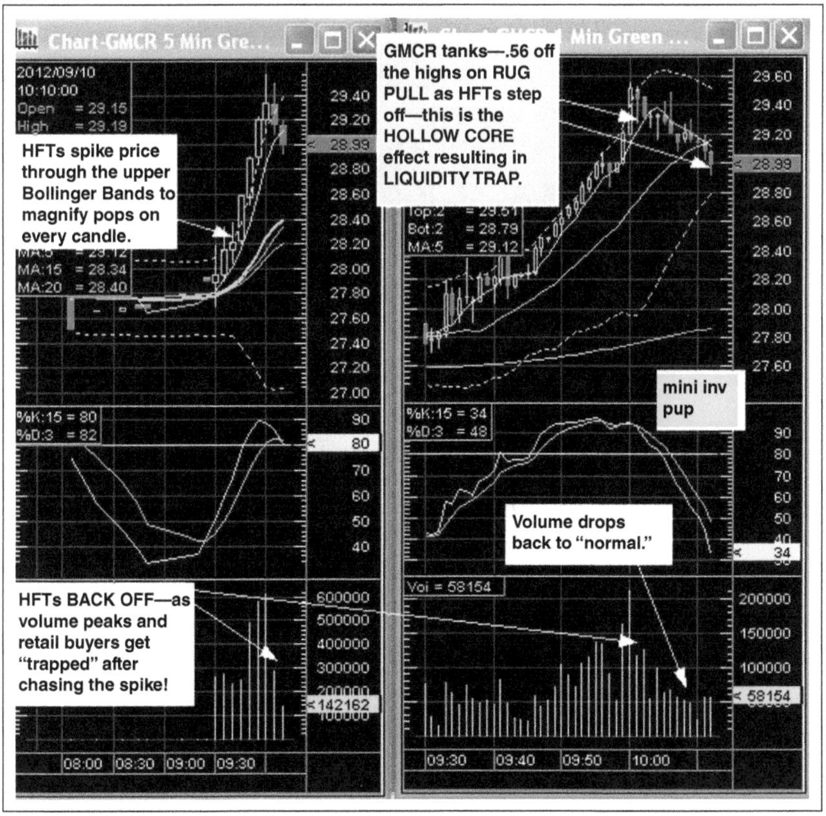

FIGURE 1.3 GMCR trade.

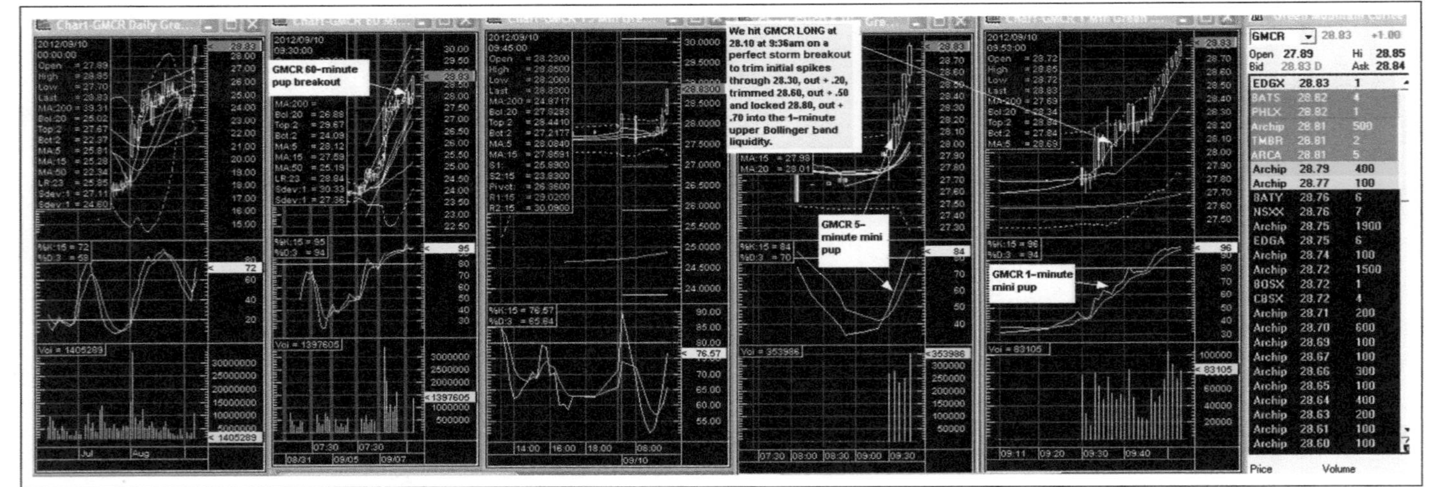

HFTs actually pushed this one even higher to 29.56 before rug pulling back down to 28.90s.

The key to gaming the HFTs is having a consistent trading method/system that feeds on volume and movement with the ability to foreshadow impending breakouts/breakdowns and can get you in at the optimum moments at the point of impact to ride the HFT-driven momentum. Play where the HFTs dwell and exit early into the momentum. Don't try to squeeze out the last drop. On GMCR, we left a lot on the table, but who cares? A normal .20 scalp ended up exiting with a .70 scaled out final exit. The problem is not getting out early . . . *it's getting in and out too late!*

Markets are rarely textbook anymore, only in hindsight. This makes detail in proper application a top priority. Proper application can often be fuzzy when you are in the eye of the storm. The boundaries of the reactions and which actions to take are matters that have to be fostered as a skill through repetition. The more you become familiar, the more you will be able to react. Moments of clarity move in unregulated cycles that must be capitalized on before they fade back into confusion. The HFTs contribute to the blurriness and chop that you see during most of the day. They stretch the extremes as a by-product of the leapfrogging nature of these programs.

The algos/HFTs profit by generating volume and magnifying momentum by luring in and trapping the greatest number of participants on the WRONG side of the trade so they can kidnap all the liquidity and ransom it out to the highest bidders.

It's true when HFT proponents claim they provide liquidity. They just provide liquidity to themselves first and ransom it BACK to the public! They don't steal liquidity, just as kidnappers don't steal their victims. They just borrow long enough to extort the highest prices for the return.

The heyday or most transparent period of the HFTs was during 2011 through the European debt crisis. While the public may assume stalled or delayed quotes were results of the overwhelming volatility and volume, the reality was a different story. HFTs literally had free rein to do whatever they wanted, most of which included infinite quote stuffing. I noticed this during the summer of 2011 when the market open would regularly stall out my quotes for 15 to 20 minutes from the open. I had five different quote sources (CobraIQ, Tradestation, E-signal, Etrade, Generic Trading, and Ameritrade) and every single one of them was stalled and delayed taking 15 to 20, sometimes a whole 30 minutes after market open to finally get the right quotes. I had Comcast and Verizon DSL Internet high-speed providers. I bought more hardware and faster boxes and yet the same problem came back. It dawned on me there was a very real problem with the exchanges or somewhere in between, but not my connections or quote providers as they were all giving me delayed quotes. This was when the HFTs were freely bid stuffing with no regard and throwing caution to the wind. For the first 20 minutes it was impossible to get correct prices; flying blind at best. The exchanges didn't admit any delays or problems, nor did the media, yet we noticed this very disruptive element showing its fist. This wasn't the birth of HFTs, but rather the heyday, as transparency reached its tipping point to a level where the regulators and eventually the public took notice (months later).

There was a rumor of an HFT algorithm sequence appropriately dubbed The Disruptor whose goal was to do nothing but bid/ask stuff the e-minis in a volatile range for a specific period of time resulting in a top-down effect of rogue ripple waves throughout the equity markets. The futures lead the equities.

The disruptor would literally blast static/white noise into the markets resonating at a violent pace to shake out as many participants as possible, which included the retail investors.

Imagine a small, shallow, calm pond without so much as a ripple. Then imagine someone taking a jackhammer to the bottom of the pond, then more jackhammers arriving to leapfrog the other jackhammers and weed whackers smacking the surface. That's what the disruptor and other similar HFT algorithms did. They hit the overnight futures to panic +/– 20–30 point S&P 500 e-minis futures gaps up and down. The damage was far-reaching. The HFTs did more damage to retail investors in 2010 through 2012 than the 2008 to 2009 market collapse. The heyday was from July through October 2011, when they tanked the SPY down to 117. Then, they floated the markets on super-light volume to 130 into the year end. Basically they traumatized and shook out most of the retail investors, and methodically squeezed out the bears on light to super-light volume. As the media, SEC, and FINRA started to catch on, they went more covert. They served more of a purpose to prop up markets rather than slam them down due to the heat from the Flash Crash. I'm sure many of these programs went belly up as well on the crazy volatility. However, their presence was there to catch falling markets and float them up. All they have to do is catch and pump to certain levels on the futures to trigger short covering and institutional buying. This was their main role for autumn-winter of 2011 all through 2012, to prop up the markets past certain price levels to keep the bulls from panicking and squeezing the bears. Yet mutual fund outflows continued to rise. The computers were responsible for more and more of the market volume. As a whole, the market volume had dropped to four-year lows as equities were hitting five-year highs. The anomaly had become the standard. Fundamentals and econ reports continued to show a flat recovery, yet markets continued to grind higher as these HFTs would come in near the end of the day to juice up the indexes. Bernanke and the Fed implemented quantitative easing 1, 2, and 3/infinity to pacify the bulls, encourage the HFTs, and screw over the bears regardless of fundamentals as each key component was getting eroded and the lower tiers were getting sold into the futures/index pops. This was the emergence of the zombie markets.

2012 and Beyond: Hybridization of Participants

True liquidity functions as a sponge that will absorb selling or buying. This is provided by willing participants who act as counterparties. HFTs aren't the root of liquidity. They are the middleman that dilute liquidity and manipulate the perception of the liquidity to serve its own needs.

Know the capacity of your pond. Being a big fish in a little pond may be an enviable position but it's only temporary. As evolution will have it, the little pond will ultimately be engulfed by a larger pond and so forth until the ocean engulfs it, or it simply dries up. This may have been the fateful oversight of my grinder buddies with the HFTs. They continued to fight them at their own game. The moral of the story is, when outgunned in battle, revert to utilizing landscape, climate, and terrain to your advantage. A dull blade is useless against a fully loaded AK-47 assault rifle in a one-on-one encounter in a closed-off space. If the landscape was in the jungle crawling with hungry crocodiles, poisonous snakes, and swarming mosquitoes, during a heavy rainstorm, then you can use the elements to tilt the advantage in your favor. As long as you don't fall victim yourself; by being prepared with the proper apparel and supplies, you could outlast your overzealous (naked and barefoot) opponent as his abilities get diminished and eroded by the elements. The longer he sticks around, the more risk he takes of getting attacked by any number of reptiles and insects.

They tried to outgun an opponent that was bigger, quicker, stronger, and never fatigues. The end result was bloody. The only formidable force to challenge high-frequency trading programs (HFTs) head-on is other HFTs or big institutional players, who are likely using some type of algo program. HFTs will just as quickly steal liquidity to find liquidity. HFTs don't absorb. The defining characteristic of liquidity is the intent and willingness to absorb. That is what liquidity is, like a paper towel absorbing spilled milk off the kitchen counter. True liquidity will absorb. This is why ECNs like ISLD and ARCA offer a rebate fee for those who buy on the inside bid and sell thereby providing liquidity. HFTs can swipe that liquidity in milliseconds or flash tons of inside bid/asks and never get hit since they can pull their orders faster than anyone can get filled.

They have the speed (milliseconds), access (direct connect to exchange servers and dark pools), and capital to leapfrog regular orders and kidnap liquidity at blazing speeds, forcing buyers to bid up and chase entries or panic out on evaporating bids on exits. They kidnap liquidity and ransom it off at elevated price levels.

In this sense, they are extremely risk averse. Rather they play the middleman to mildly absorb sellers and unload to buyers in minuscule increments. They spoof the bid/asks to manipulate perception in their favor and squeeze out the most liquidity to unload into.

Enter the Thunder and Tumbleweeds Market Trading Landscape

With the equity markets trading at four-year highs, one would assume the volume would also be keeping up. However, that is not the case as depleting volumes are trading at five-year lows. Computer-driven algorithms and high-frequency trading programs account for upwards of 70 percent of the actual daily market volume. These programs strike in spurts at specific price levels to magnify price movement at the least cost. This has resulted in a market environment that sees massive volume in compressed periods of time before vaporizing. In essence, this market produces thunderous volume generating fast momentum, which then abruptly vaporizes when HFTs step off leaving participants trapped staring at the tumbleweeds rolling by. Thunder and tumbleweeds are the new market environment.

The major pitfall of this environment is stepping into that riptide of volume by chasing price and then getting trapped in a position when the volume and liquidity dry up. Chasing thunder and getting trapped in the tumbleweeds is the common pitfall in this market.

The trick is to exit into the thunder before the tumbleweeds set in and then stay out of the tumbleweeds. While thunder can strike on any given stock at any given moment during the trading day, the market in general tends to have one single constant specific period of thunderous volume daily, that is the market open.

The first 45 minutes of the market open from 9:30 to 10:15 A.M. get the most volume of the day consistently, with the exceptions of FOMC rate decision days. The typical trading day starts off with the heaviest volume at the beginning as it tapers down dramatically through the middle of the day and tends to pick up in the final 90 minutes of the day as shown in Figure 1.4.

It's the first opportunity for the general public to react to news and developments. Many key economic reports like Institute for Supply Management (ISM), Consumer Price Index (CPI), and Michigan Sentiment get released in that time period. The volume tends to peak and then get a second wind up after the initial period from 10:15 A.M. to 11:00 A.M. That first 90 minutes is where the thunder forms and turns to tumbleweeds. This is where the biggest windows of opportunity exist to make profits and quickly. More importantly, this period also allows for opportunities to recover losses just as fast, if one is assertive enough. When one mousetrap fails, another one can be utilized during this window. After the 11 A.M. hour, the opportunities fade as the volume and liquidity fade. This doesn't means prices don't move, they just don't move in a tradable way, as choppiness and wiggles tend to overwhelm on light liquidity. Although volume tends to pick up in the last hour, much of the transparency in the markets has already been generated so the price movement can be just as choppy.

FIGURE 1.4 Heaviest and lowest volume periods during the day in this new Thunder and Tumbleweed landscape.

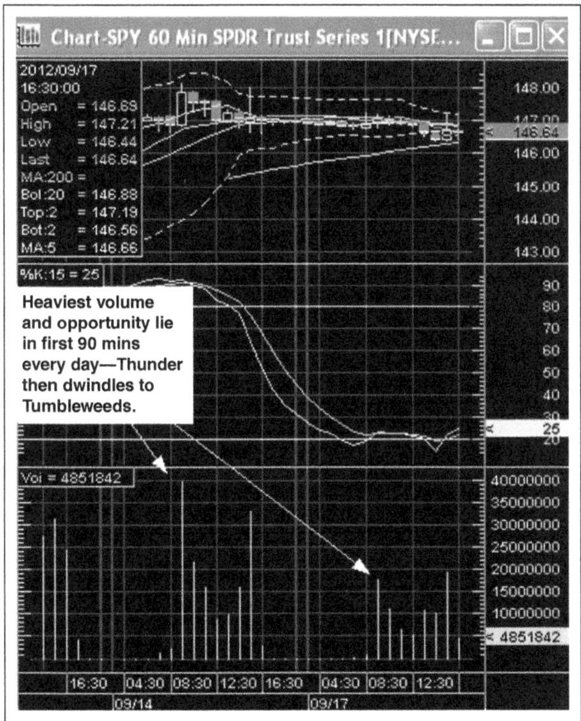

Hours and even days' worth of price movement can be found during this period and that's where traders should focus. In this market environment, *when you trade is even more important than how or what you trade.* A day's worth of gains can be made in a 10-to-20-minute time span, which frees up the rest of the day to pursue other activities. That's something everyone can appreciate. Tip the odds in your favor and stick to the thunder periods (9:30 to 11 A.M.) and avoid the tumbleweeds.

Defining Market Landscapes, Climates, and Terrains

There are three external factors that will affect your trades regardless of the specific technical setups, just as the weather can impact your drive to work. The destination remains the same, but the weather impacts your travel time, your route, and your mindset. The same routine drive to work on a clear spring morning could turn treacherous during a winter ice storm or summer hurricane. This analogy applies directly to the financial markets as there are three factors that have a direct impact on the outcome of your trades: landscape, climate, and terrain.

Landscape

Landscape depicts how the overall market ecosystem is functioning. Landscapes alter slowly, surely, and incrementally like the continental plates slowly shifting beneath the surface. The shift occurs long before the outbreak of transparency. The effects gradually materialize after the tipping point where the media and the public become aware: landscapes like the 1998 to 2000 momentum frenzy and the peak of the daytrading mania and implementation of decimalization, the real estate boom and bust cycle of 2008, the computerized algorithm/HFT infestation of 2009 to 2011, and their impact on the core mechanics of the markets and its participants. The year 2012 and forward have twisted into the thunder and tumbleweeds landscape where the remaining participants and computer programs leapfrog over each other in spurts of volume and liquidity before the landscape dries up into tumbleweeds where cannibalization of participations, liquidity, momentum, and transparency is the manifesto. It is this thunder and tumbleweeds landscape that has warranted the necessity to produce *Way of the Trade*. Landscape determines how to allocate and execute a trade.

As slick as the algo programs are, they are just programs composed of if-then scenarios. They have to be programmed by humanoids, namely programmers. They are so-called predictive only in a sense that the masses react a certain way at certain stress points, technical stress points that trigger emotions. However, with fewer human counterparties and emotions involved, the algos compete amongst themselves, usually offsetting each other in a scramble, if they are not leapfrogging. While it would be easier for me to cover each pattern setup and rules in a concrete if-then sequence, I've already done that with my prior books and notably in *Trading Full Circle*. The Law of Transparency is a double-edged sword. Once the rules are concrete and textbook, the edge comes from playing the other side. This is why classic patterns tend to fade or fail more lately because they have hit full transparency. Ironically, the paradox is that when things get too transparent, they fade, and the edge lies with the anomaly, until the anomaly is too transparent and then the classic pattern efficiency re-emerges. The name of the game is gaming the reactions of the counterparties. It's a constant shifting process that is invisible yet exists just like the wind. This sounds like a loop, and that's exactly what it is. It's a circle broken up into cycles. The easy concrete rules to play a specific pattern are not enough. If the cycle is anomalous, then the fades will override. The exceptions can easily become the norm, until they aren't. Being on the wrong side of the cycle is the surest way to blow out your account. The only way to be aware of this is by fostering your depth of knowledge, experience, and application. It's a process and journey that are beyond basic rules. The compass works until it doesn't work, and then it works again. Does this mean the compass is broken? Does this mean the compass is useless because of its inconsistency? If you think conventionally, you will say *yes*. It's broken half the time; let's find something that works all the time. Thus the search for the Holy Grail continues endlessly. Traders and investors have been so quick to ditch indicators, systems, and methods when they stop working, not realizing that the landscape is the cause of the malfunction.

If you think in depth, you will say no, it's working perfectly . . . in terms of the aforementioned, the compass is really doing one of two things . . . letting you know if we are in a classic stage landscape or an anomaly stage landscape. The compass itself *is* the indicator of what stage the landscape is in. If you realize this, then you understand how it can be used. Based on that inside information or tell, you are aware of when to put more chips in the pot and when to play defensively . . . to tread water until the compass works again. You know when to push and when to pull back. Do you see my point? It's about perspective not on the surface level, but from below . . . perspective from *depth* . . . underground. Embrace this concept that *the tool itself may only work half the time, but that in and of itself is a function of the tool.*

Climate

Climate refers to the tradability of the markets. If there is volume, liquidity, and follow-through, then I refer to this as a wet climate because it is fertile and provides nourishing opportunities. When the volume, liquidity, and follow-through dry up, then this is aptly referred to as a dry climate, like the desert that dehydrates, suffocates, and starves participants into attrition. Consolidations and make-or-break situations are dry climates, whereas breakouts, breakdowns, exhaustions, and reversals can be wet climates. Thunder is wet. Tumbleweeds are dry. Climate impacts the efficiency of the trade and plays a major role in determining whether a trade should even be warranted. Climates affect the outcomes dramatically. Climates not only apply on a daily basis with macro markets as a whole but also on a micro intraday level with individual stocks. The key distinguishing element between the climates is the presence of more active participants, which in turn spur more liquidity, momentum, follow-through, correlation intrasector and with the SPY, firmness of trends, and flexibility of price. The more participants there are, the wetter the climate. To illustrate the impact of climate, you can take a sloppy trader and an experienced veteran left to trade the same setup but separated by climate and over a series of 10 sessions, the sloppy trader will win the most. You can't attempt to change the market climate, but you can determine climate and adjust your trading to adapt to a climate change. The climate directly impacts the playing field and the outcome of your trades.

For example, a long trade made on a perfect storm breakout in a wet climate at 9:40 A.M. may reap a +.60 price move whereas the exact same setup at 12:30 P.M. in the afternoon in a dry climate may chop around for two hours giving off fake breakout and reversal signals to finally head fake toward +.40 by 3 P.M. if you aren't stopped out before then. The difference is significant. Efficient trading takes place in the wet climates. Whereas many traders will view the fast market as risky, the reality is that *risk is diminished greatly because the duration of exposure is minimized* since the price movement is rapid and direct as contrasted in Figure 1.5.

Dry Climates

Let's start with the bad news. Due to the lack of liquidity and volume in dry climates, participants thin out. This also causes very rigid stock prices and a lot of choppy head fakes resulting in stop and go action. The remaining participants tend to get panicked into positions, getting trapped and then panicked out of positions as the algo/HFT programs exterminate the humanoids.

FIGURE 1.5 Price Action in Wet and Dry Climates

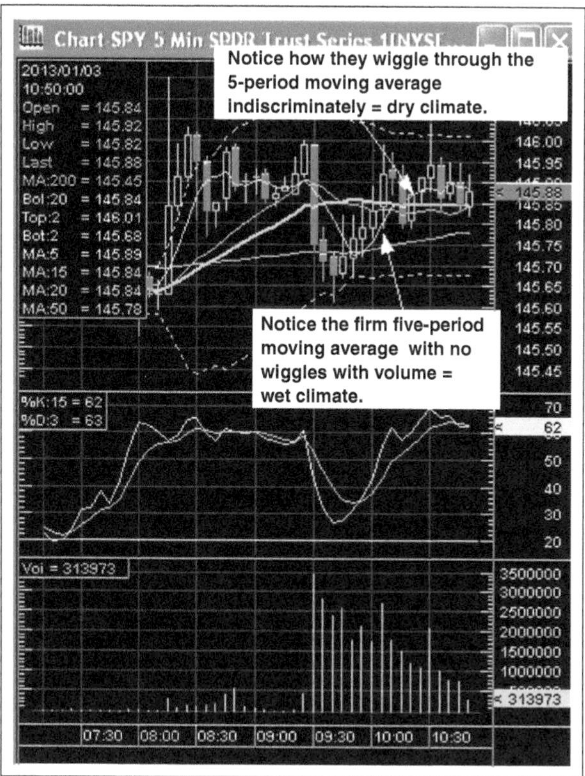

Do not chase positions long or short in dry climates. The bids may appear to be stacked and firm, but it's just a game of musical chairs. Vice versa applies on shorts where the offers appear heavy, stacked, and firm. The best method of execution is to fish the bids and asks to absorb into the flushes. This is still very dangerous as dry markets tend to overshoot past nominal levels since the objective is to panic out trend players and muscle out reversion/oscillation players. Scaling is an option but only with manageable allocations and the ability to stop out when all bets are off. It is too easy to let a scaled oscillation trade turn into a nasty reversal in a dry climate, since the slingshot coils tend to get diluted from the other participants that added into the countertrend. Therefore, it is best to avoid these periods unless you are scaling into a portfolio position trade. In a nutshell, dry climates are not forgiving and end up trapping most participants who average down. Dry climates (micro/intraday) tend to form around 11 A.M. to 2 P.M. EST most of the times. Dry climates warrant less trading, quicker profit taking, and patience to stay on the sidelines.

Dry climates = Thin liquidity with limited participants, low/falling volume, momentum cut short, inconsistent SPY and peer correlation, choppy/head fakes, thin liquidity, and rigid price movement for limited opportunities for profits, as illustrated in Figure 1.6.

Wet Climates

Wet climates have very robust and fluid price breaks generated from the abundance of active participants piling into the momentum. This creates ample follow-through and liquidity as trends absorb and deflect pullbacks. Wet climates tend to have very pronounced correlations with SPY (S&P 500 index exchange traded fund) and sector peer stocks. This allows a trader to enable defensive scaling techniques that will provide robust slingshots, allowing traders to reverse or scale up a position back to breakeven or profits. Wet climates are forgiving for those who are nimble with their analysis and reactions. The abundance of participants

FIGURE 1.6 Pinpointing the Intraday Dry Climate

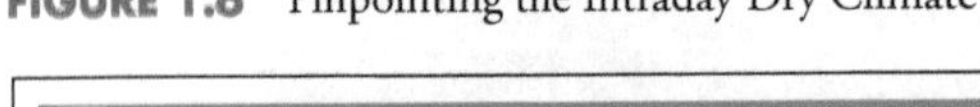

provides strong price moves with good liquidity while it lasts. The main caveat to this is that wet climates always erode back to dry climates. Therefore, it is imperative that traders unload their exposure prior to shifting back to the dry climate. Intraday wet climates consistently occupy the 9:30 to 11:00 A.M. and 2:30 to 4:00 P.M. EST of the market day, give or take 30 minutes. Wet climates provide more opportunities and warrant more size, more filter trades, and scaling profits.

> Wet climates = Thick liquidity, heavy/rising volume, strong follow-through, firm trend support, firm peer and SPY correlation, expanding ranges, and general price flexibility with expansive opportunities for profits.

The basic modus operandi is to thrive in wet climates and survive in dry climates, push and pull (see Figure 1.7).

Terrain

This refers to the type of style that best fits the environment. Markets that routinely gap intermittently up and down regularly are not conducive to position

FIGURE 1.7 The Alternating Nature of Market Climates

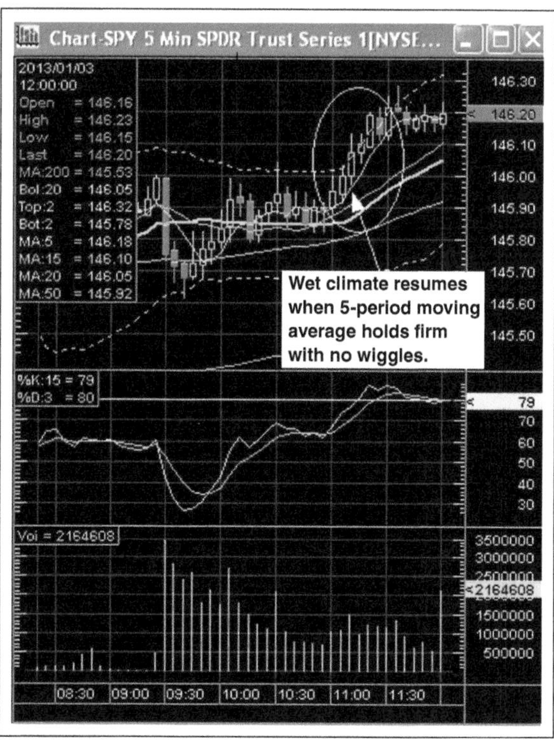

trading. This would be a scalp terrain. Whereas markets that slowly grind in one direction or another with little volatility and even volume are not conducive to scalping. This would be swing/position terrain. When markets are just choppy and unstable, usually in a wider shrinking consolidation range, then we call this a fruitless, flat, untradeable, no-man-zone terrain. These terrains are precursors to a tradable terrain so it's best to sit these out until the terrain shifts again. Terrain determines what type of trade will be most applicable.

Seasonal Macro Climates

Holiday-shortened weeks like Thanksgiving, Christmas, and New Year's, as well as mid-July and the end of August, provide an extra frustrating layer of dry climate as big participants leave for vacations and trips and close their books. Even if the indexes are up strong, the algo/HFTs steal all the liquidity leaving crumbs for the whiplashed humanoids. These periods are best to lie low for intraday trading, sticking to the morning action only. Swing traders tend to benefit better due to emphasis on the longer time frames.

The Five Laws of the Marketplace

I uncovered these five invisible laws through the years by identifying, experiencing, and connecting the constants (and violating them enough times to know they are laws!). I acknowledge, respect, and obey these laws as a matter of ritual. The literal interpretation of the laws should be followed, but try to observe how they resonate laterally across more than just the markets. They are straightforward in their definition but quite elusive in their application until you have a trading system structured to work with the laws, which I (we) do.

Law of Reciprocity

This law maintains nature's balance. In time, everything evens out. The intent is included in this law. To reciprocate is to show pure intentions supported by meaningful and equivalent actions. Karma enforces this law. Some people label it God, but even the motto "God helps those who help themselves" means to get off your rear and put in the effort to get something back!

In the markets, this means you attain by-products that are proportionate to the enduring effort you put in. The key is to make sure that your efforts are accounted for by directing them to the most efficient pipeline. Putting in the mundane work of scanning through charts and researching prospects, reading through earnings reports and conference call transcripts, while measuring price levels and then monitoring them day in and day out is time consuming but the effort gets rewarded, trust me. Through the years, I have streamlined and segmented the research process down to a four-leveled priority-based system, which I cover in full detail in Chapter 6. Working smarter comes from focusing on refining that A + B process, which I continue to do, because time spent should be time earned, as reflected in the payouts by Mr. Market.

Law of Linearity

Any tool, indicator, or pattern used to trade the markets should follow the law of linearity. In other words, they should apply equally to a 1-minute time frame, as they do to a 60-minute or monthly time frame. They should be scalable proportionately and relatively. This means that a breakout pattern on a wider time frame should react more or less identically on a shorter time frame with the only differentiating factors being the scale of the price ranges and the time to full transparency. The shorter time frames react quicker with more limited reactions on a small price range, whereas the wider time frames expand proportionately and relatively in range, duration, and price.

Shorter time frames react quicker and shorter, whereas wider time frames react slower and longer. By this metric, the wider time frames should also provide a foreshadowing effect so long as the shorter time frames converge in the same direction. What is powerful on a 5-minute time frame is even more powerful on a daily time frame. This is how we derive a somewhat predictive foreshadowing effect much like the Doppler radar used by meteorologists. This brings us upon the law of foreshadowing.

Law of Foreshadowing

The wider time frames with the identical powerful pattern formations carry the strongest undercurrents.

When a trader is too focused on the short term, he will likely miss out on the extended moves as they always appear identical initially, just as a wiggle appears identical to a reversal initially because they start off the same. The wiggle turns into a reversal because a relentless force continues to drive it past the nominal retracement levels thereby causing a reaction of stopping out the reversion players and inviting in the break/trend players.

The logic is simple, and it plays out. I believe it because I've seen it happen thousands of times. I've traded under this law thousands of times. I don't need faith because of the numerous incidents confirming this relationship. You may, on the other hand, need to start consciously observing this to get comfortable with the law of linearity. The one caveat is that the wider time frames also have more opportunities for the pattern to fall apart. The most transparent instances form when multiple time frames convey the same pattern simultaneously, which brings us to the law of convergence.

Law of Convergence

When multiple time frames exhibit the same pattern, the shortest time frames tend to be the trigger, which causes a domino effect taking a seemingly dormant wider time frame pattern into detonation mode. The effects are magnified beyond the short time frame move as the wider time frames carry the movement to greater price levels thereby magnifying the outcome. Simply put, when a powerful pattern forms on a wider time frame, it will still remain dormant until the shorter time frames turn in the same direction. This is when the transparency starts to form and participants take notice. If that wider time frame is a powerful pattern such as a pup/mini pup and the shorter time frames also contain pup/mini pups, then the detonation will form more aggressively, oftentimes in parabolic form. The law of convergence implies that most transparent movement occurs when patterns converge in the same direction on multiple time frames.

With linearity affirming that each link in the chain is just as strong as the next, and convergence affirming that detonation occurs when patterns align themselves in the same direction simultaneously, the law of foreshadowing implies that wider time frames will project the path of the shorter time frames like a Doppler radar.

Law of Transparency

This is the simplest and most violated law. Transparency is what every participant wants to capitalize on before the next guy. The purpose of trading is to capitalize on transparency before it becomes too transparent. Transparency, by nature, is elusive and fleeting. It is the proverbial window of opportunity. The law states that once transparency becomes obvious, it's too late (for that transparency). However, the opportunity to play the reversion of transparency builds proportionately as it gets more transparent. Rinse and repeat the other way. As it relates to the markets, it means catch the move early or fade it when it's too late.

Another variation of how this law applies is not just to market pricing, but also to ideas, beliefs, trends, and *apex predators*. HFTs got more media attention and public scrutiny after their flagrant activities reached the tipping point. The funny thing is they were instrumental in propping up the markets artificially at the end of the day. This formed a hollow core that would crater with any real selling pressure. This hollow core cracked during the Flash Crash of 2010 as the HFTs actually stepped away from the market, removing thousands of bids that never had any intention of buying. The crash was triggered by a fat-fingered 75,000 contract S&P 500 futures sell order that actually spooked HFT programs to step out of the market and pull their bids, leaving only the stub bids priced way out of the market to get filled. Stocks like PG sold at .01! The Dow plunged over 1,000 points in four minutes!

Their abuses were arrogant and reckless without restraint, and that violates the law of reciprocity. Break the law, and you get punished. They were scapegoated for the Flash Crash in 2010. Right perpetrators but wrong crime! This got the public aware of the existence of these programs, triggering investigations from the regulators and ultimately sanctions on spoofing.

The one constant with the markets is that no apex predator ever lasts. Once transparency reveals the existence of an apex predator, he becomes the target. In only that sense is the market efficient. Markets are not price efficient; they are only efficient in revealing transparency after the tipping point has been reached. It pays to be a ghost. Ghosts outlive apex predators.

The Profit By-Product

Why do you trade? Why do you invest? What is your GOAL?

The obvious answer is to make money/profits, right? This is the conventional answer, which means most people will give the same answer. It is this too obvious response that leads most traders right into the abyss almost effortlessly as they wear their tells on their sleeves.

Another question to pose. When is a small loss better in the long run over a big win? Or is a small loss ever better than a big win over the long run? If you answered *never* and *no*, then we need to set you back on the right track to diffuse the ticker on the time bomb that has been implanted.

If trading/investing were simplified down to an equation, it would look like this:

$$A + B = C$$

When presented with the question of what the goal of trading and investing is, the conventional answer would be profits. The C is profits as the outcome. With that perspective, the participant naturally focuses on doing anything to get C. The C is the priority that dictates all efforts. The C consumes and ultimately minimizes A and B. This is the seed planted that manifests into a curse. Everyone knows what he or she wants out of the markets; how to get there is the issue. How backwards is this? Talk about putting the cart in front of the horse.

This process judges excellence, not the outcome. Why? Because, if A and B are taken care of, then C, the outcome, is merely a foregone conclusion. Excellence focuses solely on A + B knowing that C is the simplest part of the equation. It's the logical outcome. Yet, the majority of focus for most people is on C, not the A and B.

What happens when you focus—consciously or subconsciously—too much on C?

You watch your profit-and-loss balance too closely with each uptick and downtick. Your emotions naturally get involved as you hold losers too long and winners too short. You watch your account balance more than the charts. You start to kick yourself for not taking profits earlier or taking stops earlier or for taking profits and stops too soon. The shoulda, woulda, coulda disease infects your psyche. Most importantly, your focus has been emotionally diverted away from assessing the flaws to solely cursing the outcome.

I've always admired depth—be it sports, professions, hobbies, food, wine, and so forth—that goes beyond the shallow, mainstream understanding of a genre. It takes effort to delve into the deeper understanding/appreciation that lies way below the surface. To the naked eye, the difference between a 9.6 grade and a 9.8 grade on a CGC certified issue of Spiderman #300 is virtually unnoticeable, but to a collector, it accounts for a 50 to 70 percent difference in value. The most subtle movement distinguishes a 9.9 score versus a 9.7 score in figure skating, diving, synchronized swimming, skateboarding, bodybuilding, and so forth. These are beyond the comprehension of the conventional crowd, because they entail *depth* (here we go with that word again!). It's a whole subclass that exists solely beneath the surface grouped together sharing the same appreciation.

The Model of Excellence: Shokunin

I saw a very enlightening documentary, *Jiro Dreams of Sushi* (Magnolia Pictures, 2011), which follows Jiro Ono, considered the premiere sushi chef in the world. He is 85 years old and graded Michelin three stars. Reservations must be made up to a year in advance for his 10-seat flagship restaurant, where a 20-minute meal consisting of 15 pieces of sushi starts at $350. That is the C of the A + B equation. Jiro doesn't focus on the C. At first glance, it seems eccentric, but the depth was illustrated as Jiro has stuck to a strict ritual for preparation and the tenacious, relentless pursuit of excellence for over 50 years. His interns must train for 10 years before they are even allowed to serve their first piece of sushi. The rigorous preparation of each piece of fish, seaweed, and rice is painstakingly prepared with the finest ingredients of each class. Massaging octopus by hand at room temperature after boiling for 50 minutes prior to serving, maintaining the cloudlike texture of the finest pieces of rice, meticulously fanning the richest seaweed over flames, aging the finest tuna—every detail is painstakingly repeated toward perfection at the moment it is served. They produce a seemingly simple product, fish served on top of a mold of rice. Yet this rigorous and relentless focus on the process produces a product so full of depth on an ethereal scale that it effortlessly blends each component together to magnify the purity so vibrantly that it's described as a spiritual awakening of the senses with each piece. American chef and television personality Anthony Bourdain did a segment at Jiro's restaurant, and he was literally shaking in awe as he nervously consumed each piece. Rigorous focus on the process dictates the outcome, A + B = C.

In trading, the C is obviously profits. The A and B can be ambiguous. Yet you can't arrive at C without the A and B components. A and B alone don't make C. A + B equals C. This implies the convergence, the merging of the two components.

Excellence is a condition that is generated by the efficient melding of A + B. What is excellence? Here are some situations:

1. To take a –.10 stop on a position as it pops .15 in the blink of an eye before the bottom falls out tanking it –.75.
2. To short a position that drops –.25 trimming 75 percent out into sellers and lock the final piece as it drops –.40, stalls and drops another –.40, before it climbs back +.80 and chops the rest of the day.
3. To short a position that pushed –.30 against you then –.50, to add the short there, before it collapses $1.50 while locking out a +.50 net profits in the next three minutes.
4. To take a long position into panic selling, being down –.30 before it spikes $1, while exiting with a +.50 net profit in the next five minutes.
5. To get out of a position flat as it pops +.30 then drops –.50 then pops +.20 then drops –.30 and then drops –.75 then pops +.80 then stalls in a .30 range for next two hours. Eliminate exposure in fizzle dry periods.
6. To take a long position as it slips –.50, keeping stops as it erodes another $1.

You may notice that not all of the situations produced a profit, some produced losses. The end result is still a profit. There is where most will leave it. The bottom line is what the majority focuses on, which is the C. However, the above six scenarios tell nothing about A or B.

To give it more color, let's say the allocations on the winners were double to that of the losers. That's impressive. Let's say that the headwinds were bearish as the market was sinking the whole time as the Dow Jones sold off from –100 to –225 in the above scenarios. That's even more impressive.

That additional color gives more depth to the caliber of the trades and the trader. It's that depth which only the true students of the markets can grasp. It's that depth and the focus on the process that will derive natural profits and minimize the drawdowns.

This may seem obvious and vague at the same time, but the goal is to plant the seed. Get your mind thinking from a different perspective. Imagine all the above scenarios happening consecutively. The net results are still a net profit.

Add in the rest of the context where the allocation on winning trades is double the positions on losing trades. That is excellence illustrated by the uncanny ability to generate consistency in inconsistent environments.

Grind out profits while minimizing losses consistently. It's not glamorous, but don't think for a second it's boring. Try unloading 50,000 shares of a long position in a falling market on a stock that does an average of 200,000 shares a day without so much as a ripple beyond .10 of the VWAP in a day with no market impact. That is the essence of excellence.

The point I'm trying to make is that an efficiently managed loss carries more weight than a poorly managed win in the long run. The first case reinforces a solid template that will smooth out performance in time and take measures against sustained degradation. The second case is a lucky break that sets a harmful template moving forward, as the trader will likely attempt to duplicate the outcome of the poorly managed win, especially in the face of adversity, and get plowed over sooner rather than later.

Be able to discern between a well-managed minimized loss versus a sloppy poorly managed win. Odds dictate in the long run the winner will give it all back and more to the market, whereas the risk-averse sound management that minimizes a loss will consistently be prosperous. If you can discern the difference and acknowledge the fluke nature of the win and revert back to tight management, then your performance should remain consistently positive over time. This is always a work in progress.

People, like markets, have muscle memory. They have a tendency to repeat things that are familiar to them for better or worse. It is human nature to fall into a routine that follows the path of least resistance. This is where the extra conscious effort is required to instill good habits and (re)align the course back on the right path, so that your performance smoothes out positively over the long run.

Is it really so wrong to have profits as a goal? Is it wrong to desire profits? No. It's just too obvious and as such, gets trampled during the process. The markets are a minus sum game, which means everyone can't possibly win. The majority of participants have to lose, as money gets transferred to the winning minority. The majority of participants focus solely on profits. Does it make any sense to follow the losing mindset? I would hope not.

Focusing solely on profits is what the market wants. When you prioritize profits over process, then you are easily susceptible to overlooking or ignoring flaws in your trading. As long as you are making a profit, everything must be okay—right? Failing to discern the quality of your trade management inadvertently sets the ticker on the time bomb that will inevitably expose your oversights in the most painful way.

The shallow profit motive is what the markets feed on to suck you back in or to keep you in long enough to drown and suffocate you. Markets can nudge you over that faint line where conviction turns into arrogance, which then turns into a tilt binge.

The answer to why you trade says more about the participant. The typical answer is the fallacy, usually derived through the simplest, non-effort conventional thinking. Any single flip of a coin, trade, or poker hand can rely on luck, as long as it ends there. It *never* ends there. One hand, one trade, one round, or one flip is anyone's game. If the sheep/fish wins, there will be more fresh meat on the way. That is the cycle of the food chain.

There is nothing more frustratingly misguided than a trader who thinks he's disciplining herself by being upset with a small profit as the stock rises much higher after their exit. As if the notion of being hard on themselves will somehow lead to better performance. This is the same person that will hold a losing position like a deer in the headlights during panic death drops. This same trader will then justify to himself how the position may be a good swing or investment play. The trader has inadvertently given control to the markets to determine what type of trade it will be. The market will take the opportunity to twist the knife deeper, forcing the trader to finally capitulate before it bounces. Rinse and repeat.

When you acquire the appreciation, the scale for excellence, then you realize the true goals of any trade. It's not profits. The profits should always be a by-product. The goal has to be focused on refining and improving the process. This lateral mindset is what will generate profits and minimize drawdowns consistently.

Excellence can be manifested through proper conditioning, which requires repetition and exposure in all situations and in all scenarios. This takes enduring effort and a lot of capital, unless efficiency is improved through quality training. Otherwise, blood must be shed, figuratively speaking. It can be a painfully debilitating process that most avoid. Excellent traders have what appears to be an instinctual timing mechanism that seems to get them out of harm's way, before disaster strikes. They can take many stop losses but still end up consistently profitable on the day. Outlier and anomalous situations don't shake them.

Masterful execution is only possible when one possesses an acute awareness of how the landscape, terrain, and climate influence results. To take purposeful action may appear to be sophomoric to the naked eye, but ultimately the depth of the early move finds transparency later on.

Purposeful actions produce the by-product of profits on a consistent basis. As the world collapses, they somehow walk away with profits or minimal drawdowns. As markets go parabolic, they walk away with profits or a minimal drawdown. As markets chop numbingly sideways, they walk away with profits or a minimal drawdown. See a pattern here? *Consistency breeds excellence.*

The Excellent State of Excellence

Traders who focus on continually manifesting excellence intimately realize that profits are the inevitable by-product. They acknowledge that *managing losses is as critical to excellence as managing wins.*

Those who focus solely on profits instead of the process are destined to fail. They will chase, panic, pray, and when all else fails ... gamble as desperation infests the psyche. They get minimized to the blotter where their very self-worth is based on the + or – tick of the position. Their account balance pulls the strings, and they will stay in too long on losing positions, add to losers, stop out too early on wiggles, give away their shares in panics, and get infected with the SWC disease. SWC is shoulda, woulda, coulda; it becomes a disease when it becomes latched to every trade. This disease manifests when the trader is insecure in his trading and always searching for an excuse rather than accepting the result and making the effort to work with what he has rather than what he doesn't. Looking back to analyze what could have been improved and noting the nuances is constructive. Kicking oneself nonstop so as to keep trading to make up for it and racking up losses is detrimental, especially when the climate changes from wet to dry. The same exact setup in a wet climate that produced a large fast move will sputter and chop in a dry climate later. The trader that goes in without adjusting to the dry climate will get his head handed to him, especially if he is desperately adding more size to make up for the lack of movement. The algo/HFTs will single him out and speed up his demise.

The lopsided broker stories of Microsoft's (MSFT) amazing return on investment if you bought and held it from the 1980s sets a blind eye or ignorance to the landscape changes from that period to now. The landscape was much different back then. The advent of computer algorithms and HFTS has completely changed the landscape. This should be obvious by now. These types of innuendos plant the wrong seed in the psyche.

This is degradation. Just planting a seed in the mind, with time, it becomes an embedded faulty cornerstone that will prevent the trader from evolving or maintaining consistency. Actually, they will consistently fail. That's not the consistency we are looking for. It's one we want to avoid.

Excellence ignores that. Excellence requires you to prepare before the trade and keep shoulda, woulda, coulda in check. Excellence smiles at victory, but it doesn't measure victory by profits alone. Excellence measures your reaction during the battle. Maintaining composure and foresight under fire, and the nimbleness to jump on the most optimal path at the time of the trade shows excellence. The ability to defensively sprawl scale in and out into liquidity just before the temporary slingshot bounce unravels again—this dance illustrates excellence in execution. Strive for excellence and the by-product is a foregone conclusion. Got it? Excellent . . . now let's move on.

Earnings Seasons: The Super Bowl of Momentum

I absolutely love earnings season. This is where the real action is. It is the equivalent to the Super Bowl, and it comes around four times a year lasting up to six weeks. The heart of the season is the second to fourth week with the highly liquid bellwethers that impact all the underlying peers with their reactions. The best opportunities come from gappers and dumpers, stocks that gap up big (gappers) or gap down big (dumpers) in reaction to their earnings report and guidance. It's a little difficult to define *big gap* as the size of the gap alone doesn't directly imply it will be a good prospect, especially if it is an unfamiliar thinly traded stock, which equates to less participants, which thins out the liquidity—and you know how much liquidity means to me! The existence of a significant gap up or down stirs up panic as it draws out the institutions, funds, algos/HFTs, and numerous participants in a massive eat-what-you-kill free-for-all that generates some of the highest volume days for the respective stocks. Stocks that tend to move very slowly will have periods of heavy volume and movement off the open. As for the impact of landscape, climate, and terrain, the landscape is secondary as the immediate concerns are in the now and present. The volume is magnified tremendously due to all the extra participants drawn to the gap, which means liquidity is abundant (if you are on the right side of the trade). The climate is as wet as it gets. The terrain calls for lacing up the daytrading boots (see Figure 1.8). I will go over the specifics on playing dumpers later in the book (after the perfect storms). For now, let's just focus on the general mechanics of this lovely period of spongy goodness with a cream filling.

Just a refresher, public companies report their earnings every quarter in a press release followed up with a live conference call where they often provide forward guidance, material updates, and answer questions from analysts.

The analysts who cover the particular stock will issue their upgrade/downgrade recommendations and price targets thereafter. The typical reaction will be for stock price to rise on better than expected results and/or raised forward guidance or stock falls if they missed the estimates and/or lower forward guidance numbers. This is the general flow of events, but there are always exceptions.

Stocks may gap or fall the next morning or dump and bounce, contingent on company and sector-specific earnings reports and influenced by any strong macro market movements.

I am only interested in the gapper/dumpers for the fast high-quality momentum moves via perfect storm price patterns and all their variations (which I go into in unprecedented depth in Chapter 5) in the first 90 minutes to scalp, like the trade illustrated in Figure 1.8. If any portfolio/swing positions report earnings, then it requires extra effort analyzing the results. The timing of executions and allocation still require the daytrading skillset, but may have to be tempered after the opening action with the swing/portfolio temperament to avoid panics.

Naturally the volatility cuts both ways. As fast as profits can be made, those profits can sink if you freeze or are caught on the wrong side. This takes experience not only with the patterns, but especially with the underlying stock. Many traders tend to shy away from the first 30 minutes of the open to let things settle down. In some market climates, that is a prudent thing to do. However, during earnings season when there are tons of gapper/dumpers, it is opportunity lost. This is the time to get aggressive, not in terms of putting yourself in an uncomfortable situation with too much size, but in terms of preparation and filtering down your prospects into candidates to track.

FIGURE 1.8 NAV perfect storm trade during wet climate.

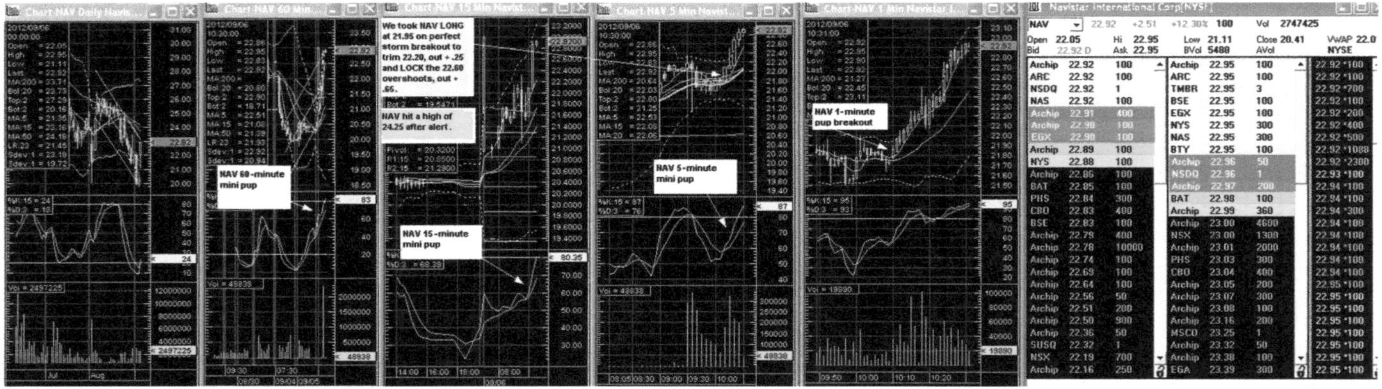

The earnings season is forgiving to those who are nimble enough to react. Such techniques as defensive sprawl scaling can be implemented to minimize losses or offensive sprawl scaling to maximize gains from a winning position. It is the climate that directly impacts the outcome. Earnings season is as wet as it gets. Having a solid group of filtered candidates on your watch list to track ensures that one broken wheel will not leave you stranded. Strange things can happen in earnings season that would almost never happen at any other time.

Immediate Crisis Panic Landscapes

When fear of an economic collapse, massive natural disaster, or terrorist incident occurs by surprise, there is a shock effect that rattles the markets as it goes into a crisis panic mode. In situations like this, fear overrides fundamentals and even technicals. In 2008, we saw the financial crisis. In 2011, we saw the impact of the European debt crisis as Greece, Spain, Italy, and France all shook the markets. The media plays the major role as they continue to spotlight doomsday further citing fear. The S&P 500 futures respond in common 20 to 30-plus handle gaps down and up.

In these cases, remember that the shorter holding periods are the most risk averse, which plays to daytrading skill. Overnight, swing and portfolio positions should have some form of a hedge. These outlier situations are where the most people get hurt as they either react emotionally with the panics or are frozen in fear. When in doubt, stay out. Remember that markets always revert back to periods of consolidation and basing. Of course, that's easier said in hindsight.

Global Influences: Europe, China, and the World

Once again, the shorter your holding periods, the more risk averse you remain. Don't overthink governments, central banks, or politics. We are playing the markets' reactions to events, not trying to predict the outcomes of events. The markets may be on pins and needles over every word coming out of Europe one week and then IBM's earnings may override Europe the next week. The market is fickle and tends to go where it wants. In 2011, the markets would react in panic when the focus was on Spain's 10-year bond rate breaking through the 7 percent point of no return. Then it would focus squarely on Washington's fiscal cliff debacle, then it would focus on Angela Merkel's comments, then it would jump around to Bernanke, then back to the European Central Bank, and so forth.

Market Sector Tier System Mechanics

How do the markets move fluidly? Equity markets are led by the equity futures, thereby making the equity futures, S&P 500, and Nasdaq 100 e-minis good lead indicators when trading equities. The SPY on a continuous feed works as a good lead indicator. There are four benchmark exchange-traded funds (ETFs) that I use to track the indexes.

The Dow Jones Industrial Average is a price-weighted index of 30 stocks and tracked by DIA. The S&P 500 is a market capitalization weighted index of 500 stocks tracked by SPY. The Nasdaq 100 is a market capitalization weighted index of 100 stocks tracked by QQQ. The Russell 2000 is a market capitalization weighted index of 2,000 stocks tracked by IWM.

Since each index is price- or market capitalization–weighted, it assigns more impact to the higher-priced/valued components. When some components appreciate in parabolic fashion like AAPL, they transform into leviathans that can lift or sink the markets solely on their own price movements. IBM in the $200s carries almost an 11 percent impact on the Dow Jones, almost twice its nearest index peer CVX at $113 and 6.5 percent. AAPL priced at $610 a share carries a market cap of $571 billion accounting for 5 percent of the whole S&P 500 market capitalization and a whopping 19 percent of the Nasdaq 100 index and QQQ ETF! First Trust realized the distorted heavy weighting from AAPL and brilliantly created an equally weighted ETF that assigns 1 percent allocation to each Nasdaq 100 component. The symbol is QQEW and averages a whopping 20,000 shares a day in volume (versus 35,000,000 average of the QQQ). Nice try . . . not.

In 2012, the parabolic rise of AAPL is also a distortion on the real performance of the SPY. With the SPY and QQQ, AAPL is the lead stock as component makers will also drag or lift with AAPL. Funds, institutions, and algorithm programs know the best way to juice the indexes are to pump the highest-weighted components like AAPL, IBM, and JPM (sector leader of the financials). When those three stocks are pumped up, the indexes will show green. When any one of those is red, they can be offset with rotation of money flow into the other two. JPM is not a high flier, but it is the tier 1 general of the banking and financial sector, which gives it lots of influence on the sector. While the indexes are rising, they use the artificial boost to liquidate and distribute positions elsewhere. This tends to work when the market tier system functions properly with leaders pulling the laggards in convergence. It's when divergence within the sectors comes into play that the dangerous misleading element comes to fruition. As misleading as the Dow Jones Industrial Average is, the media continues to chime its performance as the indicator for the overall markets.

Sector ETFs as Indicators

These equities act as a more accurate indicator for their respective sectors as they monetarily interconnect the tiers. These are most helpful when particular sectors are diverging with other sectors, which may indicate a rotation of money flow. There are lots of ETFs from different vendors. It's important to use the ones with the most volume, which should also have options contracts that can be used to lever and hedge positions. The most liquid ETFs are:

Benchmark ETFs

SPY—S&P 500 Index
DIA—Dow Jones 30 Index
QQQ—Nasdaq 100 Index
IWM—Russell 2000 Index
QQEW—Just kidding …

Sector ETFs

DBA—Agriculture
IBB—Biotech
XLP—Consumer Staples
XLY—Consumer Discretionary
XLE—Energy
XLF—Financials
XLV—Healthcare
XHB— Homebuilders
XLB—Materials
IYR—Real Estate (U.S.)
XRT—Retailers
SMH—Semiconductors
XLK—Technology
XLU—Utilities

Commodity ETFs

GLD—Gold
SLV—Silver
CU—Copper
USO—Crude Oil
UNG—Natural Gas

Bearish Leveraged ETFs

These controversial instruments have a natural depreciative mechanism. Some of these ETFs also incur additional fees on ex-dividend dates of the underlying shorted ETF. These ETFs shouldn't be held long term unless they are being used for direct hedges. Liquidity and light volume on most bearish ETFs make for wide spreads and slippage as well, so it's best to stick with the most liquid names.

Common Bearish Leveraged ETFs

FAZ—Financials Bear 3×
ERY—Energy Bear 3×
DZZ—Gold Bear 3×
SPXU—S&P500 Bear 3×
SQQQ—Nasdaq 100 Bear 3×
TZA—Small Cap Bear 3×

Breadth Indicators

This is where breadth becomes a better indicator of market health. Fewer participants mean less liquidity is spread through the markets, with most pockets of consistent liquidity gathering around the big caps and widely held stocks. This is why there will be more and more divergence with the indexes as participants continue to dry up. Sellers use the SPY bounces to liquidate positions and then panic on SPY sell-offs. This is how participants get trapped. The conventional breadth indicators would be the tick and trim data, but I prefer to see how my global watch lists as well the top-tier trading stocks perform. These can be found on the preformatted UndergroundTrader layout templates for CobraIQ users.

CHAPTER 2

The Hybrid Market Predator

The hybrid exemplifies the integration of daytrading, swing trading, and investing skillsets to create a trader that adapts to and optimally manages all market landscape and climate changes. The combination of all three skillsets generates a cumulative effect and the by-product bonus fourth skillset, portfolio trading.

The Hybrid Market Predator

The hybrid is the by-product of active evolution. The hybrid trader possesses the precision timing of execution, risk averse scaling, and technical analysis of the daytrader, the premeditative assertiveness tethered by patience and risk management of the swing trader, and the relentless investigative fundamental prowess of the investor. Whereas all three roles have butted heads in the past, now they are components that converge to manifest into a more efficient market predator that can seamlessly shift between skillsets to adapt to changing landscapes, climate, and terrain.

Algo/HFT (high-frequency trading) programs don't need to be conquered or defeated. That is a foolish way to get steamrolled. They are to be gamed to magnify profits. HFTs are awesome when you are on the right side of the pumps. When they outnumber the humanoids, you shift to swing or portfolio skillsets. When they are leapfrogging each other generating thunderous momentum, you shift to the daytrading skillset.

The skillsets enhance efficiency toward your overall performance. Swing trading or portfolio trading still requires sharp execution, timing, and analysis, which is supplied by the daytrading skillset.

Relevant Traits of the Three Skillsets

There are three skillsets needed to survive in the current and, frankly, all future landscapes. It's human nature to favor a particular skillset, likely the one you started off with, but to improve another skillset requires continued exposure and application. The skillsets complement each other and as such generate a cumulative effect to harness a by-product skillset, portfolio trading.

General Core Traits

These core traits are required for every skillset. All these core traits are addressed in the upcoming chapters.

- Adaptability to changes in market landscape, context, and terrain
- Ability to smoothly shift between skillset abilities as needed
- Acceptance of and ability to recognize and apply the five laws of the market
- Pocket recognition (execution and condition)
- Macro market analysis and monitoring
- Risk assessment and position management
- Knowledge of sectors, peers, leaders, and laggards
- Self-discipline and humility
- Composure (remain cool under pressure)
- Penchant to evolve
- Fluency with robust trading methodology *(That would be the Katana in Chapter 4)*

Daytrading Skillset

This skillset places heavy emphasis on speed as it pertains to preparation, technical analysis, reaction, and simultaneous ability to track macro market headwinds, executions, and reactions.

- Precision order execution and market/liquidity timing skills
- Pace control

- Discipline to implement closure
- Patience for triggers and conviction to step in early
- Conditioned for shortest holding periods in minutes and hours at most
- Levels 1–2 research depth *(The Four Leveled Research Techniques covered in Chapter 6)*
- Exceptional filtering, scanning, and selectivity
- Decisiveness and conviction
- Proficiency with intraday price patterns

Swing Trading Skillset

- Proficiency with multi-day price patterns
- Technical analysis skills on wider time frames
- Levels 1–4 research depth
- Acclimated to wider-range gyrations and overnight holds
- Tolerance for larger price volatility and overnight exposure
- Proficiency with positions hedging
- Patience to ride out daily trends

Investor Skillset

- Levels 2–4 research depth
- Tolerance of very large price swings
- Patience and fortitude to ride out longer-term weekly, monthly trends
- Ability to assess the bigger picture and macro trends

Portfolio Trading Skillset

This is the by-product derived from improving skills in all three of the aforementioned skillsets. Portfolio trading seamlessly fuses all three skillsets to manifest a cumulative effect.

Kurt Warner: Adversity Conditioning Model

The death of one can spur life in another. The food chain illustrates this natural phenomenon. All social, political, and market trends hit boom, bust, and rebirth cycles. The same held true for daytrading in the early millennium, will hold true for the HFTs, and so forth. The daytraders of old have mostly moved onto other endeavors, but there are those who have evolved through a hybridization process. The same applies to investors and all the incremental classes in between. Something always rises from the ashes. It parallels one of my favorite inspirational stories. The takeaway is a model that is suitable and applicable to the old school daytraders. Any growth or unlocking of talent comes from adversity conditioning as one's endurance is put to the test on multiple levels. Sometimes a talent for a particular skillset takes adversity on another skillset.

Kurt Warner was a third-string quarterback for the Saint Louis Rams who was thrust into battle when starter Trent Green tore his anterior cruciate ligament (ACL) during the 1999 preseason. The unknown Warner would set multiple NFL passing records and lead the St. Louis Rams to two Super Bowls in three years. With their Super Bowl XXXIV victory, he set a Super Bowl record with 414 yards passing and was named *Sports Illustrated*'s NFL 1999 MVP. This unheard-of no-name was given a chance and took the world by storm. *Sports Illustrated* was so surprised by his meteoric success that they placed him on the cover of the October 18, 1999 issue with the caption "Who Is This Guy?"

Warner was not a first-round NFL draft pick. In fact, he went undrafted by the NFL altogether. His short-lived NFL career consisted of trying out for the Green Bay Packers training camp after going undrafted in 1994, only to get released before the season started. He took a job for $5.50 an hour stocking shelves at a local supermarket and living in the basement of his wife's parents' house, trying to support two stepchildren while his NFL prospects faded.

Warner caught a break in 1995 when he was signed to play for the Iowa Barnstormers in the Arena Football League. He would go on to lead the Barnstormers to two Arena Bowls and be named number 12 of the 20 best Arena Football players of all time. He was signed as a third-string quarterback for the St. Louis Rams in 1998 and was shipped off to play for the Amsterdam Admirals in NFL Europe, where he led the league in touchdowns and passing yards. He was shipped back to the Rams, where he was a third-string quarterback with a piddly 39-yard season, completing 4 of 11 passes. The 1999 season was the Cinderella story, as he replaced injured starter Trent Green. From here, the by-product materialized as he went on to greatness. This explains the sequence of events, but sheds no light on how a seemingly mediocre quarterback went from anonymity to establishing one of most impressive quarterback careers in NFL history.

Further digging revealed that his time in the obscure Arena Football League, where he attained astonishing success, had awoken his skills and nurtured them to a whole new level. The Arena Football League played indoors on a 50-yard field with eight-man teams using the same size football as the NFL. The game consisted of four 15-minute quarters and a 12-minute halftime with no out-of-bounds clock stoppage, except in the last minute of each half. Everything was in fast forward mode compared to the conventional game. This required participants to double their reactions as the playing field was cut in half. This factor nurtured Warner's natural abilities to manifest evolution under extreme conditions. Another key element, salaries were $100 to $200 a game with no health coverage and no prospects of upward recruitment, the players were there simply for the love of the game, to feed the natural hunger. Arena League was the last stop for those delusional wannabes who couldn't hack it in the pros and yet couldn't accept their shortfalls. Warner's relentless enduring efforts, fueled by his passion for the game, triggered the law of reciprocity as he earned a by-product.

This landscape unlocked this by-product unbeknownst to Warner or anybody else. One day he received a call from St. Louis Rams' head coach Dick Vermeil to be a walk-on who would likely never see the playing field, but Warner accepted due to financial responsibilities. Miraculously, events happened that would result in Warner being thrust into the role as starting quarterback. This shock was initially overwhelming as demons from past failure in the NFL came back, but eventually he acclimated due to his tenure in the Arena League and then he excelled. Even Warner admitted that the NFL was like slow motion because he was used to a 50-yard indoor field. He was used to reacting in a quicker environment, which gave him an unrivaled advantage in the pocket. The AFL conditioned him to unlock his potential and nurture his talent in a way that wasn't apparent until the 1999 NFL season.

His earlier success in high school and college football was shattered when he stepped up to the NFL, where the greatest caliber of talent in the world competes. The realization that he did not belong sank in bluntly when he was cut by the Green Bay Packers. This didn't destroy his passion to play the game. His extraordinary will to push forward even as a stock boy working the night shift labeled him delusional. Yet he kept digging and digging so relentlessly that his extraordinary will was able to bend the fate of destiny to grant him a favor. The rest is legend. Warner is a very religious man whose faith in God replenished his will to keep pursuing his dream. Label it God or karma; it is the law of reciprocity at work here.

The takeaway from this applies to daytraders. While pure daytrading versus the computers for any extended duration of time is ultimately a futile endeavor, the skillsets are gold when applied during the proper landscape, climate, and terrain. The same holds true for the swing trader and the investor. Each of these styles requires a separate yet similar skillset. Similar to how mixed martial arts (such as in the Ultimate Fighting Championship [UFC]) evolved into a combined style requiring cross training strikes, grappling, and submissions developing into a hybrid fighter, the traders of today must also condition themselves in scalping, swinging, and portfolio management.

The most important takeaway from Warner's journey is that it is truly possible for a man (or woman) to will destiny to bend in his favor by exerting relentless, unwavering, and enduring effort. The law of reciprocity is at work here. All that pressure builds up, and something has to give, either the man or his destiny. In all the time he is applying the pressure, he is inadvertently manifesting and nurturing his by-product, which will reveal itself under the right landscape. This is the true reward, not a gift, because it has to be earned. Where there's a will, there is most definitely a way: the Way of the Trade (catchy . . . hehe).

There is one more takeaway from Kurt Warner: his conditioning to the faster pace in the Arena Football League transformed him into a legendary pocket player in the NFL. The key word is *pocket.* The pocket is the area that the lineman try to hold to protect the quarterback long enough to complete a pass. The pocket is always shrinking due to the opposing team trying to get to the quarterback. The pocket is dynamic and only lasts for a few seconds before it's overwhelmed. Within those few seconds, the quarterback has to remain calm, stay completely aware of his surroundings, spot an open receiver, and deliver a precision pass for completion. This scenario is similar to trading, especially trading the open. The key word is *pocket.*

Pockets, Pockets, Pockets

The key word is *pocket.* When the quarterback gets the snap to execute a play (premeditated game plan), it's no different from a trader entering a position and having to time and execute exits into pockets of liquidity before they evaporate, while simultaneous monitoring the macro headwinds.

Traders, whether they know it or not, are always searching to exploit pockets. The caliber of a trader, be it intraday, swing, or portfolio, can be gauged on how efficiently he can spot, time, and work the pockets in the market.

The pockets that pertain to execution are transparency, liquidity, and momentum. The pockets that pertain to conditions are divergence, reversion, and convergence. These pockets construct the elusive window of opportunity.

Pockets follow the law of transparency, which means they shrink as more participants spot them (and try to exploit them). Ever heard of a *crowded trade*? That's one where the pockets are destined to evaporate and with it, the window of opportunity. The assignment here is to condition you to think in terms of pockets, spotting them as they develop, and reacting while they are fresh. Repetition will alleviate anxiety and improve your capacity to effectively work the pockets.

Properly Aligning Your Personal Perspective

This concept is so important, one of the most important in this book, because it deals with the very ectoplasm of your mindset and spirit. In a nutshell, the ability to instill good habits is in your hands, regardless of outside influences. The ability to maintain a consciously objective introspection will be key to properly measuring your evolution.

I'm a big fan of the *X-Men* comic series and its spin-offs, from comics like *New Mutants* and *Harbinger* to television series like *Heroes* and *Alphas*. The surface perception of these stories revolves around a group of mutants with special innate powers labeled as outcast by the rest of society while battling the bad guys.

A deeper observation into the dynamics reveals the connection between a group of outcasts who possess unusual skills and are left to set their own perspective parameters since the rest of the normal humanoids don't relate to this set. They see events and actions in a different perspective.

Never base your performance against what the market indexes are doing on a particular day.

Depth is worthy. Anyone who digs deeper into a topic beyond the surface is making their worth. The same holds true in the trading game. The media is not the gatekeeper of transparency, but the measure of it. By the time it's reported, it's too late. It's just that conventional, but that is always the hidden agenda of the markets. Let's really delve deeper into the essence. As you know by now, I value depth highly. In *Trading Full Circle*, I suggested that pessimism keeps naive optimism in check.

The optimism shouldn't be placed blindly on expectancy every morning. This optimism can cloud judgment, dilute objectivity, and get real ugly if the trader goes on a tilt binge. That's why pessimism is a better default state in the morning. Pessimism makes you work harder on the preparation and prepares you for the worst-case scenario thereby forcing you to plan out and keep your guard up. It constantly keeps you aware that the market is capable of turning on you and is not to be trusted.

Where pessimism kills you is when you apply it too stringently on yourself for any number of perceived shortcomings like not holding a position longer through the wiggle, or not taking stops quicker. Or for not taking this or that trade. In essence, the shoulda, woulda, coulda disease infects your psyche when pessimism is misused.

The real balance lies in utilizing that optimism and pessimism efficiently, where others will, won't, and cannot. I can't stress this enough. A humanoid will look at a +.15 scalp trade on a chart three hours later and cringe when they see how it ran up two points from your exit, and ask you why you didn't ride your winner. This is the same idiot that was going to hold a 1,000-share position long as it pops +.30 into a resistance and then sells-off for –2 points the rest of the day on a grinding perfect storm downtrend. You can feel bad about lots of things. What you must not do is punish yourself for following the methods consistently but ending up with a small loss. As long as you remain faithfully consistent to the system, performance smoothes out positively, in the long run.

I'll repeat what I said earlier: *An efficiently managed loss carries more weight than a poorly managed win in the long run.* The first case reinforces a solid template that will smooth out performance in time and prevent sustained degradation. The second case is a lucky break that sets a harmful template moving forward, as the trader will likely attempt to duplicate the outcome of the poorly managed win, especially in the face of adversity, and get plowed over sooner rather than later.

Be able to discern between a well-managed minimized loss and a sloppy, poorly managed win. Odds dictate in the long run, the winner will give it all—and more—back to the market, whereas the risk-averse, sound management that minimizes a loss will consistently be prosperous. If you can discern the difference and acknowledge the fluke nature of the win and revert back to tight management, then your performance should remain consistently positive over time. This is always a work in progress.

People, like markets, have muscle memory. They have a tendency to repeat things that are familiar to them for better or worse. Human nature is to fall into a routine that follows the path of least resistance. This is where extra-conscious effort is required to instill good habits and (re)align the course back on the right path, so that your performance smoothes out positively over the long run.

The important thing is realizing when a loss was well executed or a profit was poorly executed. Only those with the affinity and passion for depth truly understand this. The difference between real-time, in the eye of the storm, in the trade versus reading a chart an hour later after the fact—even five minutes later—is night and day. Those who can't understand this become prey.

The bottom line here is that there are factors that influence the bottom line and on a consistent basis. When something is a fluke, it occurs rarely, less than 5 percent of the time. When the fluke tends to happen consecutively . . . consistently . . . that takes depth to truly understand and develop.

Appreciate the depth of well-managed trades especially well-executed stops and sprawls. Don't linger on the loss, but focus on what was done right.

Give your psyche the closure it needs, so that you can move forward with a clean slate the next day.

You have to go through every possible scenario in the markets to build that acute intuition, and it's always a work in progress. The market constantly tries to imprint misguided templates to train the participants to react in the worst possible manner.

Great traders manifest the ability to administer closure, stop, and walk, and the ability to immediately notice the most subtle divergence and take profits or reverse the trade. The ability to adapt promptly to any outlier situation is the mark of excellence.

To roll with the punches and strike during the openings, to know when to box for points and when to slug it out for a knockout—everything boils down to this simple proverb by Sun Tzu from *The Art of War*: "A skilled fighter places himself in a position where defeat is impossible, yet never misses the opportunity to defeat the enemy." This is not a hard concept to understand. That's not the point. That's the tip of the iceberg as you submerge deeper to understand the true depth of the statement.

This is the unique aspect of participating in the markets. Unless you are a portfolio manager that must meet watermarks and benchmark performance requirements, you are mostly free to participate when and how you wish. You don't have to answer to anyone outside of a spouse, and are free to beat yourself down or praise yourself up. Yet, most retail investors still react to the fear and greed emotions. They are still under the control of the markets. They are free men and women who are still shackled and enslaved to the RIGGED benchmark indices. Remember, these are price weighted, and therefore the highest-priced stocks carry the most weight. AAPL, IBM, GS, CAT, and CMI serve the most impact on the indexes, S&P 500, Dow Jones, and Nasdaq 100.

Manifesting By-Product into a Product

While we're on the topic of by-product, my own journey with UndergoundTrader.com after 11 years was instrumental in developing two by-product services that manifested out of a necessity to address the very real and separate skillsets that make up the hybrid market predator model. I include a brief, maybe not so brief, discussion on the development cycle of each service. The goal is to shed some light on how the components came together for launch. All the methods and routines I use daily will be explained in the book so you can emulate the system.

The House of Enlightenment: www.UndergroundTrader.com

It all started here. I started off launching UndergroundTrader.com in 1998 as a blog (even before the term *blog* was created) where I would update my own personal trades with narratives by ftp-ing my updates. It caught a following, especially since I was in a very popular daytrading chat room. I had issues with the moderator who would call alerts on no-volume junk, oftentimes just to create momentum, only to have everyone cannibalize each other. I got fed up with the alerts especially since I had discovered the stochastics oscillator and placed it on a 1-minute chart along with Nasdaq level 2. This is the training ground for aspiring traders who want to learn by osmosis at their own pace. All the components of the trading methodologies were developed firsthand here through numerous trades and alerts through every landscape, climate, and terrain. I continue to refine as the necessity arises. Shout out to Dodge, Gander, Wwwestlake, Wil, and the crew of old-timer members who have been stuck with me since the doors opened in 1999 (official launch of the chat room). I continue to log in and call analysis and alerts in real time as I've done since the beginning to illustrate the methods in real time. It always touches me when struggling traders end up at my house after being whiplashed and misled by the markets and services. They have been deprived of enlightenment and that's the house specialty every day all day. The house is always open, so stop in for a free trial. We won't bite (too hard).

The Passive/Assertive Portfolio Player: www.UndergroundSwingTrades.com

As the years went by and membership at UndergroundTrader continued to fall off, I realized stubbornly that not everyone has the time to spend eight hours in front of the screens every market day. People have moved on and found their own by-products. However, there was a growing interest in capitalizing on market and stock movement without having to invest the time and effort to get acclimated. Realizing that pit members were acclimated to intraday trading, the swing trades were taken by too few. This piqued my interest in delving into a hybrid daytrading/investing style that would utilize all the efficiency of precision order execution, market timing, pattern, risk, and trade management coupled with deep fundamental research-based analysis factored in the context of the current market landscape, climate, and terrain to generate a high-quality premium service that just served up the meal for consumption—taking on all the responsibility of scanning, researching, aging, and stalking candidates through a vigorous filtering process to produce the highest-quality swing trade alerts complete with allocation, limit entry/exit prices, allocations, and targets, complete with daily commentary. The portfolio approach of 10 to 30 percent allocation per play based on market conditions and technical set-ups was implemented. The majority of the initial gains would be scaled out with 7 to 15 percent profits, leaving a net 1 to 3 percent core position shares that would remain in the portfolio until targets or technicals changed. This service posts its performance on the homepage and is available for auto-trading through several brokers. This allows clients to go on with their work and careers while their portfolios were managed. This is not a cheap product, but you get what you pay for. Membership details are available at 1-888-233-1431. There are no trials for this service.

The 90-Minute Trading Day: Morning Profit Maker
www.MarketFy.com

Throughout my own trading career, I've learned to appreciate the value of a net positive day, even if it's $50 profit. A $50 profit may not seem like much, but it all depends how that $50 gain is derived. I learned the hard way to appreciate any net closed gains early on. This market landscape punishes those who take small profits for granted.

I have had days where I struggled for seven straight hours generating over 200,000 shares in volume only to end up with $100 gross profit but after the $1,000 in commissions, end up –$900 net on the day. Ironically, the days always start off with a $100 to $300 profit that I took for granted and churned myself hard. Even worse are the days where you get waxed for –$5k from the get go and spend all day grinding back to just a –$500 gross, but once again the $700 in commissions puts you down –$1,200 on the day. Let's not forget the toll these days take on your stress levels, mentality, and spirit. They drain you completely, and you still end up with a net loss due to the commission churn. The psychological drain is immense. You learn to appreciate efficient and consistent net profits. *Efficient* means quick gains from point A to point B, in and out, the quicker the better. *Consistent* means you repeat that process daily. The small gains add up in time. Most importantly, the costs on your psyche and spirit are minimal, meaning less erosion. This is something that can't be measured in profits. Remember, this is all about the process, and the outcome is a foregone conclusion.

I realized that the first 30 to 45 minutes up to 90 minutes maximum is where the best action lies every single market day. The best pattern to trade is the perfect storm in all its variations. Perfect storms need volume, which is what this time period consistently generates. Lastly, closure has to be implemented every day, either via time limit, profit/loss limit, or instinctually calling it quits due to anomaly conditions. The market will give you that $50 to $150 free every morning. It expects you to stick around and continue to play with the house's money. The longer you stick around after 11 A.M., the more likely you get sucked into the churn. Therefore, the rule is simple. Don't stick around. These simple rules and the execution of these rules helped me to create an amazing by-product service thanks to the team at Benzinga.com (Kyle, Kenny, Adam, Drew) aptly called the Morning Profit Maker on www.Marketfy.com.

This service sums up the essence of control. Sure, you can't control the market, but you can control your actions. The act of taking on a position and closing out the position is all in your hands. I do the legwork with the research, provide the watch list every morning, give color at 9:15 A.M. on the watch list and macro market conditions and then provide the alerts to get clients in and out of positions based on perfect storm patterns. The smaller your price target, the easier it is to attain and the less exposure you have to endure.

I also realized that the most fertile terrain will always be that first 30 to 45 minutes of the market day. This is where the action is. It is the discovery portion of the day for professionals as they are lenient at price levels allowing overshoots and extreme movements.

Like a chef, I gather the ingredients and serve up the meal on a silver platter waiting to be consumed. For me, it is all about liquidity and making sure my people can get in and out smoothly. Through the years, I learned that you can lead a horse to water but you can't make it drink. With this service, it allows me to do what I do best, and that is to lead my troops in and out of the markets capitalizing on the pockets of momentum offset with liquidity to grind out a nominal $50 to $150 every morning. Most mornings it's only 10 to 20 minutes of actual trading. It's that fast. Naturally, most want more. They figure if they can make $100 in 10 minutes, they could make so much more sticking around longer . . . wrong! That is what the market wants you to believe. That is the CURSE. I know because I've been there too many times. I close out the chat room regardless once the liquidity dries up in the market with or without a profit. However, the numbers are strong. It's all about consistency. It's reminiscent of the classic Iron Mike Tyson fights. After a while, people got irked because after weeks of promotion and buildup to the fight, buying the pay-per-view, getting your friends over to seriously enjoy a slugfest . . . it was over within the first two minutes of the first round, total domination. Bummer. The natural inclination was to want longer fights, to get one's money's worth.

Morning Profit Maker (MPM) can be very similar, but I cut it off after three rounds. There is no drawn-out slugfest (not usually). When things are executed seamlessly and efficiently, it happens so fast that part of you wants a little more. Trust me when I say, silence that voice. It is the market talking in your ear. The strategy is simple on the surface, but incredibly complex to someone who hasn't been down the road to hell. Remember that quote, "the road to hell is paved with good intentions." Been there, done that, too many times to care for.

MPM has cumulative stats that are available on www.marketfy.com. Just remember that we are shooting for base hits every morning, which occasionally convert to doubles, triples, and homeruns. That's great but means nothing going into the next day. It's that grinding mentality and work ethic not just for me but for the clients who log in with their coffee every morning just before heading off to work or running their businesses. This is such a perfect niche that has been perfected as a by-product though 15 years of active trading experience. This product works. Clients can just piggyback off the alerts knowing full well that my priority is to guide them in and most importantly out of positions seamlessly with liquidity. This service is available on Marketfy.com, and there is a 30-day money back guarantee. There is a live video stream of my charts as well as an interactive text chat room with optional text and e-mail delivery of trades. This service is ideal for those who want to profit while learning the methods to develop a morning income stream in less than 90 minutes every morning. Usually the perfect storm trades in wet climates are concluded in 10 to 20 minutes—we take our money and walk away. Rinse, repeat tomorrow. The reality is that catching a perfect storm in the first 20 minutes off the open can reap profits that would normally take hours to capture. Efficiency at work here generates maximum outcomes for minimal effort.

The Eight-Step Process to Turn Idea into Profit

The simple question that every trader/investor who finds an idea is . . . how do I play it (to make money)? A stock makes a new high . . . how do I play it? A stock announces an earnings warning . . . how do I play it? The Dow is selling off 300 points, how do I play it?

Transforming an idea into money involves an eight-step process:

1. Constant monitoring of the macro market conditions, not just up/down but liquidity/volume/trending or chopping. All trades are affected by market landscape, climate, and terrain.
2. Determine if the idea presents a viable opportunity—filter/qualify.

3. Analyze the risk/reward, support/resistance—technical analysis.
4. Devise a trading/strategy plan—triggers/scaling points/stops/set-ups.
5. Factor in the macro market context—convergence/divergence/fades.
6. Execute the trade—manage risk (size + set-up + duration).
7. Manage the trade—monitor the technicals with macro market.
8. Exit the trade—scale out position/down exposure into liquidity pockets.

These eight steps need to be *processed efficiently once a trade idea is found* (via newsfeed, scanner, article, or interview) to turn an idea into money. The kicker is that everything above is dynamic . . . not static. There is also a nuance factor that comes from familiarity of the nature/rhythm of the stock. There is also the expert factor as the trader has gained a feel for the stock and intuitively knows when the set-up is just not feeling right.

Let's delve into the morning ritual routine to prepare yourself for what lies ahead in the market day.

CHAPTER 3

The Morning Ritual

Repetition is the only form of permanence that nature can achieve.

—George Santayana

Your morning ritual is the most important *self-controlled* process of every trading day. It is essentially the gathering of the highest-quality ingredients (filtered prospects) in preparation for a delectable meal to consume. The adage "Eat what you kill" could not ring any truer. No matter how lazy, hungover, or busy you are, the morning ritual is a reciprocal tribute to the trading Gods to acknowledge your ante to play the game. This is where the work comes into play. Clicking the mouse is not work. Anyone can fire a pistol. Most do not possess the efficiency and accuracy of a sniper. That is the dedication and thoroughness required to ratchet up your probability and consistency in this game. The following is a step-by-step timeline of the work that needs to be done to reach the starting gate every morning. When these steps are taken in depth, the results are consistent and very quick. You can be done within 10 to 20 minutes after the open to enjoy the rest of the day. Kudos to the Morning Profit Maker service for enabling me to formally materialize and articulate this process, which is exactly what I do every morning for the service. I believe in this routine to the point of religion and thus consider it more ritual than routine. As you get more efficient in the steps, you will see the results and become a believer, too. The ritual works in so many layers to prepare for the action. Initially, you will be rigid, but the caveat is to stay loose and not overfocus too much on any single stock in the premarket. Loose and flexible is the required state of mind. Rigidity must be consciously avoided.

A professional fighter must undertake an intense training camp before each bout. Solid training camps push the fighter to his limits with special acclimated training catering specifically towards capitalizing on the opponent's flaws while maximizing the fighter's strengths. The training camp makes the difference between victory and loss. Fights are won or lost based on the effectiveness of the training camp. In fact, the actual match results are just a by-product of the training camp. The training camp is the real work.

A professional prizefighter must train 1,000 minutes for every 1 minute in the ring. Does every fighter undertake this excruciating ritual? No. Only the champions understand this. This is the modus operandi of champions. The markets don't give belts or acknowledge champions. However, the similarity exists in the essence of the preparation. You will get to a point where you know when you have put in the work premarket and during the weekend research. You will have an air of confidence because of the effort you have put in. This materializes solely in the by-product. Rather than focus on any single stock, focus on the process, and the by-product is yours. I say this from the numerous times that I set my focus on a single stock but made money on a different stock that may be tagged to the focus stock. It's about efficiency. Too much emphasis on a SINGLE stock makes you rigid. The market is all about flexibility to exterior factors tempered with rigid control with the internal factors.

I hope this makes sense. Discipline, patience, pacing, filtering, monitoring, allocation, analysis, stalking, and risk management are all internal factors you control. Stock/macro market movement, climates, landscapes, mistakes, setups, and formations are external factors you cannot and should not control.

Hunting for Prey: Headliners and Corganic

In this thunder and tumbleweeds market environment, the momentum and liquidity can surge like a tsunami and dry up like the salt flats in a matter of minutes. Eat what you kill is the underlying theme in the trading game. As a profit hunter, one must go where the action is and make sure the target has enough meat on the bones when you get there.

Playing the right stock is half the battle every morning. The key is to have a handful of candidates on the screen to stalk so that when one trigger fails, you have ample supply of alternate prey. The caveat here, however, is that more than likely the momentum will move simultaneously, so decisions have to be made quickly on the fly to drop and pursue another target or stick it out with the current hunt.

For now, let's go with the definition of two types of prey (more depth about the real prey in Chapter 7). The first is your core basket of stocks that you traditionally trade which should be aligned to the SPY or S&P 500 futures and you are familiar with, which have to be searched, tracked, and monitored organically, which I call Corganic (core+organic) prey. These are organic because they take some time to age until a strong pattern forms. They tend to move in lockstep with the futures and SPY ETF, but also can fall into those moody periods of fuzziness where setups that used to work a week ago get faded or fizzled, but will work again the next week. This can be anywhere from 5 to 20 stocks. These don't get written off, just put on the back burner until momentum returns, stocks like EBAY, SBUX, HAL, ESRX, GMCR, CAT, CMI, BIDU, SNDK, CRUS, and WDC. You should be very familiar with these stocks as they are regular go-to bread and butter candidates.

Secondly, is the headliner gapper/dumpers, stocks that are gapping up or down based on news/rumors outside of the ordinary, usually making headlines on the financial networks. You may or may not be familiar with them, but they are attracting volume and momentum due to the exceptional nature of their gaps. These candidates pop up every day on most broker/charting platforms under the Biggest Point Gainers/Losers scans. Finviz.com has a very nice market heat map, which shows bubbles of the big gappers and dumpers after 9 A.M. This is always a go-to spot for me. I don't go by percentages but more so by point value. Either way, these stocks that may trade normally on any given day are injected with steroids that bulk them up for monstrous movement, due to the disruptive nature of their gaps. We call them gappers and dumpers. The gapper/dumpers get the morning spotlight, which in turn attracts the predators allowing them to (temporarily) inherit the most tradable momentum and liquidity from the opening bell.

The Gapper/Dumper Three-Reaction Sequence

The DNA sequence of all gappers and dumpers is composed of three reactions off the market open: impulse reaction, the reversion, and the trend. The third reaction can be confirmed when it fills the opening gap level of the first reaction and continues beyond it or reverses there.

To put it more simply, conventional wisdom tends to assume stocks only move up or down at any given point in time, a coin flip that can only come up either heads or tails. This may be true from an outsiders view, but that is comparing apples to oranges. Up or down is a component of a larger behavioral pattern. A better illustration of this with the coin flip example means most gapper/dumpers, as illustrated in Figure 3.1, will either form the heads, tails, heads; or heads, tails, tails; or tails, head, tails; or tails, head, head outcome. The initial reaction occurs in the first 5 to 10 minutes, second reaction in the next 5 to 10 minutes, and third reaction in the next 5 to 10 minutes—usually—and I stress the word *usually*. Remember, we are dealing with the essence of the markets, which is fear and greed on steroids captured in a live wire. Only the nimblest of experienced traders should attempt the first reaction. The second and third reactions are for the opportunistic profit hunters. The twist is that the secondary reaction can be identical to the third reaction. I know this may sound cryptic, but gauge that first 30 minutes every morning on those gapper/dumpers, and you will notice the same pattern.

The largest number of gappers and dumpers manifest during the quarterly earnings season. When the bellwethers make the list, they pull the lower-tier sympathy stocks in the same direction providing more opportunities. In fact, I like to take the secondary laggards when the leaders are gapping since there is a distinct lead indicator to follow.

FIGURE 3.1 The Three Reactions on the Market Open for Gapper and Dumper Stocks

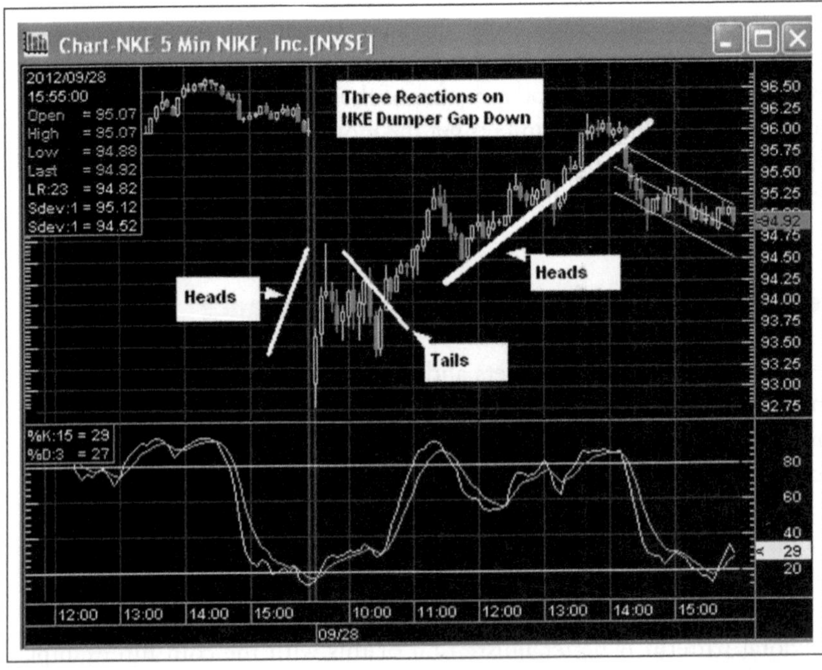

Ritual Religion

I stress the term *ritual* because it is part of my religion. It is my system of beliefs and I substitute karma for divinity. I'm a heavy believer in karma because I have seen it. I'm positive most of you have as well. I have not personally seen Jesus, Zeus, Mohammad, Buddha, Vishnu, or any other figurehead of whatever conventionalized humanoid religion. No offence to anyone who is a follower of the aforementioned, consider me ignorant, as I have not explored in depth.

As a trader, I simply choose a path of first-hand experience. I have to touch it, feel it, smell it, and basically get kicked by it; only then does it pass my litmus test. Pain doesn't lie.

What goes around comes around. Do unto others, as you would have done to you. This reflects balance. This is harmonic. This is nature. These themes encompass the principle of reciprocity. To match the effort made by a counterparty, be it a friend, spouse, relative, partner, or opponent. Nature embodies reciprocity.

Wasted Effort

The worst tragedy in this game is the misplaced effort by most of the participants resulting in the erosion of spirit and capital to the point where the only salvation is to blow out and be forced back to the sidelines.

I've seen numerous traders coming into the game with all the energy and optimism in the world, only to get stretched, drained, and corroded because they expend that energy on the shallow end of the pool. It's like taking a world-class swimmer and having her swim out of a quicksand pit. The more energy she expends, the more she sinks into the abyss. The energy was misguided. The same principle applies with the markets.

Lots of painstaking trial and error—thousands of hours and trades—have guided me to conceive my religion. As with any religion, there is a ritual that must be followed as an expression of reciprocity.

The Real Work, Don't Skimp!

This is where most go the wrong way. Here's the root of the misguidance. People tend to equate working so hard to the actual actions of buy and selling positions, constantly watching every tick of the markets, trying so hard to catch every move, and trying so hard to maximize every tick. This shallow perception of work is the downfall. In the old days, this was a truth because the market had the constant liquidity and volume where a trader could spend all day and hundreds of trades grinding back to profits or magnifying the profits. This no longer is a possibility. The high-frequency trading programs (HFTs) will always win after any extended duration. It's like the matrix; they are the Mr. Smiths of the markets. Infinite capacity and capital to capitalize on the most minute behavioral templates and patterned reactions make these robots deadly.

The real pipeline to focus effort comes in the form of preparation and research. The conventional definition of research is the laggard and frankly ignorant. Through the years, I have conceived a four-level depth research scale. The deeper the level you dig, the more time and effort it takes. However, this is where the reciprocity principle kicks in. The more effort you expend into this pipeline, the more reward you will reap as a by-product.

It may seem simple just to hit the fourth level of research every time, but the problem is that the markets are dynamic, and timing is part of the equation. It's no good to be digging through research as the technicals trigger and break out to the nominal targets while you are still reading conference call transcripts. On the flipside, shooting from the hip without at least level 1 research of quantifying the bumpers, price levels, and pattern is a surefire way to get cracked hard. Therefore a balance needs to be reached that proportionately distributes quantity of prospects and quality of prospects against the backdrop context while still having ample opportunity to react on the triggers.

Law of Reciprocity Revisited

Revisiting the law of reciprocity, everything has a yin and yang. Enduring effort will produce a by-product worthy of the effort. A by-product is not necessarily the goal, it's better than the original goal, because it's an organic outcome generated proportionately to the enduring effort put into it. This applies in life, and the markets are a microcosm of life.

I'm not superstitious, but some of the concepts may seem like superstition. I hesitate to call it faith. That's an overused label and a crutch. By definition, faith is a belief in something, which has no precedent. My religion is based on nothing but precedent. Seeing a result repeat itself hundreds and thousands of times is not faith. It is not fact because it's not precisely predictable, static, and indisputable. It's more than theory, which explains a series of phenomenon but not always. It's somewhere in between faith, theory, and fact.

Bottom line here, channel the effort into the right pipeline. You will reap proportionately to the effort you make. It's true. Talent affords you the few instances to wing it and shoot from the hip, but that is just a hall pass. Acknowledge that and never assume that is a given. Talent must be excavated then forged.

Fast and Simply Thorough (FAST) Chart Analysis

This method is extremely thorough and with enough repetition can be done in less than 30 seconds per stock, as detailed in Figure 3.2. Use this method of chart analysis preparation for your premarket watch list and anything that pops up during the day.

Bumpers are the 5-, 15-, 20-, 50-, and 200-period simple moving averages, pivot points, and the upper and lower Bollinger Bands. These are like bumpers on a pinball machine, which trigger a reaction when tested. When the values overlap with another time frame bumper, then that creates a stronger bumper. Wider time frames have the strongest bumpers; progressively, 60-minute, daily, weekly, and monthly being the strongest.

1. Cue up the stock on all seven time-frame charts; 1-minute, 5-minute, 15-minute, 60-minute, daily, weekly, and monthly:
   a. In pre/post market, only the wider time frames—60-minute, daily, weekly, and monthly—should be used for analysis. Intraday is inclusive of all seven.
2. Note any of the time frames that currently have pup/mini pup formations:
   a. Write down the bumpers on all time frames with pup/mini pups.
3. Write down any overlapping bumpers within 20 cents of each other on the daily, weekly, and monthly that are within the trading range of the current stock price:
   a. Write down any 50- and or 200-period simple moving average bumpers that the stock is trading near for the 60-minute, daily, weekly, and monthly time frames. Wider time frames have more resilient bumper price levels.
4. Filter down to two to four key overlapping bumper levels with the pup/mini pup time-frame bumpers having top priority (and noting that fact!).

FIGURE 3.2 A Premarket FAST Chart Analysis of COF Dumper Stock

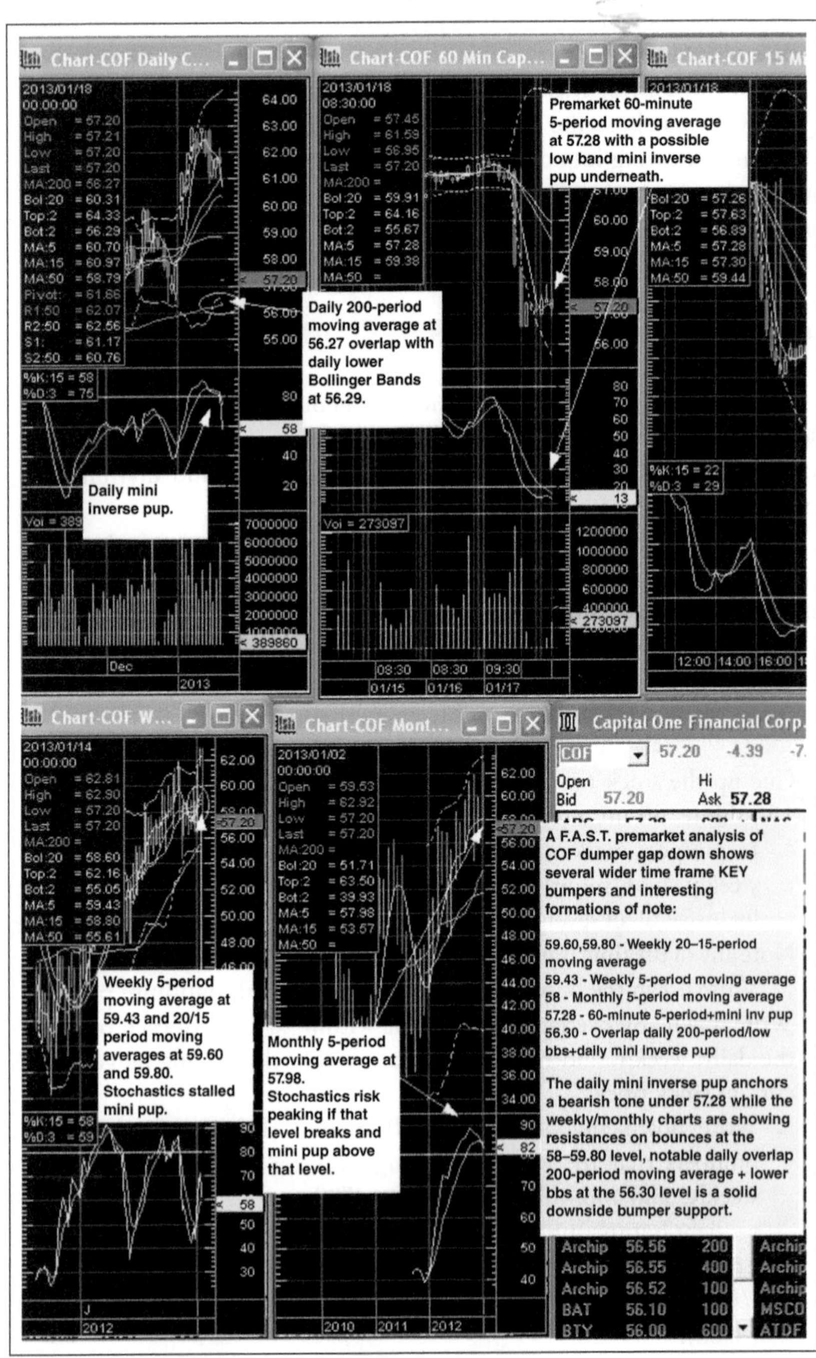

Step-by-Step Ritual Routine by Time

This may sound odd; start early around 8 A.M. on the analysis, but do not watch the premarket action too closely, especially on the gapper/dumpers. They have a way of reversing off the open more times than not. Be careful to keep your distance with these psychologically so they don't make an imprint in your frame of reference going into the open. Once you have become proficient with the FAST analysis method, during dry climates, it's beneficial to start later around 8:45 to 9:00 A.M. just to preoccupy yourself from premarket bias. Spend the early moments preparing your price levels with the FAST analysis method. Many times premarket will look like there is not a seller in sight, only to have the stock collapse on the opening bell. We want to avoid this, and mental distance is the key.

From 8 A.M. to 9 A.M. EST

Review the top-10 lists of stocks gapping the most up and down on the NYSE and Nasdaq premarket. These may be found on all charting and broker platforms. You can also get them for free on www.finviz.com or www.yahoo.com/finance. These stocks generate the most headlines and exposure on Bloomberg and CNBC along the way, which generates more interest and volume, especially when the CEO gets scheduled for an interview.

From the headlining gapper stocks: Pick out four to five stocks with more than 50,000 share volume premarket that you are familiar with. Average trading volume should be over 1 million shares trading above $10. Stocks under $10 require very specialized knowledge of the specific stock. Since the ranges tend to be smaller, more allocation risk is inherent with these cheapies. The momentum tends to fall off much quicker causing newbies to get trapped in positions. Only the very experienced should play stocks under $10. For the largest gaps up or down, always have one sympathy/laggard stock within the sector that tends to move together with the gapper.

The laggards are one of the best trades because of the natural tendency for money to flow top down in a sector when a leader is excessively strong or weak. The strongest convergence with the laggards will be the first 45 minutes. Afterwards, the leader and laggard may diverge once volume falls off. Always try to include one laggard stock in the watch list, like the proverbial single bullet in the chamber.

From the organic tracking stocks: Pick out four to five searched organic stocks that you have been tracking. Go through your market minder of

50 to 100 stocks for ideas. If you don't have a list already, place all the headliner stocks from prior days onto this list.

These could be stocks that had a very strong trend the prior day or stocks that have daily mini pups yet to detonate due to the shorter time frames like the 60-minute stochastics not converging yet. Remember that one day's trash can be the next day's treasure and vice versa. The highest-quality organic stocks are ones with daily pup/mini pup formations yet to detonate because the 60-minute stochastics haven't crossed in the converging direction. These are sleeping giants and should be tracked.

The prior week's worth of gapper/dumpers are good sources of organic prospects as well. While these stocks fade from the spotlight, oftentimes the setups trigger in the following days, or erosion forms as volumes drop back to normal. My favorites are gappers/dumpers that consolidate for a full day or two as they base for reversion back to weekly and/or monthly Bollinger Band levels. In the trade example with HLF detailed in Figure 3.3, I stalked this one for five days as it sold off continuously for eight straight days falling way under the weekly and monthly lower Bollinger Bands. I noticed very strong seller pressure at the 28.60s resistance that would not only reject but collapsed the stock on heavy volume every time it tested. This is all data collected from the constant monitoring and aging for the right opportunities. This big slab of beef would be enough to feed on for many days.

FIGURE 3.3 Headline dumper stocks such as HLF can provide more opportunities for organic trades even after the initial headline day.

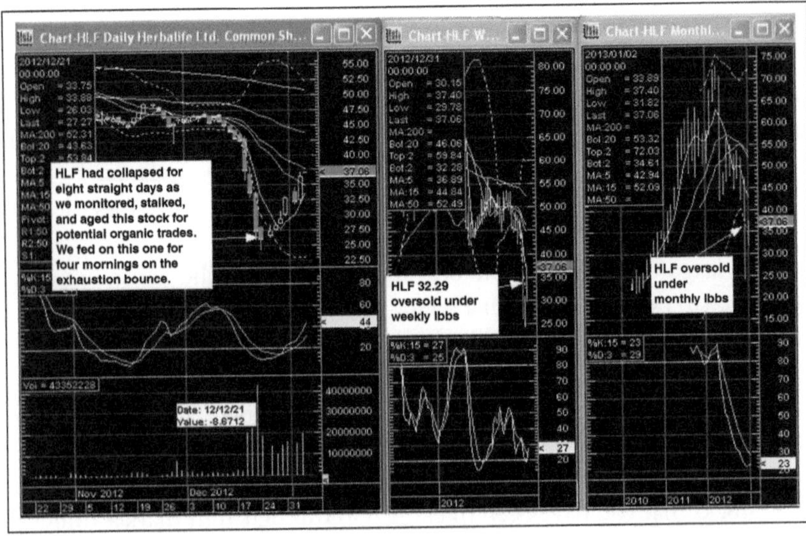

The following trades were provided for my MPM members at www .Marketfy.com via Morning Profit Maker service.

On Monday 12/24/2012, HLF gapped up once again to the 28.50s levels going into the open with a potential perfect storm uptrend against the resistance (Figure 3.4). Once the market opened, it immediately proceeded to collapse on heavy volume as the 5- and 15-minute mini pups got exhausted and dejected. HLF cracked through the 60-minute 5-period moving averages, which triggered an impulse inverse pup breakdown panic as bottom buyers were getting vaporized. HLF tried to hold a support at 26.50 as the 1-minute chart had three consecutive green counter candles that peaked at a 1-minute star. The body low of the succession of counter candles was around 26.30 trigger, which meant a 26.30 price break would trigger a 1-minute inverse pup in addition to the 60-minute inverse pup, 15-minute stochastic down and 5-minute mini inverse pup which equates to a perfect storm breakdown. The trigger formed as HLF collapsed through 26.30 clear to 25.80s where they attempted a hammer. *We hit the SHORT at 26.17 into the flash coil* which managed to flash tick up to 26.50s as we were cueing up to add at 26.60s. This sucked in bottom catchers only to headfake them back down on the 1-minute 5-period moving average break under 26.05, which caused a collapse to scale out at 25.85, out + .32 and 25.62, out + .65 profits on a 4-minute trade! This is the magnitude of price movement on perfect storm patterns. The trade took four minutes to execute in and out with fast profits, but that was because I stalked it ORGANICALLY for five days beforehand. The preparation pays off; that is the law of reciprocity.

On Wednesday, 12/26/2012, HLF gapped back up premarket with a perfect storm breakout pattern (Figure 3.5). Unlike the 12/24 perfect storm, this one had the muscle of a 60-minute mini pup going into the open, as opposed to an indecisive 60-minute make or break the last time. That heavy time frame in mini pup carries massive clout as the anchor. I knew 28.60 would still be a resistance, but if they held the perfect storm above 27.60, then that 28.60 would be a magnet to rechallenge the resistance, at which point it rejects or squeezes out the shorts. Either way, we have upside to the prior resistance level. We took initial entry long at 27.53 anticipating the breakout on the 1-minute mini pup trigger, but it got faded, and we stopped out at 27.33, out –.20 as I noted the falling volume on the 1-minute chart. Although the 5/15 and 60-minute were still in mini pups, that 1-minute mini pup fade was an early sign of sellers trying to get aggressive early on. The perfect storm can't detonate without the 1-minute stochastics fuse being lit. As we waited on the sidelines, we noticed the 5-minute stochs coil back up as the 1-minute stochastics coiled too. The counter candle trigger was at 27.67 breaks;

FIGURE 3.4 HLF trade on 12/24/2012.

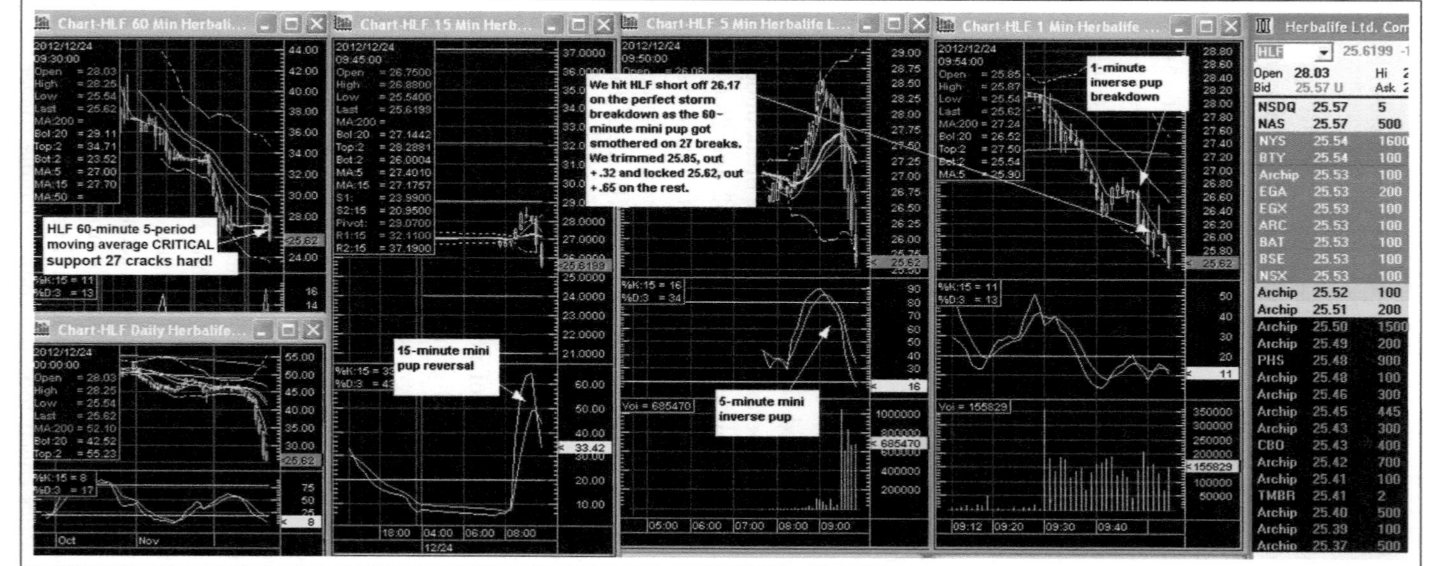

FIGURE 3.5 HLF trade on 12/26/2012.

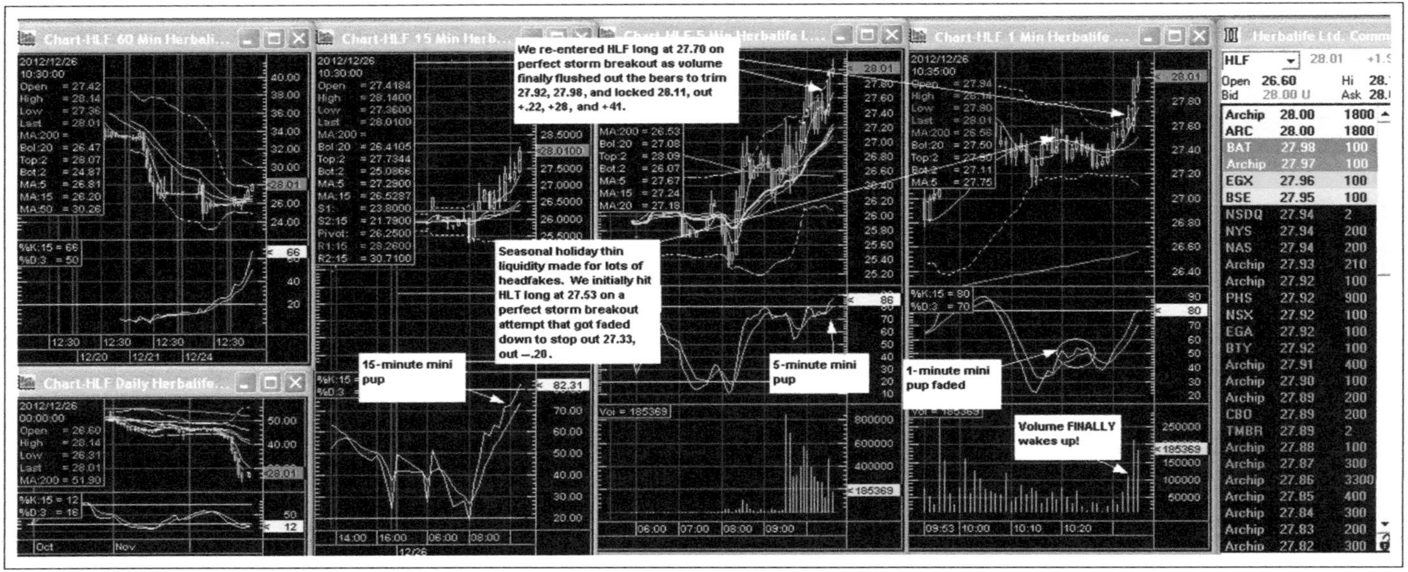

we reentered the *LONG at 27.70 on DOUBLE shares* allocation as the perfect storm breakout redetonated. We went double the prior size because the 15-minute showed to be the boss chart with a mini pup, which never wavered. Our original setup was still proven valid through the 1-minute failure, now the 1-minute was crossing back up and most importantly was the *rising 1-minute volume bars!* That was the dead giveaway they were looking to squeeze this time. HLF spiked on a panic squeeze allowing us plenty of liquidity to sell into the 27.92, 27.98, and 28.11, out +.22, +.20, and +.41 as all the new shorts got squeezed. HLF eventually climbed up to 28.60s and rejected hard again to low 27s, déjà vu?

The next day, Thursday 12/27/2012, we opted to play NKE's stock split, but continued to monitor HLF. HLF held a higher low from the prior day above 28 and proceeded to challenge 28.60s again and got rejected again but only pulled back to 28.20s to consolidate the rest of the day. Hmm . . . HLF is making higher lows but still holding that 28.60 resistance . . . hey, that 60-minute formed a pup breakout into Thursday's close along with the 15- and 5-period moving average make it a perfect storm going into tomorrow.

On Friday, 12/28/2012, which stock do you think we played off the open? Exactly. HLF gapped up premarket through the 28.60 resistance level, but that was just premarket (Figure 3.6). It did the same thing on Monday only to get flushed down to lower 25s. The difference this time is the higher consecutive lows the past three days in addition to the 60-minute pup formation into the market open along with the 15- and 5-minute mini pups and the day long basing at the 28.20 to 28.50 level yesterday. With the 28.60 prior resistances, we calculate that 28.80 is the coil break resistance. Since HLF gapped up to 29.10, the main concern would be if that 28.80 and then 28.60 would hold pullbacks. If 28.80 cracks, HLF could collapse –.50 easily. After the market open, we took HLF long at 28.99 on the 1-minute pup trigger attempt, but SPY was selling off, and HLF was losing volume again. We took a quick stop at 28.82 out –.17 to avoid any risk of a collapse on that 28.80 if it broke. The SPY continued to sell off, but ironically HLF continued to hold that 28.80 very firmly. We re-entered the LONG at 28.97 on heavier shares for the 1-minute stochastics cross-up and counter candle body high break trigger at 29.02 to tick. Sure enough, the 1-minute cross up triggers a massive volume spike to sell into the liquidity at 29.11, out +.14 and lock the 29.24, out +.27, for a third day of feeding.

Once again, the five prior days of stalking paid off in multiple tasty meals. Organic stocks require more work to track, but they can feed you for days. Put in the work to monitor, stalk, and age until ready to eat, and you eat what you kill in this game!

FIGURE 3.6 The Final HLF Trade on 12/28/2012 on the Sequence

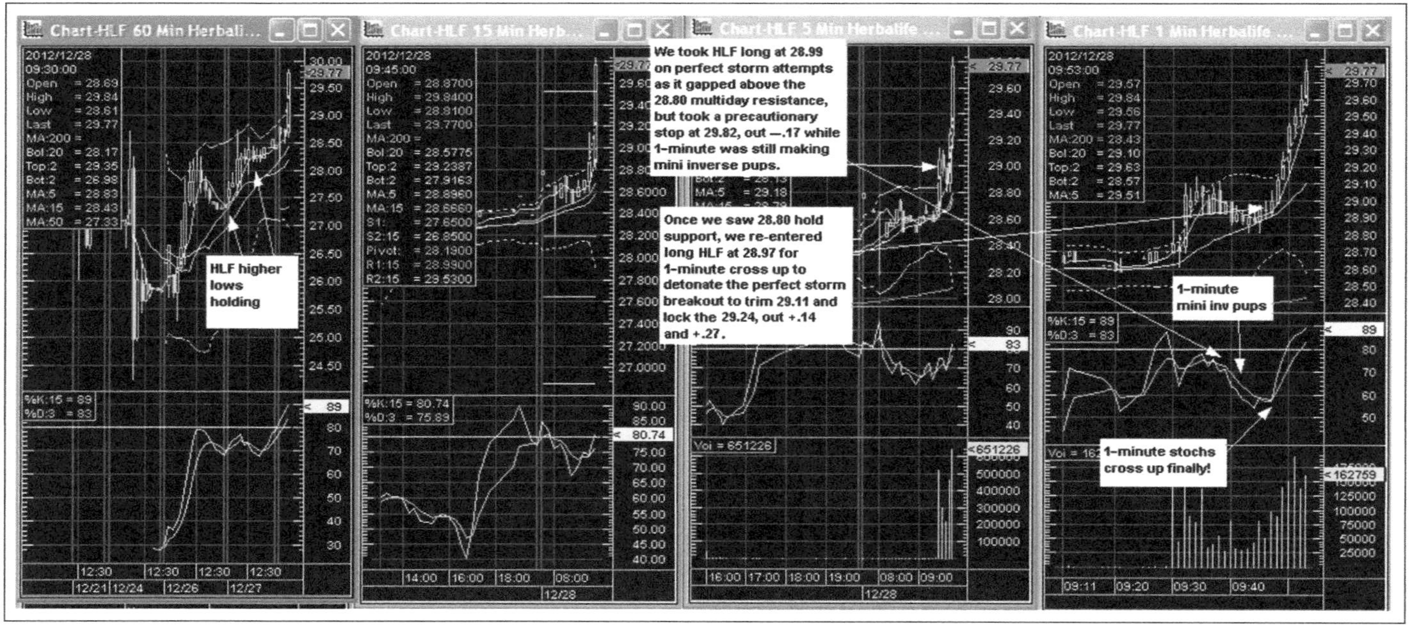

Don't worry about the trade patterns or terminology for now. I will go over pups, mini pups, and the infamous perfect storm breakout/breakdown patterns in complete full-color detail in the upcoming chapters.

1. By 9 A.M. EST: Have 8 to 10 prospects on the watch list. From this list, filter down to 4 to 6 stocks with the strongest setups. This is your A team. Keep the others as the back-up B team.
2. The priority of the filtering goes like this: Perfect storms, double pup/mini pups, double to triple overlapping bumpers, excessive gaps, laggards.
3. By 9:15 A.M.: Have your A-team set up by allocating a set of charts to each in addition to the SPY, which is the macro market *headwind-indicator*. Depending on your screen space of course. If you are only working with a single screen, then dedicate a market minder to the A team list and the B team.
4. Do a FAST analysis of the SPY: The SPY is your tailwind. Many traders will use the e-mini futures.
5. By 9:28 A.M.: Set the egg timer for 17 minutes and take a bathroom break. For me, this is the longest period of the day, as the minutes seem to stretch for hours. It is too easy to get sucked in too early on the wrong side during the early minutes especially for those who strain their eyeballs watching the premarket action too closely. Aside from the specific setups, there is a thin psychological tightrope that we walk every morning between complacency and assertiveness, fear and aggression, conviction and stubbornness to successfully navigate consistently to ride the storms.
6. After 9:30 A.M.: During the opening sequence, you will be overwhelmed due to the spikes and rug pulls happening simultaneously on your watch list. Relax, take a deep breath and let things play out. Always remember there are ultimately three reactions on gapper/dumpers. The first reaction is that violent spike or dump off the opening bell. The first reaction is rarely played. That's in the hands of the HFTs and big institutions. Let them duke it out. It's the reversion (second reaction) or the trending move (third reaction), we are always looking to play. The mistake with newbies is to chase the first reaction. That is the purpose of the first reaction. The first reaction is to squeeze desperate shorts on pops or panic out scared longs on dumps, inevitably, you also get traders who chase the squeeze or chase the shorts on rug pulls. These traders may catch the runner at most 2 out of 10 times. A 20 percent probability is not what we ever want to play. The first reaction will always peak out, then get the reversion move on the

second reaction where the bulls and bears clash resulting in the third action which is the resulting trend. The third reaction is what we want to play in a dry climate. The second and third reaction can be played in a wet climate. In very rare instances, the most experienced traders can play the first reaction, but that takes a premarket entry in the wettest of climates backed firmly with the SPY in a converging direction.

In dry climates, it is imperative to let the opening 15 minutes grind by to avoid getting chopped and steamrolled over on sprawls. In wet climates, the playable action can come in anywhere from 5 to 10 minutes after the open. It is always going to be safer after 9:45 A.M. But remember that safety comes at a premium, usually, a more expensive price or dilution of momentum.

Evaluate the Climate

The climates will impact your results. There are always outlier stocks that are the exception to the overall climate (like the aforementioned HLF trade sequence), but be prepared for the general market impact. If you happen to hit the exceptional stock, you will still be prepared to capitalize with less risk. Never get into the bad habit of assuming the exception is the rule. Don't assume you can play the identical setup the same way in a dry climate as you did in the wet climate.

The wet climates are fertile and provide quicker reactions, longer follow-through, larger overshoots, and longer windows of liquidity. Wet climates usually form during the earnings season. Wet climates allow for more allocation of shares, defensive sprawling, and more scaling in and out to proportionately maximize profits efficiently. Ironically, the dry climates appear safer due to the longer time needed for setups, but that is what makes them more dangerous, as the size of the ranges is smaller and wiggles are more prevalent. Wet climates move fast, which initially scares traders who are not prepared. That's the fault of the trader. Wet climates are where the fast profits are made. It's the dry climates that are the most dangerous, as they will chop mercilessly while the range tightens.

The dry climates provide smaller windows of opportunity, have shorter durations of liquidity, more limited range, and contain more chop. They are notorious for lack of convergence between the time frames; for example, a 60-minute and 5-minute mini pup but 15-minute mini inverse pup—d'oh! Ultimately, this will smooth out in one direction but it takes time.

Dry climates usually form in between earnings seasons. Dry climates can be unforgiving so if you aren't at a high level of proficiency with the methods, use stops rather than defensive sprawls. Dry climates are meant to tread water and limit drawdowns, with less allocation of shares. The irony here is that the ranges will be smaller and the moves will take longer to play out as volume falls quicker. This would logically imply increasing your allocation of shares, not decreasing them, to maximize the smaller ranges. This is what hurts traders, as the smaller ranges don't provide very much liquidity. The duration is spread longer for transparency and trend movement. Remember that risk is composed of allocation of position tempered with duration of holding time. Therefore, the smaller shares are taken due to the probability of having to hold longer due to the choppiness and time necessary for transparency to show. A trader who takes larger allocation more times than not will end up getting stopped out both ways and shake his head (while cursing the stock), only to return 30 minutes later as the stock ground higher. It's the climate, stupid. You have to adjust to the climate. One more very important step, wait 15 minutes after the open! Since the setups take longer to form, the three reactions naturally take longer as well. Whereas in a wet climate, the third reaction can kick in as early as 9:35 A.M., in a dry climate, it may not form until 10:15 A.M. Meanwhile, stepping in too early often results in getting chopped hard. The setup is the same, but takes longer to form in dry climates.

Let's move on to the real nitty-gritty! Prepare to receive your weapon. . . .

CHAPTER 4

The UndergroundTrader Trading System: The Katana

Choose your weapon . . . actually, I've already done that. I've compacted the UndergroundTrader trading methodology into a single word that symbolically embodies the essence of the system at multiple layers, simply put, the Katana. It's a weapon . . . deadly sharp, meticulously balanced; painstakingly hand crafted and reciprocally reliant on the individual's skillful application during encounters.

The Katana consists of basic component indicators assimilated in the right configuration to craft a symbiotic set of tools. These tools allow the user to visually interpret, track, and foreshadow price action. Most importantly, they reveal powerful, specific price patterns I've discovered called pups and mini pups. Once users get immersed in pups and mini pups, they will be able to track and trade the most powerful formation called the perfect storm, which I will review in exhaustive details and all its variations in Chapter 5.

Recommended Online Direct Access Broker: Cobratrading.com

I recommend Cobratrading.com and the CobraIQ direct access platform. The rifle charts were developed on this platform. The stability of the platform, especially during heavy volume periods, is second to none, and they have the best-personalized customer support on the planet. I HIGHLY recommend that traders use them over the conventional mass-marketed online brokers you regularly see on television. It boggles my mind that for the deep pockets these big firms have, they still can't put together a seamless and intuitive trading platform. I also have to point out that unless you are trading over 4,000 shares on average per trade, it is most cost effective to go with a per share pricing commission plan as opposed to a flat rate fee.

This is common sense but not always obvious. When you are exiting/scaling out a 400-share long position in three exits; for +.20 on 200 shares, +.30 on 100 shares and +.40 on 100 shares for a total profit of +$100, do the math. At $10 per trade, you are looking at –$30 in commission, for a +$70 net gain. That's 30 percent of your profits going to the broker, whereas a per-share commission rate of .004/share would calculate to a total of 800 shares (400 shares bought and sold) for a commission of $3.20 or only 3.2 percent of your total profits! Multiply that times 20 days a month (one roundtrip a day in the morning) and you are looking at $600 in commissions versus $64! This is whether you have profits or not. The commissions alone can be a detrimental barrier to success if they are too expensive, which MOST of the popular platforms are. When you are in a trade, you should not have to limit your scaling out of a position because the commission would eat up the gain anyway! How about when you don't want to take a small stop loss because you don't want to be hit with the commissions and would rather wait for the position to come back your way? Or decide to hold out a little longer on exiting shares because you don't want to give your gain to the broker? In all scenarios, it's a case of nonmarket influences hindering your efficiency. Don't be passive on the commissions. The wrong commission schedule will dampen your profits during peak profit cycles and burn like lethal acid in an open wound during drawdown periods. Heed my words or find out the hard way. 'Nuff said!

Moving on, let's get started with the components and tools of the Katana. The basic chart is a variation of the stochastics and moving averages with Bollinger Bands.

Configuring the Rifle Charts

Most charting packages and online brokerage platforms should have the basic indicators necessary to create our basic chart aptly titled the rifle chart, illustrated in Figure 4.1. This chart is composed of the following indicators: stochastics, simple moving averages, Bollinger Bands and (optional) pivot

FIGURE 4.1 The indicator components of the rifle chart.

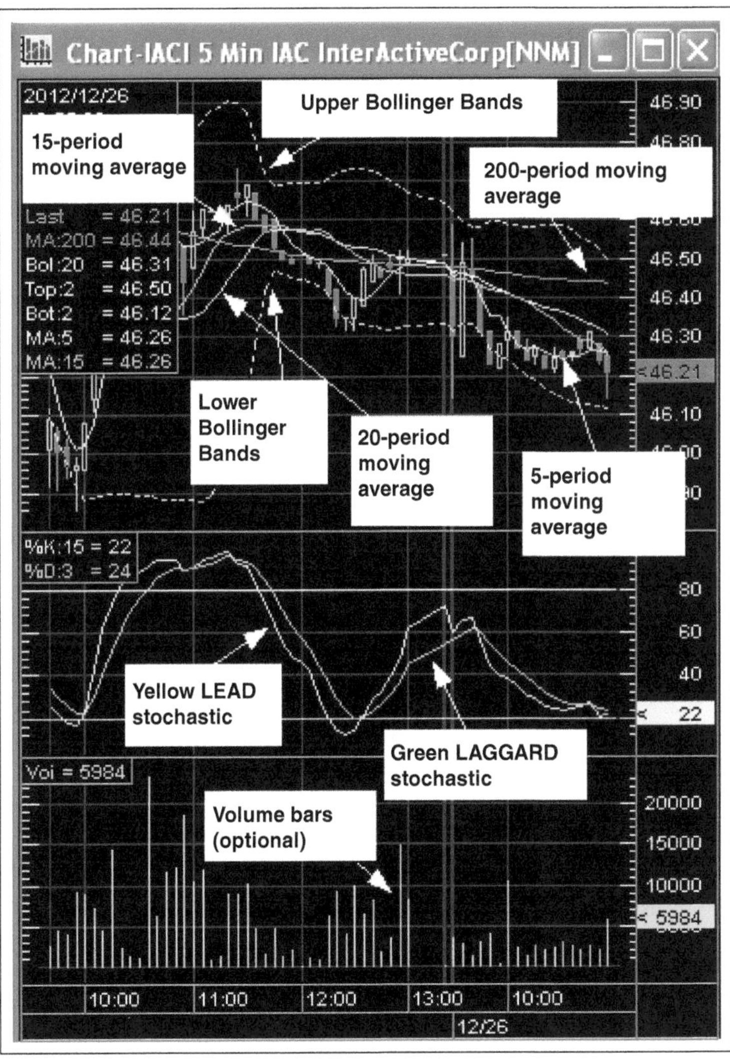

points, and volume bars. Most of the charts in this book are off the CobraIQ platform, so the configurations are set to that platform. They should be similar to most of the other broker and chart platforms in the market as far as the basic indicator components. It is the synergistic outcome of the tools and accuracy of the price level calculations that tends to establish CobraIQ as the de facto standard for me.

These directions apply specifically to the CobraIQ trading platform at Cobratrading.com. Other platforms will typically follow along these lines of setup as well. If you already have a CobraIQ trading account, then you can simply ask Chadd Hessing for the UndergroundTrader layouts that are already preformatted personally by myself and are the identical ones I use. Check them out!

Set-Up Directions

1. Open up a New Chart Window
    - Set to Candlesticks
    - Set to Include Pre/Post Market Data or Continuous Data
2. Add Indicator
    - Choose Simple Moving Averages
    - Configure to 5-period simple moving average (repeat step 2 for each below)
        - 15-period simple moving average
        - 50-period simple moving average
        - 200-period simple moving average
3. Add Indicator
    - Choose Stochastics Slow
    - Configure settings to 15,3,1 for smoothing
4. Add Indicator
    - Choose Bollinger Bands
        - Configure to 20-period and 2 Standard Deviations
5. Save Chart as Default (Congrats! You now have the rifle chart as your default)
6. Open up a New Default Chart Window
    - Change Time Frame to 1 minute
    - Repeat Step 6 for each of the following time frames: 5-minute, 15-minute, 60-minute, daily, weekly, and monthly charts.
7. Open Level 2 Window
    - Link level 2 Window to all seven time-frame charts (assign the same Link/Group letter to each chart)

Optional

8. Add Volume Bars (on 5-minute and 1-minute charts)
9. Add Pivot Points (on the 15-minute chart)

Congrats! You now have your first set of rifle charts with all the necessary time frames. Repeat these steps again for each new set of rifle charts you want to have.

Figure 4.2 illustrates the complete seven time-frame charts linked to a level 2 screen which gives you a complete bird's eye view of the battlefield. I suggest having at least two sets. One set is for your trading stock and the other is for the macro market headwind-icator SPY (or e-minis futures, if you prefer) as showed in Figure 4.3.

Understandably, these charts hog up a lot of screen space, which is why I recommend having a dual monitor setup for your trading computer and a separate dual monitor setup for your newsfeed/chartroom/research/scanning computer. I utilize seven screens on three different boxes, and that is still considered minimal. Realistically, you can only focus on so many stocks with the needed intensity anyway. The rest are for scans and research. Also, you can minimize the weekly and monthly charts, as you will likely be gauging those only once a day to see if your stock is trading near any relevant price ranges or if there are any pup/mini pup patterns. The 1-, 5-, and 15-minute charts are your most immediate charts thereby requiring the most screen space (Figure 4.4), then the 60-minute and daily. This applies especially for intraday trading and when you are executing swing trades for entries or exits.

I have a three-screen main layout as shown in Figure 4.5, which allows me to track two full-time frames stocks along with the SPY and gappers/dumpers, options, and over 100 stocks on my market minders. See what works best for you.

The Role of the Bumpers: Moving Average Breakouts, Breakdowns, and Trends

I will often refer to the moving averages and Bollinger Bands as bumpers throughout the book. The term *bumper* has two applicable meanings. Each moving average represents a dynamic support and/or resistance price level that serves as a *speed bump* when the stock price reaches it. Like bumpers on a pinball table, they will elicit a reaction when touched. These levels will eventually either deflect or get pierced through. When a moving average bumper gets pierced, the stock price moves toward the next bumper for another reaction; deflection or piercing.

FIGURE 4.2 The complete seven time frame charts linked to a single level 2 order entry screen.

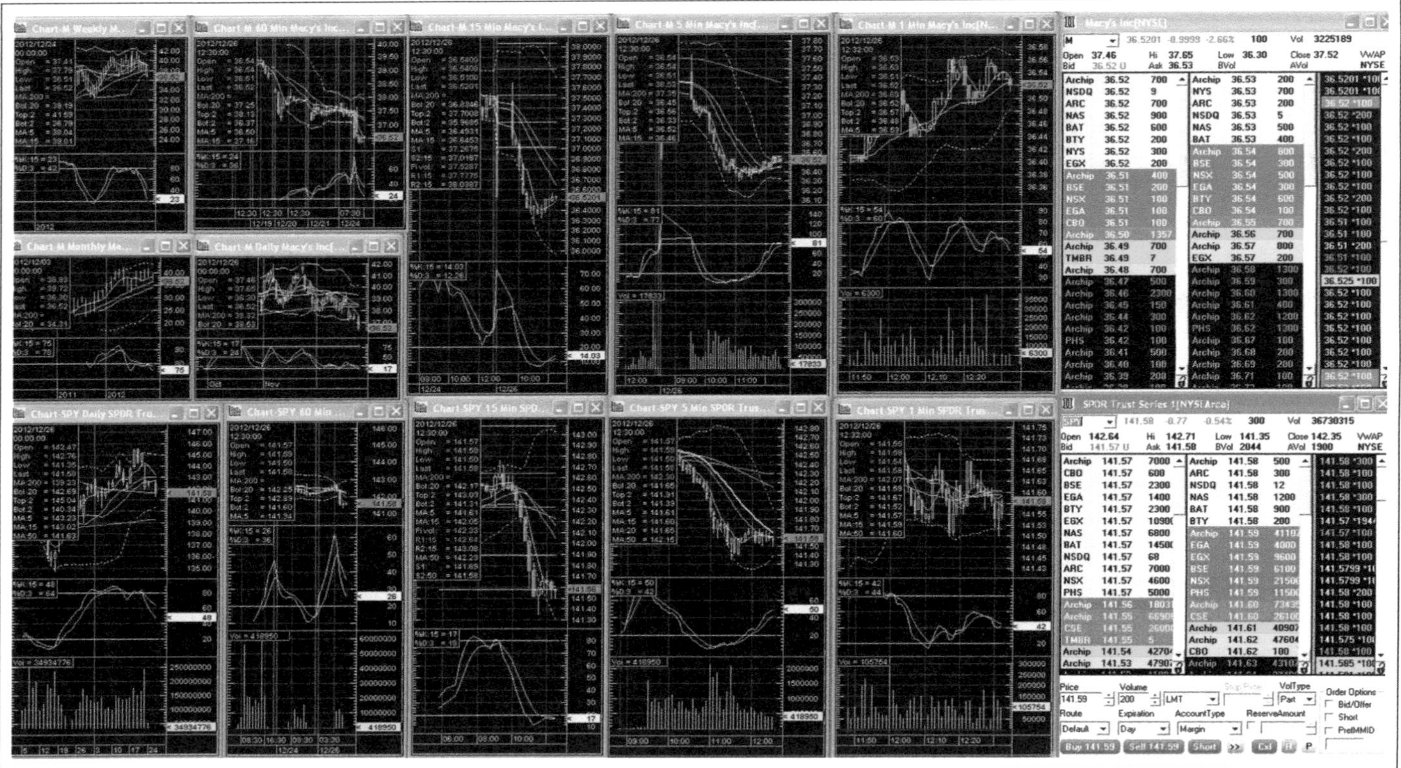

FIGURE 4.3 The focus stock and its seven time frames on the top row linked to the level 2 while having the five intraday time-frame charts for the SPY, which represents the general market headwinds. When overlapped above each other, it's easy to visually determine if the stock is correlated with the SPY or fading it.

FIGURE 4.4 A single-screen layout for traders who use a laptop or are limited to a single screen. This screen is composed of the 15-minute, 5-minute, and 1-minute charts linked to the focus stock's level 2 in the upper row and the SPY on the lower row.

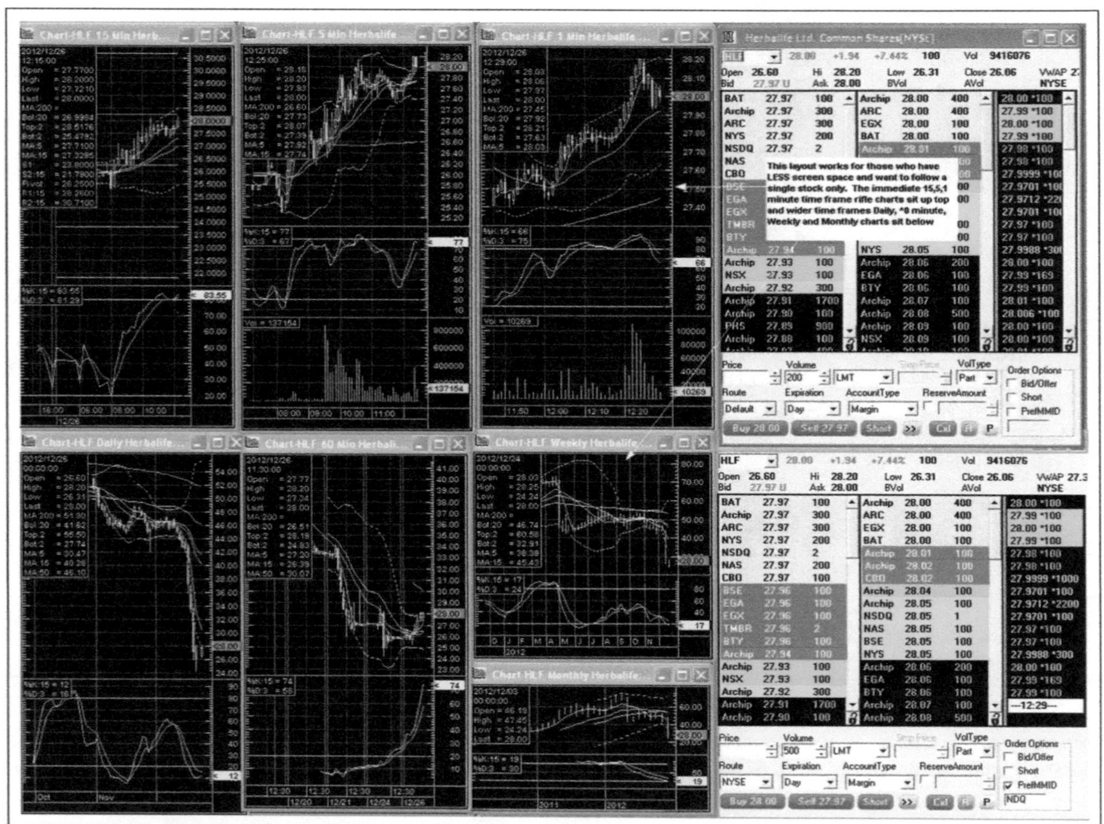

FIGURE 4.5 A three-monitor layout template that I presently use on my main system. All of the preformatted templates are available for clients of www.cobratrading.com.

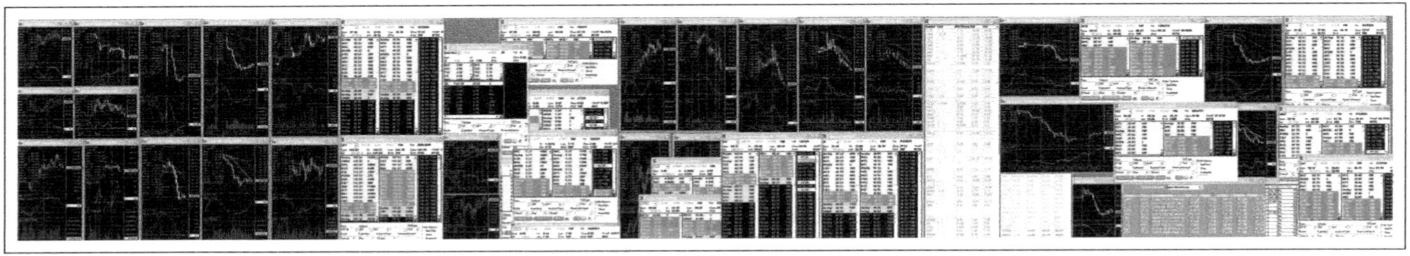

The significant moving averages that I use are the simple 5-period, 15-period, 20-period, 50-period, and 200-period moving averages. The 5-period is the leading (moves first) moving average followed by the 15-period moving average. When a 5-period moving average crosses over the 15-period moving average up and higher, or starts to rise up and away from the 15-period moving average (Figure 4.6), it forms a *breakout*. As the stock makes higher highs indicated by the rising 5-period moving average and higher lows indicated by the 15-period moving average, this is an *active uptrend*. The distance between the 5-period moving average and 15-period moving average is called the *trend channel*. If the stock no longer makes higher highs but stalls around the 5-period moving average, the 15-period moving average will usually continue to rise and close the distance to the 5-period moving average. This is considered an *inactive* or *stalled uptrend*. If the 15-period moving average stops rising and goes sideways/flat with the 5-period moving average this forms a *consolidation*. Stalled uptrends are where pup breakouts can form to thrust the stock to a higher price range, more on that later.

If the 5-period moving average crosses down and lower through the 15-period moving average, this is called a *breakdown*. As the stock makes lower lows and lower highs via 5- and 15-period moving averages, respectively, this is called an *active downtrend*, as shown in Figure 4.7. The distance between the 5- and 15-period moving averages are called . . . that's right, the *trend channel*. If the 5-period moving average goes flat because the stock is not making new lows, the 15-period moving average will continue to fall thereby closing the distance. This is a *stalled downtrend*, that will either form a *consolidation* by going flat with the 5-period moving average, or reverse if the 5-period moving average crosses back up and higher through the 15-period moving average, or form an inverse pup breakdown to collapse the stock to new lows.

The 20-period moving average acts as a secondary bumper to the 15-period moving average specific to situations. Don't forget to watch the history of the moving averages earlier in the day or to note which time frame is not experiencing any wiggles or headfakes at which moving averages. Stocks have muscle memory and tend to hold significant price levels as supports or resistances instinctively if they get tested with volume.

The larger 50- and 200-period moving averages are bigger speed bumps with bigger reactions, which makes they significant since they may only be reached occasionally, whereas a 5-/15-/20-period moving average gets reached many times a day. As a rule, the wider the time frame, the more significant the bumpers since they will be reached less frequently on a day-to-day basis.

FIGURE 4.6 A consolidation breakout.

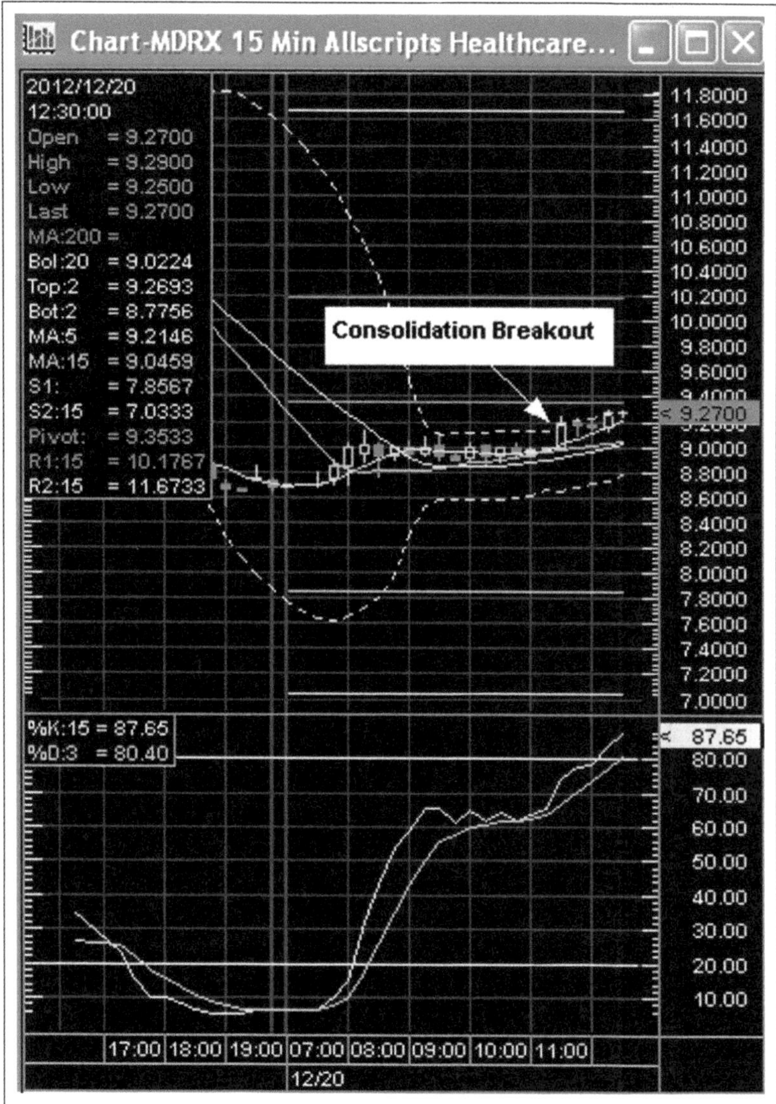

The Four Parts of Trends: Consolidation → Break → Peak → Exhaustion

If you were able to follow the aforementioned description of moving average trends, breaks, and consolidations, then you probably noticed that the cycle of price action is the four parts of trend. There are four parts to any

FIGURE 4.7 A breakdown and ensuing downtrend.

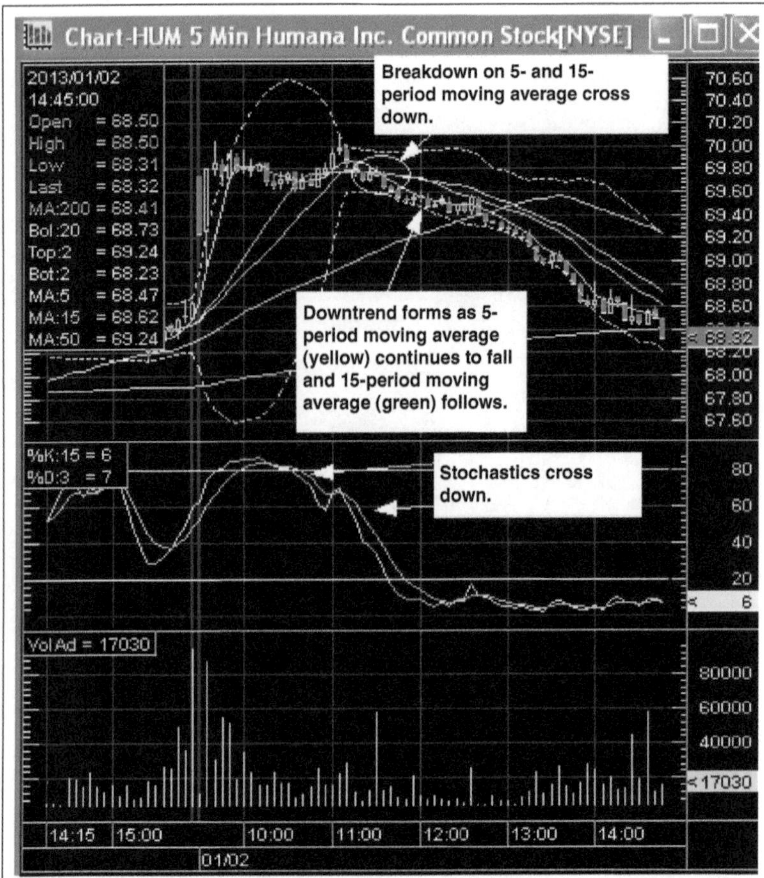

price trend cycle that continues to repeat itself (Figure 4.8). The mechanics don't change, only the magnitude, duration, and direction of the trend. The four parts are consolidation, break, peak, and exhaustion. After the exhaustion phase, the price will stall (synonymous with consolidation) then resume or reverse the trend with a breakout or breakdown. The consolidation can take shape in a three-hour choppy basing or a brief 10-minute stall and resume or reverse by a breakout or breakdown. Either way, they still operate through the four parts of trend. The break, peak, and exhaustion are playable. Stay out of the consolidations as they are very tight, thin, and full of headfakes.

FIGURE 4.8 Each stage of the four parts of trend.

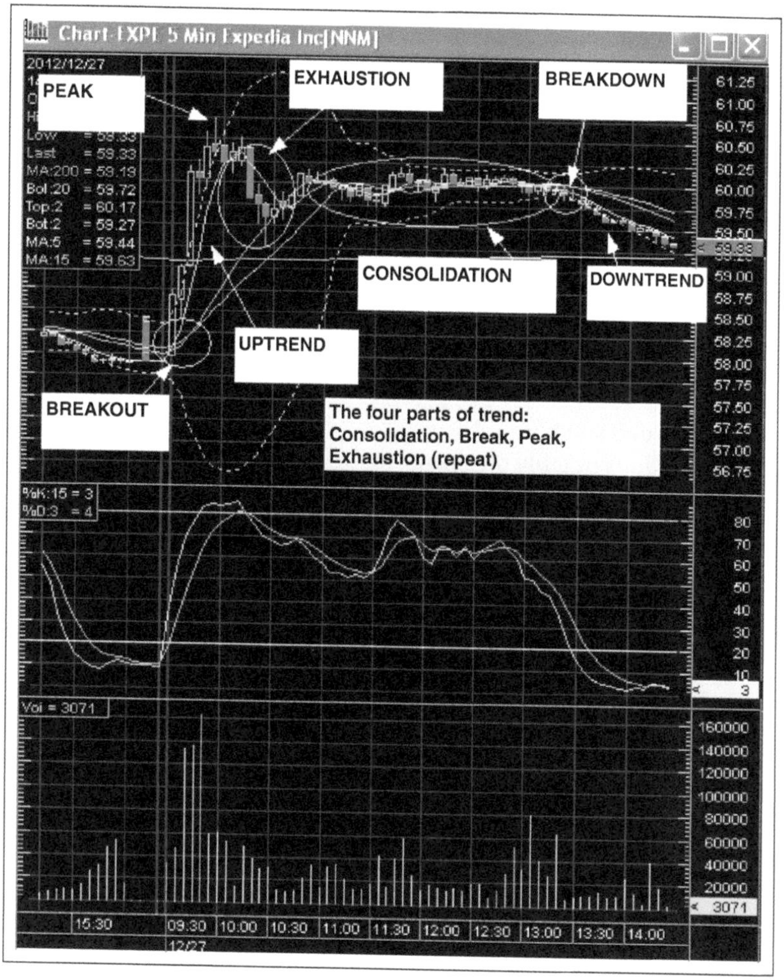

The Role of the Bumpers: Bollinger Bands

The Bollinger Bands consist of an upper Bollinger Band and lower Bollinger Band also referred to as the upper and lower envelopes. There is also a middle Bollinger Band represented by a 20-period simple moving average. Bollinger Bands serve as nominal price targets during trending cycles. The upper and lower Bollinger Bands represent the nominal upside and downside price range. During an uptrending cycle as prices move higher, the 5-period moving average will hold support on pullbacks causing the stock to bounce higher as the upper Bollinger Bands expand in unison. During downtrending cycles, the lower Bollinger Band will slope lower in union with the 5-period moving average, which rejects every bounce attempt. Each time the 5-period moving average fends off break attempts, the momentum of the trend continues thereby expanding the respective Bollinger Band.

The Bollinger Bands will contract and constrict when the price range tightens as volatility thins out and expands during breakouts/breakdowns as trends form and volatility rises. Like the heart, the Bollinger Bands contract and expand, and contract and expand, and so forth. The differentiating factors are the inconsistent durations of each motion. The very tightest contractions become so transparent that the expansion breaks are an open bandwagon that every participant expects to jump on, transforming into self-fulfilling prophecy. The inevitable expansion triggers every conventional entry signal. Very tight contractions notably on the 60-minute and daily are the rarest instances and should be given the most attention. *The general rule is, the tighter and longer the contraction, the greater the expansion. The widest time frames generate more powerful expansion in terms of magnitude and duration.*

Contracted Bollinger Bands indicate a consolidation/basing (Figure 4.9), which provides less risk for entries on the range break expansions. However, they are notorious for headfakes and false break attempts; therefore, it's best to avoid playing them until the break is confirmed. Contracted Bollinger Bands are precursors to impending breakouts and breakdowns. The challenge is to simultaneously be aware of and monitor while abstaining from playing them. When the break comes, the stock will no longer penetrate the 5-period moving average as it holds a trending support. It should start to slope away from the 15-period moving average in the direction of the trend as the Bollinger Band expands. This is the trend taking form and triggering the entry either on the break or small pullback.

The Slope Effect

The Bollinger Band sloping is a very useful characteristic to monitor during a trend move. Active trends have the 5-period moving average and Bollinger Bands sloping together in the same direction. When the trend shows any signs of exhaustion, it is the shorter time frame Bollinger Bands that will actually stall and hook against the 5-period moving average, as illustrated in Figure 4.10. This motion indicates that the nominal target is actually diminishing in value. This is a very subtle but effective and *often unnoticed* early

FIGURE 4.9 The nontradable, choppy, and ambiguous nature of a consolidation with contracted Bollinger Bands in a dry climate.

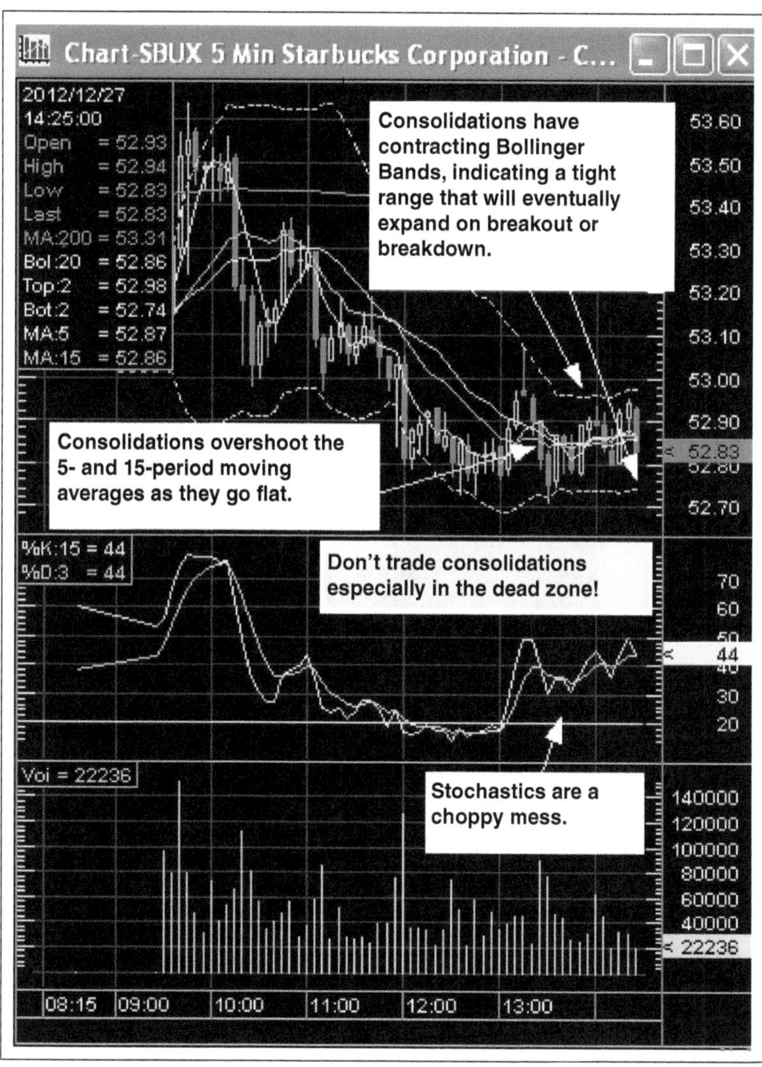

reversal signal (at least temporarily). It is prudent to react before the transparency gets full-blown by the time the reversal gains more traction.

The 5- and 1-minute Bollinger Bands are the best time frames to indicate an early reversal, which gives the trader a heads-up to scale out or exit the position or consider stepping in for a trend reversal trade. When the 1-minute upper Bollinger Band slope stalls and hooks down, it's a sign of

FIGURE 4.10 The slope change of the Bollinger Bands can give a powerful heads-up to an impending trend reversal.

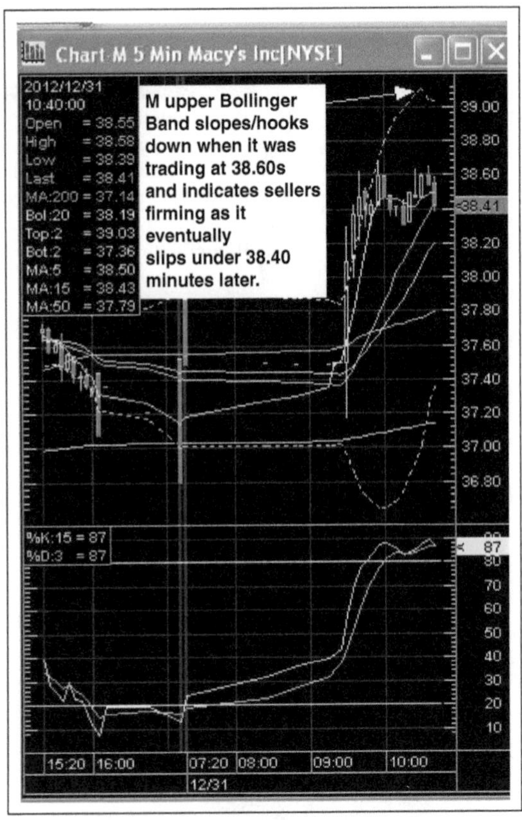

an oscillation move against the 5-period moving average uptrend. When the 1-minute lower Bollinger Band slope stalls and coils back up, it is an early sign of a possible bottom and exhaustion move back up. This doesn't always result in a complete trend reversal, but it does indicate an exhaustion-tightening move is nearing and measures need to be taken on existing positions.

The 60-minute and daily Bollinger Bands follow the +/– .20 rule. When stock prices exceed the 60-minute or daily upper Bollinger Bands, there is a .20 of buffer against the overshoot. Once the price surpasses that critical additional .20 coil level, the momentum actually increases. For example, if a stock ticks above the +.20 level, then the stock can go parabolic as gravity no longer applies. This is due to the sheer panic by the bears jumping over each other to cover. It's like breaking through the atmosphere into space entering a no gravity zone. The same applies in reverse when stocks fall more than –.20 under the 60-minute or daily lower Bollinger Bands, this causes panic amongst the bulls who rush to exit out of their positions. Stocks get extreme beyond the +/–.20 Bollinger Band levels as volumes rise on the panic from the reversion to the mean players.

When stocks eventually exhaust and return back over the Bollinger Bands on pullbacks, gravity makes up for lost time in a hurry on uptrends and slingshot bounces on downtrends. Therefore, once a stock breaches the +/–.20 tick beyond the 60-minute/daily Bollinger Band level, it tends to stay beyond that level for an extended duration of time, and pundits will use the level as a de facto momentum support for as long as possible. It is in these cases where the upper Bollinger Band becomes a support bumper and where lower Bollinger Bands become a resistance bumper. These are the outlier cases that occur usually on some news/rumor event catalyst and usually found in abundance during the earnings reporting seasons.

The Weekly and Monthly Moving Averages and Bollinger Bands

These are the widest Bollinger Bands that we use, and they carry the most weight. They act as the last line of support and resistance and rarely get pierced or remain pierced for too long except in the cases of extreme earnings reactions. When stocks gap up or down beyond the weekly and monthly Bollinger Bands, they will usually try to fill the gaps back to the Bollinger Bands on the weekly and monthly. Treat them like major bumpers with the +/–.20 rule in place for most stocks trading under $200.

They may not apply every day, but when the weekly/monthly bumpers are tested, they provide a valuable edge that can be used for early entries or to fortify a confirmed entry in confidence. Any pup/mini pup patterns further strengthen converging intraday trends and bumpers, shown in Figure 4.11. As they say, it's better to have a gun and not need it than to need it and not have one.

The Role of the Stochastics

The stochastics measure the direction of the momentum like a tachometer. They are composed of two oscillators; a lead %k and laggard %d. They are measured on a scale from 0 to 100 called bands. The 20 and 80 bands are significant bands as they indicate oversold (20 band) and overbought (80 band) levels. When both stochastics fall through the 20 band, the stock is considered

FIGURE 4.11 Useful and powerful weekly and monthly time-frame charts when the stock is trading in proximity of overlapping bumper levels.

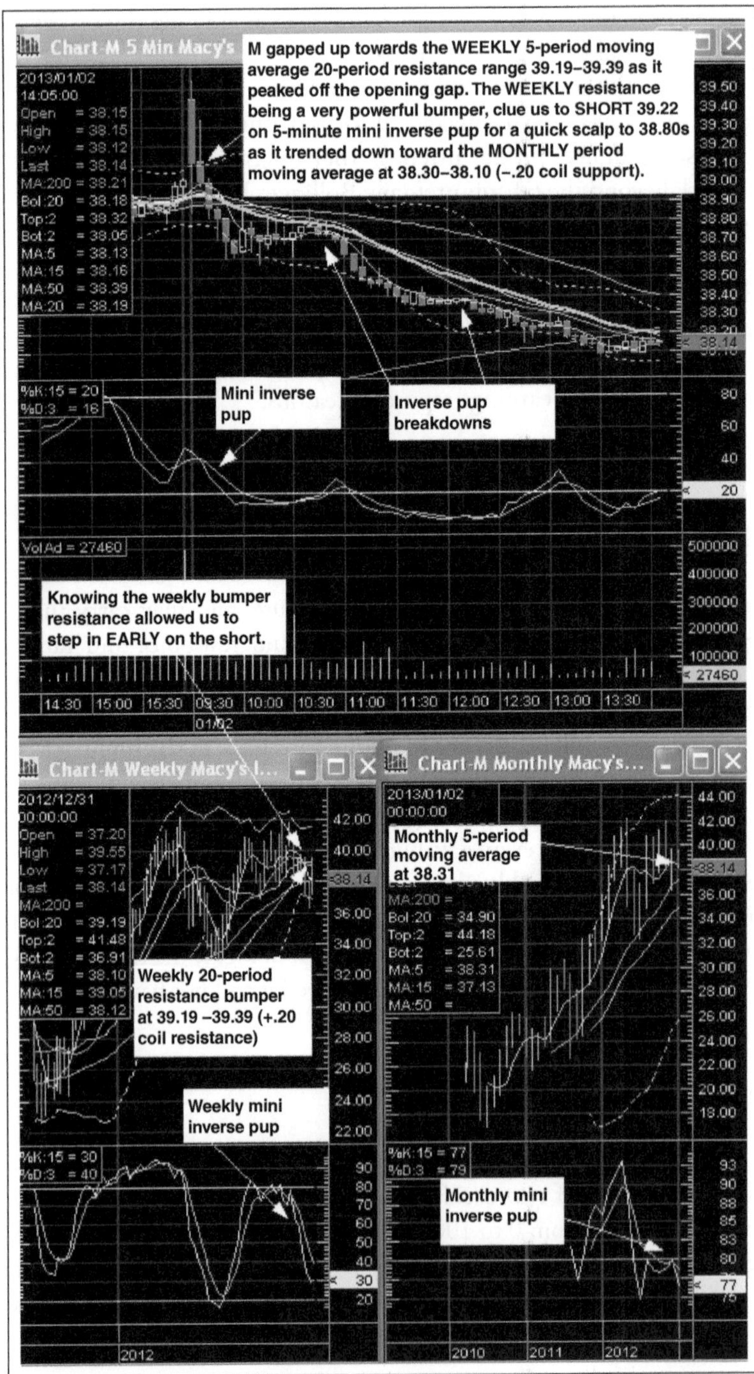

to be in oversold range. When both stochastics rise through the 80 band, the stock is considered to be in overbought range. However, stocks can often remain in extended periods of oversold and overbought levels. Reversals back up through the 20 bands are conventionally considered buy signals, while reversals back down through the 80 bands are conventionally considered sell/short signals. These are conventional assumptions and we know where conventional thinking gets you . . . in the gutter.

The argument against the effectiveness of stochastics has been the lack of consistency when these conventional buy and sell/short signals trigger. For example, a trader who took XYZ long at 53.30 on a 1-minute 20-band stochastics cross-up may have gotten a nice spike to sell at 53.70 for a +.40 profit in the morning. The same trader may take the same long again in the early afternoon at 53.30 on an identical 1-minute stochastics 20-band bounce, but this time it only bounces +.10 for the full drawn out 1-minute oscillation to the 80 band, which rejects and proceeds to collapse –.50 against him for a –.40 loss. In both cases the stochastics were identical buy signals on the 20-band cross up bounces but resulted in completely opposite outcomes. This argument is valid. I know, because I followed this belief too, until hundreds of hours down the road I discovered the need for a trend indicator, which was the moving averages. The moving averages gave the clear reasoning why two identical stochastics formations resulted in two opposite reactions. In the first example, unbeknownst to the trader, he took a fine entry long into an existing uptrend pullback that resulted in a +.40 profit on the price spike with the stochastics on fresh morning volume. In the second example, the trader took the same buy signal but entered into a downtrend. The 20-band stochastics bounced to the downtrend resistance and rejected, forcing the stochastics to cross down plunging the stock price with it. This was my first taste of the symbiotic relationship between moving average and stochastics and the early steps toward ultimately creating the rifle charts in the coming years. Just as significant was my discovery of pups and mini pup patterns. I can't understate that necessity is the mother of invention. The aforementioned examples shaped the early clues to discovering the pup and mini pup price patterns. So without further delay, let's get to the nitty-gritty!

Spotting and Trading Fades

Throughout this book, I will mention fades. When the SPY rises on an uptrend, this usually lifts most stocks higher as well. Vice versa, when the SPY falls on a downtrend, this usually pushes down most stocks as well. When I say most, I am referring to the correlated stocks starting from sector leaders on down.

Spotting the fade is a skill you develop from watching how a particular stock reacts when the SPY or futures and/or sector peers are rising and falling. There is a natural delay as lower tiers take more time to move based on the magnitude of the leaders within a sector. However, when a stock rises as the SPY falls, that is initially considered a buy fade. When a stock falls while the SPY rises, that is considered a sell fade. Sell fades indicate aggressive sellers, and buy fades indicate aggressive buyers. The purpose of spotting a fade is to allow you the opportunity to step into position with the fade when the SPY reverses the immediate direction, thereby propelling the fading stock farther in the direction of the fade. For example: if SNDK is buy fading as the SPY sells off, then SNDK should bounce stronger when the SPY bounces and vice versa if SNDK were sell fading into a SPY bounce, SNDK should fall harder when the SPY falls back down. This is just a rudimentary explanation as there are many factors involved in determining if a fade exists and whether it's playable. Up until my discovery of mini pups and perfect storms, fades had to be eyeballed on the level 2 screens. However, they can now be visualized and interpreted quicker thanks to the stochastics moving average charts and the utilization of pups and perfect storms. In fact, one of the main qualifiers with perfect storms is the resilience of the fade when the SPY moves against the formation for a temporary period of time.

Not all fades are the same. Fades are usually temporary, awarding the plunder to the first set of participants able to spot and capitalize on it. The law of transparency eventually sets in as the fade fizzles out or even reverses when transparency gets full blown or if the SPY moves against it for an extended period of time. Fades are limited in time.

The process of forming a fade is akin to boiling water in a pot with the lid on. It builds up steam as the reversion and oscillation players push against the fade only to get smacked hard the other way when the SPY turns in the direction of the fade. These build up pressure that ultimately releases in a violent price move. Unless of course, it fizzles out as the volume erodes as participants thin out and lose interest. In the case of the latter, it probably wasn't a very good qualified fade to begin with. Fades need to have volume, just as pups and perfect storms need volume. This is why fades are intricate components of perfect storms. The fade often acts as a heads-up to the impending confirmation and early heads-up on the trigger, as illustrated in Figure 4.12.

If a stock is actively downtrending while the SPY is actively uptrending, then we call this a sell fade. If a stock is actively uptrending while the SPY

FIGURE 4.12 CREE stock in the top row is sell fading against the SPY in the bottom row.

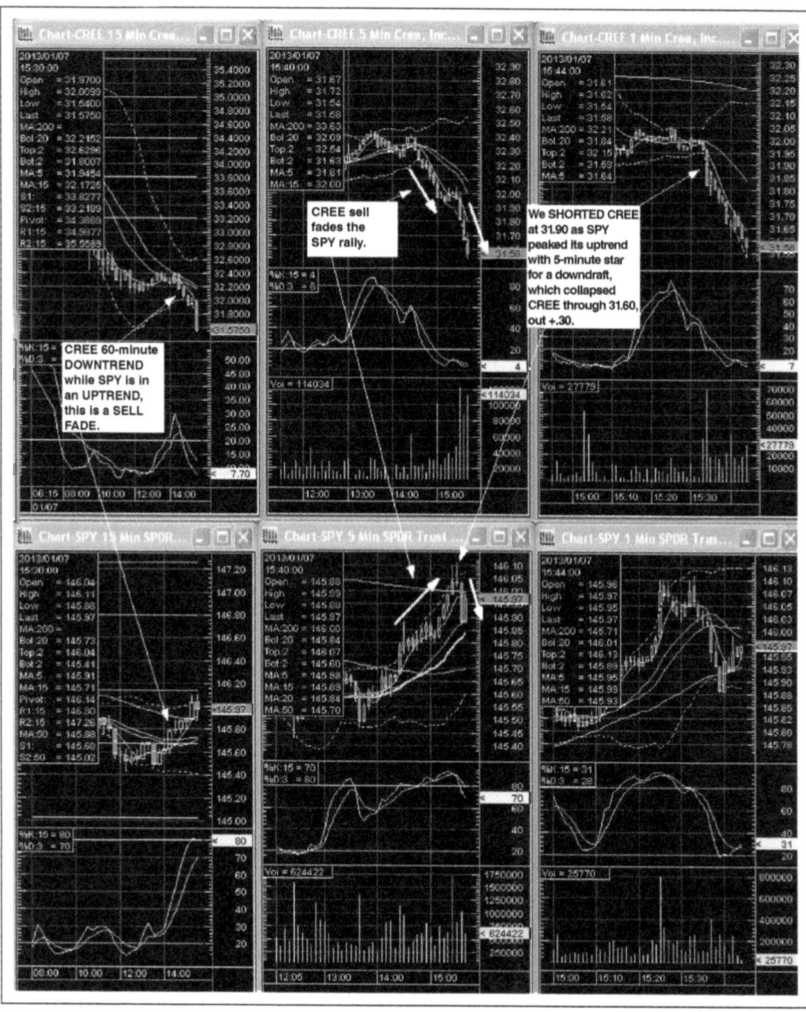

is actively downtrending, then we call this a buy fade. The key word here is *active* trending where the 5-period moving average(s) are rising or falling with a distinct trend. If the moving averages are flat and or volume is light/shrinking, then it could just be a wiggle but nothing out of the ordinary yet. The stronger the volume in the stock, the more transparency forms on the fade. The best visual way to determine the existence of the fade is to overlap the chart to compare with the SPY. When two or more time frames are actively trending opposite to the active trend of the SPY, then it's officially a fade especially if there is rising volume.

Fades indicate the presence of exceptionally motivated large orders needing immediate liquidity to fill. The best liquidity comes from fading into the direction of the SPY's active trend. Fades will eventually revert back to aligning with the SPY once the large orders are filled.

If a stock is sell fading, then it should fall harder when the SPY peaks and/or exhausts. If a stock is buy fading, it should bounce harder when the SPY bottoms and/or bounces. The opportunity presents itself by using the shorter time frame charts to time an entry into the fade as the SPY exhausts.

Be aware that fades are temporary conditions that will eventually revert back to following the SPY. If the fade gets too excessive against the SPY, then it could turn into a laggard once the heavy orders are liquid and the threat of a fast reversal looms. In some cases, the fades are done purposely to set a trap to lure in more participants at excessive levels only to reverse it back hard and smoke out the chasers. As long as you manage to scale out before the 1-minute stochastics turn, you shouldn't get trapped too often.

The Two Most Important Price Patterns: Pups and Mini Pups

Now that you have the rifle charts, you are empowered to accurately track the two most important price patterns in the markets. These are the core uranium particles that ultimately detonate the perfect storm patterns, which are covered in Chapter 5. They are also core to the methodology and require a firm understanding of the mechanics and applications. These are the pup and mini pup patterns. The rifle chart components work symbiotically to identify these patterns as they develop.

The Pup Breakout Pattern

These form on stalled trends where the 5-period moving average goes flat while the 15-period moving average continues to close the distance to the 5-period moving average and closing the trend channel generating steam like pressure, as shown in Figure 4.13. The smaller the trend channel is, the less risk on entry at the 5-period moving average, since the secondary support is the 15-period moving average. Eventually the buyers figure this out and step in with volume above the 5-period moving average indicated by candle(s) closes above the 5-period moving average, which panics the bears to cover

FIGURE 4.13 The pup breakout pattern.

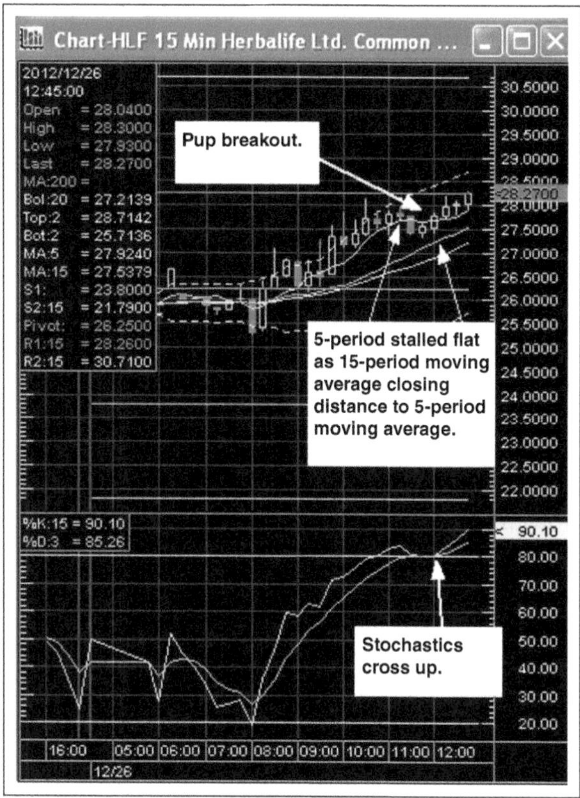

their short positions, which causes more buying. The result is a pup breakout that thrusts the stock to higher price levels and re-activates the uptrend.

This is what happens with the moving averages, but if you were only to use the moving averages alone, you would get shaken out too many times. This is where the stochastics comes into play. The stochastics' cross-up is what confirms and validates the pup breakout. Symbiotic relationships are beautiful. If the stochastics have not crossed, then it is considered a make or break situation. These happen during the consolidation/stall–period. The danger of stepping into a long position during a make or break is that the pup breakout attempt could just headfake and result in a breakdown. Step in front of the stochastics' cross-confirmation too many times, and you will have your own mental breakdown. Therefore, the general rule is to wait for the stochastics' cross to confirm before buying your position long. The exception to the rule is if there is a wider time frame pup in place and you are scaling into your long position on the smaller time frame stochastics pullbacks. If you are new to the methods, then start with the general rules to form a solid base of knowledge before delving into the exceptions. Note that I said general rules, not conventional rules!

Pup Breakouts *trigger* on stalled/flat 5-period moving average + rising 15-period moving average + candle(s) close above 5-period moving average + stochastics cross-up + volume rise = target to upper Bollinger Bands or next viable bumper

The Inverse Pup Breakdown Pattern

As the name implies, these have the identical mechanics and dynamics as pup breakouts, just in reverse/upside down. They are breakdowns that form at the stalled point of a downtrend where the 5-period moving average goes flat while the 15-period moving average continues to move lower closing the distance to the 5-period moving average. The bulls are trying to fend off the bears by holding the line literally at the 5-period moving average. As the 15-period moving average closes the distance, it builds up steam and releases to the downside as the 5-period moving average resumes the move lower as the bulls panic for the exits. The stochastic cross-down confirms the inverse pup breakdown in addition to candle(s) close below the 5-period moving average and volume rise as Figure 4.14 illustrates.

Pup breakdowns (called inverse pup breakdowns) *trigger* on stalled/flat 5-period moving average + falling 15-period moving average + candle(s) close below 5-period moving average + stochastics cross up + volume rise = target to lower Bollinger Bands or next viable bumper.

The Mini Pup Breakout Pattern

Just as the pup pattern forms on stalled trends, the mini pup pattern operates in the same fashion but with the stochastics. The mini pup looks like a pup in shape but is formed on the stochastics. The %k lead stochastic will stall as the price peaks and pulls back to test the 5-period moving average indicated by a red candle(s). These are called *counter candles*, since they are counter to the trend. They are reversal attempts that suck in premature bears to short ahead of the impending stochastics cross down; see Figure 4.15. This happens during the exhaustion stage of the trend. As bears lick their chops for a tasty sell-off, the stalled/flat 5-period moving average continues to resiliently hold its ground long enough for the stock to pierce the body high of the counter candle(s) which causes the lead %k stochastic to slope back up (instead of crossing the laggard %d back down). This immediately

FIGURE 4.14 The inverse pup breakdown pattern.

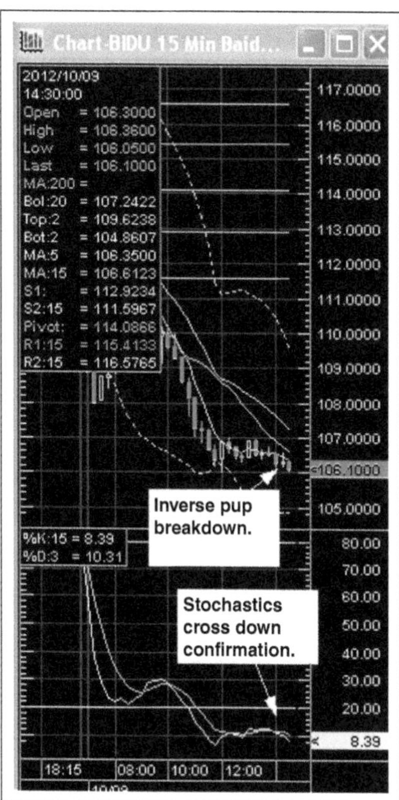

panics the bears to cover their short positions and shakes buyers off the fence as they race for liquidity as the stock spikes on a breakout as the uptrend resumes toward the upper Bollinger Bands or next viable price bumper as illustrated in Figure 4.16.

Keep an eye on the clock as the candle close for that time frame nears. This is where the bulls will make their move to push the close above the counter candle body highs. This will cause the 5-period moving average to update higher at the candle close which rumbles the ground hard enough to flush out the bears. Usually, you can take your longs once the counter candle high is pierced, but the safer entry is on a candle close above. Since these moves can be drastic, you may not get a decent entry if you wait for the candle close, just piercing the price level is enough to trigger the mini pup and subsequent reactions. Volume should also rise on the breakout. The volume is integral to the breakout.

FIGURE 4.15 The very important counter candle triggering a mini pup breakout.

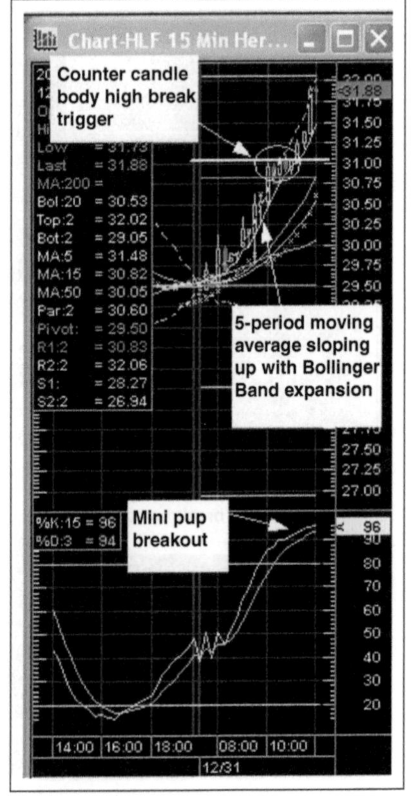

Mini pup breakouts *trigger* on price breaks through the body high of counter candle(s) above the 5-period moving average + %k lead stochastic slope up + %d laggard stochastic continues rising + volume rise = target upper Bollinger Bands or next viable bumper.

The Counter Candle(s) Trigger

Please pay very close attention here. The counter candle(s) will be the price trigger for mini pup breakouts and mini inverse pup breakdowns. They are absolutely essential for the trigger, so you must have an absolutely FIRM UNDERSTANDING of these candles.

Up until *Way of the Trade*, the trigger on the mini pups was the %k lead stochastics slope up with a candle close above the 5-period moving average. Through thousands of trades, I have discovered the most exact price trigger

FIGURE 4.16 A stochastics mini pup pattern with counter candle buy trigger.

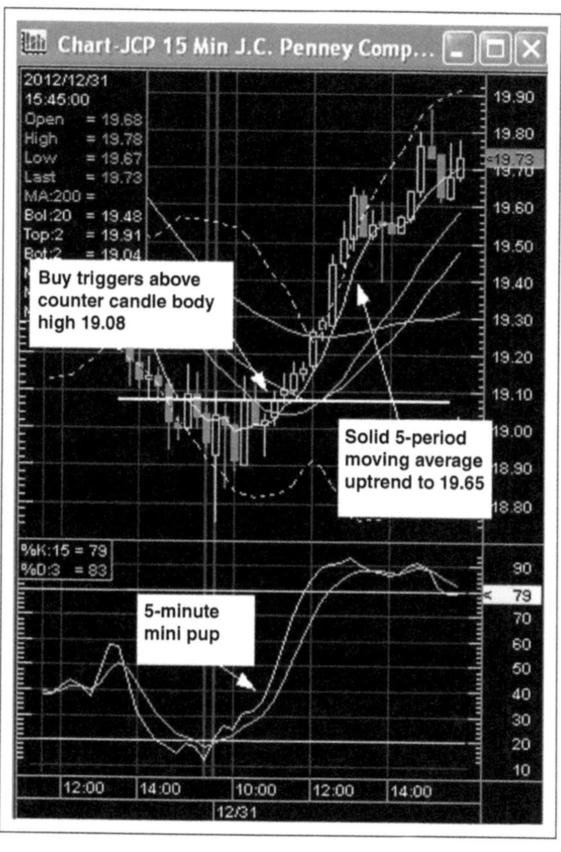

that will often PRECEDE the stochastics movement. These are what I call the counter candles, and the only reason the mini pup even exists. Without counter candles, the stochastics oscillation would never stall since there would only be continuous green candles nonstop. We know that isn't possible. Therefore, in an uptrend, you will get a series of green candles before a red candle representing the sellers/shorts will form. This red candle(s) is the counter (trend) candle, since it goes against the uptrend. On downtrends, it will be a series of red candles and then a green counter candle(s).

The counter candle(s) are the most important price trigger with mini pups. It is the counter candle trigger that allows the %k lead stochastics to hook/slope up rather than cross the %d laggard down. This slope up causes a headfake panic for the counter trend players, who then panic to exit their positions, which in turn panics buyers to come off the fence (during breakouts). The opposite happens during breakdowns, of course, as the %k lead stochastic hook/slopes back down without crossing the %d laggard stochastics up. This causes the bulls to get headfaked and panic out of their longs while bears rush to short the breakdown. The price trigger is always based on the counter candle.

The basic counter candles appear counter to the moving average trend and set the line in the sand for the trend resumption trigger based on the price of the body high break on uptrends and body low breaks on downtrends. Remember that counter candles only apply when there is a trend in place and are not applicable during consolidations or basing periods.

Counter candles tend to follow Fibonacci series as to when they show up. Fibonacci series started with prime numbers that add into each other starting with 1, so it goes 1, 3, 5, 8, 13, 21, and so on. Counter candles tend to show up at the third through fifth candle in the trend series. This means if there are two green consecution candles, then often the third candle will attempt to be a counter candle. It is not confirmed until the candle closes red. If it closes green, then look for the fifth candle in the series. If the fifth candle closes green, then look for the eighth candle and so forth. Very rarely do you get past the eighth candle, but when you do, that is when the trend is becoming excessive and due for an exhaustion tightening at the very least to rest. I'll review shorting excessive slow grinds later.

Back to our example in Figure 4.17, let's say that after three green candles in an uptrend (make sure it is in an uptrend meaning 5-period moving average is rising and holding support), the fourth and fifth candle closes red. That

FIGURE 4.17 The mini pup buy trigger on counter candle body high breaks.

means that some sellers are taking profits and some bears are thinking the stock is due for a pullback and short simultaneously. The high of the body of the counter candle in an uptrend is the price trigger for a mini pup. That is the point where we can assume the bears started shorting the stock in hopes of covering lower into the sell-off. At this point, the sellers push the stock back down to test the 5-period moving average support. If they successfully break it with another red candle close, then that puts the stochastics in jeopardy of crossing down and the trend in jeopardy of a reversal. Healthy mini pups usually will hold support at the 5-period moving average and deflect any tests there. While many traders will use pullbacks to the 5-period moving average to enter early long into the selling, this can be risky since there is no confirmation that the downdraft has concluded and naturally if the 1-minute stochastics cross down (%k lead crosses the %d slow back down), the early buyers get trapped as the stock collapses.

The better early entry is measuring the value of the body high of the counter candle. If there is more than a single counter candle, then use the highest body high of the sequence of red candles for the trigger line for the price and be prepared to buy a few ticks above. If the stock bounces through the counter candle high, that panics the shorts to buy cover, which then sucks in more buyers as the stochastics does the %k hook up forming the mini pup pattern and squeezing the stock back up to resume the active uptrend towards the next bumper. The reason why you should take the long entry a tick above is that the 1-minute candle closes very fast (every 60 seconds!). Once the 1-minute candle closes above the counter candle trigger, it accelerates even faster as more shorts panic to cover, which puts you in a precarious spot of trying to chase an entry competing against the algos/HFT programs with their 30-millisecond fills. Which means you won't get filled at a decent price or pay too much.

On uptrends, the long trigger is a tick or candle close above the body high of the counter candle, as shown in Figure 4.18. If there are more than two counter candles, then the highest body high of the counter candles is the break trigger, see Figure 4.17.

On downtrends (Figure 4.19), the short trigger is a tick or candle close below the low of the counter candle low. If there are more than two counter candles, pick the lowest body low of the counter candles as the break trigger.

Counter candles are formed counter to the direction of the 5-period moving average during a trend and against the prior series of candles. There has to be a trend in place in order to have something to counter and reverse against.

FIGURE 4.18 Uptrends require a counter candle body high break to trigger the stochastics mini pup for that time frame.

In most cases, this will be pretty straightforward; however, in situations of channel tightenings where the 5-period moving average is actually closing the channel towards the 15-period moving average, the technical definition would be a downtrend, BUT, the 5-period moving average is moving counter to the trend itself by sloping toward the 5-period moving average. When

FIGURE 4.19 Downtrends require a break below the body low of the counter candle to trigger a mini inverse pup.

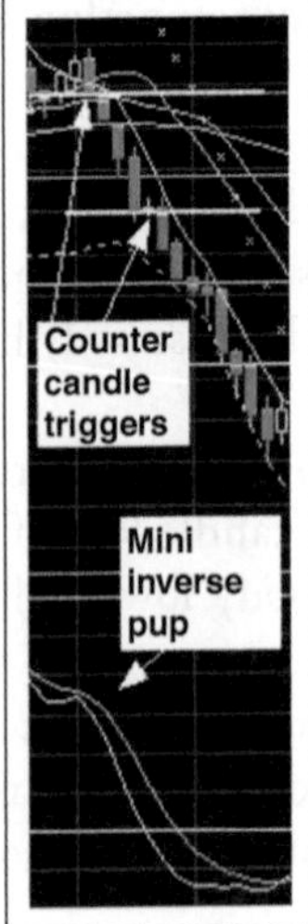

the stock price gets back up through the 5-period moving average, then the countertrend candles will be red or dojis, as illustrated in Figure 4.20.The dojis can be green or red. It can get a bit tricky during channel tightenings. Just remember that counter candles stall the 5-period moving average then price triggers when they fail, thereby continuing the 5-period moving average trend triggered by the mini pup.

There may be more risk in taking the early entry on a tick break exceeding the counter candle as opposed to waiting for a candle close confirmation, but the reward is also greater since the confirmation candle is often a very large candle that assures a more expensive entry. There are ways to mitigate the risk when two or more wider time frames have existing mini pups, which leaves the 1-minute as the trigger for a perfect storm breakout, which is covered in Chapter 5.

FIGURE 4.20 The advantage of having a hammer candle for the counter candle.

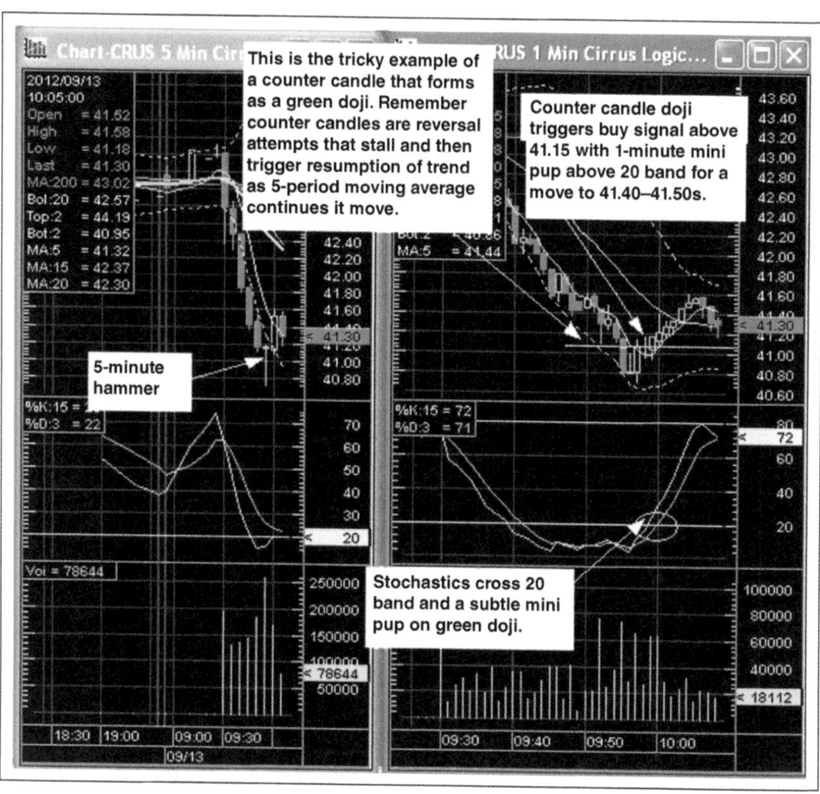

Although many traders are at ease paying a higher cost for more security on the entry, be aware that this eats into the nominal profit if you end up chasing your entry too far or without taking quicker profits. With the algos/HFT programs, it pays to be early as the leapfrogging magnifies quickly in terms of price, which is good if you are in early, and bad if you are chasing, and worse if you are on the wrong side. If mini pups are the fuse, then counter candles are the matchstick.

The Mini Inverse Pup Breakdown Pattern

This stochastics pattern forms on breakdowns, countertrend tightenings, and downtrends. The mechanics are just flipped to reflect the bearish nature of the pattern. The 5-period moving average plays the pivotal role of being the lead resistance that rejects bounce attempts in a stalled downtrend. The pattern triggers after the 5-period moving average resistance fends off break attempts and the stock falls back under the counter candle(s) body low, which causes the %k lead stochastic to slope/hook back down rather than cross up (see Figure 4.21). This flushes out the panicked bulls as the stochastics acts like a trap door that opens right up.

Mini pups are market tested at reactive inflection points to force the hand of transparency. The beauty of mini pups is that they offer market-tested protection by defending the 5-period moving average long enough to reverse back through the counter candle body triggers. This provides a solid stop price provision on 5-period moving average breaks and targets at the Bollinger Bands or next viable bumper. The stochastics points the way with the %k stochastic slope/hook.

Stairstep Mini Pups

When mini pups happen in succession within the same oscillation, we label them stairstep mini pups. The succession indicates that the counter parties are still trying to make a stand since the initial mini pup break isn't as violent, giving the impression of weakness. The smaller initial price break movement makes these so dangerous in that the counter players are tricked into complacency as they assume the break is already losing steam. In reality, they are getting set up for a much more magnified price move as a result of their complacency. Stairstep mini pups tend to grind slowly and incrementally towards a final climax on the 80/20 band breaks, where the largest, fastest, and most voluminous part of the price move is generated, as the stubborn (and beaten down) counter parties capitulate in sheer terror.

FIGURE 4.21 The counter candle acts as a price trigger for the mini inverse pup.

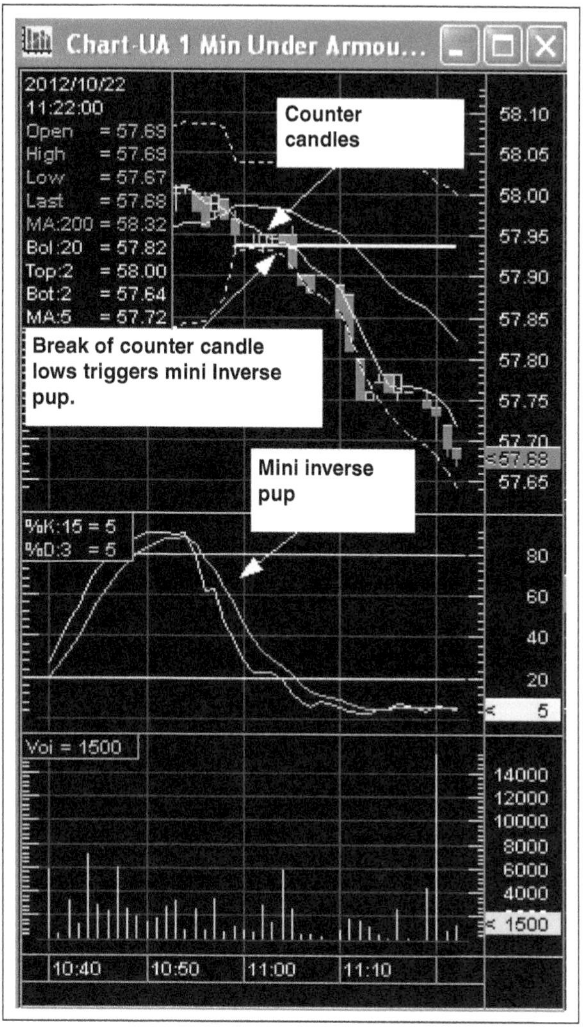

Pretzel Mini Pups

With a typical mini pup, the %k stochastic shouldn't touch or cross the %d before it slopes/hooks on the break. However, there are instances where the %k lead stochastics actually kisses or crosses the %d initially and then headfakes by crossing right back in the direction of the trend. The squiggly stochastics resembles a pretzel, which is why I call them pretzel mini pups, shown in Figure 4.22. The initial stochastics failure occurs when price

FIGURE 4.22 A pretzel mini pup.

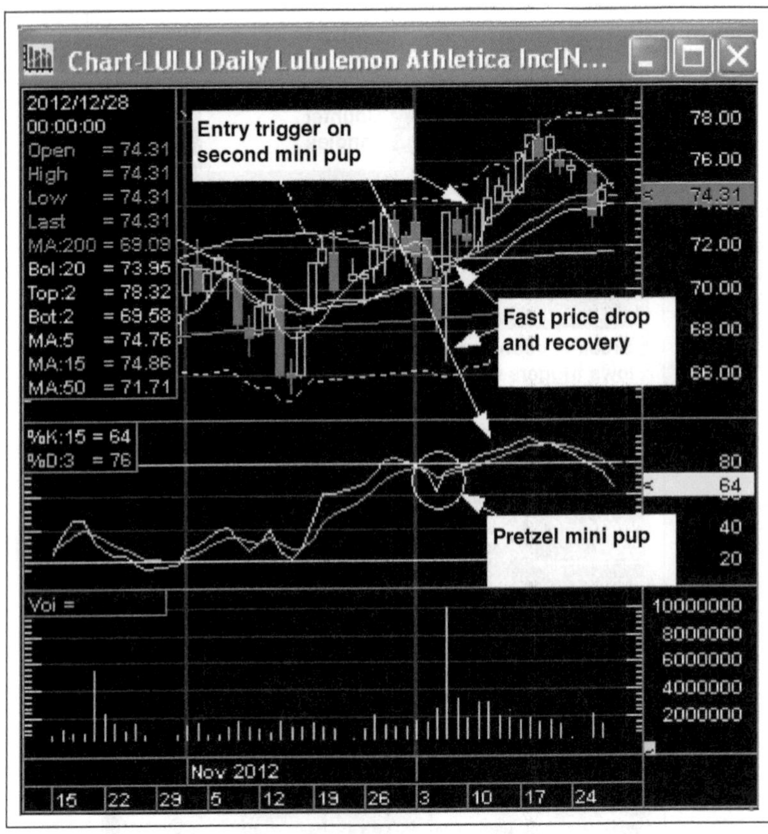

pierces through the 5-period moving average (and sometimes the 15- and 20-period) so fast that it panics in more counter players only to get flushed out on the recovery as the mini pup forms on the break of the counter candle trigger. These are tricky patterns that can also be a result of macro market choppiness or big gaps up and down as well. They really only can be identified afterward, unless there are wider time frame mini pups foreshadowing the shorter time frame mini pup. Either way, they are nail biters for sure, and the best way to play them is to step in on the next mini pup trigger.

Mini inverse pup breakdowns *trigger* on price breaks through the body low of the counter candle(s) below the 5-period moving average + %k lead stochastic slope down + %d laggard stochastic continues falling + volume rise = target lower Bollinger Bands or next viable bumper.

Mini Pup Reversal Fades to Channel Tightenings

When a mini pup breakout loses its 5-period moving average support and fails to regain it via rejected counter candle(s), then it can actually form a mini inverse pup tightening where the prior 5-period moving average support becomes the resistance as it slopes countertrend to close the distance towards the 15-period moving average. This is called a channel tightening, as the mini pup is inverted to close the distance to the next-lower bumper. This happens after large gaps or an abnormally long and obnoxiously extended mini pup. The upper Bollinger Bands will give the earliest signal with its slope stalling flat or hooking down against the 5-period moving average.

The same applies when a mini inverse pup breakdown loses its 5-period moving average on buying pressure and fails to regain it after counter candle sell attempts failed to break the 5-period moving average, the 5-period reverses its role to become a support as the stochastics reverse to form a mini pup for a channel tightening towards the 15-period moving average as shown in Figure 4.23. This happens on dumper gaps and extended min inverse pups. The initial clues of the impending channel tightening can be found on the lower Bollinger Band slope reversals against the trend.

Combination Pup and Mini Pup Pattern

Every so often, you will come across a single time frame chart that forms not only a pup breakout, but the stochastics confirmation comes in the form of a mini pup as well. Naturally, these are even stronger signals with extra protection on the 5-period moving average support. Consider these as bonus patterns and take advantage of the profit opportunities when they form as illustrated in Figures 4.24 and 4.25.

Stinky 2.50 and Five-Level de Facto Price Bumpers

I've pointed out this phenomenon ever since the equities market moved to decimalization pricing. The .40, .50, and .60 price level on every 0, 2, 4, 5, 7, 9 price level plays a de facto price bumper. The easier way to figure this out is go in 2.50 increments like 20, 22.50, 25, 27.50, 30, and so on. Each 2.50 level gets a .10 overshoot at the .50 price level of the whole number. Therefore 17 would have a 17.40, 17.50, and 17.60 stinky 2.50s range.

FIGURE 4.23 The transition from mini pup breakout that peaks and exhausts to reverse into a mini inverse pup as the 5-period moving average slopes down.

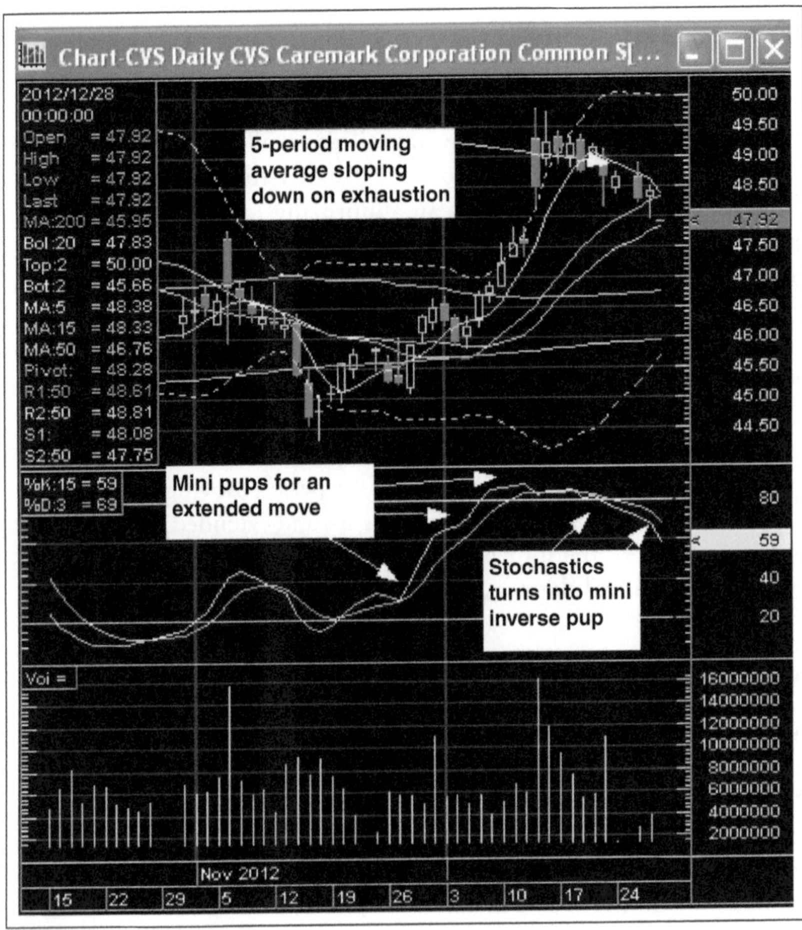

The stinky 5s represent the five incremental levels with the same .50 price level overshoots of +/–.10 but also apply to the whole number preceding. Therefore, 20 level would be 20.50 +/–.10 resulting in 20.40, 20.50, and 20.60 being the stinky 5s levels, and 19.40, 19.50, and 19.60 being the lower stinky 5s levels.

These stinky bumpers were originally called sticky to describe how prices tend to have a hard time breaking into the range, but once they enter, they have a tough time breaking out of the range. These are enhanced speed bumpers that act as initial resistances when tested and then strong supports when broken. When they overlap with other bumpers, it solidifies the levels even

FIGURE 4.24 A combination moving average pup breakout that also contains a stochastics mini pup.

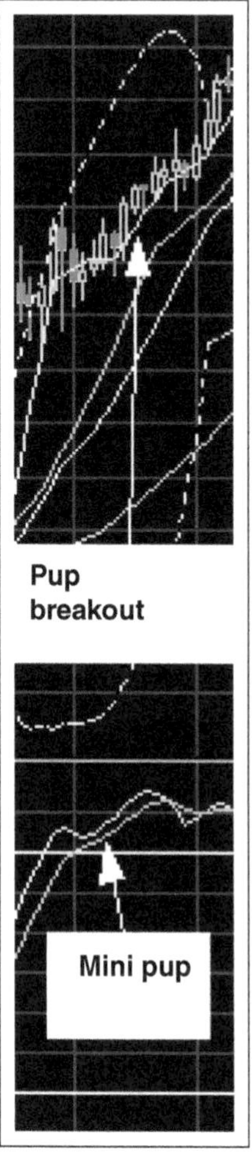

stronger. These are good areas to take profits or use as stop loss triggers when broken.

The (Only) Three Candlesticks I Use

Much thanks goes to Steve Nison for introducing candlestick charts to the masses. His books are the premiere references to these price tools, and I highly recommend them for anyone wanting more depth of knowledge.

FIGURE 4.25 Another combination pup and mini pup breakout on the same time frame pup.

I tend to stick to three candlestick patterns when it comes to the methods, and these are the reversal candles known as hammers, shooting stars, and dojis. The significance of the candles relies on the number of preceding trend candles and then the following candle. I tend to give relevance only to those reversal candles that have at least three or more succession candles before it. Additionally, I prefer to have these reversal candles form at some significant bumper support or resistance price level usually around a Bollinger Band or overlapping support/resistance levels.

Hammer candles form at price bottoms indicated by a long tail usually twice the size of the body closing at or near the highs (Figure 4.26). They are confirmed hammers when the following candle(s) close higher than the body high of the hammer. The general rule is to enter longs above the hammer candle's body high and trail either the body low or the tail/shadow low breaks.

Anytime the highs of stars or lows of hammers are surpassed with subsequent candle(s), they risk getting declawed with an extra-strong trend

FIGURE 4.26 Hammer candles.

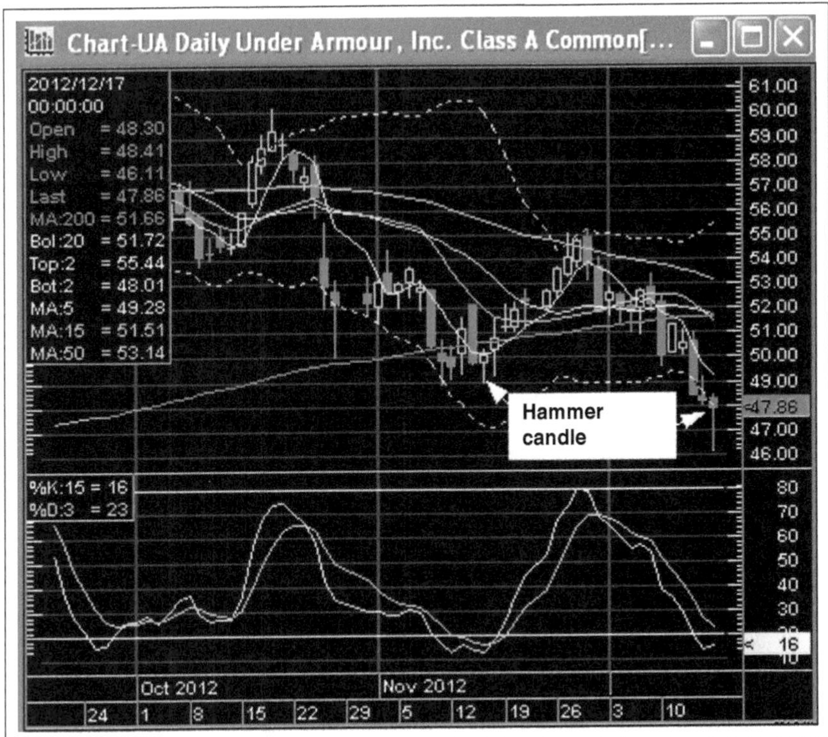

continuation push as the reversal candle players get flushed right out (often times with pup/mini pup perfect storms). These highs and lows also become break triggers if and when they get surpassed later. This is why it's important that there be as many preceding trending candles prior to the reversal candle.

Shooting star candles form at price tops indicated by long tails usually twice the size of the body, which closes at or near the lows (Figures 4.27 and 4.28). They are confirmed shooting stars when the following candle(s) close lower than the body low of the star. The general rule is to short under the body low of the shooting star candle and trail the body high or tail/shadow high.

Dojis are reversal/continuation candles where the body open and close are nearly identical to form a small or no body, resembling a + sign as shown in Figure 4.29. This forms a line in the sand based on the body closing price where the reversal/continuation is confirmed based on where the following candle(s) close. Doji candles can form on uptrend or downtrend

FIGURE 4.27 Shooting star candles form reversals at the peak of the price move.

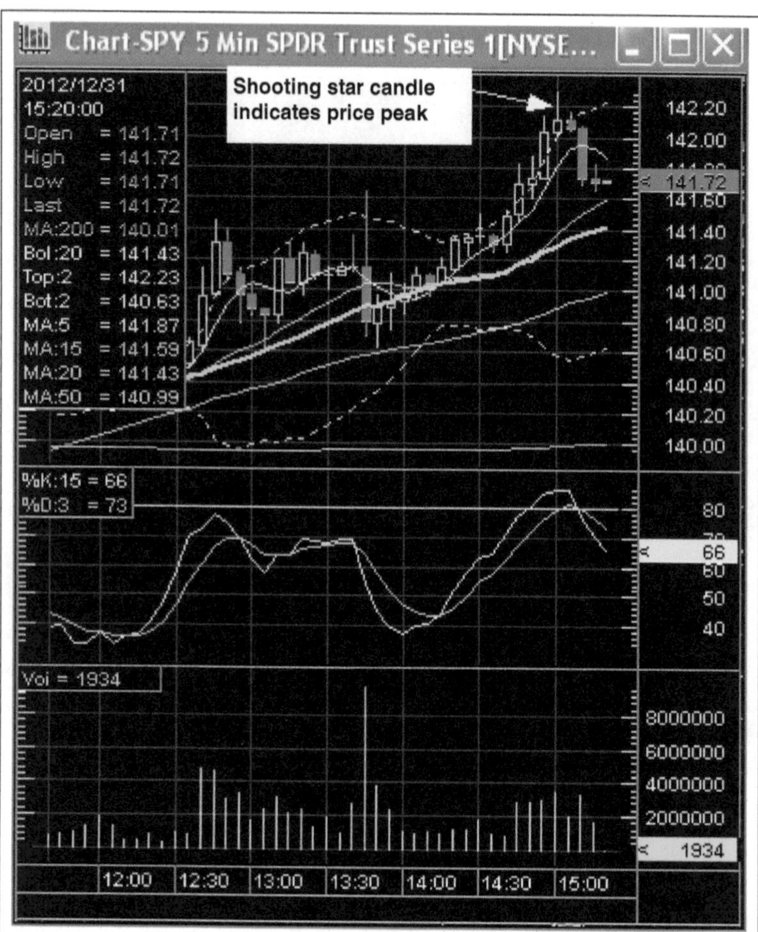

reversals and continuations. The doji is more significant when there are more trend candles preceding the doji. They are insignificant during consolidations. Unlike hammers and stars that indicate a capitulation bottom or blow-off top, a doji shows literally both reactions resulting in a minuscule body that injects uncertainty and doubt onto the side of the immediate trend.

If a doji forms at the peak of an uptrend, then the candle closing price acts as a resistance and reversal underneath and a support and continuation above (Figure 4.30). If a doji forms at the bottom of a downtrend, then the candle closing price acts as a support for the reversal bounce. If the stock falls below the doji line in the sand, then it acts as a resistance

FIGURE 4.28 Shooting star reversal.

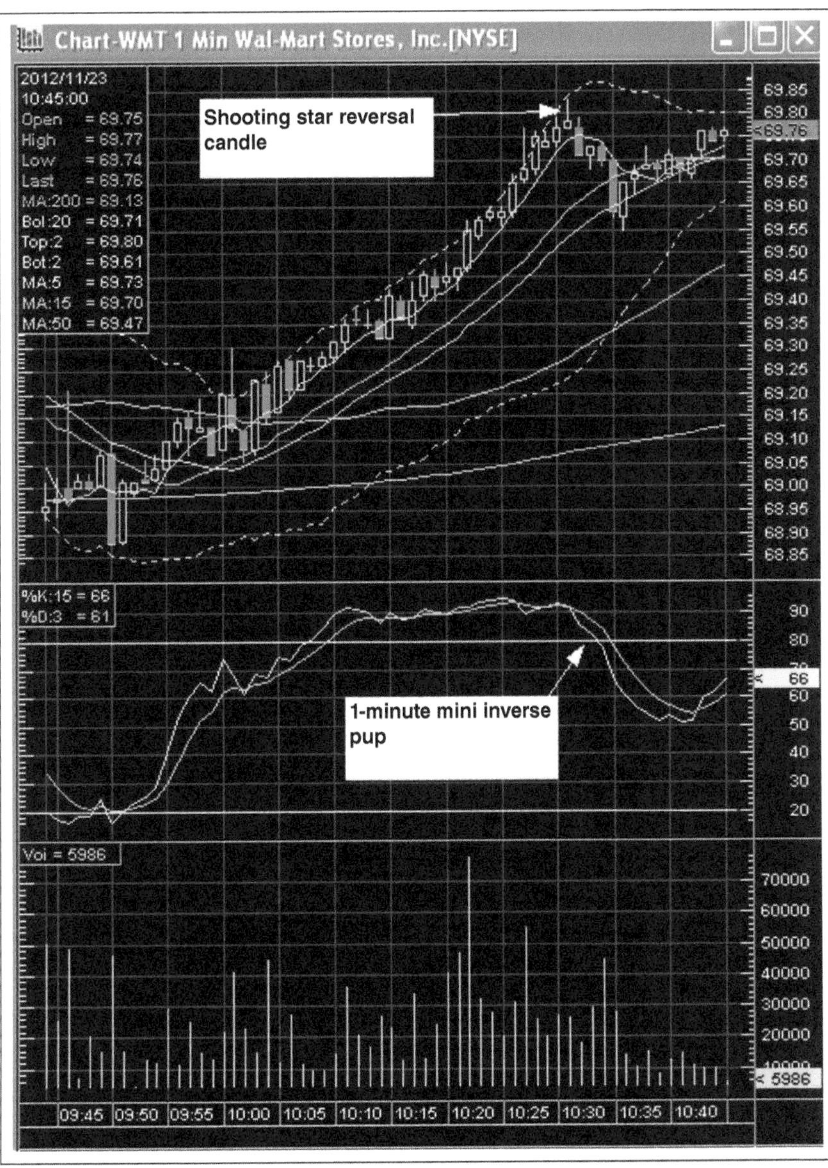

on the downtrend continuation. The doji close line in the sand remains a significant price level when there are more than three trend candles leading up to it. If the line breaks later on in the day, it can add more velocity to breakout or breakdown.

FIGURE 4.29 Doji candle.

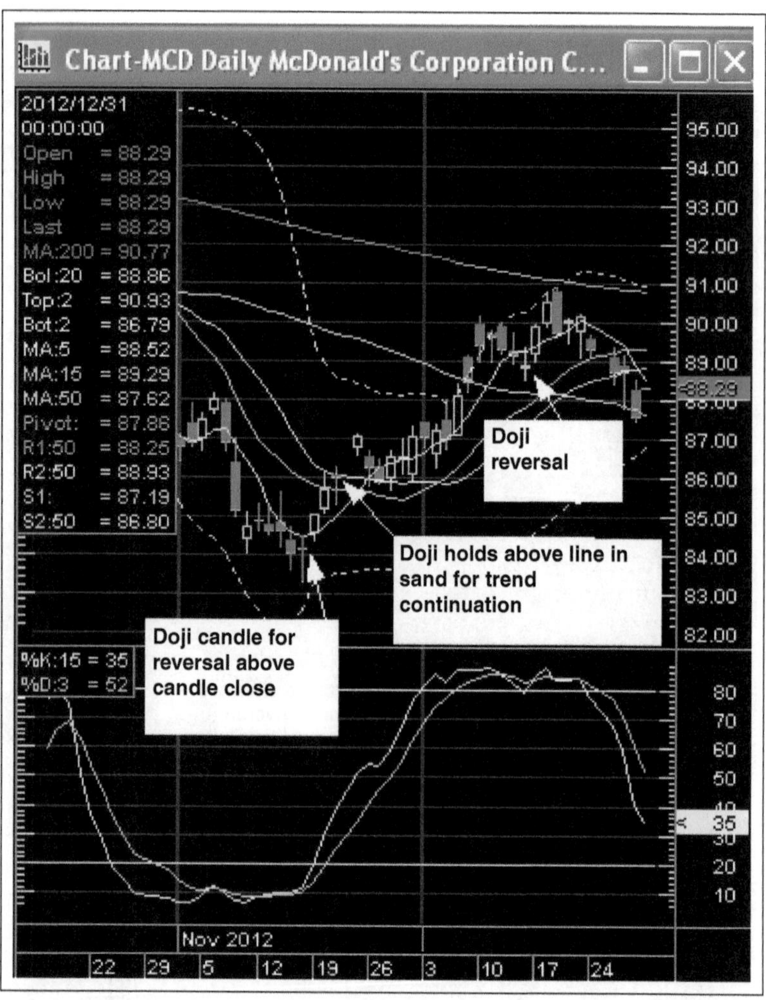

Massive Volume Spikes

When volume spikes five or more times the regular volume, it will cause a hard knee-jerk price move via breakout/breakdown. When the volume reverts back to regular sized, the price will either completely reverse the trend or hold the new range with relatively little pullback before it explodes to the next leg.

With volume, there are two types of heavy volume spikes. One type is the capitulation volume spike that puts in a reversal (tops and bottoms).

FIGURE 4.30 Doji reversal candle forms at the peak and initiates a subsequent two-candle price pullback that absorbs the pullback and grinds the stock back up through the doji candle body for a pup and mini pup breakout.

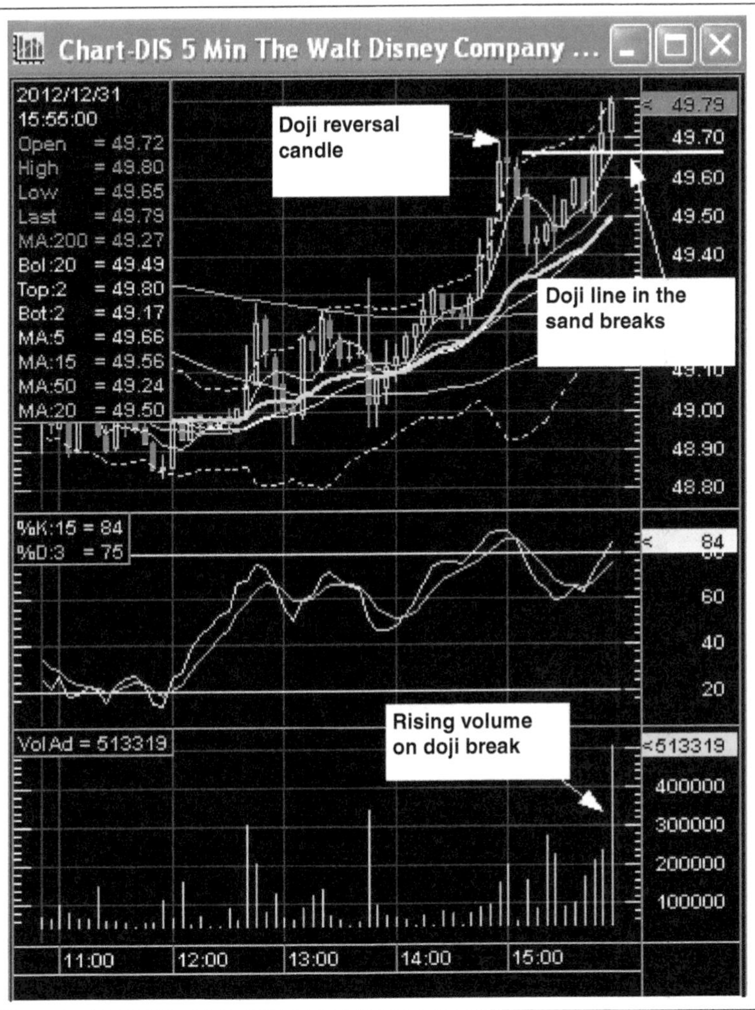

The other is the heavy volume spike that pushes up a stock and then tapers off while the stock holds the new range long enough for the stochastics to coil back up for the next leg up on uptrends as shown in Figures 4.31 and 4.32. The opposite applies for downtrends but ironically, they tend to occur less frequently.

The heavy volume spikes that form during a stall-period are generated from the big boys loading up on shares that eventually will be cheap.

FIGURE 4.31 A massive volume spike that forms a pup breakout from the 36.40 range to a new range at 37.

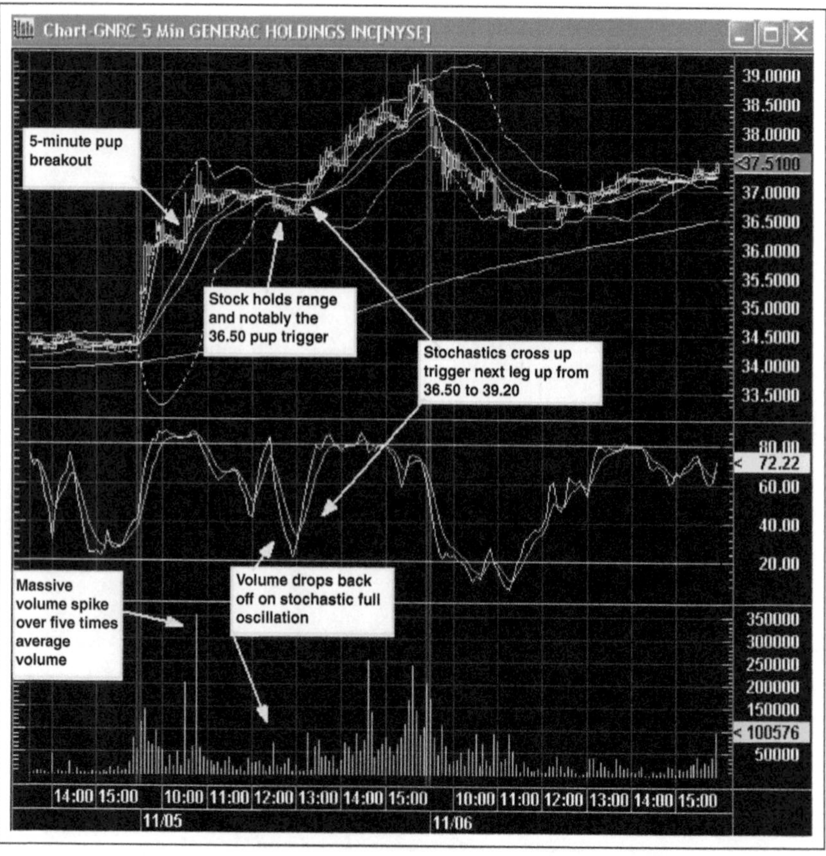

Professionals don't accumulate that many shares in full transparency unless they are planning to jam it much higher after the exhaustion and shallow pullbacks, which suck in overzealous shorts/bears.

The clue comes from how well the price holds the new levels as volume falls back down to normal levels usually accompanied by a stochastics reversal, as seen in Figure 4.33. If it holds the range, then it's solid. If a shooting star, doji, hammer reversal pattern forms, then be prepared for a reversal based on how the next candle forms. When a series of massive volume spikes are placed incrementally, they create a very strong uptrend sequence as shown in Figure 4.34.

FIGURE 4.32 Short a massive volume spike in deadzone during the consolidation on INFY that launches the grind to 52.

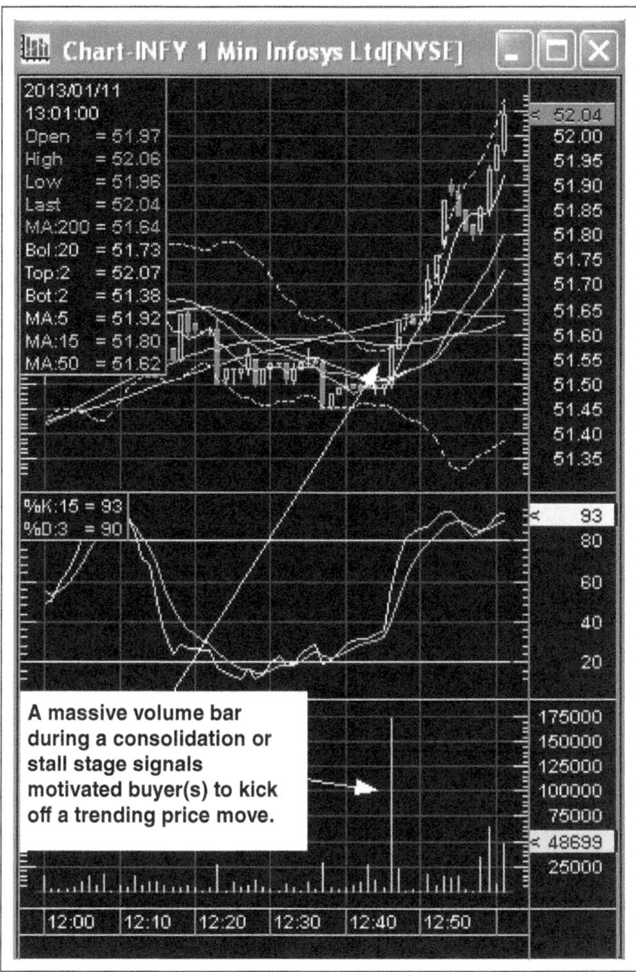

Mischievous Mistick Manipulation

The mistick has become more and more prevalent through the years. A mistick is a trade made way out of the market anywhere from .50 to 3.00. It's a single trade that shows up on the time of sales that is either a late post or erroneous tick. Whatever the excuse, the growing instances of these occurrences are suspect and go beyond conspiracy to the point of purposeful

FIGURE 4.33 The massive volume spike on the TNAV daily chart that lifts the stock to a higher range before breaking out two months later to new highs.

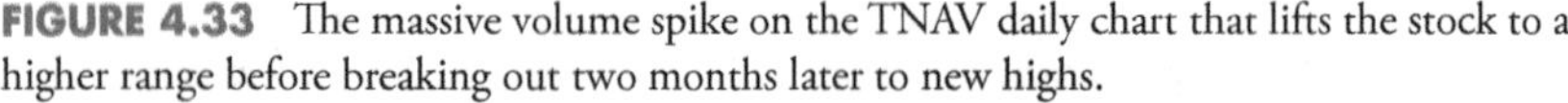

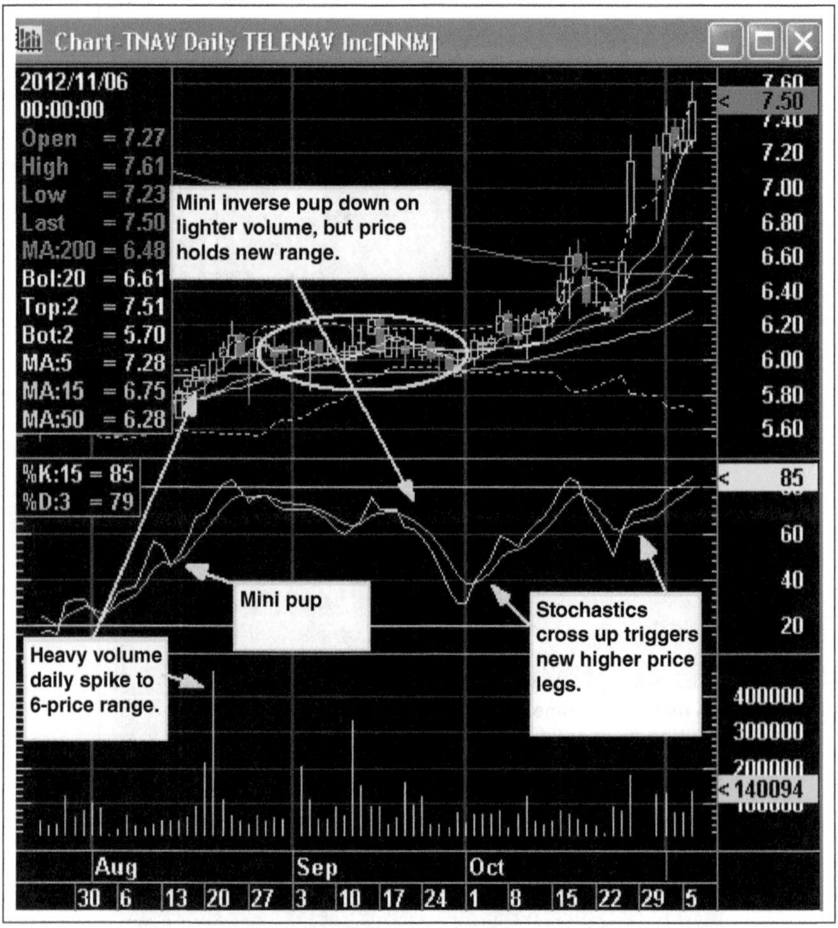

manipulation. Some quote platforms allow you to manually erase the mistick. Most platforms require the quote provider to fix the mistick. When a crime is committed, the first question is "What is the motive?" When you understand the motive behind placing these misticks, then you will also agree they are not mistakes but attempts at manipulating the perception on the charts to trigger knee-jerk reactions from participants including the algorithms.

As time goes on with each chart time frame period close, the effects of the mistick get diluted and return to the normal direction. However, until the candles smooth out, the mistick initially triggers a reaction.

FIGURE 4.34 The trend reversal due to the series of well-placed massive volume bars on the SPY.

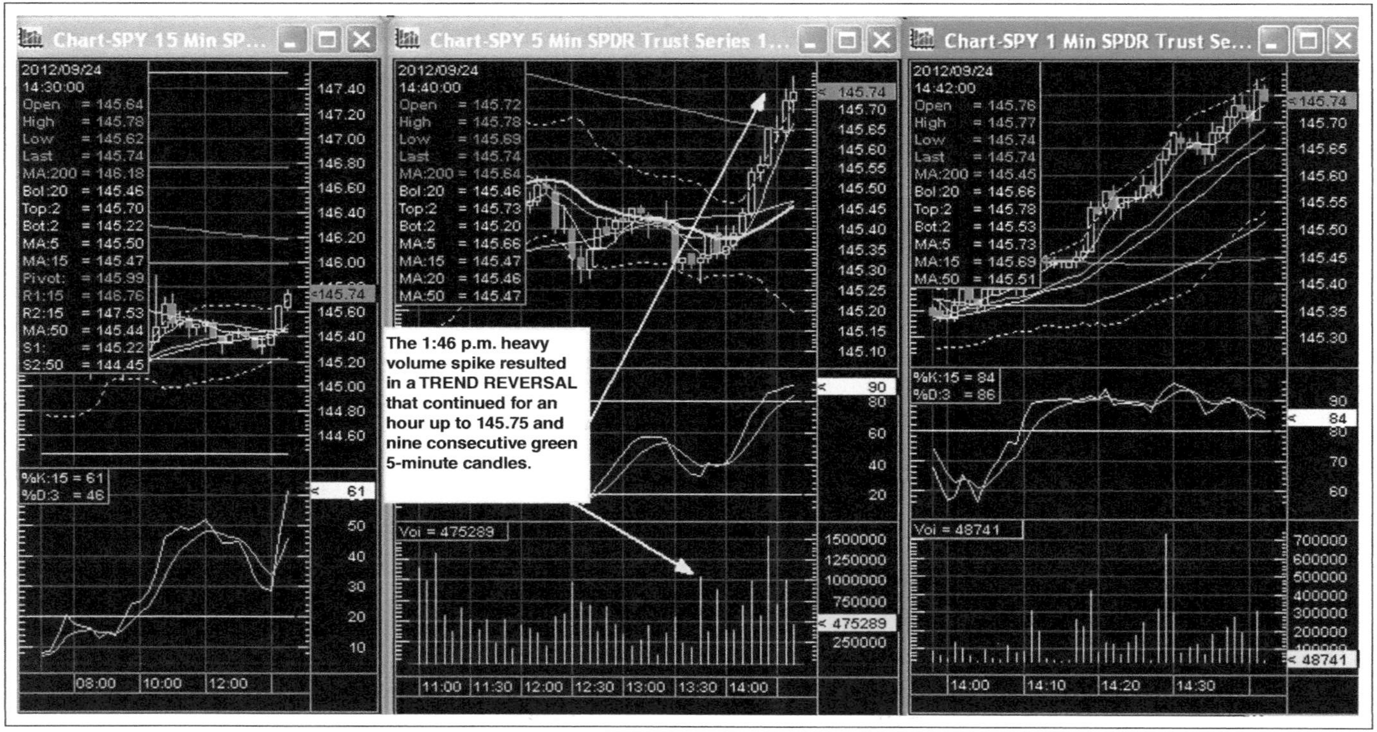

The rule of thumb to keep in mind when misticks trigger way below the trading price, is that the motive is to give perception of a bottom by painting a fake hammer, as shown on the HTS example in Figure 4.35. If the mistick is ABOVE the trading price, the motive is to give the perception of a TOP as shown by the P example in Figure 4.35. The stochastics will immediately lift, and then the subsequent trades at the true market price will then take it back down. Desperate shorts will place big misticks way above the market price especially in uptrends to create a shooting star candle effect that will peak the stochastics and the Bollinger Bands. This is done to create shooting stars, spinning tops, or dojis in an attempt to shake out the longs and suck in

FIGURE 4.35 The mistick on HTS to 27.33, which paints a hammer candle reversal on the chart and tricks participants including algo/HFT programs to buy the hammer and provide temporary liquidity for the trapped long to unload some shares. The mistick on P paints a shooting star by trapped bears to cover some shorts on the knee-jerk selling the candle triggers.

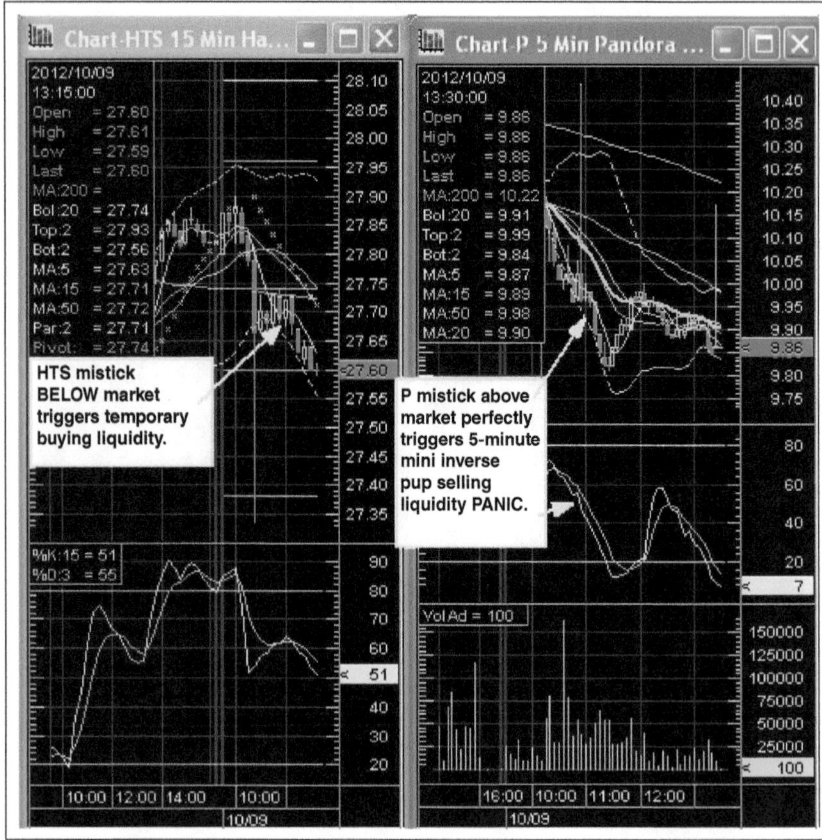

more short sellers to panic as many longs as possible, likely for the perpetrator to cover into the sellers before it reverses direction back up. Observe the sequence on the SPY premarket.

As seen in Figure 4.36, the perpetrator(s) were able to trigger a lone mistick at 143.40s when the inside market was 141.79 to 141.80 to trigger knee-jerk selling from the mini inverse pups they temporarily created on the 1-minute and 5-minute charts causing a sell-off to 141.70 (Figure 4.37), which they likely covered their positions into. What is the definitive motive?

FIGURE 4.36 SPY premarket mistick.

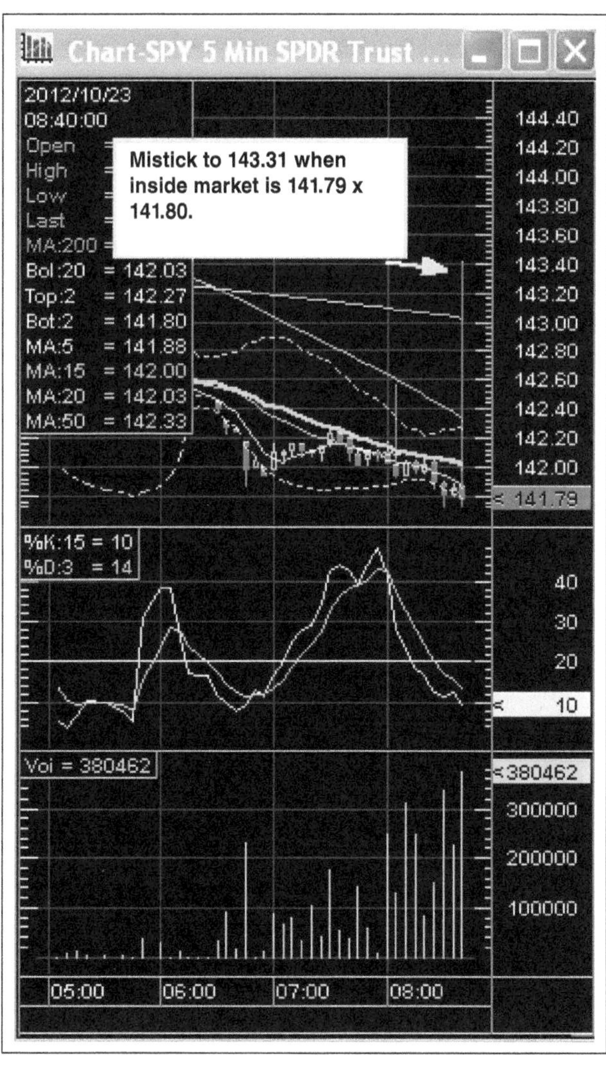

FIGURE 4.37 SPY mistick sequence continues.

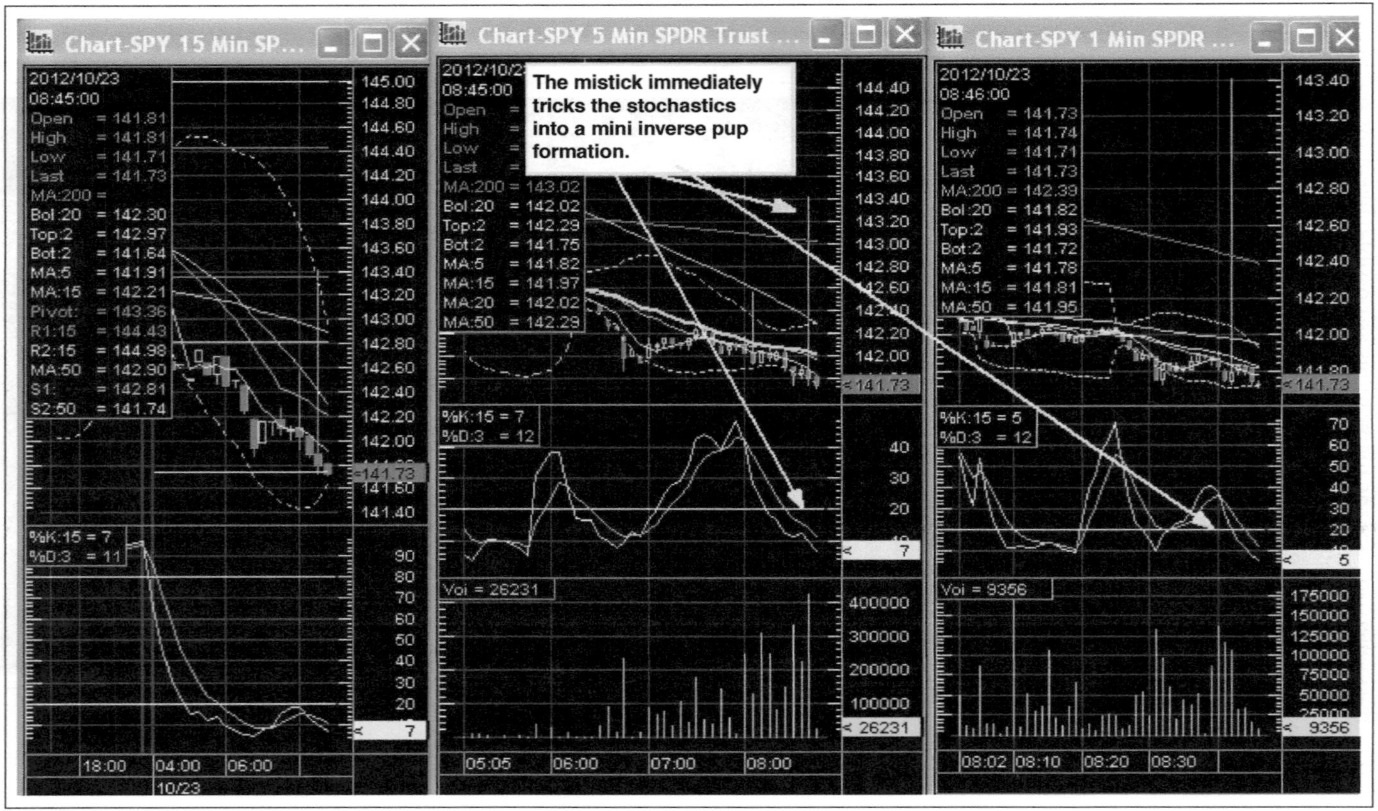

Liquidity. The shorts knew a reversal was looming around the corner and needed LIQUIDITY to cover into. Therefore a single mistick away from the market as a loss leader would generate substantial panic volume to cover their shorts into. It costs them –$160 on 100 shares (143.40 – 141.80 = 1.60 × 100 shares) to generate over 300,000 shares of selling liquidity to cover into!!! I hope you see how profitable misticks can be.

Afterwards, the SPY resumed its normal path back up to 142 (Figure 4.38). The motive was to manipulate a knee-jerk short-term panic to cover their shorts before the impending reversal bounce triggered.

On the flipside, if the mistick is made way BELOW the trading price, the motive is to give the perception of a BOTTOM. The stochastics will immediately fall and then spike back up with the next series of trades at the real market price. This is done to create hammer candles to knee-jerk shorts into covering.

As mentioned, these misticks are a temporary situation as they get smoothed out in time with more candle closes. In rare instances, they can have a self-fulfilling effect if the mistick isn't too far away from the market and is timed perfectly. The farther away from the market, the more extreme the short-term reaction, and the quicker it reverts back to normal and less believable. These are risky as they can get flagged if there are too many, so they are placed very strategically.

There are algorithm programs that trigger based on candlesticks, chart formations, and trade prices. These algos are usually the target of these misticks. This is the one time a humanoid watching can notice the mistick and not get panicked. However, since the algos have the firepower, humanoids can still get flushed out of their positions as collateral damage. Eventually, the algos will smarten up to these if not already.

On the flipside, if the mistick is smoothed out, the counter reaction to the mistick can be substantial, as it may backfire even harder on the perpetrator. The perpetrator is likely institutional or a market maker with an alibi and access to post late trades, or access prints on dark pools, unlike retail traders. There are so many of these that it's virtually impossible to track them all during the day. The most blatant are misticks on the index ETFs or even rarer on the e-minis. Benchmark index/futures misticks are as risky as a bank robbery in broad daylight during a crowded lunch hour. They will resonate more since they will influence batches of stocks tied to the index, but the media will catch that quickly.

Misticks directly affect the stochastics and the Bollinger Bands, notably the slope of the Bollinger Bands. These are the most sensitive of our indicators. The moving averages, due to their nature of being the average, don't get affected too drastically, unless it is way out of the market.

FIGURE 4.38 SPY mistick knee-jerk over as it resumes its natural bounce.

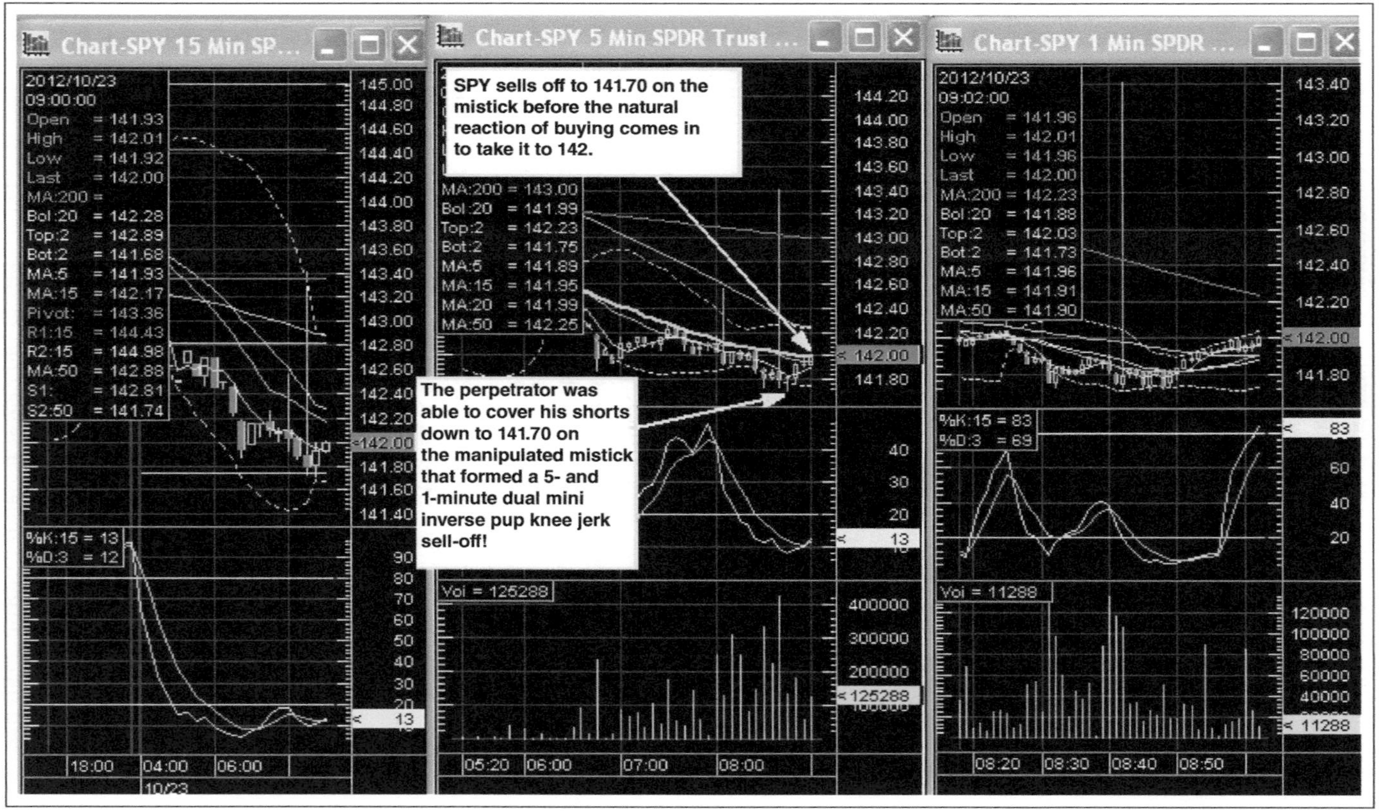

The most important factor in dealing with misticks is having multiple time frame charts up as does my system. While the mistick may have a dramatic initial effect on the shorter 1-minute and possibly 5-minute time frame, the 15-minute, 60-minute, and daily time frames don't blink much. There is an important distinction between a mistick and a heavy volume spike or lean. The differentiation factor is the volume. Misticks are usually 100- to 500-share single trades. You can simply click on the candle of the mistick to see the volume or scroll back on the time of sales. Remember, don't mistake a natural shooting star with heavy volume and multiple trades versus a single print mistick. This distinction is shown on Figure 4.39 as the out-of-the-market pricing may appear to show a mistick, but real trades were actually forming a real shooting star.

Let's go back to the scene of the crime. What is the motive for a perpetrator to place a mistick out of the inside market? The motive, the reaction,

FIGURE 4.39 Real trades that should not be mistaken as a mistick.

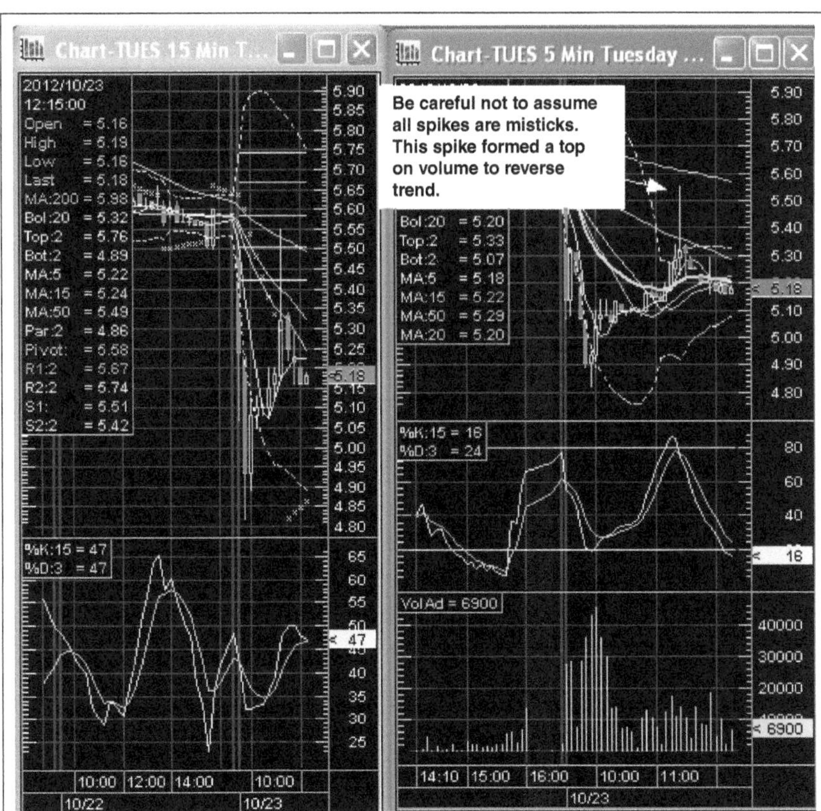

and the reversion back to normal. If you are LONG a position and a mistick triggers BELOW the market, the motive is to prop up the stochastics and slope up the Bollinger Bands for another leg up. This will be indicated on the stochastics with a 1- and/or 5-minute mini pup. That is your clue to LOCK OUT profits into the impending spike. There is a reason for that mistick placed below market, which is likely due to the lack of sustained liquidity and momentum, which the perpetrator is trying to offset. It is likely going to be a limited spike, so take your money off the table.

Now that we are aware of misticks, the real question is how do we trade with misticks?

Before we answer this question, revert back to the original premise for the trade. What was the BOSS time frame formation? Let's say you are long on a 15-minute mini inverse pup. That means the 5-period moving average is the BOSS support. Usually misticks will revert back to normal trading after three 5-minute candles and one 15-minute candle. However, remember that we are not playing detective here with the perpetrator; we are only focused on the REACTION of the OTHER PARTICIPANTS to the mistick. If the HFTs take the mistick for reality and hit the exit doors, you will get trapped playing hero. The short-term 1-minute charts will give initial guidance on the immediate action, and then the BOSS time frame dictates the rest. If the BOSS time frame changes, then exit your position and exposure completely. Otherwise, always trim down 50 to 75 percent exposure, especially if the mistick works in your favor.

If you are LONG a position and the mistick prices BELOW the current market pricing, then immediately trim down your position on the spike and revert to the 5-period moving average on sequential bumpers to the BOSS time frame bumpers (i.e., 5-minute 5-period moving average, 15-period 5-period moving average, 60-minute 5-period moving average, etc.) on the charts that have a mini pup in place. Exit out 50 to 75 percent of your position on the 1- and 5-minute bumpers. Exit out the rest of the BOSS time frame if stochastics get reversed.

If you are LONG in a losing position and the mistick comes ABOVE the market price, that will trigger more sellers as the stochastics get peaked out and reversed. Refer to the BOSS time frame. The question will be to either defensively scale (sprawl) or trim/eliminate exposure.

Think a few steps ahead. How can you game the misticks to take a position? Misticks below the market also give you a clue that the longs are getting desperate and trying to generate liquidity to sell into. If you know the motive and understand that only the market makers or institutions can place these misticks, this is a clue toward the impending direction of the market. Taking advantage of these clues can be profitable. Once again, the caveat is to make sure you have multiple time frame charts to view the complete context. Here is an example of a trade we made on ASML utilizing the desperate premarket high mistick.

The 15-minute stochastics had already formed a mini inverse pup along with the 1-minute mini inverse pup. The problem was the 5-minute stochastics was still manipulated up from naturally crossing down, due to the mistick being placed seconds before the 5-minute candle close. However, knowing that the mistick was a desperate attempt to prop up the stock and generate buying liquidity, we shorted the stock on the 1-minute mini inverse pup even while the 5-minute stochastics were up. We were able to scalp out nice clips as ASML ultimately sold off to the 53.30s by the end of the day.

In a nutshell, just remember that misticks placed *BELOW* current trading price are meant to fake a hammer/bottom designed to coil up the stochastics like a slingshot (Figure 4.40).

Misticks placed *ABOVE* the current trading price are meant to fake stars/tops designed to push down the stochastics.

Misticks mostly affect the shorter time frames such as the 1-minute and 5-minute time frames. The 15-minute and especially the 60-minute time frames take misticks in stride as the wider time frames will smooth them out.

The Essence of Stops

Right here I want to fortify in your brain the belief that STOPS are simply a PAUSE in your trading. What you lose in money, you BUY in time and transparency. Remember that. *STOPS BUY TIME and STOP THE BLEEDING*—and with it, TRANSPARENCY. Please write that down and tape it somewhere you will see constantly.

Idiotic Blanket Rules: Don't add to losing positions. Ride your winners and cut your losers. The trend is your friend.

These are smug, generalized, and conventional hindsight statements, which you shouldn't even waste a second contemplating. It is these kinds of general so-called rules that infect most traders from the get-go. Let's be realistic. The whole concept of dollar cost averaging is based on adding to losing positions if performed on individual stocks. How can you ride your winners if they start off as losers that you should have cut? The trend is not your friend if you got sucked into chasing a long position as the trend breaks down. As for trend, there are seven time frames, each with a trend;

FIGURE 4.40 The ASML short trade we implemented knowing the below market price mistick is a sign of desperation by a trapped bull looking for liquidity to exit his long positions. We know the coil is temporary as the market figures it out and will resume back down.

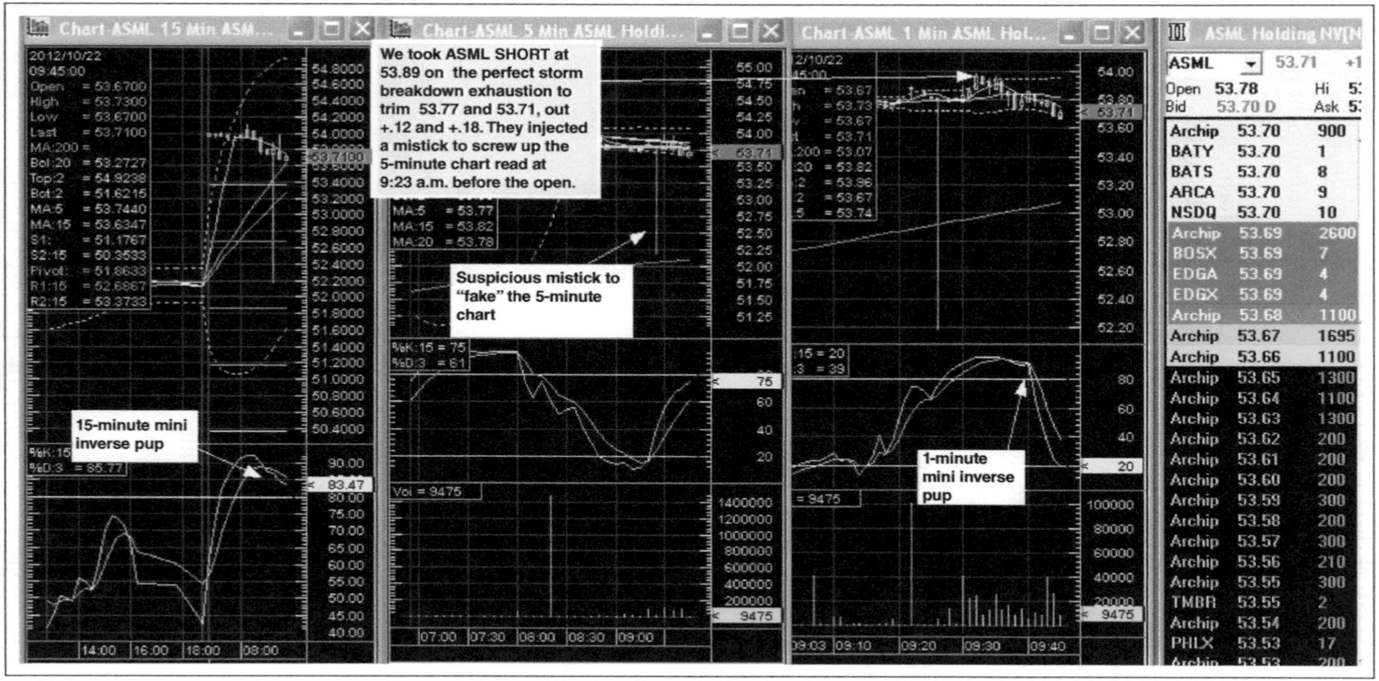

which time frame are they referring to? These are generalizations usually spoken after the fact.

Markets are getting less and less textbook in their behavior. This is just a by-product of the participants (computers and humanoids) striving to acclimate and react faster than everyone else. The outcome tends to create lots of chop sprinkled with shorter periods of transparency. Outcomes tend to get perverted to a point where the best liquidity comes from fading the patterns. This works only so long until it gets too transparent, thereby trapping the other side and flushing them out as the classic pattern plays out.

The real effort should be expended on being able to notice and react when patterns are getting distorted or playing through almost textbook-like.

I regularly add to losers to average out the price for the stock and take advantage of wiggles on the underlying trend. When the outcome is profits, then it is considered masterful. When the result is deeper losses, it's considered a stupid newbie mistake that violates the rule of "don't add to losing positions." Whereas the reality, is not the adding part, but the failure to exit into the short-lived reversal while the average price basis has improved temporarily.

The advantage of the individual lies in the ability to maintain absolute control over one aspect, his or her actions. An individual can decide to stop out and walk away for the day. The market hates that. The market, very much like a casino, can only feed if the participants have exposure, just as a casino can only work the house odds if the player is still on the property. Just as a casino will grant comps for shows, meals, and rooms, the market will generously front the proverbial quarter knowing it will get dollars back from MOST of its participants. Markets strive on pumping hope-ium into the playing field with its well-timed bounces and rug pulls. Performance can be measured on too many scales. There are over 8,000 publicly traded companies on the U.S. exchanges; why does everyone focus on just 30 of those stocks known as the Dow Jones Industrial stocks? Because it provides a conventional benchmark to compare your performance to the standard. The S&P 500 is supposedly the more sophisticated benchmark as it contains 500 stocks, which spreads out the exposure, but in reality, it's a matter of how 5 to10 major components are juggled to offset the rest of the PRICE-WEIGHTED index to give the illusion of market strength or weakness. The majority of retirement funds are funneled into those index component funds, which keeps the illusion alive. We saw in 2008 what happens when redemptions come into the market—absolute collapse. Ignorance is bliss . . . but it's just numbing like morphine and ultimately deadly. The markets of the 1990s are worlds different from 2000, which is worlds different from 2012. The participants have evolved, and markets are mutated. The same historical routines and performance are hindsight quarterbacking at best and fatal at worst. With so many indexes and benchmarks, what is the real reality? It's simple. It's what you walk away with. Your own reality is your profit and loss. It takes work to grind out profits because it's so easy in hindsight to assume you should have held a position longer to get more profits and cut a position quicker to have minimized the losses. There is no absolute, and that makes everything subjective to personal interpretation. This is the reason why you must set your OWN parameters of performance and action. In essence, your own religion so that you are walking away with a constant flow of profits from the markets. Sitting through a 50 percent drawdown and recovering simply by ignoring your statements and having faith in the market's historical track record of outperformance is misguided faith.

There is so much material that misguides people. Alas, I'm not here to fight that. My goal here is to give you a more realistic perspective should you choose to accept it. The ultimate proof of life is your personal performance.

Less Is More Applies More Than Ever

Unlike casinos where players may grind out a positive expectancy, if they play flawlessly for extended periods of time, the markets are the opposite. The longer you go head to head with the physical activity of banging those buy and sell buttons, the lower your probabilities of winning. I never thought I'd say the law of diminishing returns ever applied to trading, but with the over advantaged algo/HTFs, thunder and tumbleweeds landscape, and commission, the consistent momentum periods after the open are limited. The key is knowing when and how to strike and taking diligent action to attain closure.

Over the decades, I know when I've put enough time and effort on my research to satisfy the law of reciprocity. I know when I've surpassed the gate. Interestingly, it's not measured in time, but *the effort is time consuming, thus making time a qualifier by default.* For example, on the weekend, I spend six to nine hours on my weekly report, which includes breaking down aged and stalked prospects and level 4 research on two to three prospects for my swing trade clients. This six to nine hours can't be fluffed or faked. The reports are only the shallow aspect. I realize that the real depth can only be touched after clearly surpassing the shallow surface. To get sucked purposely into the zero gravity depths of research is a wonderful state. It's like being a kid all over again, as I read through conference call transcripts, read the message boards and any articles to open up and expand the panorama on multiple levels of the essence of the company and the crosswinds with the underlying stock.

STOPS and SPRAWLS

When a position moves against you, you have three options: wait, stop, or add. The wait portion should be a deliberate effort to wait and not because you are too frozen in fear to take a stop out.

Which option you take depends on the previous depth tempered with the current reality and a dash of foresight and action, which is 80 percent of the equation. Even though the three options appear to be actions, they are simply options until the decision to apply is made, triggering a purposeful action. Remember this, inaction is an action albeit a passive, indecisive, irresponsible action likely as a result of the deer-in-the-headlights syndrome, confusion, or prayer, unless it is deliberate.

Remember, inaction if consciously taken, is meant to buy time. Buying time simply means to buy transparency at the cost of erosion of existing position(s). Always remember the other way to buy time without the erosion and stress is to take stops.

That sounds simple, but it's all contingent on the context and the depth of the setups that triggered your entry into the position—don't forget that! If your premises are still intact, then you should wait and give it another 5-minute candle close. If the shortest time frame has reversed but the other time frames are still intact while aligned with the SPY, which is moving in your direction, then it is more prudent to wait as well.

If two time frames consecutively fail, then you must make a decision to STOP or SPRAWL, as demonstrated in Figure 4.41. How you decide is based on the strength of the time frames that still support the initial premise as well as the macro context. Remember that the wider time frames carry the most weight BUT are dormant until the shorter time frames converge in the same direction to trigger and detonate the awakening of the sleeping giant.

The only way to take a proper action in the heat of battle is by being sufficiently prepared before the battle. The preparation should compose of the fast chart analysis for each of your watch list stocks in addition to the SPY. The fast chart analysis is inclusive of all the significant price levels (bumpers) along with any pup/mini pups in the vicinity. If you have a lead peer stock, then make good and sure you have run analysis through that stock as well. It's better to be overprepared than underprepared.

If you are not sufficiently prepared, then take the stop and run the fast chart analysis. Do not ever sprawl if you honestly didn't investigate the depth beforehand. This is where most blowouts occur. You can't fake it in the markets for any duration. You may get lucky, but the crap will always hit the fan, and the market will always expose you.

FIGURE 4.41 How we took a stop on the initial short on EBAY and used that information to play a reversal long trade on EBAY.

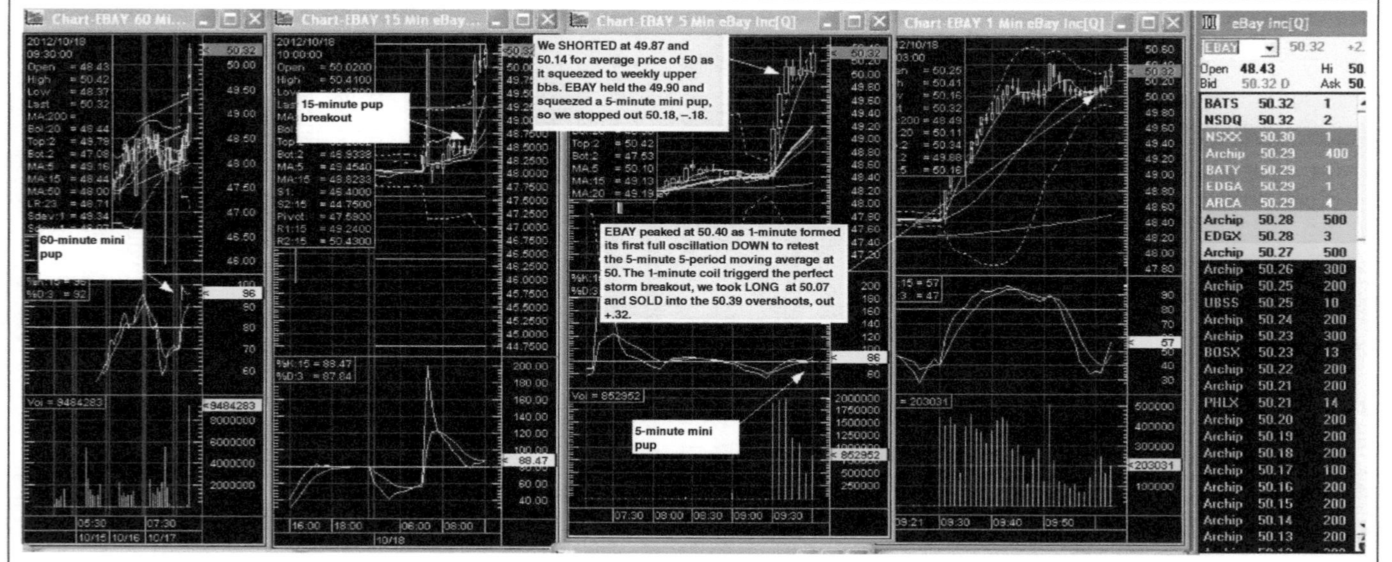

Research level 1 depth is sufficient (see Chapter 6 on the four-level research process) with the fast chart analysis, but any deeper research can be time constraining during the trading day.

Sprawls are the definitive way to gauge the caliber of any trader. As they say, the nature of people's character is how they hold up under pressure and adversity. During the Internet/daytrading mania where markets skyrocketed during 1999–2000, anyone who held for any duration made money. Those good times came to an abrupt end as newbies got vaporized when the market went to decimals as profit margins got squeezed with liquidity continuing to dry up.

Handling stops and sprawls takes practice to develop the intuition for deliberate reaction before full transparency hits the market. This is the type of practice most people don't want to practice, but the ability to stop and sprawl is almost a full skillset of its own.

First and foremost, stops and sprawls are defensive tactics (Figure 4.42). They are meant to limit damage and if executed with precision can also create profits. Obviously, stops and sprawls are not ever the goal of a trade. They are a necessary part of the game. However, no system of trading is complete without methods for dealing with the inevitable drawdowns.

There are many factors involved. Understand that you must acknowledge and take action during the pockets of liquidity. The purpose of a DSS (defensive sprawl scale) is to average your share position only in a situation of extreme panic (to capitalize on the panic) to exit out into the reversion pocket (Figure 4.43). Let's get something straight, stops and DSS mean you are on the WRONG SIDE of the trade, simple as that. The reason you may not stop out is because the panic reaction is so great that the liquidity completely vanishes. Always remember, the goal is not to get out at the original entry but to lessen the damage and maximize that pocket of reversion without overstaying the coil.

Don't add to a position out of hope alone. When traders can't distinguish between a DSS and OPS (offensive pare scale), they cling to hope and use any reasons to justify the position.

OPS: Offensive Pare Scaling

This is a proactive action taken from a position of strength. OPS is the same action as adding to a position but more so to maximize the nominal (limited) range of the potential movement. If you knew the probability for a .10 move on a stock was 95 percent, what would you do? What you SHOULD DO is maximize the leverage to take advantage of the move, fully aware of

FIGURE 4.42 The defensive sprawl scale trade on ARMH to capture some profits on what could have been a large stop loss when a massive volume spike formed out of the blue.

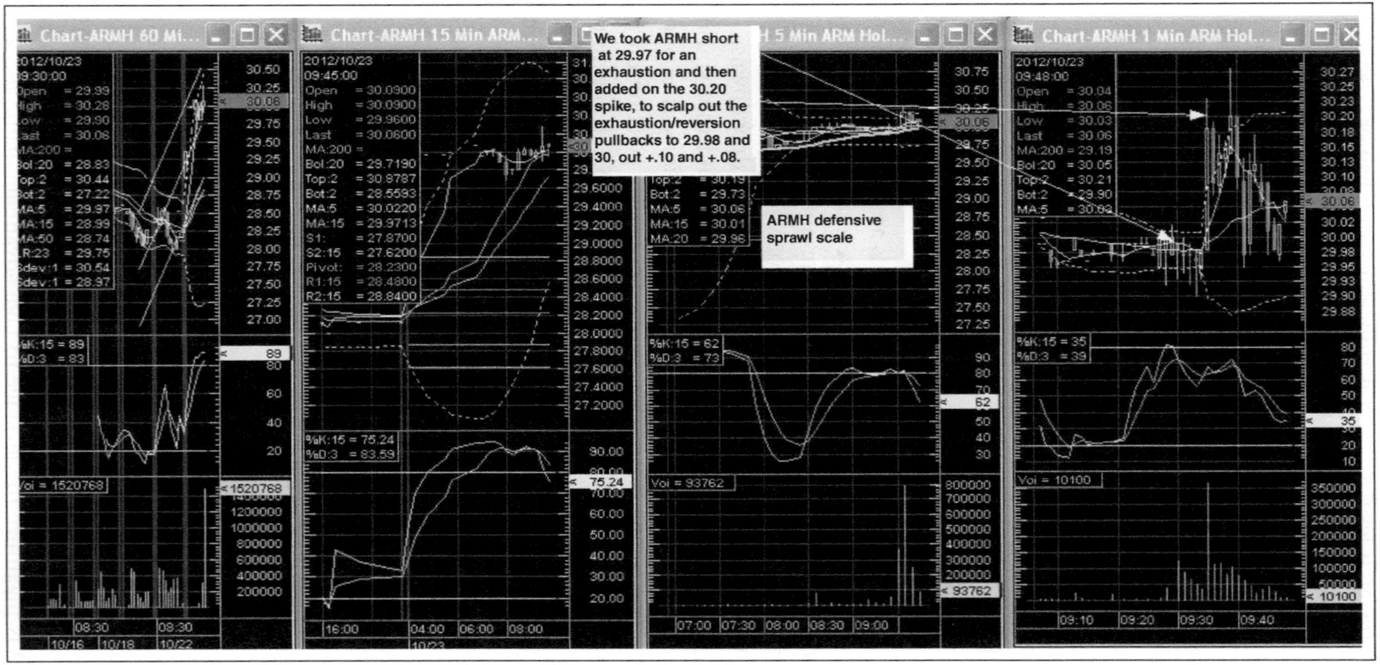

FIGURE 4.43 A defensive sprawl scale trade to minimize losses and a reversal trade to score profits.

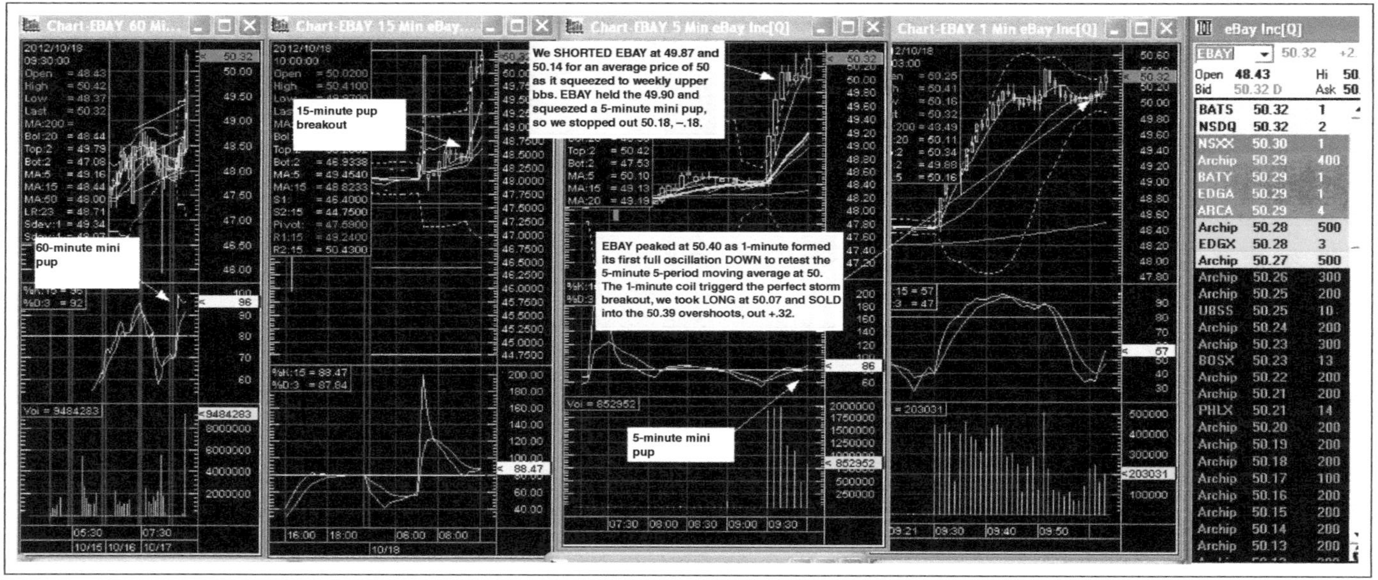

the limits and prepared to sell into the liquidity. I am not talking about a typical .10 spread chop move but a 4–5 lane perfect storm in a stock where the nominal direct movement to the next bumper lies .10 to .15 away. This is very important to be able to distinguish between a trend move and chop. An underlying perfect storm pattern is the key to this distinction, but most traders will just assume it's a spread chop. The aficionados of depth will have the foresight to realize the price move may be limited, but the formation will assure the move is made and proactively take advantage of it. The fact that others do NOT see the DEPTH of the inevitable yet nominal nature of the move is the ADVANTAGE. The range of movement is the last factor to be concerned with. If probability of a price move is the highest priority, then comes the nominal range of that move. While a .10 to .15 move in a stock seems identical to the naked eye, there is a major difference between a wiggle of .15 and a solid, heavy liquidity thrust. One is random, and one has intent. The one with intent carries the liquidity.

This reiterates the lack of depth that most human participants gauge with price action. This flaw should be considered an advantage. One .15 move is not the same as another .15 move.

Figure 4.44 demonstrates the offensive pare scale trade from a position of strength as we added to our position because we already factored in the limited remaining nominal upside left in the position; however, the probability of hitting that upside of a .15 price move was extremely high, over 90 percent. While AMRN wiggled .15 effortlessly off the open, the same wiggle when the 5-lane perfect storm formed turned into a trending move. The difference is liquidity. A random chop or wiggle carries no liquidity, whereas a deliberate perfect storm grind carries massive liquidity. The liquidity overrides price.

Slow Steady Grinds: Stop Out

If the move against you is a slow grinding trend, then stop out. Slow grinds tend to continue grinding until a climatic volume peak. Keep in mind that slow steady grinds are often developed by perfect storms, which you don't want to be on the other side of unless they have climaxed. Slow steady grinds are tempting in that fills are relatively easy, but you have to step back and observe the chart and the tight range grind meaning the lack of wiggle on the 5-period moving averages and the nominal upside on the rising upper Bollinger Bands (on uptrends). The major problem with trying to add short shares into a slow grinding uptrend is that the peak hasn't hit and may not hit until much later. They are deceivingly easy since the movement

FIGURE 4.44 Offensive pare scale trade on AMRN maximized profits on a high probability (90 percent) target with minimal nominal price gain (.10 to .15 reward).

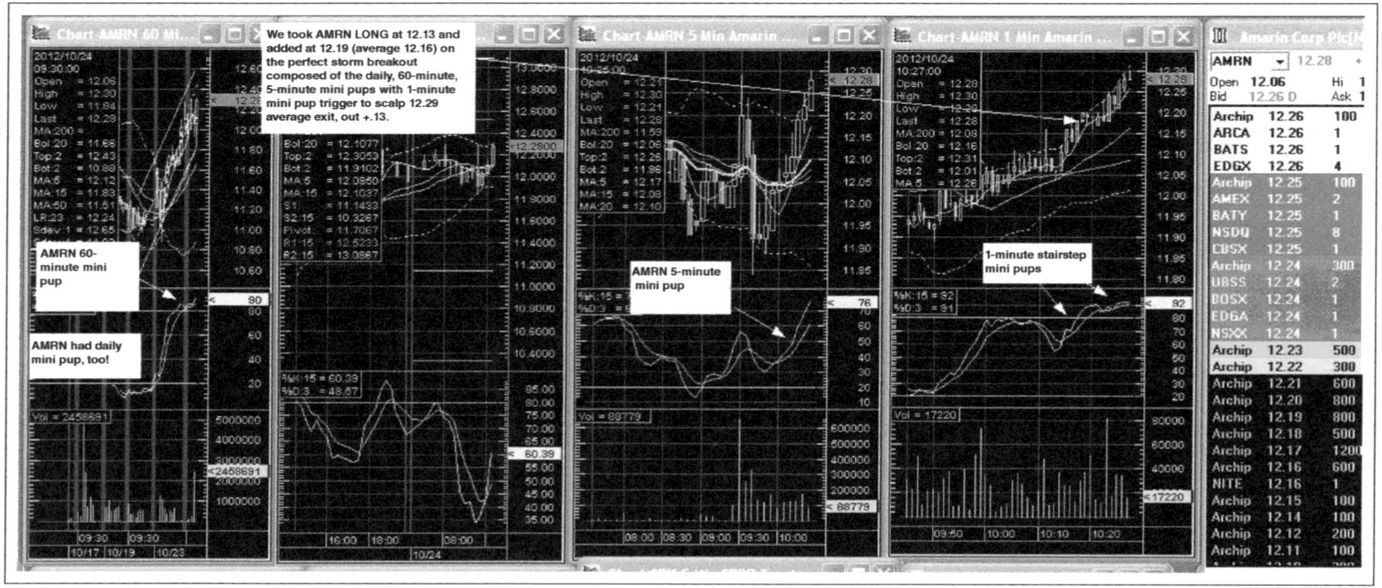

seems so minimal against your position initially as the grinds are incrementally small. However, the transparency only makes itself apparent at the climatic peaks. This is the point where shorts get squeezed out and final buyers come in off the fence. However, that can occur much later after you are deeply in the red, and the reversal may be minimal. Ideally, it is the climatic peak you want to short, IF there is enough "meat between the bones." This meat is the space (price difference) between the bumpers like the upper Bollinger Bands to the 5-period moving average. This distance should be divided by three to derive the nominal scalp amount. Therefore, if you are shorting a stock and the upper Bollinger Bands hit and the 5-period moving average is .15 lower, then the nominal scalp is .05. If you are –.20 on the trade position already, there is no point in sprawling and adding to the short especially if it is after the opening 45 minutes, as volume tends to fall off. This is a sketchy situation where one can easily get sucked in and trapped much like quicksand. The more you struggle and try to add to the short, the deeper you sink. Avoid all that by stopping out when there is no meat between the bones.

Excessive Slow Grinds: How and When to Short

In the counter candle explanation earlier, I mentioned that when a trend continuation candle sequence goes to the eighth candle or beyond (seven or more straight green candles on uptrends or seven or more straight red candles on downtrends), they are getting excessive (Figure 4.45). Whenever the slope of the angle of the 5-period moving average is more than 45 degrees accompanied by a 1-minute stochastics above the 80 bands for more than 30 minutes, it's definitely excessive.

Beyond the seventh continuation candle is when things get excessive and you can start looking for exhaustion shorts. Remember when shorting exhaustions, you want to make sure that you are shorting against a resistance bumper(s) for protection. Make sure that you start with the 1-minute chart and work the bumpers upper Bollinger Bands to 5-period moving average to 15/20-period moving average. Check the 5-minute 5-period moving average as that is oftentimes where an overlap support bumper sits like the 5-minute 5-period moving average and 1-minute 20-period moving average. Remember to always be covering near the next bumper. Having a 1-minute mini inverse pup triggered by a 5-period moving average rejection then shorting the counter candle break is the safest play (Figure 4.46), unless you have a shooting star on a wider time frame like a 5- or 15-minute chart.

FIGURE 4.45 How we caught the exhaustion on an excessive slow grind in WMT and the propensity for counter candles to attempt at Fibonacci price counts.

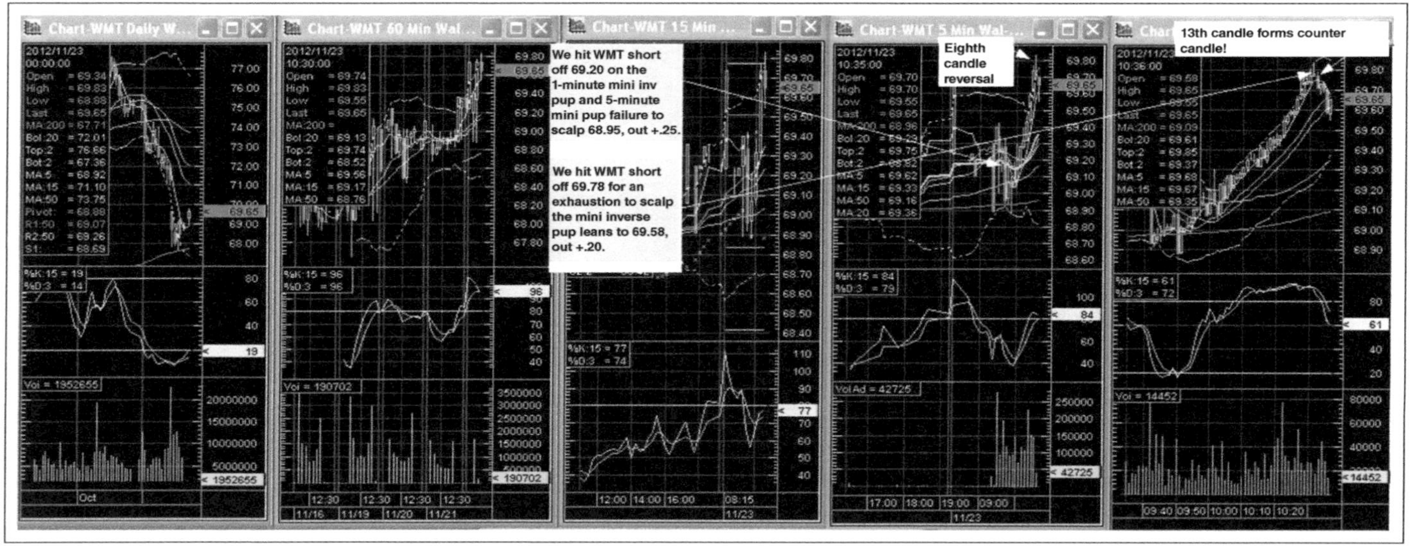

FIGURE 4.46 Excessive slow grinds.

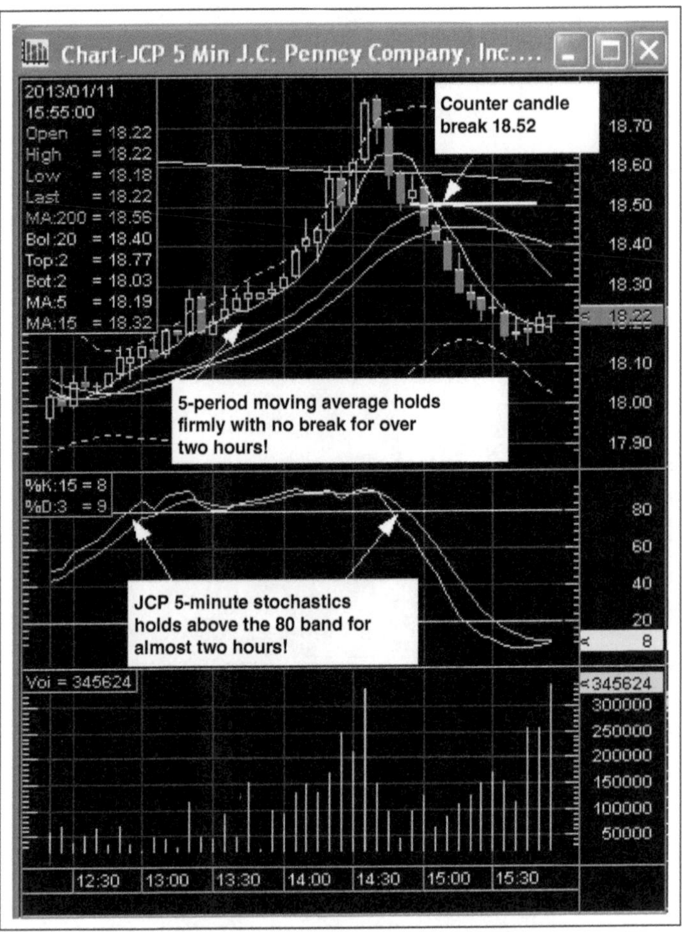

Early and Mid-Stage Perfect Storms

Very much like the slow grind, these are perfect storms that are either building up steam deceivingly displaying weakness until they enter the stage 2 explosion completely trapping the early shorts while sucking in early buyers like a vacuum (on breakouts) culminating into a high volume, parabolic price spike. The vice versa applies on breakdowns. There is no point in fighting these as they move too fast and continue to grow. The best remedy is to stop out early or reverse the position to ride the perfect storm. For the very experienced, there is sometimes a POCKET to sprawl into temporarily only to catch the temporary wiggle to unwind the position completely. Overstaying and ignoring the pocket pullback opportunity will only compound the bloody damage. For most traders, it is best to immediately stop out when a perfect storm is developing against their position while it's still early.

Knowing that a perfect storm relies solely on the 1-minute trigger is your escape hatch to stopping out before the damage gets too bad. A five-lane perfect storm can be forming, but it is still DORMANT until that 1-minute stochastics trigger crosses in the direction of the storm. When that fuse is lit, it's a mad dash for buyers to enter and shorts to cover. It is imperative you recognize the importance of taking action and not freezing up when the 1-minute is about to cross up. Take your stop and cut off the limb before it infects the whole body. Stops are just a pause. The bright side is that once you have taken the stop, you are now free (on many levels) to consider re-entry with the perfect storm and ride the natural flow and trend of the stock. Remember, you CAN'T reverse a position, until you are FREE of the position. While there are hedging methods, which I will discuss later, this is not a factor here. The stop loss is not only meant to limit the losses, but it buys closure. Once you have this closure, you are no longer chained to a wrong position and dealing with the stigma, stress, and tension. Most importantly, you are free to take the correct side of the trade. In fact, I always state that the best person to intimately know the strength of a stock is someone who is short and the best person to intimately know the weakness of a stock is someone who is long. This is the real inside information. *This inside/insight information can only be purchased at the cost of a stop loss. The key is keeping that purchase price low* so that you can capitalize on it multifold by taking the other side. This is another subject that I will delve into, the reversal trade. I am talking in baby steps here, but ultimately remember that in death, there is life.

Stop losses are a topic that is very misunderstood, and this is the perfect time to dig into the essence of stop utilization. Let's be realistic here; people hate taking stops. It's an admission of guilt. It's the acceptance of a loss. The distinction between a paper loss and a real loss is made by closing out the position. *It's not a real loss until you stop out* is a misguided belief stemming from the reality of not actually registering the loss on your taxes unless it is taken by closing the position. This works as a negative justification to holding onto bad positions. The reality is that your capital and buying power are affected whether you are closed out or not. Losing positions tend to cause the most tension stemming from ego, fear, guilt, shame, or paternal/maternal nature. These are all shallow surface-level factors.

On the flipside, many people tend to prioritize their stops so much that they overlook the pockets of liquidity to take the profits and only react (with good discipline) when their stop losses get hit. While the discipline and intentions are very good, the tight-fisted focus tends to harness tunnel vision on the downside. After enough stops get hit, traders lose their motivation and figure the market is only out to catch their stops. This becomes a self-fulfilling prophecy, which in turn reverts them back to the other scenario of not accepting stops—rinse and repeat.

What we have here are two ends of the spectrum where stops either won't be taken or are the only things being taken. The search for a middle ground is futile. The real search entails depth and requires digging for . . . the underground (hehe, cliché but justified).

Meandering beyond Comfort Zone Threshold

If the tension is too great and you stopped watching the charts and are totally focused on your profit/loss column, then you have materially shifted to overfocus on C. In these cases, you should immediately stop out of one third of your position to bring down your stress levels: 80 to 90 percent of your attention should be on the charts, not your losses. If you find yourself completely focused on your profit/loss column, then you should immediately stop out of one third of your position. If you are still focusing too much on the p/l then stop out another one third. Usually, these are situations where you surpassed your comfort zone due to overexposure, meaning too many shares. *You can't trade effectively with too many shares. It's like trying to swim with sandbags tied to your ankles.* You will worry too much about sinking rather than completing the race.

Your comfort zone is involuntary and only you can honestly assess when you are meandering beyond the thresholds of your comfort zone. The less shares you have, the less exposure you take on and the less your tension levels should be.

Three Levels of Stop Mindset

On a shallow level, the purpose of a stop loss is to prevent further bleeding of capital by eliminating exposure, sophomore.

On a mid-depth level, the stop loss is a pause in your trading that buys you time, which in turn buys you transparency and the freedom to react without being chained to a losing position, senior.

On the undercurrent depth level, the stop is merely a tester weather balloon expected to pop but not without extracting intimate details of the veracity of the direction. This is a loss leader meant to feed information towards the *greater trade*. At this level, the trader will not flinch to reverse or add on to a trade, because the initial entry was just a tester. This is the deepest depth of stop utilization efficiency. This depth requires preparation (awareness of the context and bumper levels), experience, premeditation (actions already game planned out mentally to each scenario), and unflinching reaction control (ability to execute without freezing or tilting) of the greatest magnitude, samurai.

> Adversity has the effect of eliciting talents, which in prosperous circumstances, would have lain dormant.
>
> *Quintus Horatius Flaccus*

What to Do after a Disaster

No matter how consistent you get, no matter how long your winning streak is, inevitably, you will get spanked on a trade or series of trades that vaporize weeks or a month's worth of gains. It's inevitable. It's an anomaly and should be treated as such.

However, there are very specific actions you MUST take after one of these ROGUE WAVES smacks you. If taken too seriously, it could jeopardize your mindset dramatically. If not taken seriously, it would lead to more damage. I interpret these trades as ROGUE WAVES. Although they are anomalies, they can happen on any given trade. The bids evaporate so quickly on a long position that an effectively well executed defensive sprawl scale can backfire as the market continues to chew right through those bids in a massive panic, stopping you out with a nasty drawdown equivalent to several weeks of profits.

These incidents should occur less than 5 percent of the time, but the key is taking the right precautionary steps afterward to ensure it doesn't repeat too soon. When these happen, it's a sign that the market is showing you who's boss. Acknowledge it. It is could be a sign of a possible landscape change in the works.

Ignoring it and brushing it off could lead to a repeat. Overthinking the monetary losses inadvertently can cause you to go on TILT as you try to make them back quicker. If you repeat the missteps, it only gets worse! These reactions are only natural as fight or flight kicks in subconsciously . . . ignore or run away. These are the worst actions you can take! I know firsthand, trust me!

The Three Steps for Proper Re-Setting

Rather than call this recovery, I like to use the term re-setting. Recovery implies getting back to even or back to the status quo. I believe that pain and trauma are a necessary part of evolution in the trading game. Each recovery should raise the skillset and improve one's threshold in the process. The more accurate word is re-set. This is not the traditional meaning defined as starting over from the beginning; rather it's the process of re-setting the broken bones properly so they can heal and strengthen. It is re-setting the proper template and routine so that as muscle memory takes over, you stick to good habits and prevent a mutation. Re-set not reset. Focusing on the proper re-setting process goes beyond just recovery. Recovery is one of the by-products, as well as rebuilding, fortifying, strengthening, and evolving. By re-setting properly, you will reset the internal timer ticker set to blow out. This process involves three painstakingly crucial steps.

Step 1: Be the Hammer Candle

If you are on TILT, chances are it's impossible to stop. You are too far gone. Telling yourself that you have to stop won't work. Giving yourself an out, is the only way short of getting punched in the face. On your next smoke break, tell yourself that you are done after a single winning position. The position size must be half of the last trade. If that trade stops out, then half it again on the next trade and continue to half it down. Singles trades, not sprawl scaling either!

Notice, I said position, not trade. This means as soon as your trade is green, you immediately lock out and stop. One positive trade, just one, even if it's for $1. Once that is done, you turn off the computer and the television and go do something until the market closes or in extreme cases, until the ENN's close at 8 P.M. EST. The physical closure will put a cap on obsessing over how the trade could have turned out if you stuck around longer, or where the market is going or how your p/l looks. Close it all out. As long as you end with a single positive trade, no matter how small, you end the day with a silver lining of a possible turnaround, like a hammer candle. Notice the analogy, of a hammer candle, which implies a capitulation bottom. The hammer candle in and of itself is not confirmed until the next candle close. Understanding this, your trading stop with a positive trade, only puts a stop to the bleeding. The confirmation of a bottom and reversal will only happen after the next few days. You achieved the first step of taking yourself out of harm's way and ending with a positive trade.

Step 2: Be the CSI (Crime Scene Investigator)

After you take yourself out of harm's way, there are two pivotal steps that must be taken to correctly heal the wound: the investigative analysis and the actions moving forward. This is the only path to closure.

You have to investigate the situation and honestly answer these specific questions. Be the crime scene investigator. Assume a third party stance. Rather than just study the homicidal trade in question, start from the prior two to three days of trades. Any detective will want to know the context leading up to the crime. In your case, the prior two to three days of trades perhaps up to five days of trades must be checked.

Was there an increase in defensive sprawl scaling leading with the prior trades? If so, this is a sign that you may be stepping in too early on the trades, not giving enough time for confirmation. With the defensive sprawling, did the trades resume in your direction after your exit or against your scaling direction? If the stock continued lower after your buy scaling and exit, then you were playing countertrend. Although, your exit was great, the proper trade would have been to short into the small bounces, especially if the pattern was a perfect storm breakdown. You were on the wrong side of the trade and got out just in time.

If the trade reversed in your direction after you exited, then you got in too early. Had you waited a bit longer, you could have gotten a better entry and a confirmation or perhaps an offensive scaled add from a position of strength. Once again, the trade itself was right, but the timing could have been better, causing less wear and tear on your psyche. The path of least resistance is always the correct (more correct) path.

If there was too much defensive sprawling leading up to the fatal trade, then you have your footprints. Defensive sprawling is a sign that either you or the market is not converging. It is an early sign to ease up on the gas pedal and likely wait a little longer for confirmations. *The 10- to 15-minute egg timer rule is great for this* (details on that in the following paragraphs).

Rogue Waves

Was the error a sudden price reversal on a strong pattern; that is, a perfect storm? Was there any clue from the peers or from the SPY of the reversal; that is, SPY was in a perfect storm breakdown, you went long a stock in a perfect storm breakout? Vice versa, going short a strong stock with a perfect storm breakout but SPY was in a perfect storm breakdown.

In these cases, the two will eventually converge, but you may have stepped in too early or stayed in too late.

Self-Imposed Error

Did you sprawl correctly but didn't cut your exposure during the REVERSION POCKET? This means you overstayed. It's a matter of timing, and you missed your window to exit.

The remedy is to make sure that you are not trying to break even on the trade, but to use the 1-minute reversals to exit out into liquidity unless the 5-minute reverses as well IF the trade is a trend fade.

Reaction

Too early
Too late
Froze

These are the rogue waves that can happen literally out of the blue. This is different from the error of fading a strong pattern that suddenly gained massive momentum against you.

Was the error on your part fading a strong pattern, underestimating the overshoots, too much scaling against the trend, or just not taking the stop signal fast enough?

Step 3: Take the Prescription

The prescription is the conscious, purposely taken actions, which are required in order to HEAL and STRENGTHEN moving forward. Just like a broken bone, it must be re-set properly in a cast to allow for proper healing. Care must be taken to not put the injury in harm's way. Doing so allows the natural healing process, physically, mentally, and spiritually, to complete. Trading is no different. The problem is when traders don't realize they have an injury and continue to do the same routine. Ultimately, the injury will reveal itself in full transparency in the form of TILT-ing or blowing out the account. By then, the erosion is so great that it will take more time and effort to heal properly. Unfortunately, it is only at this point where traders are completely knocked (forced) out of the game (involuntarily) that they finally realize the existence and the extent of the injury. Remember the essence of the trading game is spotting transparency early and reacting BEFORE it becomes too transparent. This applies on multiple levels. The surface level understanding applies to markets. The deeper, often overlooked, level applies to your own performance. A + B = C. C not only represents profits, but also the efficiency of A and B. The transparent warning signs come from C.

There are always subtle clues before the finality of full transparency sets in. This is what trading is about, but the same aptitude is applied internally as well, such as the ability to spot the early signs of hairline fractures . . . and being able to distinguish between a normal drawdown and something deeper that is causing interference with the A and B. This may go unrecognized in the early stages, because C is producing the nominal by-product. The final transparency comes when C craters.

Spotting deficiencies in your trading early is the key toward prevention and smooth healing.

My rule of thumb is three deviations are a warning sign, five deviations are the emergency. This means that if you are averaging $100 profits a day for the past 20 days, then a –$300 day is a warning of possible hairline fracture. If you hit a –$500 day or higher, then it's time to take the three-step recovery plan. Ignoring these signs will result in mutation and stagnation that will eventually lead to blow out.

Once we have identified whether the problem was the landscape or you, we move towards calibrating the mechanics of filtering and execution, but there is also one more element that must be addressed. This is something that affects on a DNA level. You have to purposely widen your prospects. You have to DOUBLE to TRIPLE the prospects. YES. At least 50 to 75 percent MUST be organically searched NOT situation prospects. This requires manually scanning post-market and pre-market through your watch lists, not news items.

Purposely Add More Stocks to Watch List and Minders

This action purposely deals with one of the elements that underlie all tilting, the feeling of being closed in, trapped, and abandoned down to that single stock you are getting waxed on—that nagging feeling that since you have invested your time and capital into this play, you get tunnel vision and stick around too long allowing emotions to take over for the worse. The proverb, "Don't put all your eggs in one basket," applies here. Therefore, the second-most-important thing is to expand your basket so that your options are not limited to 3 to 5 prospects narrowed down to 1 to 2 after the open, but 7 to 12 prospects narrowed down to 6 to 10 after the open. We are adding more baskets.

Quick recap—the three remedies for affliction are . . . counteract, diffuse, and/or dilute. The purposeful action of doubling or tripling the prospect list directly incorporates the third remedy, dilution. Focus is great, but dilution is required to prevent you from watching the leaves while the forest is moving. Additionally, once you've triggered and executed your first trade, keep at least three prospects in the visual sight for the same purposes. One of the reasons to trim allocation is not only to cap your exposure, but also to allow for spreading out the exposure should the filters trigger identical setups or hedge on inverted setups. Make sure to review "Level 1 Research Process" and "Level 2 Research Process" in Chapter 6 to attain the key price bumpers and fundamental catalysts before you engage the trade sequence. *This preparation must purposely be done beforehand to bypass falling into the same trap.* Be very aware, this is not the usual routine preparation, but extra preparation is needed. The extra effort must be made post- and pre-market to expand the list of prospects with organic patterns going into the next day. This is where the EFFORT truly counts. The misguidance is the belief that one should scan on the fly and shoot on a whim to make back losses. This takes no real effort; this is not the currency of effort that the market recognizes. Usually the on-the-fly trades are likely chasing situations with high/low lists common to all scanners. When stocks make these lists, transparency is full blown so you are likely getting in at tops on longs and shorting bottoms. Clicking the mouse is not quantifiable effort. It's a shortcut attempt that rarely pays off and when it does, it's sure to damage you in the long run.

The way to fight is to manually SCAN and research to depth level 2 to expand the prospect list into the next day 7 to 10 corganic to headline gapper/dumpers. This may seem like more extra work, but that is what's required to climb out of the hole in every sense, mentally, physically, and spiritually. When presented with more options, one is no longer shackled. By implementing the mechanical rules of decreased exposure, quicker profits or stops, no sprawling, and permission to take multiple positions, you will be too preoccupied to fall into tunnel vision—provided you have the skill sets down. If you are a newbie (be honest), then forget about the last paragraph.

Step-by-Step Healing and Recovery

As instructed, no matter how bad you tilt, end the day with a single positive trade, no matter how small, to put in a hammer. A small victory is necessary and ends it there.

Remember, a hammer candle alone means little without the next series of candles to confirm a bottom and reversal. For the trader, this means it's essential to close with small profits, for the following days. The profits will be smaller because the allocation sizes must be trimmed down. This is opposite the reaction of taking more risk; we want to take less risk both in terms of *the filter, entry, exposure, and exit.*

The filter should be only the highest probability perfect storms. Only play the highest probability pattern end of story.

The allocations should be cut automatically by 25 to 50 percent. We are proactively cutting the risk by cutting the amount of exposure.

The entry is based on the 10- to 15-minute egg timer rule. No trades are taken no matter how awesome they are before 9:40 A.M. EST and preferably 9:45 A.M. This is to get two to three 5-minute candles of transparency on the charts before stepping in. This will prevent jumping the gun too early where it can have the most damage and still give time to prevent jumping in too late at the end of the move if the pattern is strong. It also gives time for initial momentum to fade and truly test the resilience of the trend.

The exits are taken on the first oscillation and bumper overshoot or stops taken on the 1-minute reversal. No defensive sprawling.

This is to prevent overleveraging or any temptation to go back on tilt. As much as you are following the rules, if you add to a position against you, then it's easy to have a déjà vu moment, and that's the last thing we want to prevent. Keep stops tight and losses small. If your stop was too tight, you can re-enter once the 1-minute turns back in your favor as the trigger, as long as the perfect storm is intact.

The Unconditional Three STOP Rule

If you get stopped out, you cut your capital allocation by 20 to 25 percent. If you get stopped out three consecutive times, then you are done for the day.

At this point, be proud that you stuck to the game plan and didn't go on tilt. There is something wrong with the market or with your head. Go back and repeat steps 2 and 3 after the market/electronic communications networks (ECNs) close and start again the next day with a clean slate and less allocation. If your head is not there, then take a day or two off. Sometimes, that's the only thing that can remedy as you are just too tangled in the eye of the storm. There is nothing wrong with that. It happens to the best of traders.

Believe this: Consistency always smoothes out the anomalies in time. This is the essence of good trading and good traders. They will always have the occasional crazy trade that backfires hard, which could eat up a month's worth of gains.

DSS: Defensive Sprawl Scaling

Another misguided statement is "Don't add to losers," implying you should not add to losing positions. The problem is that a loser is usually recognized in hindsight when the pattern has completely reversed against a position. However, the difference between a wiggle and a reversal depends on the time frame and how it is managed. A breakdown on a 5-minute chart could be a wiggle on the 60-minute chart. Therefore, the prudent action might be to add on sell-offs to key 60-minute support levels to average the cost of shares and align with the more dominant wider time frame. By the time the 5-minute time frame turns back up, the breakout extends to new highs. It is the confusion during the heat of battle that causes traders to freeze up like a deer in the headlights. When a 1-minute fails, then the 5-minute is the next safety. If that 5-minute fails, then the 15/60 minutes are the next safety. When all four lanes reverse, then it is a reversal unless you are swing/portfolio trading, which focuses more on the daily, weekly, and monthly. This may sound a bit confusing, and to anyone stepping into a position unprepared, it is confusing, which is not the place you want to be. This is why the preparation of plotting out the playing field and all support/resistance bumpers ahead of time is crucial. Preparation is not just to satisfy the surface layer of the immediate entry and exit, but also to be aware and ready to react in case the setup turns into an anomaly situation against you.

The action of adding to a position moving quickly against you is called sprawling. If you ever watch a fight in the Ultimate Fighting Championship where a grappler/wrestler is pitted against a striker, the grappler will try to take down/tackle the striker. The grappler's terrain is on the mat, where he can submit or ground and pound his opponent. The striker's terrain is on his feet, launching powerful punches and kicks looking for knockouts. When a grappler charges in to take down a striker, the striker must do his best to stay on his feet long enough to create some distance to launch strikes. This skill is called sprawling. Sprawling is an aggressive defensive action to counteract the opposing force long enough to cut exposure with minimal damage and in some cases to optimize share price and buy time for the wider time frames to detonate, thereby magnifying profits.

Effective sprawling is an essential skillset that will buffer missteps if executed soundly, as demonstrated in Figure 4.47. Sprawling takes instinct not only to add to position but most importantly to unload the overweighted position. The comfort zone will be tested with the added shares, so it is imperative to not stay overleveraged for too long a duration to the point where

FIGURE 4.47 Details of our defensive sprawl scale trade in QCOM.

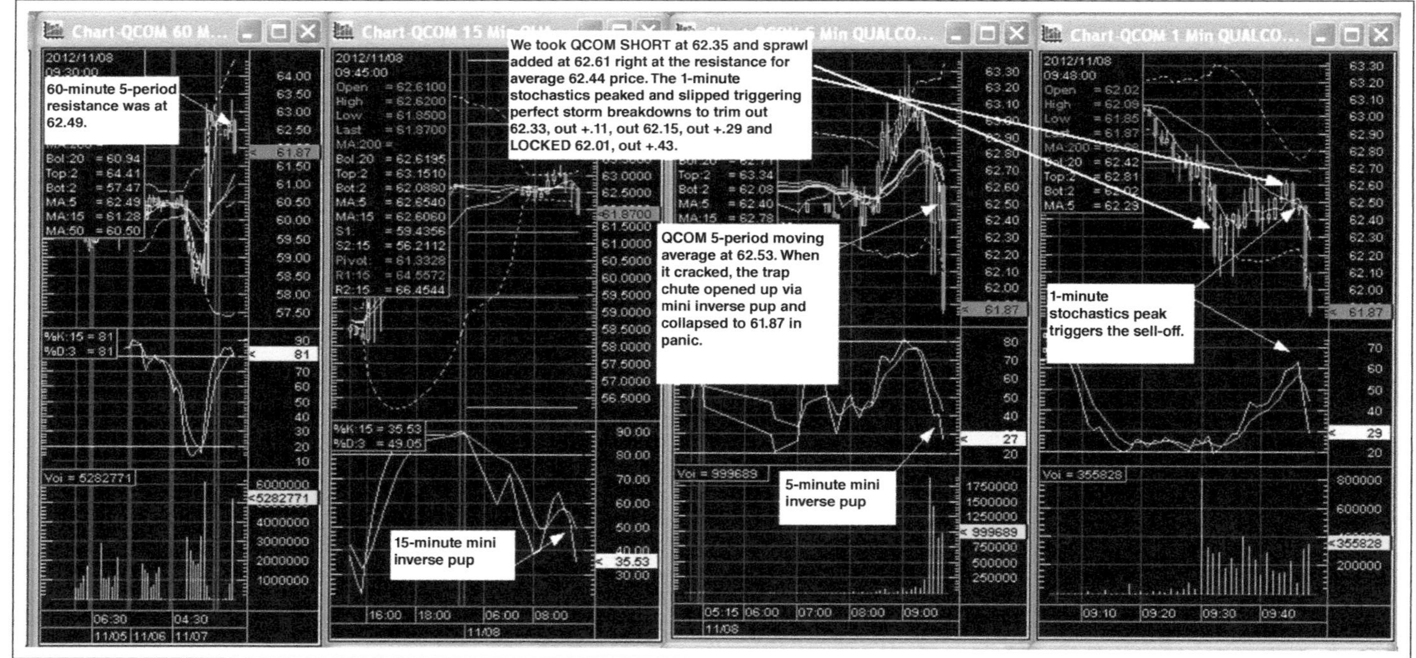

the emotions will kick in prematurely. Therefore, the timing and placement of the add/scale in shares is most crucial. It is most important to add at the point of 1-minute reversal or near an overlapping bumper resistance while 1-minute stochastics are at high bands (80 band or higher), so that you are not stepping in too early. The key rule of thumb is to wait for a 1-minute coil back up through the 20 band on longs to add, or peak and slip through 80 bands to add to shorts. If there are wider time frame overlap supports (two to three key bumpers), then one should add on the initial overshoots since a hammer confirmation will be much higher. Sprawls should not take more than a max three adds. Beyond that, it means you are sloppy with entries or sloppy with the exits.

The problem most traders fall into when sprawling is not the adding part, *but the exiting part.* They tend to trip over the intent of add-ins, especially when they step in too early before the reversal.

DSS Rules and Checklist

The DSS trade involves adding to an existing position at a better price to reduce the cost basis for total position. This involves adding to your original position at various price levels during a rapid panic situation. This is called defensive because your position has turned red and liquidity has dried up; thus the stage is set for a panic. Rather than stopping out in panic, you work on the panic of others and scale in one to two additional positions at strong overlapping bumper levels. The stronger bumpers are based on the wider 60-minute, daily, weekly, and monthly (if the stock is trading near those ranges). There are two scenarios where you can use a DSS. Either you are playing an exhaustion tightening countertrend trade on an excessive momentum move as the stock continues to move against you, or you take a position at the point of impact that immediately turns against you for a steep fast move. The DSS trade is not meant to score a profit but to minimize the damage. The most important aspect is the exit(s), then followed by the add-ons. The stock should still be in a wet climate and preferably a panic situation and not in a slow grind.

1. Must be a wet climate.
2. Stock has to make a *fast panic* move against your position to an overlapping bumper level. The faster and farther the move, the more room for a snap-back reversion.
3. 1-minute stochastics should usually sit at an extreme band ready to reverse.

   a. For long positions, the 1-minute stochastics should be under the 20 band.
   b. For short positions, the 1-minute stochastics should be above the 80 band.
4. Add to your position:
   a. A reversal candle is always helpful (hammer, doji, star).
   b. Monitor and time with the SPY 1-minute charts converging in your direction (e.g., if you are DSS long, then try to time add-ons on the 1-minute SPY bounce and vice versa on shorts).
   c. Early add: You can add into the panic if it tests overlapping bumpers before the 1-minute stochastics reverses. This provides you the better price fills but is susceptible to further moves against you until the stochastics reverse.
      i. If the move continues against you, then evaluate your position and consider another add at the next overlapping bumpers or an impact add for better confirmation.
   d. Impact add: Add to the position as soon as the 1-minute stochastics cross back through the 20 band (on longs) or below the 80 band (on shorts). This will be a costlier position add with a more shallow reversion, but carries a higher probability.
5. Exits: This is the most important aspect of DSS. Since these are reversion trades, you are only expecting a temporary snap-back that lasts the duration of the 1-minute stochastics oscillation. Be aware of the bumper levels on the retracements, and be sure to exit just ahead of those levels as they test, usually the 5-period moving averages. You can scale out if the 1-minute stochastics continues in your favor but is approaching a bumper resistance. Don't look at your blotter or try to figure out your average price, focus on the trade and getting the most price improvement into liquidity while it is still present. You are using leverage here so it is of the highest importance that you trim that leverage back down sooner not later.
6. If you can't take a stop loss under normal circumstances, then do not play DSS trades.

Remember that when you enter a position and it moves against you, there are three actions to take: wait, sprawl, or stop.

The waiting should be done in increments of the BOSS time frame candle close periods. Waiting is actually buying time. If the BOSS time frame is the 5-minute chart, then 5-minute increments are usually required to let the pattern play out, unless a very sharp heavy volume reverse forms that cracks through multiple bumpers.

The sprawl is another term for scaling in/adding shares to average cost basis for defensive/offensive purposes.

This allows the seasoned trader to minimize damage and/or maximize gains if exits are executed efficiently. Seasoned and disciplined traders who are acutely familiar with the underlying stock, the setup, and the methods, should only execute the sprawl trade. This is because the trader is taking on a double sometimes a triple allocation. Leverage works both ways. Most importantly, sprawling should never be performed by newbies who are just trying to average their costs with no exit plans.

The difference between a meticulously executed defensive sprawl trade versus a trapped humanoid just emotionally adding to a losing position lies in the mindset.

The pro intimately acknowledges the essence of risk in the trading game is a perpetual balancing of exposure and duration. Under these terms, the goal is to eliminate all risk preferably with a profit, but that is not the mandatory requirement. The mandatory requirement is complete eradication of risk.

CHAPTER 5

The Perfect Storm Pattern Trade

In this chapter I will provide the most comprehensive details of the strongest price pattern I have ever played, bar none. This pattern is linear across all time frames and all financial markets and instruments. I have discovered that the true depth of these patterns goes beyond just playing the straight single breakout or breakdown setup but expands into several variations of which the fade reversal is twice as strong as the traditional perfect storm. This is a by-product of my journey that I am honored to share with you. Let's get to the nitty gritty.

What Is a Perfect Storm?

Simply put, this powerful pattern forms when three or more pups/mini pups (or inverse pups/mini inverse pups) form and converge simultaneously on three or more separate time-frame charts (of the seven total time frames).

In meteorological terms, it's the equivalent of three or more storm fronts converging into a massive nor'easter like a superstorm (Figure 5.1). Very similar to the weather version, perfect storms are tracked with the charts and contain a Doppler forecasting effect when the wider time frames lie dormant (for the time being).

FIGURE 5.1 A three-lane perfect storm breakout.

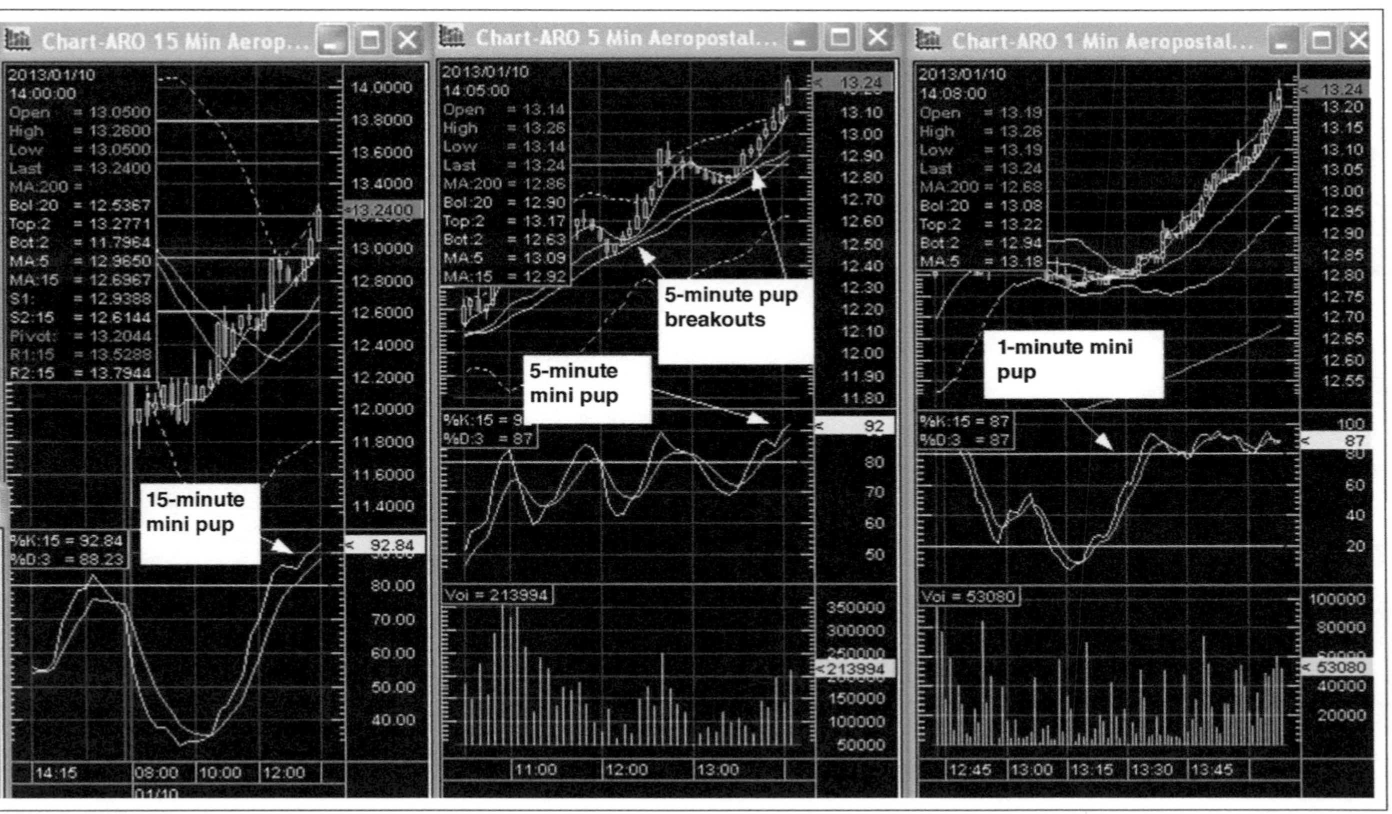

In trading terms, these are fortified patterns composed of the single strongest patterns (pup/mini pups) that converge in a direction with triple the strength. When the pup/mini pup components form on the widest time frame (i.e., daily, weekly, monthly), the moves can last for days to weeks.

I have touched upon perfect storms in my earlier books and qualified them as the highest probability setups, which were as proportionately rare to find as they are powerful (Figure 5.2). This was my assumption for many years. It wasn't until the advent of the high-frequency trading program (HFT) infestation that I reverted back to the strongest pattern weapon out of necessity. To my amazement, I discover that perfect storms form every market day, but they have to be searched out. They tend to move simultaneously with the macro market and sectors and then disperse by the time they hit the scanners. They can be very elusive, yet bountiful as they literally move in packs. When playing one perfect storm, there are simultaneous perfect storms triggering as well.

Perfect storms follow the law of transparency. Transparency and opportunity are inversely correlated. Time improves transparency while simultaneously diminishing opportunity proportionately. When perfect storms attain maximum textbook transparency, it's too late to step in. Unfortunately, that is when most traders witness a perfect storm, after the fact. However, this doesn't mean there isn't a way to make money. I'll get into that later.

I spent the latter part of three years focusing solely on every aspect of perfect storm patterns. My quest resulted in the creation of a system that should reap at least a perfect storm daily. Much like mining for gold, it takes excavation of a lot of dirt to filter down to the pieces of gold, to catch a playable perfect storm. People do tend to get lucky and stumble on a playable perfect storm. While that particular trade may play out profitably, it is nothing more than a gift. Accepting a reward and earning a reward are completely different situations. As in everything in life, effort is what earns the rightful prize and by-product. Anything less is a gift. Don't look a gift horse in the mouth, and, most importantly, acknowledge when you are presented a gift. Never assume that gift was earned when it wasn't. A gift is a wake-up call, oftentimes not a positive one. It means that for whatever reason, you received profits, which you rightfully didn't deserve. Going back to what I wrote earlier, the market LOVES to give small change, knowing it will make back many times what it loaned out.

There are different types of perfect storms that will produce different magnitudes of reactions. There are three different stages and three different types of perfect storms. There are three ways to play perfect storms. We'll cover all of these in this chapter.

Since this pattern and variations thereof will be your main strategy, it's important that we go over every aspect in rigorous and repetitive detail to drill the strategy into your psyche.

FIGURE 5.2 A rare seven-lane perfect storm breakout.

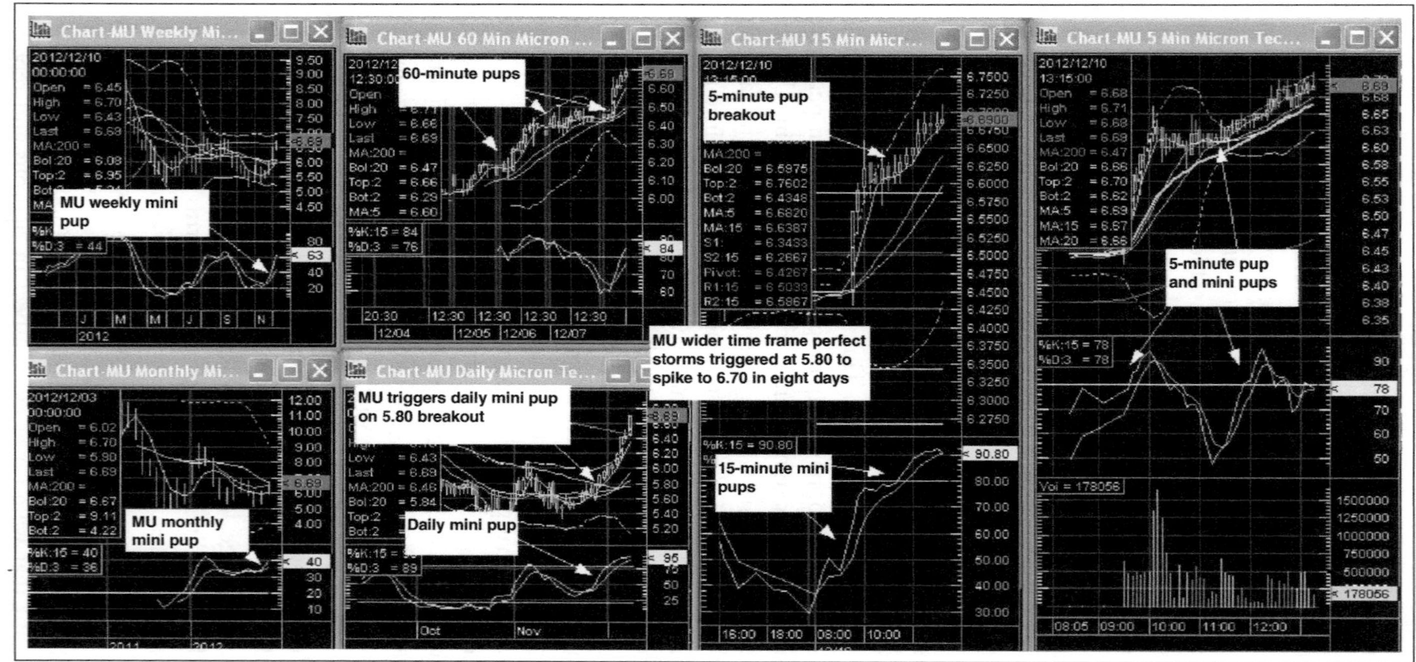

Basic Formation

The rifle charts pinpoint perfect storms at every stage of development. Proper application of these charts is essential for success, so make sure that you are thoroughly acclimated with the pup and mini pup formations.

Let's get started with the basic formation. For learning purposes, the first priority is grasping the concept, identifying the pattern, and witnessing the impact/aftermath. I'm going to thoroughly cover as much depth as possible making this the largest and most significant chapter in the book. My best advice is to chew (thoroughly) and digest in small pieces.

Proper repetition develops familiarity. Repetition becomes more effective as it becomes more mundane/boring to the conscious mind. This is because the designated beneficiary is not the conscious mind, but the elusive subconscious state. This is the state where actions and reactions become natural/instinctive. For better, or worse, repetition is SOLELY in your hands. I hope that you are motivated enough to utilize repetition.

Next comes experiencing the riptide-like force of the storm. Perfect storms can move viciously due to the leapfrogging and magnifying effects of HFTs in addition to the institutions, market makers, and retail traders/investors trying to pile in.

Just so I don't have to constantly repeat the vice versa applications in run-on sentences, please note that my explanations dealing with pups and mini pups referring to breakouts and uptrends also apply to the inverse pups and mini inverse pups for breakdowns and downtrends. Just as many texts will for the sake of simplicity use "he" rather than inject "he or she" into every sentence. By definition pups and mini pups are breakout/uptrend patterns, whereas the inverse versions are breakdown/downtrend patterns.

Remember that pups form on the moving averages and mini pups form on the stochastics. Perfect storms develop when three or more time frames (out of seven) form simultaneous pups/mini pups. The wider time frames carry more clout in terms of formation and significance of the bumpers. The intensity grows with more time frames forming pups/mini pups.

Perfect Storm Profile

A perfect storm pattern develops when three or more pup/mini pups form simultaneously in the same direction. This results in a significant price move that breaks the price range. The speed of the breakout/breakdown is one of the most obvious effects in addition to follow-through, volume, and liquidity as seen in Figure 5.3.

FIGURE 5.3 A perfect storm breakdown short trade.

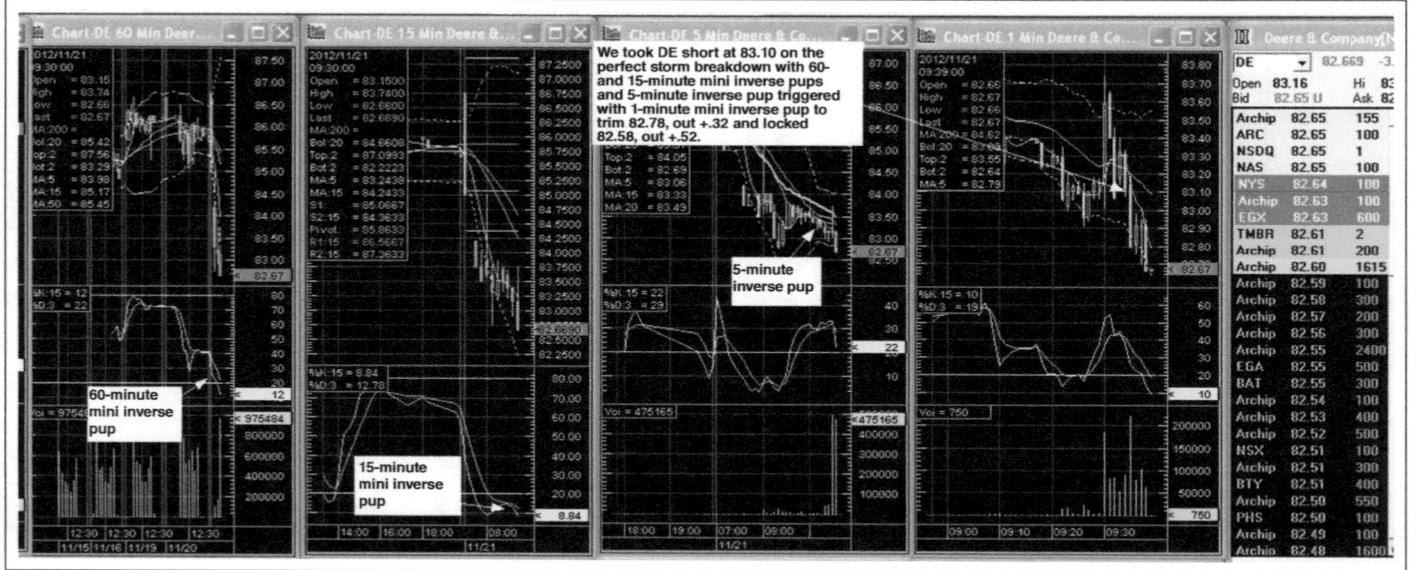

The Three Stages of the Perfect Storm: Dormant to Detonation

Perfect storms have a life span broken down into three stages. Stage 1 is the early dormant stage where two of the time frames (daily, 60-minute, 15-minute, 5-minute) have a pup/mini pup pattern formed but remain dormant until the third time frame forms a pup/mini pup with the 1-minute stochastics cross trigger. The 1-minute itself can be the third time frame if it forms a pup/mini pup as the trigger.

When the 1-minute triggers by having stochastics cross up on breakouts or down on breakdowns, it commences stage 2, the impact and detonation stage. This is where the full fury of the perfect storm pattern takes place as the three pup/mini pups are unleashed led by the 1-minute stochastics.

As the stock reaches its target bumpers, the 1-minute stochastics will eventually exhaust and reverse. The reversal should pull back to the 5-minute 5-period moving average. If the stock holds support off the 5-minute 5-period moving average long enough for the 1-minute stochastics to cross back in alignment with the trend, then it resumes the perfect storm until the next 1 minute oscillation peaks and reverses again stalling out the perfect storm until the 1-minute stochastics resume the direction of the perfect storm trend. When the pup/mini pup time-frame charts reach above the 80 band stochastics on longs or below the 20-band stochastics on shorts, they reach the final stage.

Stage 3 is the late stage of the perfect storm where the final climax move detonates for a final peak (Figure 5.4) and ultimately a reversal that causes the pup/mini pups to erode and reverse. When entering stage 3 perfect storms, be aware that you are entering near the end of the move and should be taking our profits or stops sooner, not later. The nice thing about stage 3 is that when it reverses, you still have the three levels of protection in the form of three or more 5-period moving average supports that provide liquidity to close out the position. However, if you fail to notice the late stage and liquidate your position, then you could get trapped when the perfect storm finally reverses. Once you have a firm grasp of perfect storm stages, you should rarely be caught off guard. Many times the stage 3 of a perfect storm can often step up a stage 1 early stage of a reversal perfect storm, which then starts the stage cycle all over again in the opposite direction.

The Three Perfect Storm Outcomes

When perfect storms detonate, they will produce three outcomes. The first and preferred outcome is the break and trend where the trade plays out as

FIGURE 5.4 A four-lane perfect storm breakout.

Each time-frame chart is considered a lane. Perfect storms require at least three lanes to have pups and/or mini pups. The preferred break and trend outcome is assured with more lanes. When more lanes are present, the reaction is more robust and powerful.

planned with rapid price acceleration, momentum, and follow-through complete with volume and liquidity. This is the break and trend outcome and the most favorable outcome we seek.

The second outcome would be chop and wiggle. This is where the trigger forms a small initial price move that fizzles out as it chops on shrinking volume and thin liquidity. The lack of volume and follow through erodes interest in the stock. This is common during dry climates. Pay attention to the clock to measure when the 5- and 15-minute candles close to update the moving averages. When the candle close creates no additional price movement and volume spikes, then it may be reverting back to flat consolidation or a potential third outcome. The consolidation simply requires more time to resolve. You should either stop out or trim down your position due to the additional duration of time this trade may require. It's very important to be ready to stop out or reverse the trade if you spot early signs of the third outcome.

The third outcome is a fade and reversal. It's imperative that you keep a close eye on the 5- and/or 1-minute volume as that will be the distinguishing factor between choppy second outcomes or a solid fade. A fade will actually absorb the perfect storm break attempt as volume rises but price is restrained and starts to erode towards the opposite direction. Usually it was also fading the SPY direction. When the SPY reverses direction, the fading perfect storm gains more momentum on the reversal and eventually gets muscled into a full-fledged reversal that traps the participants and panics them out in the other direction as they chase liquidity for their stops. Since perfect storms are the highest caliber patterns, it takes a tremendous amount of muscle to smother them out and reverse them. This means the reversal should be twice the strength of a break/trend outcome. If you are long a fading/reversal perfect storm, then you should play the reversal trade as soon as you stop out. The quicker you exit before the other participants, the more profits you capture when they are forced to panic out.

Spotting Perfect Storm Opportunities with the Anchor Time Frame

The best way to spot these formations is to work down from the widest intraday time frames, which are the daily and 60-minute charts. These time frames provide the anchor for the intraday moves. From there, it is three more time frames that need to converge/align in the direction of the pup/mini pups. It may sound complicated, but no more complicated than dominos naturally tipping over sequentially into each other. It's simply the natural sequence.

Start by scanning through the daily and 60-minute charts looking for any pup or mini pup formations. If both the daily and the 60-minute contain pup/mini pups in the same direction, that means you are already two thirds of a perfect storm. If only the daily or 60-minute has a pup/mini pup, it is important to make sure the stochastics direction is aligned with the direction of the other time frame's mini pup. Since the daily and 60-minute take the longest time to shift trends and stochastics direction, you want to make sure they are pointed in the same direction first before even considering the prospect. The wider time frame will always carry the clout that the shorter time frame has to converge with.

For example, if XYZ has a daily mini pup, but the 60-min stochastics are falling, then the daily chart is dormant. The 60-minute chart can take one to three days to converge with the daily pup/mini pup, so keep it on a lower-priority minder for the next few days. This is the process of aging the meat. Make sure to monitor it every morning for the 60-minute stochastics convergence.

Moving on to current prospects, once you find a daily pup/mini pup with an aligned 60-minute chart, then gauge the lower time frames for any pup/mini pups and direction convergence on the stochastics and moving average trends. The key here is having two pup/mini pups lined up/prepared, so you can focus on the third pup/mini pup, which will be triggered by the 1- and/or 5-minute charts. The full impact of the move happens when consecutive time frames simultaneously have pup/mini pups or at least converge in the same direction for charts that don't contain pup/mini pups.

The PS Code

We can describe the perfect storms by labeling them first with the time frame M,W, D for monthly, weekly, daily and 60, 15, 5, 1 for time frames and p, mp, a for pup, mini pup, and aligned. Add an I to p and/or mp to represent inverse (breakdown/downtrend) versions.

The combination of daily mini pup + 60-minute pup + 15-minute pup + 5-minute aligned + 1-minute mini pup = perfect storm breakout. It can be coded as a Dmp, 60p, 15mp, 5a, 1mp PS (perfect storm). As long as there are 3 p/mp (pup/mini pups) and 1 or 2a (aligned), the perfect storm ignites (Figure 5.5).

Safety

Since perfect storms have at least three or more intertwined pup/mini pups, they tend to be very lenient when they fail and bountiful when they

FIGURE 5.5 The shorthand way to delineate a complete description of any particular perfect storm chart.

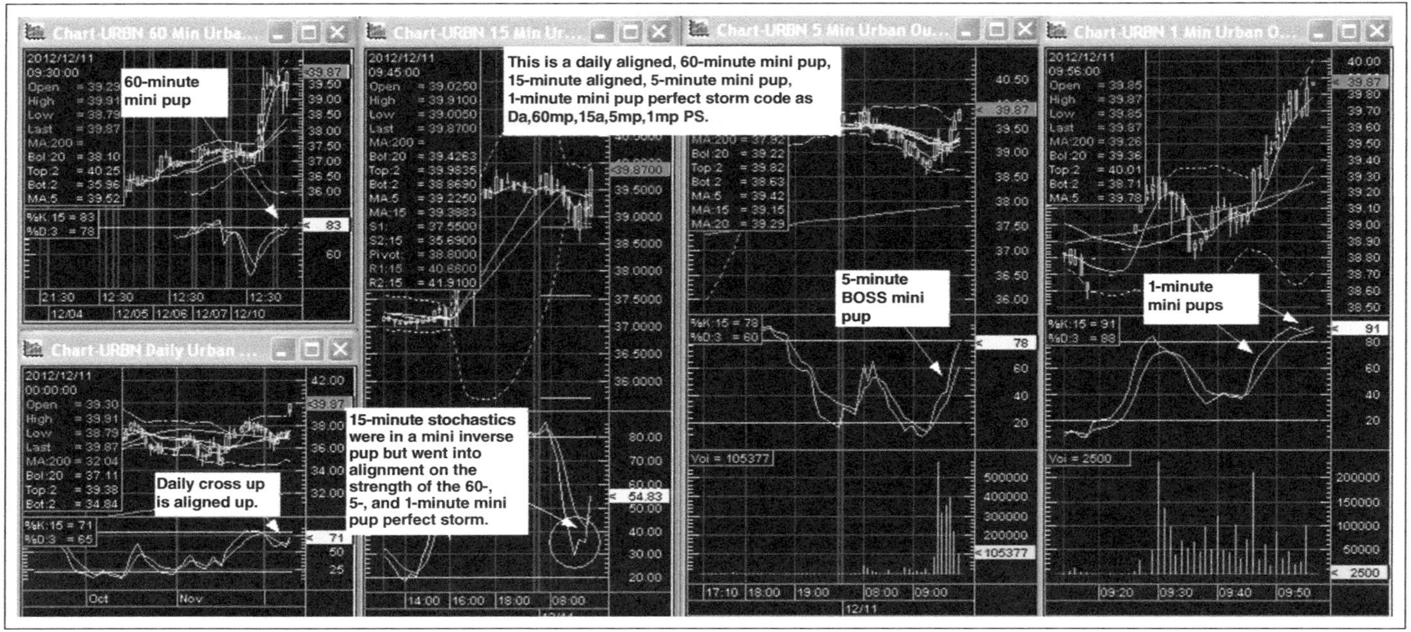

reverse, IF you are aware and assertive enough to react (Figure 5.6). Both qualities are required together. Having consecutive time-frame charts with pup/mini pups gives multiple layers of protection, but waiting too long to stop out or reverse will only compound the damage as you will be chasing liquidity on exits and playing right into the dynamics of the inversion. The main reason why reversals are so powerful is due to all the sheep that finally decide to throw in the towel at the thinnest point of liquidity triggering panic.

Education will build your awareness, but repetition is what makes you assertive. Being aware that you are in the path of a Mack truck is a start, but it takes assertiveness to take action and move out of harm's way.

Since we use the SPY as the main indicator of the macro market climate, it is important to gauge if the perfect storm is correlated and aligned with the SPY or fading the SPY. This can be determined by overlapping both sets of charts and comparing. The double-hedged sword sequence is an advanced play that is composed of two opposite perfect storm patterns. It's an inverse pairs position where two uncorrelated stocks happen to have opposite perfect storms allowing for the expert trader to use the SPY movements to capture pockets of profits on opposing fades before one side finally reverts back into SPY alignment.

Volume Hungry

Perfect storms thrive on heavy volume. Conversely, light volume is the proverbial kryptonite as there are so many more headfakes and wiggles. On lighter volume, the fades are much harder to gauge as liquidity thins out. It takes more time for them to form. If the wider time frames are in pup/mini pup patterns, they don't detonate until the shorter time frames converge with aligned pup/mini pups. Whereas a perfect storm breakout setup produced a large move in the morning, that identical formation can develop during the deadzone period (11:30 A.M. to 2:30 P.M.) and produce nothing more than headfakes and wiggles. They fail to generate the volume and therefore end up getting reversed back down. They will also fail to breakdown and end up getting reversed back up oftentimes off the wider time frame supports. This cycle repeats itself as it continues to thin out the participants, volume, and liquidity.

However, if the pattern develops again post deadzone in the last 90 minutes of the day, the odds increase as volume returns into the market. The volume makes all the difference. The closer towards the end of the day, the more volume will naturally grow, as shown in Figure 5.7.

FIGURE 5.6 How lenient perfect storms can be with stops and reversals as long as you are aware and do not hesitate to react! WSM initially started off as a long position for a tightening perfect storm, but sell faded the SPY bounces as the muscling down became apparent. We were able to stop out and reverse the trade to the short side with double allocation to score a profit.

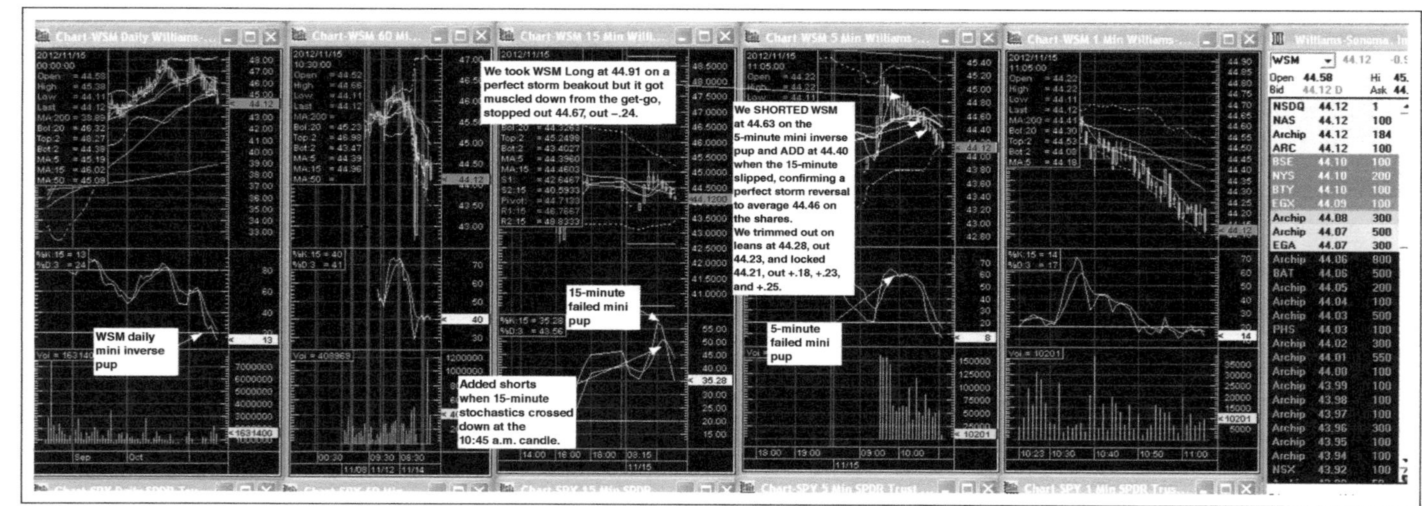

FIGURE 5.7 How powerful perfect storm breakouts can be as long as there is rising volume.

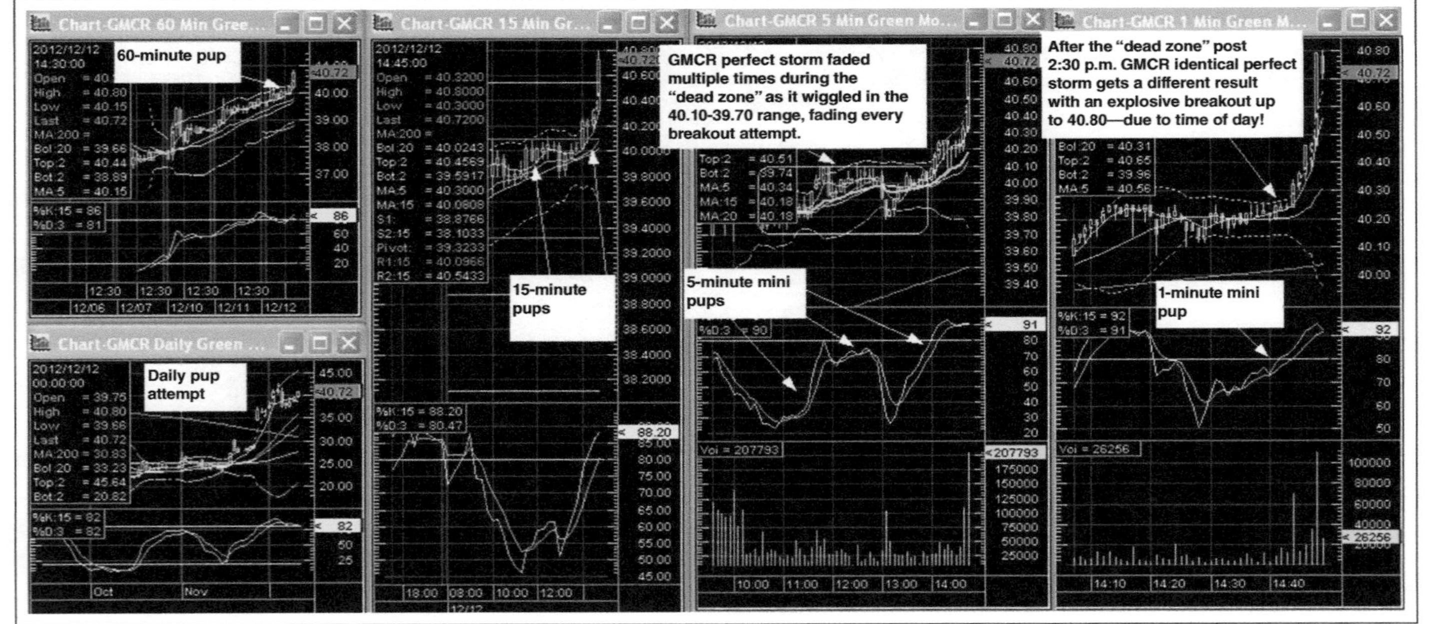

It is because of this thirst for heavy volume that the most opportunities to play perfect storm patterns will be during the heaviest volume time period of every trading day, the morning open (9:30 to 11 A.M.). Heavy volume exposes any strong buy/sell fading thereby giving an astute and assertive trader early transparency and the opportunity to profit from it while it's still fresh and robust. Heavy volume is the truth serum.

As you get further into the trading day, dilution and erosion become the bigger problem. Stocks either catch rigor mortis with virtually no price movement, or chop back-and-forth headfakes as algo programs try to generate what liquidity they can by purposely fading break attempts (temporarily) through the deadzone. The algos know the most effective way to trigger volume and liquidity in a tumbleweed landscape is to shake out the breakout/breakdown players at the top and bottom of ranges. They do this because the volume is so thin, making it relatively cheap to flush out the limited number of participants within the range. Once this routine gets familiar to participants, what do you think the algos do? They not only let the breakout/breakdown manifest but will pump it hard and flush out the oscillation players. This is the mechanics behind consolidation break perfect storms. They fade the break attempts, converting breakout players to switch the oscillation theme only to finally break it hard against them. When do you suppose this happens? During the high volume periods off the open or post deadzone.

The algos/HFT programs profit by generating volume and magnifying momentum by luring and trapping the most participants on the WRONG side of the trade so they can extort the vital liquidity lifeline needed for their exits. That statement should ring a bell. It was mentioned in the first chapter. This sucks if you got sucked in on the wrong side, but is amazing if you are on the right side, as long as you use the liquidity for your own exits.

Determining the Boss Time-Frame Chart

Back in the early era of electronic day trading, 1990s to 2003, Nasdaq level 2 was the most powerful tool due to having an ax market maker who would tip his hand on the direction of a stock by fading a price level long enough to convince participants to join him. Due to the rise of the electronic communication networks (ECNs) and dark pools, market makers no longer attempt to give any transparency as their roles have diminished. While level 2 is still a tool employed to measure the depth and price levels for order executions, the algo programs and HFTs with their millisecond speed and quote stuffing (yes, they still do!) has rendered it useless for transparency purposes. The recurring theme of necessity being the mother of invention has allowed me to use a more powerful version of an ax, not with level 2 but with the rifle charts.

The new embodiment of the ax market maker lies in the form of a boss time-frame chart. Just as an ax market maker was spotted because he would either be a buy fader into selling pressure or a sell fader into buying pressure long enough to exert his will on the direction of the stock price, a boss chart has the same fading prowess. Boss charts indicate the presence of a determined/motivated market participant(s) willing to absorb pressure from its peer charts to establish the dominant position in the price action. This usually occurs as a result of big trade orders being worked when volume is heavy or at the hands of the algos when volume thins out.

While the larger time frames, like the daily and 60-minute, in most cases overpower the shorter 15-, 5-, and 1-minute charts, there are instances where a shorter time frame will singlehandedly support or resist against a perfect storm long enough to muscle and convert the other time frames into its direction as demonstrated in Figure 5.8 and Figure 5.9. It's just that the boss chart usually tends to blend in as it conforms in most cases with the general direction of the other pup/mini pups in a unified perfect storm. The boss chart only reveals itself when it gets tested, by fading the direction of its peer time-frame charts.

While the boss chart's 5-period moving average will be the price level that fades in most cases, it is the boss chart's stochastics that is the key factor. While the boss chart will protect its 5-period moving average, it's the stochastics alignment that determines the outcome of the fading.

One of two outcomes will prevail when the boss chart fades the perfect storm attempts. Either it will be so determined during the fade that it will outlast the pressure and convert the other time frames in its direction, or it will fade the pressure to build up steam and finally release it upon aligning it back in the direction of the other charts, which generates a powerful perfect storm.

The Basic Method of Playing Perfect Storms

This checklist is specific to perfect storm pattern trades. This list represents the basic mechanics for intraday perfect storms. The complete trade execution process from start to finish is detailed thoroughly in Chapter 9. To play wider time frame perfect storms for swing, prioritize and confirm pup/mini pups on the 60-minute, weekly, and monthly charts; then proceed with the checklist.

1. Determine the type of perfect storm (trending, consolidation break, tightening).
2. Determine which time frames have existing pup/mini pups starting with the daily and 60-minute anchors, then 15- and 5-minute charts.

FIGURE 5.8 The early signs of a boss frame chart on the SPY.

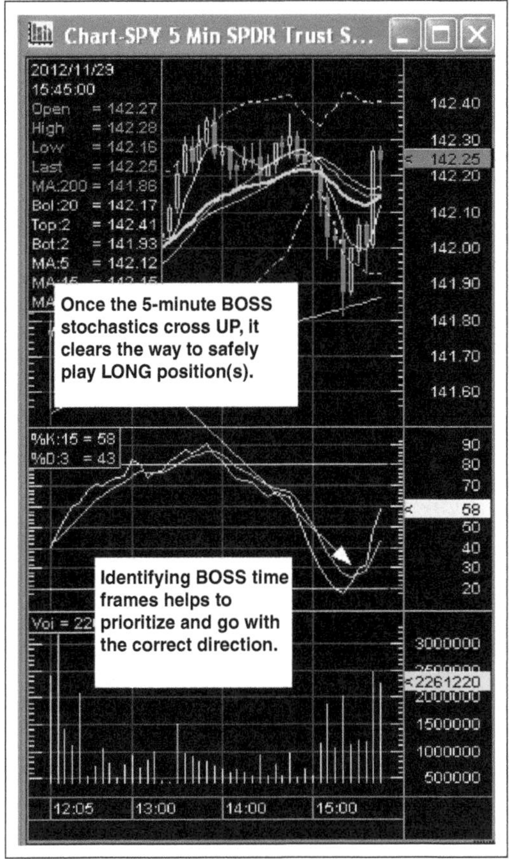

The 1-minute chart is the trigger, so make note of its position on the stochastics.

3. Determine if there is a BOSS time-frame chart, which is the chart that has firmly maintained the 5-period moving average without wiggles or the one preventing momentum to follow through.
4. Determine and identify if there is a leader stock or a sympathy peer stock correlation. This can be confirmed if the chart formations are identically correlated in pattern and direction.
   a. If your stock is the laggard or sympathy to a leader, then follow the leader at inflection points (breaks and reversals) for advance notice of impending moves on your laggard stock.
   b. If your stock is the leader, then be prepared for the opportunity to play the laggard stock(s) for additional profits.

FIGURE 5.9 The 5-minute boss time frame on the SPY.

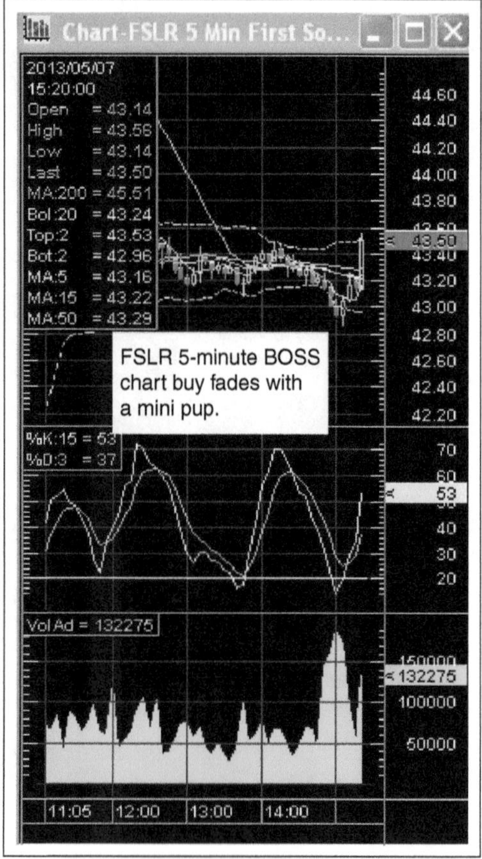

5. Note the 5-period moving average values and next target bumpers on each chart containing a pup/mini pup.
   a. Measure the meat between the bones by assessing the nominal price move to the next bumpers to determine if entry is worth the risk.
   b. Determine proper position allocation based on the stock rhythm, probability, and duration.
6. Monitor the SPY macro market technicals and note if aligned or fading
7. Assess market climate and environment (wet/momentum or dry/limp).
8. Wait for the 1-minute trigger to align with the peer pup/mini pup charts.
9. Enter position on the 1-minute trigger signal on the break of the counter candle body high for longs/low for shorts.

   a. Strive for 20/80 band stochastics cross entries.
   b. If taking longs above the 80 band, make sure there is a mini pup and be mindful to sell into buying liquidity before the stochastics peak and cross back under the 80 band and 5-period moving average.
   c. If taking shorts under the 20 band, make sure there is a mini inverse pup, and be mindful to cover into sell-offs before the stochastics cross back up through the 20 band and through the 5-period moving average.
10. Be mindful of the proximity of the near-term supports/resistance bumpers as well as the stochastics levels on the pup/mini pup charts.
11. Continually monitor the SPY for market headwinds and correlation.
12. Exit position into liquidity as it nears target bumpers and/or extended stochastics levels. Wider time frame swing trade perfect storms still utilize intraday exit methods but focus on the immediate 60-minute and daily bumpers, then the weekly and/or monthly bumper targets.
   a. Stop out if the pattern fades or fizzles.
   b. If the perfect storm fades the SPY on relatively strong volume, then identify the boss time-frame chart responsible for the fade to consider either a full/partial stop exit and/or reversal trade.
      i. If the perfect storm reverses too fast, then consider a defensive sprawl entry at overlapping bumper support/resistance levels to average cost basis for a reversion scalp to minimize loss.
      ii. If the SPY continues to trend, then the boss chart could finally turn back into alignment triggering a stronger unified and laggard price move at which point more experienced/aggressive traders can implement an offensive scale sequence to add to the position to maximize profits.

The checklist may appear to be pretty labor intensive and complicated. It is a thorough breakdown of the thought/action process that in time can be done in seconds if you have already prepared properly ahead of time with quick analysis of your watch list prospects before the opening bell. Otherwise, it may take a few minutes if it's a new prospect and you are starting off cold. Remember, more lanes equate to more strength in the perfect storm as Figure 5.10 illustrates.

How to Trade the Three Types of Perfect Storms

There are three types of perfect storms: trending, tightening, and consolidation break. Although they share the same structure composed of three or more simultaneous pup/mini pups on different time frames, the actual type

FIGURE 5.10 A five-lane perfect storm breakout on AKAM.

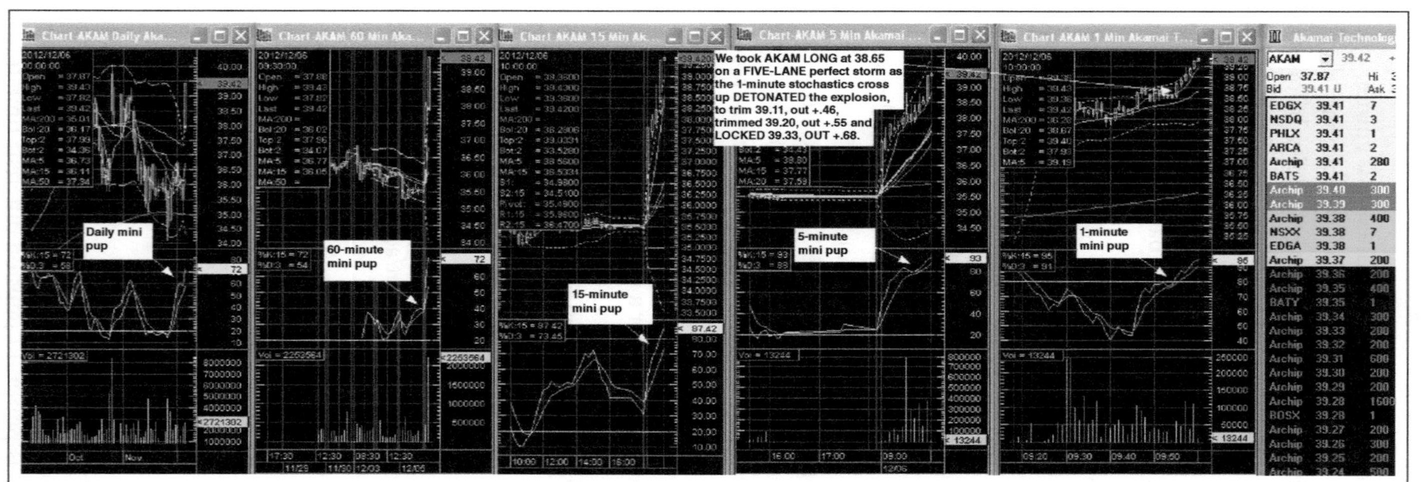

The more pup/mini pup time frames contained in the perfect storm trade, the more powerful it becomes.

of perfect storm is determined by the context in which it forms. Each type of perfect storm has its own set of nuances. I will go over each type of perfect storm in detail and how to trade it.

The Trending

The *trending perfect storm* is the classic form of the pattern, where all intraday time frames are aligned in the same direction/trend indicated by the moving averages and stochastics. The wider time frames establish the dominant trend, while the shorter time frames act as triggers to facilitate a unified directional trending price move.

These types of perfect storms provide opportunities for entry/re-entry into the larger trend by stalking the shorter time frame pullbacks that develop into pup/mini pups that will often result in breakouts to higher price ranges on uptrends as shown in Figure 5.11 (or breakdowns to lower price ranges on downtrends (Figure 5.12)). The 5-period moving average will provide the pullback support and bounce area that traders should be monitoring.

How to Play Trending Perfect Storms

On trending perfect storms, your goal is to either step in early on the pullback to the 5-minute 5-period moving average before the 1-minute stochastics cross back up, or at the impact stage on the coil off the 5-period moving average with the 1-minute stochastics cross trigger or late stage on extended 1-minute stochastics mini pups above the 80 band on longs and below the 20 band on shorts. It's important that you don't make it a (bad) habit to chase perfect storm entries in dry climates as liquidity can dry up quickly. Late entries should only be considered in very heavy volume wet climates like the market open only.

Early Entry:

1. Wait for pullbacks to test the 5-period moving average as the 1-minute stochastics oscillate against the 5-minute chart.
2. Enter position at or near the 5-minute 5-period moving average just ahead of 1-minute stochastics cross.
3. Scalp/scale out position into the bumper target levels as the perfect storm resumes on the 1-minute stochastics cross back in alignment with the perfect storm direction. Use the 1-minute oscillation to exit into the next bumpers.

FIGURE 5.11 A trending perfect storm breakout.

FIGURE 5.12 A trending perfect storm breakdown.

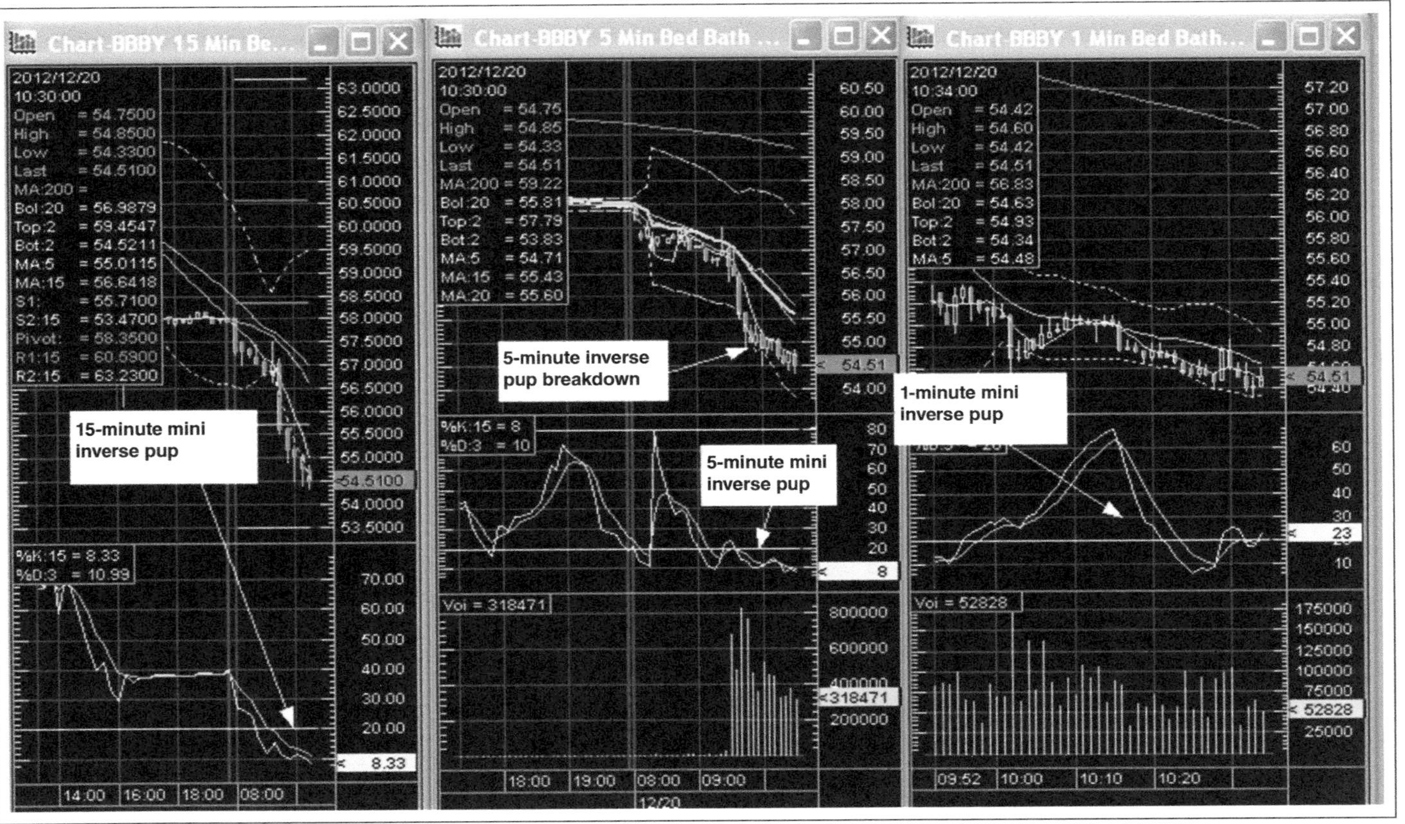

4. Trail the 5-minute and 1-minute 5-period moving average breaks on remaining shares until scaled out.

Impact Entry

1. Wait for pullbacks to deflect off 5-period moving average and 1-minute stochastics to cross back in direction of the perfect storm (up for longs and down for shorts).
2. Enter position after stochastics cross.
3. Scalp/scale out position into the bumper target levels as the perfect storm resumes on the 1-minute stochastics cross back in alignment with the perfect storm direction. Use the 1-minute oscillation to exit into the next bumpers.
4. Trail the 5-minute and 1-minute 5-period moving average breaks on remaining shares until scaled out.

Late Entry

1. Confirm a wet climate, expanding Bollinger Bands and nominal profit potential by measuring the room to the next bumper.
   a. Don't bother playing late entry perfect storm breakouts when the 5- and 1-minute upper Bollinger Bands are less than .20 to .30 away from the 5-period moving average bumper.
2. Enter position on 1-minute counter candle body high price break with 1-minute mini pup through 80 band on longs or cross below 20 bands stochastics on 1-minute counter candle body low price break and 1-minute mini inverse pup on shorts.
3. Exit position into the bumper target overshoots before the 1-minute stochastics exhaust and reverse back through the 5-period moving average(s).

Trading the Sympathy/Laggard Perfect Storm

As mentioned earlier, when a stock makes a big gap up or down based on earnings or some fundamental catalyst, that momentum oftentimes spreads to the sympathy and laggard stocks within the sector. This allows traders to use the main gapper stock as a lead indicator and play the laggard(s) for the belated move. Many times, the lead stock may move too fast to capture a decent entry price, so the laggard gives an opportunity to step in before it also gets overpriced as demonstrated in Figure 5.13.

The Tightening

The *tightening perfect storm* is a counter trend formation that pits the shorter time frame 1-, 5-, and 15-minute charts against the trend of the wider time frame 60-minute and/or daily charts. On uptrends the tightening perfect storm forms after a peak is reached and exhaustion sets in as it reverses against the trend of the wider time frame (Figure 5.14). These will form at the Bollinger Band to the 5-period moving average or the 5-period moving average to the 15-period moving average. They tighten the trading range by selling off in a countertrend manner to the opposing bumper at the 15-period moving average and 20-period moving average. These will have shorter time frame trends that move against the wider time frame trend.

The most powerful version of a tightening perfect storm involves a BOSS time frame with a distinct 5-period moving average SLOPING DOWN by

FIGURE 5.13 How to use a leader stock to trade the laggard.

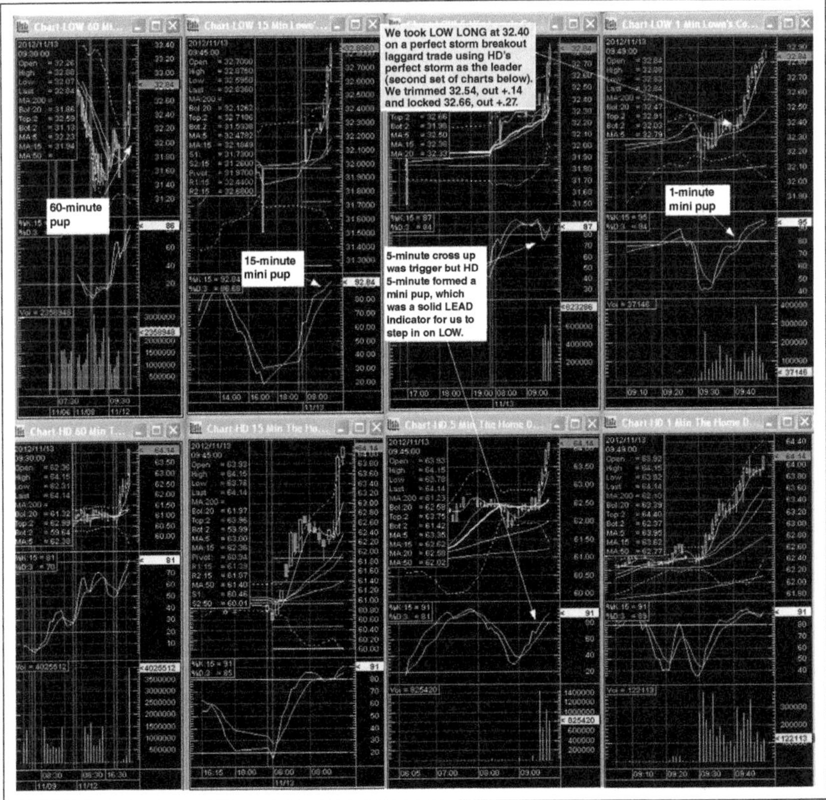

FIGURE 5.14 How tightening perfect storms form after a stock peaks and exhausts.

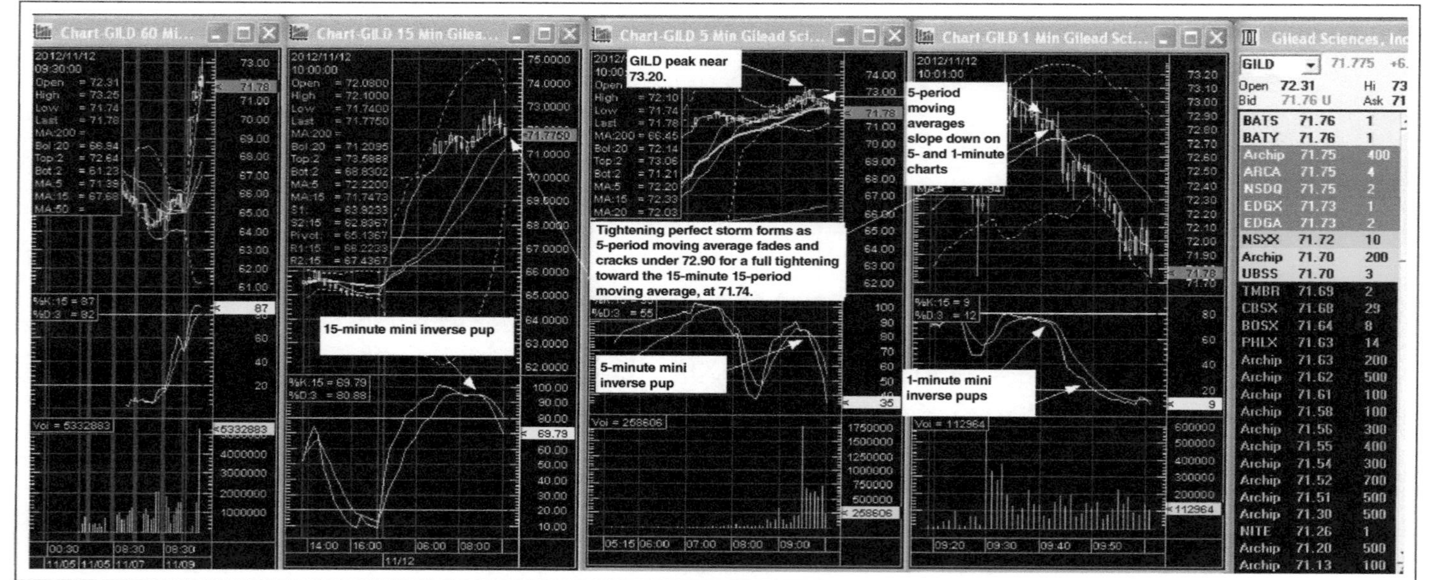

consistently rejecting every attempt to break back through that 5-period moving average. The wiggles should be minimal as the 5-period moving average caps and smothers out all bounce attempts. In the best cases, there will be less than a few pennies of overshoot slippage.

Remember that just because a stock peaks and slips, that doesn't qualify it as a tightening perfect storm. It has to slip UNDER the 5-period moving average and then reject the bounce attempt back up through. It is upon this rejection that forms the counter candle and then a mini inverse pup at the break of the body low of the counter candle. This can happen on any single time frame, but the simultaneous formation across three time frames is what makes it a perfect storm, which seals the fate of the tightening to the 15/20 period moving averages.

In a *downtrend tightening*, this requires the stock to bottom out, oftentimes indicated by a hammer candle, and coil back up through the 5-period moving average, whereas a solid down trending perfect storm will reject the bounce attempt at the 5-period moving average and continue back down. Once the 5-period moving average is initially pierced, the bears will try to push it back down through the 5-period moving average, but soon find out that it has become a solid support that is sloping up. This will cause the bears to panic to cover their positions driving up the price of the stock as the stochastics form a mini pup thereby sealing the fate of the bears as the stock moves towards the 15-period moving average target bumper. If they break the 15-period moving average bumper, then the 20-period moving average is next and then upper Bollinger Bands. The key is the sloping/rising 5-period moving average that sustains pullbacks long enough for stochastics to coil a mini pup as detailed in Figure 5.15.

The tightening perfect storm forms after the peaked highs and bottomed out lows of trending perfect storms. They peak/bottom out and then start their exhaustion reversion/reversal pullback. The term *tightening* refers to a reversal against the wider trend, whereas a trending perfect storm is aligned with the wider times. These are countertrend to the wider trend but are exhaustive to the shorter time frames (Figure 5.16).

The shorter 15-, 5-, and 1-minute time frames will appear to be a trending perfect storm except that they are opposing the 60-minute and/or daily trend, which could change if the 5-period moving average crosses the 15/20 period moving averages down. Remember, trending perfect storms have the wider time frames *aligned with* the shorter time frame mini pups. A tightening perfect storm has shorter time frames *opposing* the wider time frames until the 15- and 20-period moving average supports are tested and either coil and resume trend or collapse and reverse trend.

FIGURE 5.15 A tightening perfect storm where the 60- and 15-minute charts are both in downtrends while the 1-, 5-, 15-, and 60-minute stochastics form mini pups counter to the 60- and 15-minute charts The profits targets are the 15-minute and 15- and 20-period moving average bumpers and the 60-minute 5-period moving average bumper.

FIGURE 5.16 A tightening perfect storm breakdown after the 60-minute chart peaked out.

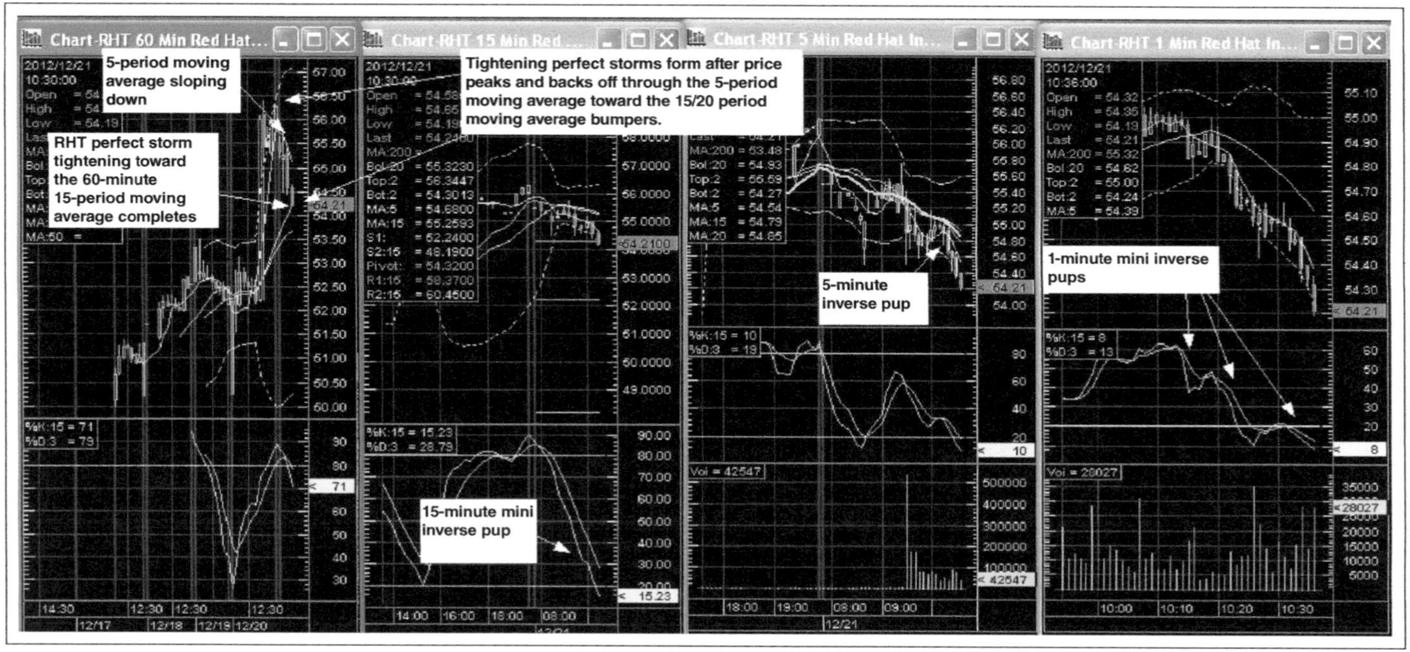

Whenever playing a tightening, it is very important that you are taking profits near the target tightening bumpers. Just like the rule of playing any tightening pattern, take your profits into the liquidity because they could disappear quickly after the nominal tightening target level is reached as Figure 5.17 shows. With tightening perfect storms, the threat and magnitude of the recoil is much stronger. Once 15-period moving averages are hit, they tend to coil back to the 5-period moving averages to retest against the sloping down and ultimately decide the fate of the trend.

Tightening Reversals

Tightening reversals are extensions of the tightening perfect storm where the trend actually reverses after the normal tightening target areas (15- and 20-period moving averages) are exceeded causing the 5-period moving average to cross over the 15-period moving average.

Channel tightening completes after the 15- or 20-period moving averages are hit on the wider time-frame charts. When they break through the last bumper and create a 5-period moving average crossover through the 15-period moving average, this creates a trend reversal (Figure 5.18). The key is to have the sloping 5-period moving average that rejects all pullback break attempts. *Channel tightening perfect storms come at the tail end of trending perfect storm peaks.* If the channel tightening completes but continues to move in the counter trend direction until it changes the trend, we refer to it as a tightening reversal. These trend reversals can ultimately turn back into trending perfect storms as long as they meet the qualifications of three simultaneously triggered pup/mini pups. This goes back to *the trending perfect storm* mechanics aforementioned.

How to Play Tightening Perfect Storms

1. Note the wider time frame bumpers, notably the 5-, 15-, and 20-period moving averages.
2. Note if there is a reversal candle, shooting star, hammer, doji at the peak/bottom.
3. Note where stock is trading in relation to the wider time frame bumpers.
   a. Confirm which wider time-frame chart is doing the tightening, and market those bumpers as targets (e.g., 60-minute downtrend but 15-, 5-, and 1-minute perfect storms mean mark 60-minute 5- and 15-period moving averages as target bumpers).

FIGURE 5.17 The dangers of not scaling out your positions on dumpers.

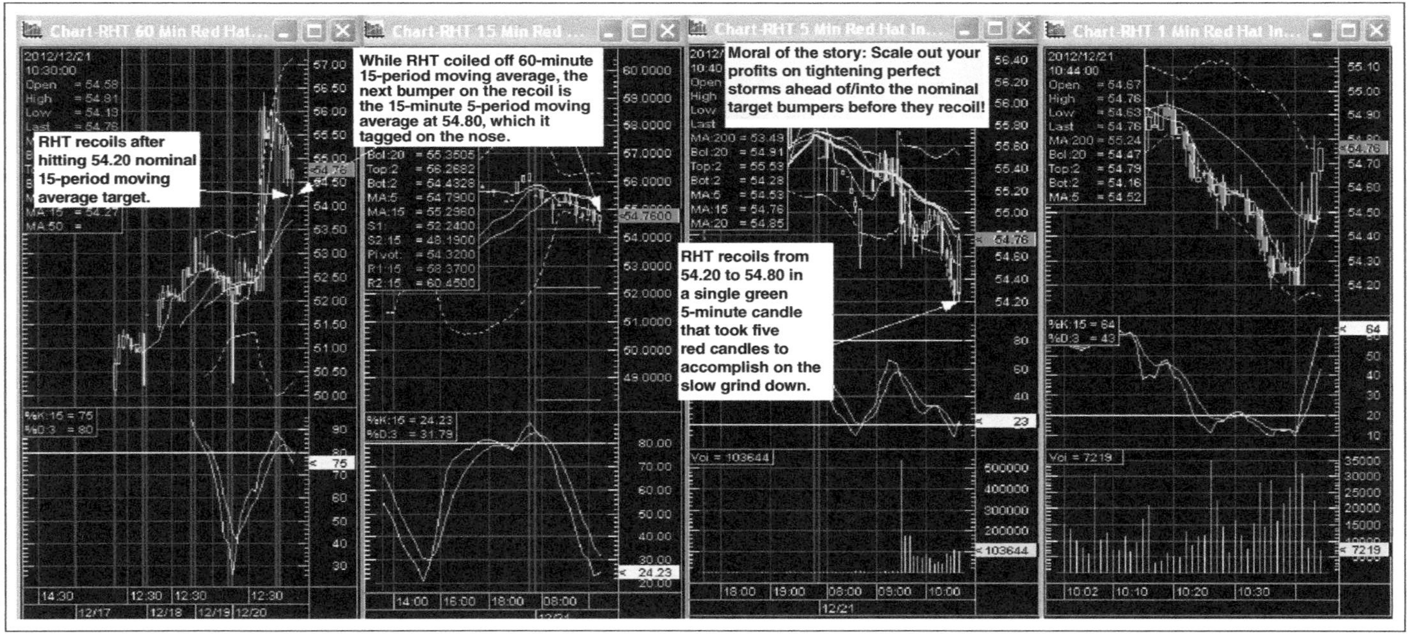
Chart-RHT 60 Min Red Hat...
RHT recoils after hitting 54.20 nominal 15-period moving average target.
Chart-RHT 15 Min Red ...
While RHT coiled off 60-minute 15-period moving average, the next bumper on the recoil is the 15-minute 5-period moving average at 54.80, which it tagged on the nose.
Chart-RHT 5 Min Red Hat In...
Moral of the story: Scale out your profits on tightening perfect storms ahead of/into the nominal target bumpers before they recoil!
RHT recoils from 54.20 to 54.80 in a single green 5-minute candle that took five red candles to accomplish on the slow grind down.
Chart-RHT 1 Min Red Hat In...

FIGURE 5.18 A trade on JPM perfect storm tightening reversal.

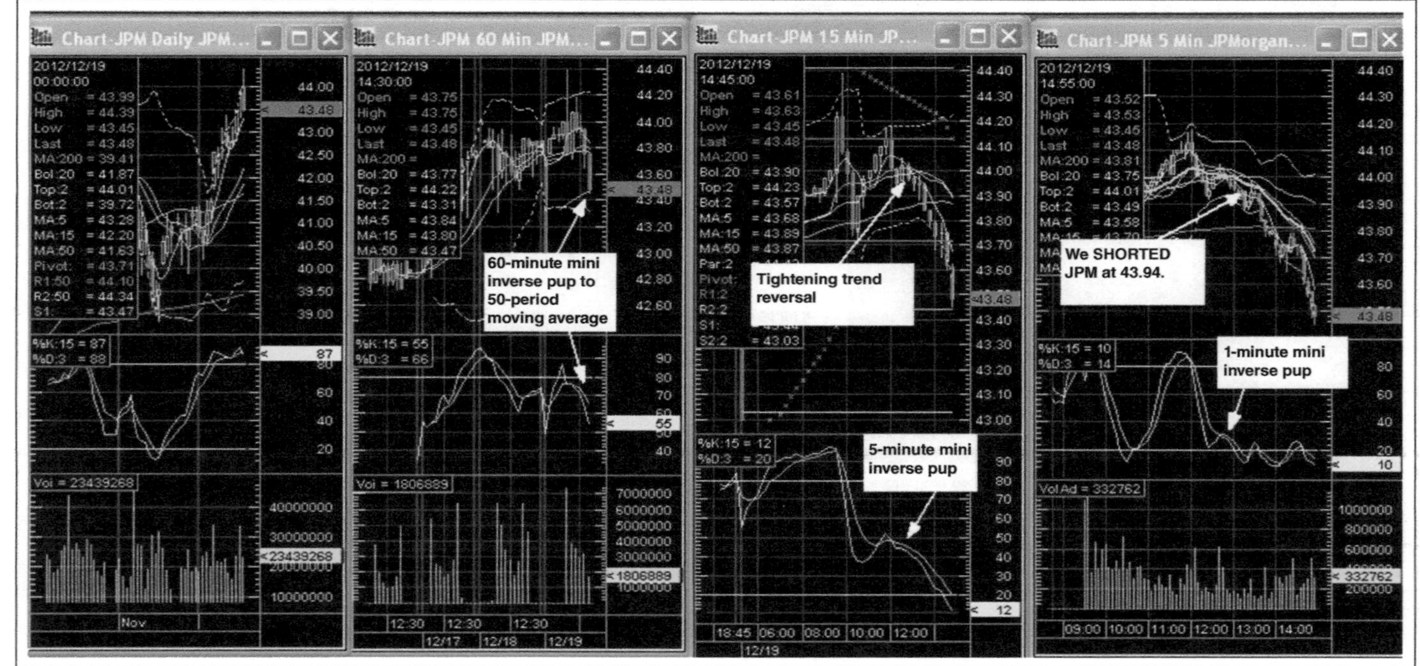

4. Gauge the shorter time frames, 15-, 5-, and 1-minute, to see where the stock is trading in relation to their bumpers.
5. Spot the two pup/mini pups charts and measure the 5-period moving averages and the next bumpers (upper/lower Bollinger Bands/50/200 period moving averages, if they lie ahead of the bbs).
6. Confirm the 5-period moving average sloping up on downtrends and down on uptrends.
7. Determine if the 15- and 20-period moving average target bumpers have enough meat on the bones. This means there is enough room to nominal target bumpers to make it worthwhile.
8. Factor the time period of day and market climate.
   a. Opening 90 minutes, wet climate, heavier share allocation.
   b. Deadzone—dry climate, lighter share allocation.
   c. Closing 90 minutes—dry/wet climate, lighter share allocation.
9. Calculate your position size allocation based on comfort level, market climate, familiarity with stock, potential upside, and downside risk.
10. Await 1-minute trigger and enter position.
11. Manage the position by monitoring it along with the SPY and any lead/peer stocks.
12. Scale out positions into target bumpers before stochastics reverse.

The Consolidation Break

The *consolidation break perfect storm* forms after the trading range has compressed into a long base with flat 5- and 15-period moving averages that eventually form a breakout/breakdown. The basing period lasts for hours (on the 5- and 15-minute charts) to days (on the 60-minute and daily chart).

This tends to be the safest type of perfect storm due to the very long aging process of basing in a tightly defined range. When the breakout happens (Figure 5.19), it is usually foreshadowed by the wider 60-minute and daily time frames, which act as anchors as their bumpers should not break. Entry can be on the range break or entering on pullback with a shorter time frame mini pup. However, the problem with the latter method is that the breakout may be slow and solid enough with no wiggles or explosive with very few wiggles due to all the basing. Therefore, the earlier entry on the range break is preferred since most will assume it's just another identical wiggle and likely not give it credence until it is too late and then rush to get into a position at much higher prices. This is what limits the pullbacks on the consolidation break perfect storms. It's a slow building perfect storm that tends to take

FIGURE 5.19 A consolidation breakout trade.

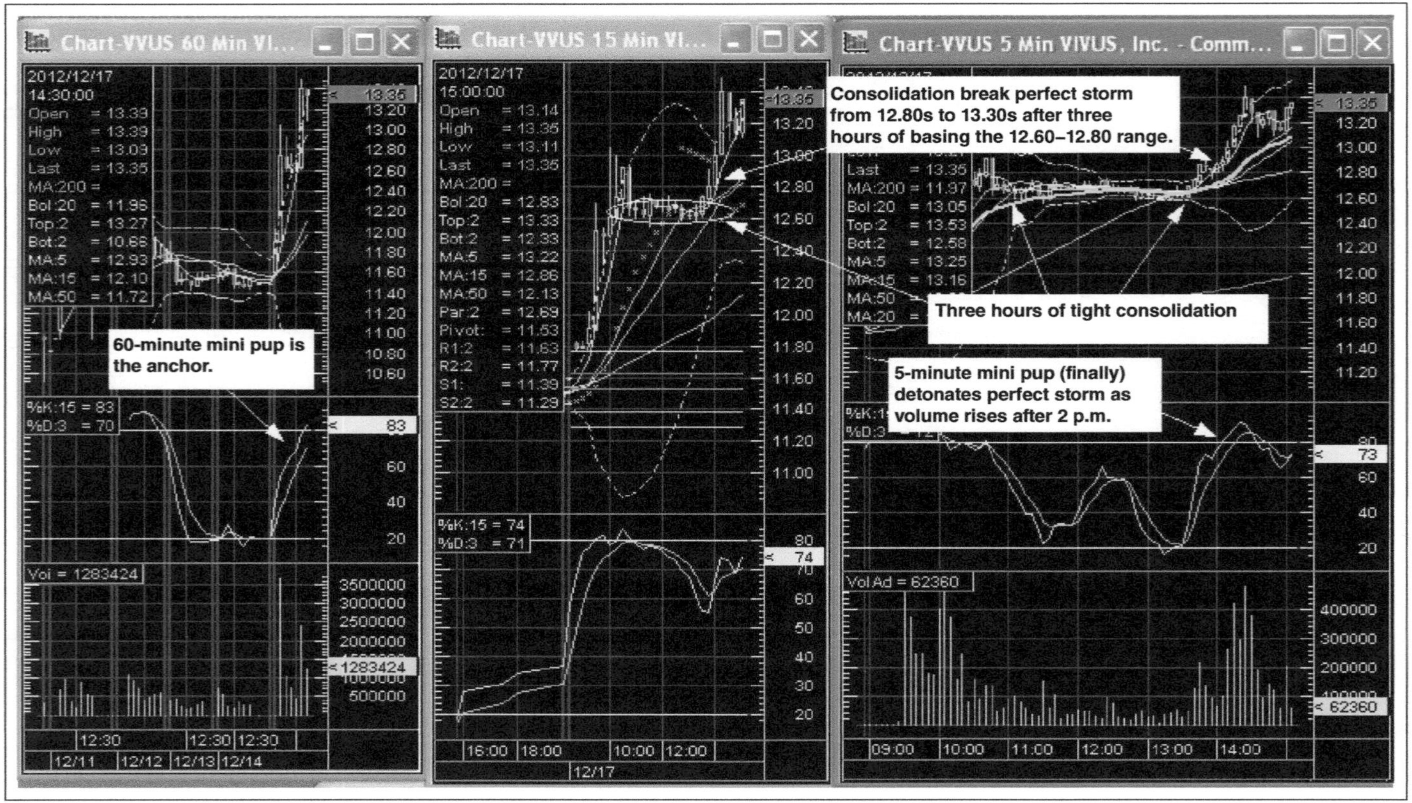

most participants by surprise due to its extended period of basing, which still creates lots of headfakes and wiggles up until the point where that long wiggle turns out to be a breakout. Once again, by having the 60-minute and daily charts available, they give you a heads up on the direction of the break. It's simply a waiting game on the shorter time frames to trigger either in the morning as a result of consolidation the prior day or in the post deadzone period after 2 P.M. EST where the volume picks up again.

On downtrends (Figure 5.20), the wider time frames forecast the direction of the perfect storm with a mini inverse pup, while the shorter time frames continue to chop in a tight range for hours until volume picks up on the actual breakdown. Sometimes these can take a 20 band stochastics cross down to finally crack the range, triggering panic to the downside as the perfect storm finally detonates.

Patience is the key when playing consolidation break perfect storms since they take so long to base in a tightening range. They often form in the last 90 minutes of the day (after 2 P.M. EST) as volume picks up post-deadzone or the first 90 minutes of the next morning as the basing goes into day 2. Those are the two heaviest volume periods in the trading day, and where there is volume, there will be perfect storms. The longer (timewise) the basing takes, the stronger the break (Figure 5.21).

These are the best aged organic trades since all they require is enough time to hold a tight range until the heavy volume period is reached. Gappers or dumpers usually make the best consolidation break candidates. Therefore, even if you played the initial perfect storms on the gap up or down, the opportunity to play a consolidation break often presents itself later in the day or the following day. Therefore, you should routinely put these on the secondary minder list to continue to track or stalk. It's akin to taking the leftovers from a hearty meal and making a delicious stew the next day. These are all ingredients that can continually be recycled and recharged if aged and monitored properly.

How to Play Consolidation Break Perfect Storms

1. Note the wider time frame bumpers, notably the 5-, 15-, and 20-period moving averages.
2. Note if there is a reversal candle: shooting star, hammer, doji at the peak/bottom.
3. Note where the stock is trading in relation to the wider time frame bumpers.

FIGURE 5.20 A consolidation perfect storm breakdown.

FIGURE 5.21 A consolidation breakout pattern with the 5-minute counter candle trigger price levels.

4. Gauge the shorter time frames 15-, 5-, and 1-minute to see where stock is trading in relation to their bumpers.
5. Spot the 2 pup/mini pups charts and measure the 5-period moving averages and the next bumpers (upper/lower Bollinger Bands/50/200 period moving averages, if they lie ahead of the bbs).
6. Determine if target bumpers have enough meat on the bones. This means there is enough room to nominal target bumpers to make it worthwhile.
7. Factor the time period of day and market climate:
   a. Opening 90 minutes, wet climate, heavier share allocation.
   b. Deadzone—dry climate, lighter share allocation.
   c. Closing 90 minutes—dry/wet climate lighter allocation.
8. Calculate your position size allocation based on comfort level, market environment and climate, familiarity with stock, potential upside, and downside risk.
9. Await 1-minute trigger and enter position.
10. Manage the position by monitoring it along with the SPY and any lead/peer stocks.
11. Scale out positions into liquidity at bumper levels before the 1-minute stochastics exhaust and reverse.

Repeating Nature of Perfect Storms

That about sums it up. Stocks have muscle memory, so the participants tend to repeat their reactions resulting in perfect storm patterns repeating themselves, perhaps not daily, but once you get the feel of the rhythm of the moves, you can play them with consistent familiarity as indicated on our trades with identical perfect storm setups on GMCR, on 11/28/2012 shown in Figure 5.22 and 12/5/2012 shown in Figure 5.23.

It's logical why patterns repeat themselves if you narrow it down to the individual participants that make up the market. The nature of trading is to find early transparency. This early transparency is based on who can recognize and react quickest. When you are familiar with something, it cuts your reaction time. Therefore, anything that remotely feels familiar is seen as an advantage over the next participant. This is a double-edged sword because the algos are playing on that natural flow. Whereas the familiarity with a pattern makes you money by stepping in early during the morning, that same familiarity with the same pattern can be to your detriment during the deadzone as you get flushed on every entry. Just as you figure it out and adapt to the oscillations at the range tops/bottoms, they flush you again as

FIGURE 5.22 GMCR detonates a perfect storm breakout on 11/28/2012.

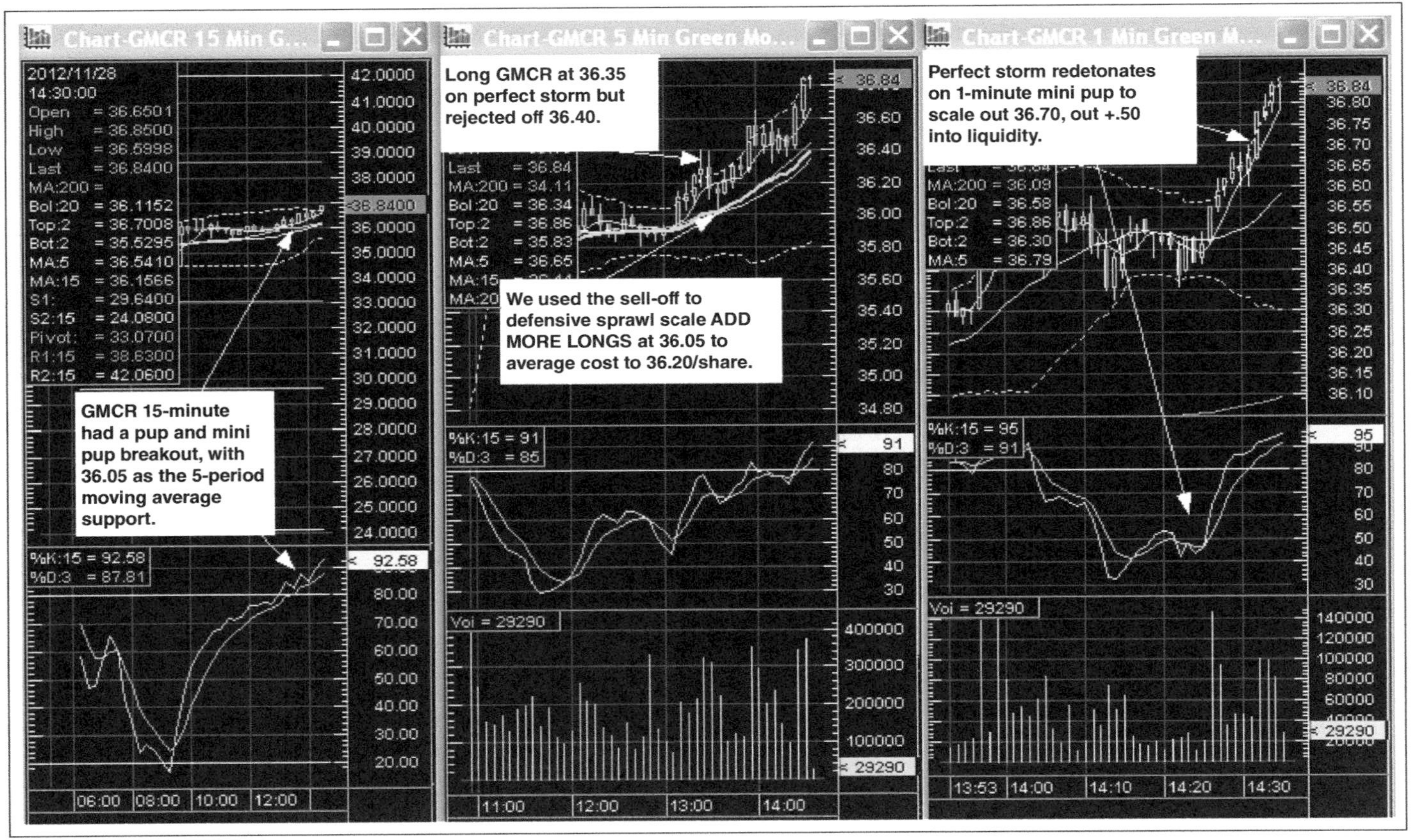

FIGURE 5.23 GMCR triggers an identical perfect storm breakout on 12/6/2012. This illustrates the muscle memory–like repeating nature of perfect storms.

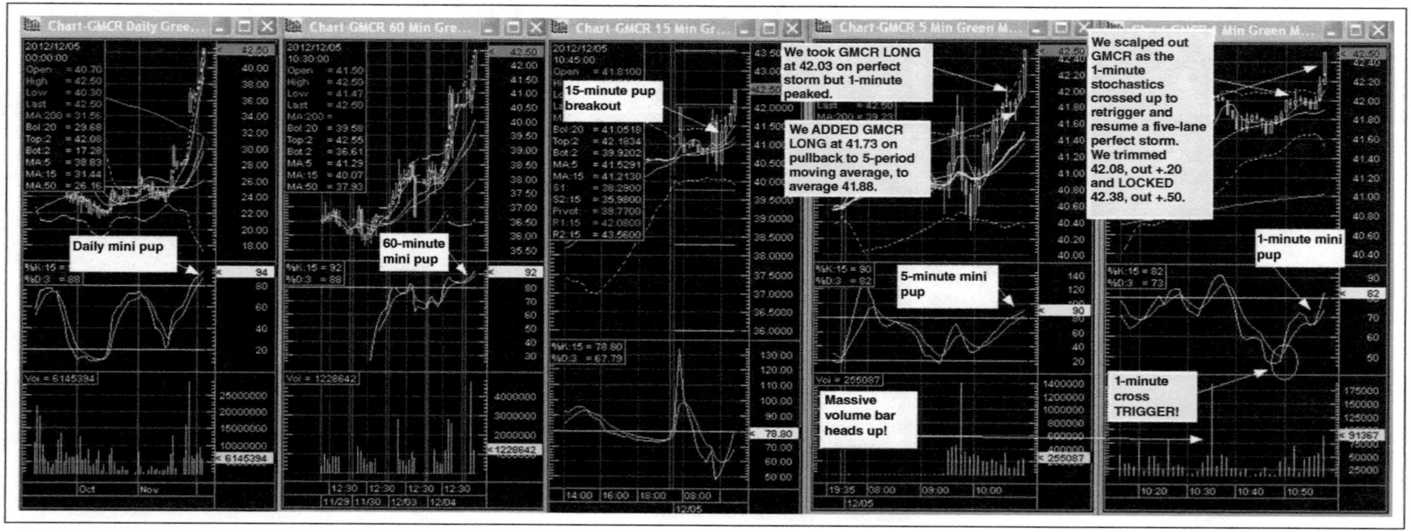

the trend finally breaks out, trapping you on the wrong side of the trade. You anticipate oscillation, they trend. You anticipate the breakout, and they oscillate. You finally convince yourself it's an oscillation, and they break out against you.

This is how you get pecked away in the deadzone market period. The SAME pattern that worked off the opening 45 minutes will FIZZLE and CHOP during deadzone for the sole purpose of chopping or tiring you out. When the breakout resumes post deadzone, you will either be too frustrated and worn out to believe the pattern as it explodes without you, or end up trapped on the wrong side expecting an oscillation but getting flushed as the real breakout plows over you.

Double-Hedged Sword Sequence Trade

I'm sure you've heard the term double-edged sword. Occasionally, I will pull a double-hedged sword sequence play (DHSS). This opportunity occurs when two stocks on my watch list form perfect storms simultaneously in opposite directions. The perfect storm breakout stock buy will buy fade on SPY selling and spike on SPY bounces while the perfect storm breakdown stock sell fades SPY pops and collapsed on SPY selling. This is a directional trade that takes a position in both directions. Unlike the antiquated pairs trading method of shorting the laggard and buying the leader, this is not market neutral. If you want market neutrality, then stay in cash.

This is a hedge over a hedge, which makes them inversely directional. The SPY is the lead indicator to scale out on both sides. The caveat is if the SPY trends firmly, then one side could go into laggard mode to catch up to the market. Therefore timing and most importantly share allocation are crucial. I like to spread the exposure equally initially and then ride the dominant stock should the SPY trend firmer.

On 11/6/2012 (election day), the SPY had a modest gap up. My watch list consisted of about five stocks. SNDK was an organic setup that had a daily mini pup in place, which needed the 60-minute 5-period moving average at 45.31 to break to wake up the 60-minute mini pup and then the 15-, 5-, and 1-minute charts to converge to detonate a perfect storm breakout with a daily mini pup anchor, which increases the probability to the highest level. I also had a headliner gapper prospect, which was HAS. It gapped up excessively on a partial takeover rumor sometime next year by DIS. I had noted if HAS got above 38.50, then I would be interested in shorting since I needed that 15-minute stochastics to cross back down.

A few minutes after the market open, we took SNDK LONG at 44.37 on a five lane perfect storm (Figure 5.24), which consisted of the 1-, 5-, 15-, 60-, and daily mini pups. The SPY had gapped into the open and then saw initial selling, which provided liquidity for entry back down to 44.30. As I was waiting for the SPY to absorb the selling and coil, I noticed that HAS had touched a low at 37.50 and squeezed parabolic style up to 38.70 to rug pull back down to 38. This is the quickest and dirtiest way to reverse a high band (above 80 band) stochastics, the 15-minute stochastics in this case. Oftentimes, you will see a mistick try to emulate the same effect to no avail on the wider time frames. The convincing factor was the classic 5-minute mini inverse pup that formed when 38 held resistance along with the 1-minute mini inverse pup coming down. This was too good to pass up. This was a high-grade sell-fader. It would be a good hedge for the SNDK long in case that failed, since HAS was excessive in the gap and fading short-term SPY coils. We took HAS SHORT at 37.81 on wiggles up 38 rejection (Figure 5.25), which then triggered the 15-minute mini inverse pup.

At that moment, we had two live perfect storm positions in opposite directions composed of the SNDK perfect storm long shown in Figure 5.24 and HAS perfect storm short showing in Figure 5.25. The double-hedged sword sequence play manifested itself. Unlike the defunct pairs trading strategy, these are multifisted, multilayered, directional setups on opposing sides that provide wide pockets of liquidity to carve out profits as the SPY oscillates. A perfect storm pattern requires the strongest single time frame pattern called a pup/mini pup to trigger at least threefold simultaneously. That means each layered time frame provides a concrete backstop. This gives solid follow-through on completions and thick pockets of opportunity to abort on failures.

As the SPY rallied, we scalped out HAS on leans to 37.68, out +.13 and scalped SNDK into liquidity at 44.52, out +.15. This was a fast trade that lasted less than eight minutes total. The SPY continued to rally and SNDK eventually squeezed up to the daily upper Bollinger Bands through 45, while HAS made a panic dump to 36.80s later. Amazingly the inversion sequence actually lasted for several hours after we were long gone, even as the SPY continued to rally a strong uptrend into the close.

As a rule of thumb, profits should be taken quickly in the event the SPY forms a lasting trend move. The fade sequence may last for minutes to hours. It's all based on the driving factors behind the move technically or fundamentally. The more the SPY trends in one direction, the more the fading position risks a strong reversal. The normal pup/mini pup rules apply in these situations. This takes an advanced understanding of perfect storms and their

FIGURE 5.24 SNDK leg of double-hedged sword sequence trade.

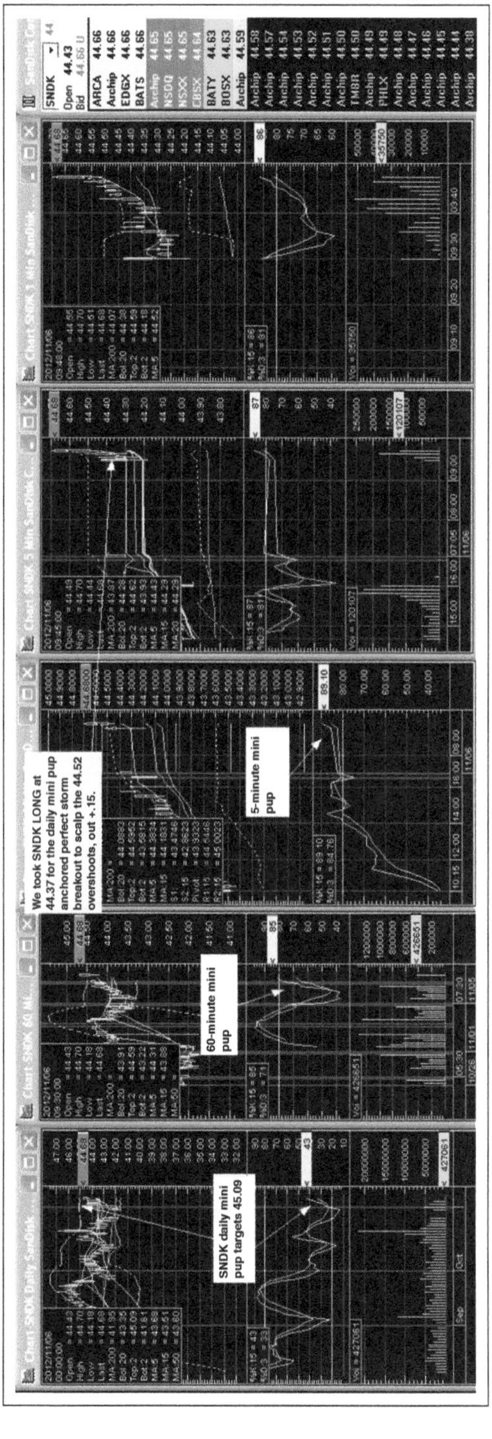

FIGURE 5.25 HAS leg of the double-hedged sword sequence trade.

components, and experience, in addition to knowing the underlying stock rhythms. Don't get it twisted. This can backfire hard if you catch them too late or don't manage the trades efficiently.

Another rule of thumb is to use an organic pattern play on one leg and a headliner gapper/dumper on the opposing leg, as the aforementioned example illustrates. Personally, I only care about probability, not duration. *Risk is based on allocation size and duration of exposure.* You can offset the other tentatively, but the longer you hold a position (duration), the risk continues to grow, which can be offset by trimming the allocation. In this HFT-driven market landscape, the risk of a rogue wave always looms, especially when the transparency peaks. I prefer to take the money while it's in front of me and walk away. Closure is a wonderful thing, and it feeds consistency. The first 30 to 45 minutes of the trading day give you that opportunity. Stick around past 11 A.M., and you are in a lot rougher neighborhood after dark.

How to Execute DHSS Trades

The DHSS is a play I've developed through the years out of necessity. Perfect storm patterns tend to form simultaneously. Therefore, to capitalize on them, you need to step in on multiple setups. A hedged-type setup works even better since you are not stuck in one direction. If your preparation is thorough, meaning your watch list is composed of a solid balance of situation and organic stocks (core trading stocks that are screened organically; discussed in more detail in Chapter 7) for long and short prospects, then you will occasionally find simultaneous situations where one stock is buy fading firmly towards a perfect storm breakout while another stock is SIMULTANEOUSLY sell fading firmly toward a perfect storm breakdown. The fades are based on the context of the SPY. In this situation where you are presented with opposite perfect storm patterns, the opportunity for a DHSS presents itself, the double-hedged sword sequence play.

If the SPY bounces, the buy fade triggers a perfect storm breakout to the upside to profit on your long entry while the sell fade stock continues to sell fade until the SPY exhausts its upside bounce and reverses down, which triggers the perfect storm breakdown on your short trade giving you profits on the short side.

This is the opposite of the conventional (sophomoric) and worn out pairs trade where you would buy a tier 1 and short a tier 2 in the same sector to scrape the minimal divergence which is the spread (which the HFTs will scoop up from you long before you hit the buy/sell button). It's an easy strategy that is wrought in slippage and screws over most traders who attempt it on a surface level. This play is so outdated, worn out, and infested by too many participants and algos that it's not even worth mentioning. Frankly, it's a wimpy misguided market neutral play where the computers have taken all the edge out of, just like opening order trades are the same joke.

The double-hedged sword sequence requires more effort in preparation and execution, and experience always helps. It capitalizes on the immediate divergence rooted in SOLID perfect storm patterns in opposite directions, not on the coincidental off chance that the specialist mispriced an opening price or a tier 2 tail wags the tier 1 dog. Perfect storms have DEPTH through multiple time frames. They only form when there is a significant force in the market that is desperately trying to camouflage its intent too hard and to no avail.

A hedge is technically supposed to be market neutral. But a double hedge is actually directional, just like two negatives make a positive and vice versa. The beauty of this play is that you win regardless of market (SPY) direction. If you long a perfect storm breakout and short a perfect storm breakdown, your long spikes when the SPY rises, while the short fades the SPY until it peaks and pulls back or reverses, at which point your long buy fades and holds its ground while your short profits as the stock collapses. The only caveat is the duration of the FADE and the SPY direction. The rule of thumb is to use the SPY spikes to trim the longs and the pullbacks to trim the shorts to capitalize on both sides. The danger is if the SPY continues to grind in one direction so long that it causes one of the trades to turn laggard and reverse, which eats into the profits of the other, or if they both exhaust and reverse. This is why TIMING is of the essence. These should be considered short-term trades, even though they can last for hours.

On the surface level, this play appears risky or neutral as the longs will be offset by the losses in the short position and vice versa, but that is the surface level appearance to the conventional crowd, which is what prevents it from becoming an overcrowded trade. Overcrowding by nature forces transparency. The depth of the perfect storm pattern is overlooked, which is great for us.

The best candidates naturally contain perfect storms on both legs. Excessive gap takeover rumors are great for the exhaustion short leg versus organic perfect storm breakouts. The other alternative is to take the opposite trade directly with the SPY on strong fades. The allocation and timing of exits makes or breaks this trade.

Is this more risky than a single directional trade? Yes, so manage the risk by spreading out the allocation proportionately. This means you have to be familiar with how the stock trades so that you can allocate the proper shares factoring in the nominal move targets to the next bumper on both sides.

A lot of the risk is offset because both trades have perfect storms. As long as you can manage your exits, they should give you a more than adequate amount of time and liquidity to close out both legs profitably.

DHSS Trade Process

1. Find two stocks with opposing direction perfect storms: Corganic and Headliner gapper/dumper with opposing perfect storms.
2. You can do this by overlapping or comparing the intraday trading time frames daily, 60-, 15-, 5-, and 1-minute.
3. Monitor the SPY trend direction and bumpers.
4. Execute entry position in the perfect storm stock that is aligned with the SPY using the 1-minute trigger.
5. Confirm that the other stock is actively fading the SPY direction with an opposite perfect storm.
6. Execute entry position in the actively fading stock with opposing perfect storm on the 1-minute trigger just before the 1-minute SPY exhausts and reverses.
7. Alternate exits by scaling out when the 1-minute SPY stochastics move in the same direction.
    a. For example: Sell the aligned perfect storm long when SPY bounces on the 1-minute chart. The other stock should be sell fading the bounce. Then cover the short leg after 1-minute SPY peaks and sells back down, which should collapse the sell fading stock.
    b. Keep in mind the duration of the fade has to be monitored carefully. If the SPY proceeds to trend strongly, then the fader may eventually re-align with the SPY. Therefore it is imperative that you work to exit the position or scale it down before this happens. You may opt to ride some of the aligned stock's perfect storm if the SPY maintains an extended trend move. Ultimately, the fader will revert back in alignment with the SPY; your goal is to be completely out before that happens.

CHAPTER 6

Optimized Four-Level Research Process

Through the years, I've gone the whole gamut of methods and routines to research for information on stocks. It's easy to get overwhelmed and side tracked as hours can go by to only produce morsels of interesting information. Yet these morsels of information oftentimes turn out to be the most compelling elements to the story. They are the by-products produced from going through the process of research. As a result, I've streamlined my own research methods to extract the most relevant, compelling, and useful information.

For most of the earlier years, I've only focused on just the price elements of stocks and believed that the charts are all that mattered. After all, we are trading in a stock market, not a company market. We should only concentrate our attention on the price action and pay little attention to the operations of the business. The chart technical formations and price levels trumped the fundamentals. A company is what you interact with and a stock is a three- or four-letter symbol represented by the price action. The price action is all we need to concern ourselves with. Fundamentals have little bearing on the stock price with the exception of news and earnings. Of course, I was only concerned with intraday trading during this time.

It wasn't until I pressed further into overnights, swing trades, and portfolio positions that I realized the role of fundamental analysis. For one, they help you sleep well at night with positions providing a psychological support buffer and backstop.

Fundamentals shape perceptions and valuations of stocks while revealing the motives behind price action, while technicals are an X-ray that tracks the structures behind the price movement. While intraday trading lends more to technicals, swing trading and investing require an insight into the fundamentals. It's best to arm oneself with an affinity for both aspects of the game. I've optimized both technical and fundamental research into a four-level research process that addresses all skillsets.

Thorough research is rewarded by extending the path a little more as you connect the dots as more ideas and connections get generated as it speeds up, more ideas and connections. In the meantime, you are harnessing your capacity for information and the speed at which the synapses make connections. It's magical to see where you end up. There have been numerous times I start off researching a biotech stock that takes me to a tech stock and a whole sector, which leads me to a subsector, which leads me to a retail niche sector and so forth. Each time making a new connection increases my ability to synthesize and connect faster not just with stocks but with news, culture, personal matters, coincidences, and so forth. All it takes is a spark to generate a fire. The greater your affinity, the more receptive it becomes, like lighting a spark in a room soaked with gasoline . . . kaboom . . . enlightenment!

It's human nature to learn; just look at babies and how curious they are, getting stimulated as they discover the world around them as they continue to gather more knowledge. Somewhere along the way as adults, it's easy to lose that stimulation as the urge for safety overshadows our natural urge to discover and learn. We are either bored or overwhelmed but rarely challenged at that sweet spot stimulation trigger. This is something that can't be dictated or assigned. The sweet spot can only be discovered organically. It is a very personal aspect, specific to the individual journey. Research is associated with mundane, drudgingly slow, and boring work. It doesn't have to be. The profit motive that the market incites is sufficient to motivate. I want to elaborate that fear and greed are what tend to motivate people into pursuing research. Either you are treasure hunting or stressed over a losing stock position and decide to justify your reasons for holding. Preferably, you don't find yourself in the latter situation too much more after learning the four-level process. Research works best when it's premeditated. It is used for preparation and should be performed prior to every type of trade. Please remember that little distinction moving forward.

Level 1 Research Process: Spot Technical Analysis and Headline Search

This is the research you will be utilizing most often. It is literal thinking based and is basically a gathering process of key information. The emphasis is on quick technical analysis and with fundamental analysis limited to news headlines. It's all about immediate on-the-fly analysis in the shortest amount of time to sufficiently prepare you for action. Level 1 research should take between 30 seconds and three minutes per stock, contingent on whether step 2 is needed. With experience, your speed and efficiency will continue to improve as you cultivate this element of the day trading skillset.

Step 1: FAST Chart Analysis (Requires Rifle Charts)

This step was outlined in Chapter 3 for analyzing your premarket watch list. Naturally, this step can be used any time for any new stocks you are monitoring. Just remember to leave out the 1-, 5-, and 15-minute time frames during off-market hours.

1. Enter symbol on level 2 to bring up the seven time frame charts:
   a. Premarket, post-market, and weekend analysis should be limited to just the 60-minute, daily, weekly, and monthly. In other words, leave out the 1-, 5-, and 15-minute charts unless you are tracking the stock intraday.
2. Spot and note the nearest overlapping bumpers within the .50 to 1.00 range of stocks.
   a. Make special note if the 200- or 50-period moving averages are involved for any time frame chart.
3. Spot and note if there are any pups or mini pups in the 60-min/daily/weekly/monthly charts.
   a. If so, then mark the supporting bumper (5-period moving average on breaks and 15-period moving average on tightenings) and the next bumper target levels.
4. Write down the most overlapping bumper levels and any mini pups along with corresponding support/target price points.

Step 2: Headline Search

This step really applies to the headliner gapper/dumper stocks. If the stock isn't showing a gap or significant price movement, then it's okay to end it with step 1. Intraday, the price action often precedes the news or rumors.

1. Run the stock symbol on your newsfeed to pull up any headlines or press releases.
   a. BenzingaPro.com—This is the quickest and most thorough news feed that will provide headlines, news, rumors, peer action, articles, SEC filings, and analyst activity within seconds to minutes of release. They focus on the significant items that may be impacting the stock.
   b. Yahoo.com/finance—This feed is free but lagging on speed of posting up news headlines. Check the headlines and also market pulse.
   c. Finviz.com—This is another free site that posts the headlines from the major newswires, but expect a delayed result.
2. Determine the news catalyst causing the big gap up or down. Reference Chapter 7's "Most Significant News Situations" rundown if you aren't sure. Go through the list to see which applies.
   a. For earnings-related gapper/dumper, note down whether it was an earnings beat by how much, or miss by how much on the earnings per share (EPS) and revenues. Write down the guidance if provided and whether it was lowered, inline, or above.
      i. Conference call effect—Find out if a conference call has already taken place on dumpers. Many times, stocks with gaps down will bounce into the conference call on optimism. This applies heavily to stocks that report earnings in the premarket. Conference calls usually take place at 5 P.M. EST, 8:30 A.M., 9 A.M., 10 A.M., or 1 P.M. EST.

This is the extent of the level 1 research. You should have the mental playing field complete with the significant price bumpers along with patterns and the news catalyst responsible if there is a significant gap up or down. This information is sufficient to trade with if you choose.

Figure 6.1 is a great example of level 1 research applied to a premarket dumper stock EAT, which reported in-line earnings with raised guidance resulting in a gap down. The company scheduled a 10 A.M. conference call. The FAST chart analysis identified the weekly mini pup and the various significant bumpers from 31 up to 32.22, which was the weekly 5-period moving average overlapped with 60-minute lower Bollinger Bands. This analysis takes no more than two minutes to spot the price level playing field going into the market open.

As you can see on Figure 6.2, the research pays off because EAT proceeds to bounce off the daily 50-period moving average bumper at 31. The 5-minute stochastics cross up shortly after the open driving the price towards the weekly 50-period moving average at 31.38 where it chops

FIGURE 6.1 The premarket fast chart analysis notes.

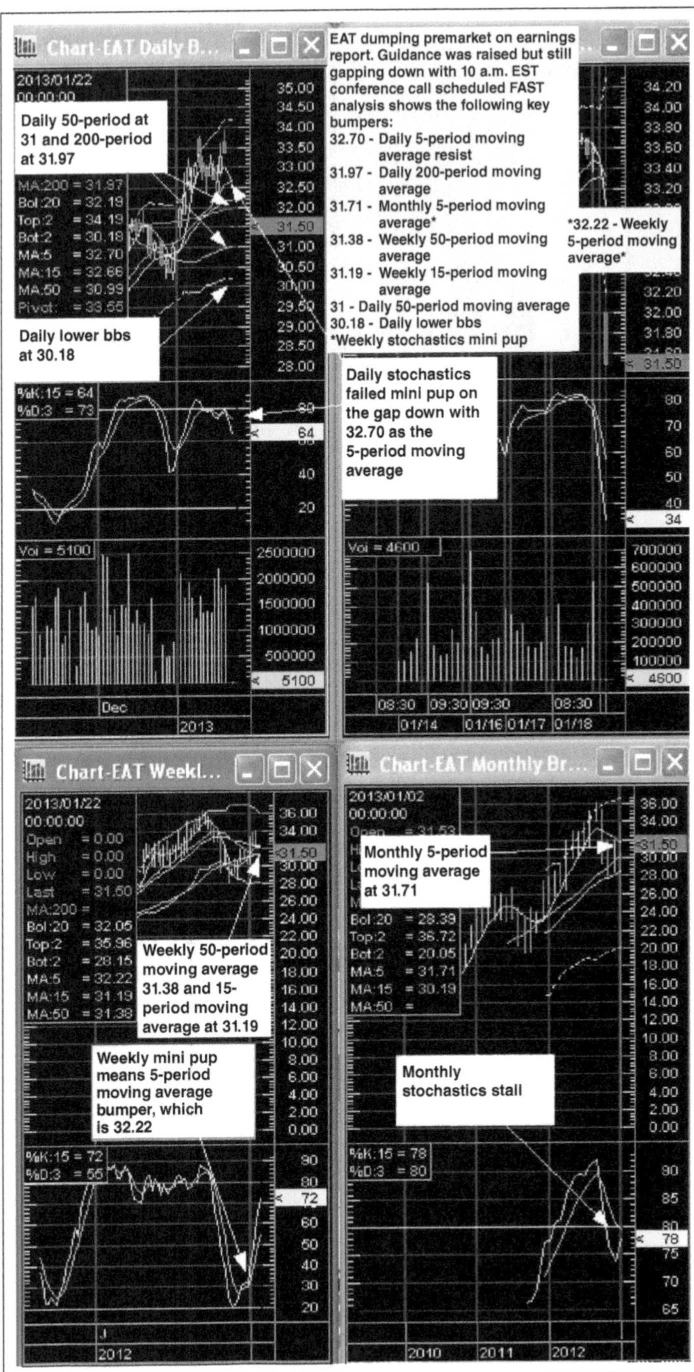

FIGURE 6.2 EAT demonstrates the conference call effect.

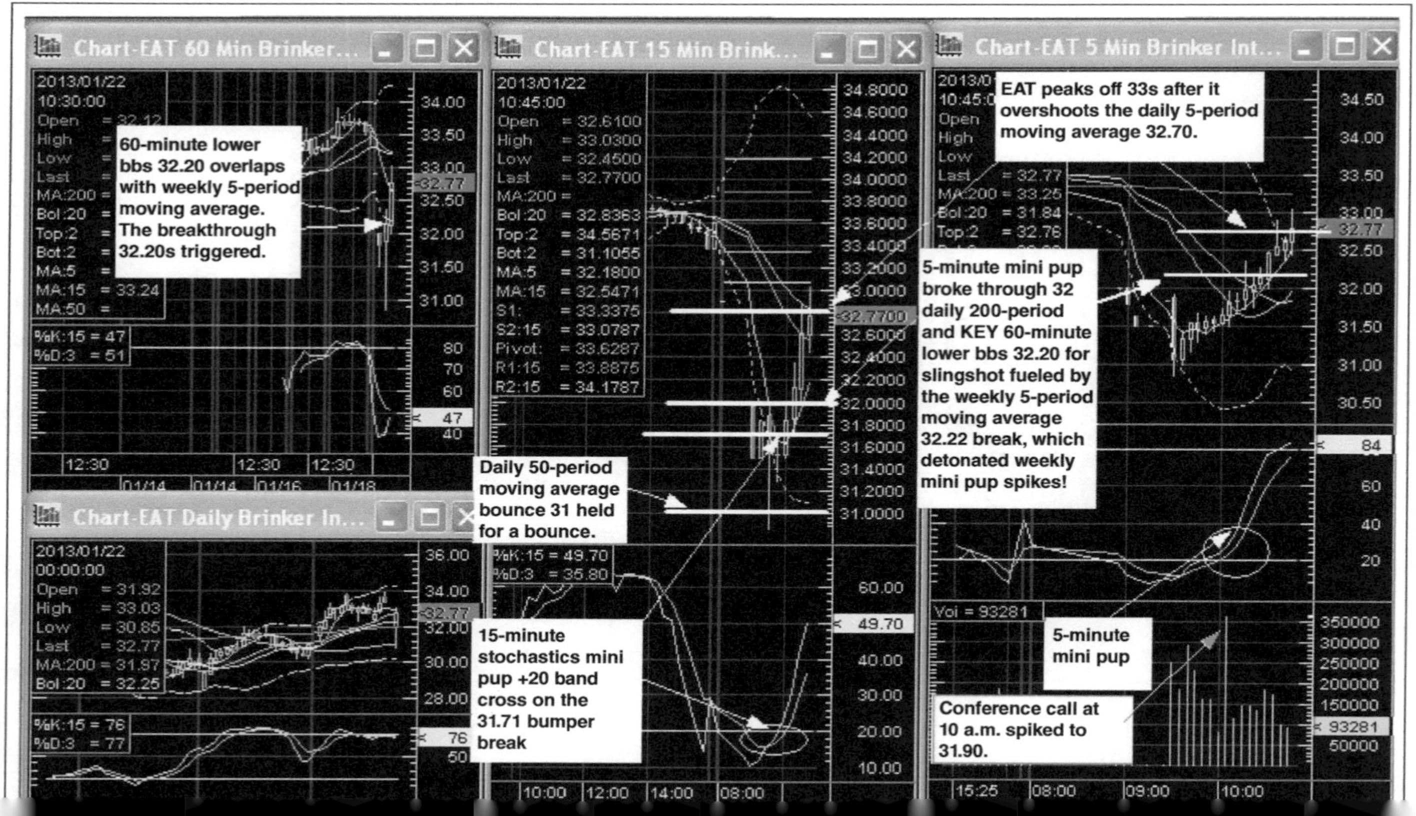

around. As that level broke higher, the 5-minute stochastics proceeds to cross the 20 band as EAT works itself to the 31.70 monthly 5-period moving average bumper, where it overlaps with the 15-minute 5-period moving average resistance which caused a knee jerk back down to 31.38, the weekly 50-period moving average. That stalled the 5-minute stochastic but didn't cross down because EAT proceeded to absorb sellers at 31.38 and bounced back to the 31.60–.70 resistance level up until 10 A.M. EST, which was the scheduled conference call. EAT formed a 5-minute mini pup on the 31.70 break to squeeze the price up just shy of the daily 200-period moving average at 32. This was the *conference call effect,* the bounce into the conference call. Incidentally, EAT had an upbeat conference call which allowed the 5-minute mini pup to couple with the 15-minute mini pup and 20 band cross up as the 1-minute formed a mini pup (not shown on these charts) to trigger a powerful perfect storm tightening that penetrated the 60-minute lower Bollinger Bands at 32.20, which alone could trigger a slingshot bounce, but also the weekly 5-period moving average at 32.22. Why is the 32.22 bumper significant, you ask? The weekly stochastics were in a mini pup formation and a break above its 5-period moving average detonates an impulse perfect storm spike. Couple that with the 60-minute lower Bollinger Band slingshot spike, and the result was a short squeeze to rally through the 32.70 daily 5-period moving average up to 33.05 peak! All these levels were spotted and prepared for ahead of time using the level 1 research! We played longs from 31.42 to 31.66 on the 5-minute mini pup spike into the 15-minute 5-period moving average bumper for a +.24 scalp. Level 1 research pays for your efforts.

Level 2 Research Process: Digging Deeper into Fundamentals

This includes level 1 research and digs further into the stock-specific news and financials. This is still mostly a literal thinking process that entails expanding the scope of information gathering. This research can be utilized premarket, during, and post market. It's useful when considering overnight trades or ranging all day. This exercises the swing trading/investor skillset. Have a research folder on your computer to write down your notes and links per company. I prefer to keep it on the computer as opposed to a notebook simply for access purposes. This process can take anywhere from 10 to 30 minutes per stock.

Step 1: Gather and Screen Financial Statistics

1. Go to www.yahoo.com/finance, enter your stock symbol, and click the Profile link to read the general overview of the company. Then click the Financial Statistics link to review the numbers.
2. Write down the following metrics (if applicable):
   a. Price/Earnings
      i. A single digit p/e can be compelling (except banks and financials!).
   b. Quarterly Revenue Growth (yoy):
      i. 0 to 10 percent is solid, 10 to 30 percent is fast, over 30 percent is hypergrowth.
   c. Quarterly Earnings Growth:
      i. 0 to 20 percent is strong, 20 to 50 percent is fast, over 50 percent is hypergrowth.
   d. Total Cash per Share
      i. If cash per share is trading at or above the stock price, it is very compelling (except banks and financials).
   e. Total LT Debt:
      i. No long-term debt is preferred, not always required.
   f. Book Value per Share:
      i. If trading higher than stock price, then compelling value play (except for banks and financials).
   g. Operating Cash Flow:
      i. Positive OCF is preferred.
   h. Short Percent of Float:
      i. Make a note of anything over 20 percent.

Step 2: Check for Insider Buying or Selling

1. Check Yahoo! Finance and Finviz.com to note any recent insider buying within the last three months, especially large purchases in the open market near the current stock price. Note the price levels and gauge to see if it acts as a support area.
2. If there is nothing but insider sells, then it's a negative, especially if it involved the CEO, CFO, or COO. Note those price levels as possible price ceilings (but not always the case). There is less emphasis on insider selling because there are so many reasons for this, including predetermined automatic programs, tax selling, secondaries, and so forth. There are lots of justified reasons for selling that aren't detrimental. It's only a concern if the stock is also selling off.

Step 3: News and Analyst Scan

1. Check for any significant news or analyst ratings change in the prior days to weeks. The significance is determined by any gaps or large price moves on the day of the release.
2. Check for any rumors.
   a. Go to Benzinga.com or BenzingaPro.com and enter in the symbol.
   b. Check the Market Pulse and Message Boards on Yahoo! Finance.

Step 4: Mark Any Unfilled Gaps on the Daily Chart for the Past Six to Nine Months

It doesn't matter how far away the current stock price is. Note the gap price levels and put them on an Alerts minder.

1. Go to www.finviz.com and enter your stock symbol in the search box. This should pull back a year or so of daily candles. Note any significant gaps in the price chart and mark the gap top and the gap bottom in the succeeding days.
2. Check the date of the gap for news. Note the news item and material impact (i.e., earnings warning lower guidance by 20 percent).

Step 5: Add Fibonacci Retracement Levels on Daily Charts

Most trading and chart platforms carry the Fibonacci retracement chart tools. The site www.tradingview.com offers free charting with lots of free indicators.

1. Add the Fibonacci retracement levels from the highest daily price down to the lowest price for a one-year range. If the stock is trading at or near 52-week highs or lows, then pull up the weekly and monthly charts and apply the lines for two or more years.
2. Note the .718, .618, .50, .38, and .23 price levels on the daily and weekly charts. Keep those prices handy to note any overlapping with other daily, weekly, monthly bumpers that you did on the FAST chart analysis. They add an extra layer of support or resistance to enhance existing bumpers when they overlap.

Step 6: Quick Peer Check

This step is used to gauge whether your stock is aligned with or fading the sector and or peers. If it's a laggard and the peer leaders are strong/weak, then that warrants a swing position for the imminent delayed move, provided the wider time frames are set up.

1. If your stock has peers, do a FAST chart analysis with just the 60-minute, daily, weekly, and monthly charts on two similar sector stocks to gauge if the peers are also aligned and flowing in the same direction with your stock, unless your stock is a laggard trade.
2. If no peers, then skip this step.

This should be sufficient to give you the warm and fuzzies to carry positions overnight or swing trade a few days tempered by the chart technicals first and the fundamentals second.

Level 3 Research Process: Mining Perspectives

This includes level 1 and 2 research and then pushes for more depth beyond just the focus on your stock, but also the industry/sector and peers within. Up until now, most of the effort has been effectively gathering information. This level opens up the door for contrasting perspectives by reading through articles and message boards. Be careful not to jump completely onboard one perspective but to keep an open mind weighing both bull and bear debates to ultimately derive your own perspective of the company and its standing among its peers. This is the start of the lateral thinking process.

The investor skillset is prevalent in this process. This process takes anywhere from 30 minutes to an hour per stock.

Step 1: Gauge the Sector and Peers

1. Look up the exchange-traded fund (ETF) for sector; http://etfdb.com/etfs/ is a good ETF database tool to check which ETFs contain your stock. If not sure of sector, then click the Competitors link in Yahoo! Finance and enter a competitor symbol in the ETF database. From there, click the sector-specific ETF to show the other components in the sector. Make sure it is a sector-specific ETF. If it is a general industry ETF, then there is no need to pursue any further. Some stocks won't have direct correlating peers. If that is the case, don't sweat it and move on to step 2.
   a. Run a level 2 research process on each peer stock to determine placing.
      i. Run a FAST chart analysis on the 60-minute, daily, weekly, and monthly charts for two to three peers.

   ii. Determine if your stock is a laggard, mid, or leader in sector.
   iii. If leader, then look for laggards.

Step 2: Read Articles and Message Boards

1. Go to Message Boards on www.yahoo.com/finance/ for your stock and read messages posted for the past two weeks. I know most of the posts are spam, personal attacks, cheerleading, and plain garbage, but with any luck, there may be a few insightful posts. If the message board is active, it will also give you a sense of the sentiment by the sheep. Ultimately, they get trapped on the wrong side. Less active message boards can mean less transparency.
   a. Check the Market Pulse link on Yahoo! Finance as well to read any insightful posts or comments.
2. Go to www.Benzinga.com, and type in your stock symbol to pull up any articles for the past three months and read them, take notes on any significant points, and save links.
3. Go to www.seekingalpha.com, and type in your stock symbol to pull up any articles for the past three months and read them.
   a. Read the comments after the articles. These tend to contain much more intelligent discourse than the cheerleading garbage on Yahoo!. Take notes on any significant points and save the links.

Step 3: Check for Any Upcoming Catalysts

1. These can be positive or negative catalysts; the only known detail is the date. The speculation and rumors can stir price action and volume in the days leading up to the date.
   a. New product/service launch dates
   b. Special event/announcement on set date, with no further details
   c. Regulatory and legal rulings dates
   d. Patent expirations
   e. Proxies and shareholder votes
   f. Major industry conference presentations
   g. Company-sponsored analyst days

Step 4: Check Options Activity

1. Go to Options on Yahoo! Finance and check for any particularly large transactions for the next three strike prices that are not hedged with the

opposing call or put. You are looking for 1,000 contracts or more priced at least .50 or higher. The larger the volume, the greater significance to indicate a directional bet or a spread position.

These steps should expose you to market sentiment on your stock and its placement within the sector and peers. You should have an idea of whether your stock is underperforming as a laggard or leading the sector. You should also have an idea of how correlated the peers are to each other by comparing and overlapping the 60-minute, daily, weekly, and monthly charts. Most importantly, you will invariably form an opinion on the stock, good or bad.

Level 4 Research Process: The Juicer, Full Immersion

This level includes research levels 1 through 3 and pushes the journey further towards full immersion. There's deeper information gathering in this stage that entails reading through conference call transcripts and digging into the SEC filings. This is the deepest level of research and sufficient for swing, investing, and portfolio trading. This is where maximum lateral thinking gets utilized. The previous research levels are the literal information-gathering process that includes chart technicals, fundamental data for stock and sector, secondary analysis from articles, opinions, message boards to shape your perception of not only the stock, but the company, sector, and business model. With level 3 process achieved, you should be familiar with the general scope of the company's model and sector as you dive deeper into the specifics. You will find yourself referring back to some articles at times, which is why it's important to have noted the links carefully. The goal here is to go through the final information-gathering with a magnifying glass noting anything significant. Break it down into positives and negatives. Imagine if you were pitching this stock, what relevant points support your position (long or short)? The level 4 research process can take anywhere from two to four hours depending on how extensive your digging. If you haven't already, start by going through the company's website to inspect the operations, sector details, products/services and partners, distributors, and customer base.

Step 1: Read Latest 10-Q and 8-K Results of Financial Operations and Conditions Report

The 10-Q quarterly report is more comprehensive and audited, but comes out about one to weeks after the 8-K. You can find them via the SEC Filing link at www.yahoo.com/finance or www.investorshub.com and type in the stock symbol to search. If possible, start with the latest 10-Q first and then the latest 8-K preliminary quarterly report. If an 8-K is the latest report, then start with the prior 10-Q and then move on to the 8-K. The 10-K is an annual report, which is the most preferred report if it is the latest report; then that's all you need. Start reading! As you read through, note the following details on a word document or write down in your research files.

1. Read thoroughly through the Management's Discussion of Financial Conditions and Results of Operations to grasp the nature of the business and the sector and risks including legal proceedings faced by the company.
   a. Is the company in a growth expansion, slow down, stagnant, recovery, turn around, or death spiral cycle?
   b. Compare to peers and apply to overall sector/industry.
2. What are the revenue streams: Break down revenue segments:
   a. Are more than 30 percent of revenues sourced from a single client/distributor/customer? This can be a problem down the road when too reliant on a few clients (e.g., PLAY from AAPL, ZNGA from FB, MITK from FISV—all stocks got destroyed as a result).
3. Determine book value: Found on Key Statistics at Yahoo! Finance: Stock trading below book value lends to a compelling undervalued situation and tends to act as a backstop.
   a. You can manually do this as well with the latest 8-K to double check yourself, especially in cases where the earnings are just released.
      i. Find stockholders' equity value on the second-to-last line on the balance sheet. Find total outstanding shares on the Key Statistics link on Yahoo! Finance. Divide stockholders' equity by total outstanding shares for book value.
4. Review cash flow statement: Revenues' rise should equate to rise in cash flow:
   a. If cash flow is decreasing while revenues are rising, check if operating margins are shrinking. This could be a case of too much discounting.
   b. If cash flow decreases while revenues rise and operating margins show no discrepancy, then check capital expenditures or any one-time expenses.
   c. If cash flow from operations is less than investing activities, this could be rising debt. Investigate.
5. Owned property or real estate? Found on the balance sheet under assets/property and equipment.

   a. Does the company outright own its buildings/store property or real estate? This is an underlying asset often overlooked with retailers; technology companies like data centers.
6. Patent/intellectual property assets:
   a. How many patents owned and in pipeline? (e.g., NOK several thousand tech patents)
      i. If possible, search for an estimated value of patents. This can be found in the Intangible Assets section but is completely subjective. Also Google search something like "value of Nokia's patents" and see if there are other options and values placed on them or peer comparison.
   b. Any current or future lawsuits regarding patents? (e.g., TIVO patent settlements. RMBS ongoing patent litigation setbacks. VHC increasing patent litigation settlements after winning against AAPL).
   c. Any major patents expiring? (e.g., GMCR's K-cup patent expires September 2013).
7. Read the most recent 8-K filings aside from the quarterly report for any material changes. This was likely done with level 3 research, but double-check for new 8-K filings.
8. Read the Notes to Consolidated Financial Statements and Loans Payable section:
   a. Find details on existing options or warrants issued during secondary or private offerings.
      i. Warrant/option/conversion price levels can play a significant role in the price action.
   b. Review existing loan notes (e.g., 13.8 percent senior secured convertible note) especially if they are secured convertible notes.
      i. Interest rates above 10 percent are detrimental.
      ii. Convertible notes should have conversion provisions detailed. Convertibles are usually detrimental to the company as they open up the possibility of the holders to short the stock to box their position and cover upon the cheaper conversion price. Read the details of the terms very carefully in regards to how, when, and how much they can or will be converted. A fixed higher than market conversion price is slightly better but still doesn't prevent the holders from shorting the stock. Be careful on stocks like this! (ETAK had endless warrants and convertibles that snuffed out the stock from 4s to 1s.)
9. Does the company have activist major holders?
   a. Check the 13G filings and major owner's stakes.

Step 2: Review Latest Conference Call Transcript

1. Find latest conference call transcript (if available) at www.seekingalpha.com or on the company's website under investor relations:
   a. Transcripts are more detailed, but if the audio version exists, listen to it and follow with transcript.
2. Read/listen through the complete conference call (stay awake).
3. Take notes regarding:
   a. Guidance for the next quarter or year on revenues and earnings.
      i. This is usually found in the press release but should be stated in the conference call in most cases, unless the company doesn't issue guidance (jerks).
   b. Gauge the tone from management. Audio conference calls are more transparent for this: upbeat, accommodative, responsive or monotone, ambiguous, inconsistent, dodgy or self-effacing, downbeat, gloomy, or a combination. This is purely subjective, of course.
   c. Any reference from management to competitors and leaders in the field (e.g., INAP CEO stated they were moving more into cloud services like their competitor RAX). This sets a good leader/peer connection for stock sympathy play.
   d. Questions and answers session with analysts and investors:
      i. Any questions that stump management or pry more color or new information not previously detailed in the company filings or press releases.
      ii. Comments and concerns brought up by analysts especially from the bigger investment banks and research firms (e.g., Goldman Sachs, Morgan Stanley, Merrill Lynch/Bank of America) as their recommendations carry the most reach.
      iii. Same applies for any large fund managers on the call.

Step 3: Find the Sexy

The sexy refers to the compelling hidden catalysts that could spark a significant price move if and when the market discovers it and prices it correctly. These can range from takeover/acquisition prospects, overlooked/undervalued product pipeline/components/assets, compelling growth engines, and correlation with current market themes.

1. Is the company a potential takeover target? By competitor, private equity, management, activist hedge fund, or investors?

a. Find a historical template: Search for recently acquired similar peers in the past year. Then figure out the metric used for the acquisition price (e.g., three to five times sales? 10 times earnings? How much premium to market price?). Compare the peer to your stock in terms of sales, growth, cash flow, and debt and then apply the metrics used to the acquisition to your stock. The further back in time the acquisition, the less valid the comparison may be, but it can still be used for reference. Acquisitions tend to generate themes that the market embraces for a duration of time; for instance, cloud computing company acquisitions were hot in 2010 to 2011, but this doesn't mean they will collect the same premium in 2013. The theme of that period had a major impact on the price. Determine if the theme is still relevant. This may not be an apples to apples comparison, but it still adds to the story, especially if the comparison is compelling. (e.g., cloud computing theme from HPQ and DELL bidding war for 3PAR in 2010 spurred a flurry of cloud computing acquisitions by GOOG, CA, CRM, IBM, CSCO, etc.).
    i. Speaking of themes, is there a current market theme the company fits into? (For instance, past themes included internet mania, fuel cells, stem cells, alternate energy, solar stocks, cloud computing, organic foods, etc.)

2. What compelling factor(s) of the company are potential price catalysts, not priced in by the market?
    a. Are there undervalued assets: property, inventory, products?
    b. New applications of existing products?
    c. New product pipeline (prior to rollout)?
    d. Activist shareholders?
    e. Possible spin-off of division?
    f. Monopoly situation unrecognized by market?
    g. New acquisition that enters company into new market segment/niche?
    h. New stock market theme experiencing massive interest and surging money flow into sector?
        i. New regulation or laws that directly benefit company (e.g., Obamacare, mandatory airbags, cell phone and text-while-driving bans)?

Any combination of the factors increases the sexy quotient. These aren't sure things, but are logically possible, which is more beneficial than already transparent factors.

Step 4: Process the Juice

You may find that you already started to experience this step during the level 3 research process. That is great. It means the juices have started to flow naturally. Level 4 is where you take the information and start processing it to shape the story. What factors make this a compelling position to take long or short? Be the pitchman that is trying to convince someone to buy or short the stock.

Analogous to using a juicer machine, you've selectively gathered the various highest quality raw ingredients for processing. As the machine grinds through the pulp to extract the rich nutrients from each ingredient, it produces a meticulously hand-crafted organic concoction rich in fiber, purity, and nutrients to nourish and replenish your mind and spirit.

The goal here is to let the lateral thinking juices flow to articulate what is uniquely compelling about the company and/or stock price very much like an analyst who has to pitch the stock to institutional investors. What makes this stock compelling? What makes it sexy? What are the catalysts? How are the financials? The audience is the market participants.

Metabolize all the relevant information components you gathered in the first three steps to manifest your own picture of the company and the stock.

1. Construct your version of the story that supports the premise of the trade.
2. Detail the wider time frame chart technical patterns and bumpers:
   a. Include a macro assessment as well with the SPY.
3. Detail the pros and cons:
   a. Include valuation details and compelling financial metrics.
   b. Include revenue and income, historic and projected growth rates.
4. What is the fundamental angle of the trade? Undervalued/laggard, turnaround/restructuring, undiscovered baby giant, takeover candidate?
   a. Include the sexy factors/catalysts.
   b. Provide some comparables as historical templates.
5. What price range makes this a viable trade?
6. What is the upside of the trade based on technicals, valuation, duration, and the stop-loss provisions (price and indicator)?
7. What are some alternate trades to consider based on this story?

The Afterglow Effect

Immersive research will always lead you down many forked roads that transition you to other facets of the company. As you read through the information, you will get little tidbits that will compel you to chase another path and perhaps another stock or sector—don't cut it off. This is the natural flow that is fed by the instinctual desire to learn. Make sure to take notes. This is MOST important! I can't stress this enough. Don't pay any mind to the notion of getting sidetracked. There is no such thing. You may look at the time and realize you just spent three hours going in a total different direction with different stocks. That's great. Get immersed in depth and get lost from the traditional track. Level 4 research opens the pathways to new realms, new stocks, new compelling stories, and their catalysts. Let things flow naturally and embrace the path as it twists and turns into other directions.

To embark down the conventional path and then forge your own direction(s) is the essence of this journey. Don't cut yourself short. It takes the process of the first three levels of research to get to level 4. Don't discount your efforts. It raises your awareness and stimulates your senses. This is such an intense endeavor that I've struggled to even be able to label it.

As you go through the press releases and SEC filings, you may run across a majority stakeholder or activist fund that leads you to their major holdings, that leads you to another compelling stock in another industry. Do you see how the law of by-product is in play here? Many times, I started off in one direction that opened up more paths and more directions, which led to more compelling ideas, better ideas, and better stock plays. It is rarely ever a straight line. As you read more, you will shape your own picture but always remember that the audience is the market participants. Whether your perception is correct or totally off base will be determined by stock price action, which is determined by the perception of the market participants. This is the most exciting aspect of level 4 research. It is an uncharted journey that dangles the prospects of mining for something the market has yet to discover, overlooked, or left for dead. It opens up new doors and new worlds rich with content and information. This is where the dopamine gets flowing. Craft a personal and organic vision of the company in the context of its peers and the overall markets. Immersion of information produces the osmosis effect where your mind gets acclimated to the process. The process gets more efficient with more repetition. Bottom line, the more you research, the more efficient you will become at researching.

You know you've performed level 4 research sufficiently afterwards. You will have an overwhelming sense of satisfaction and fulfillment of the knowledge and enlightenment you've procured, not because it was required, or given as an assignment, but because you craved it. You fed the hunger. This is awesomeness.

CHAPTER 7

How to Prey for Playable Stocks to Trade

Playable stocks should have momentum, follow-through, price movement, volume, and liquidity. They are elastic, not rigid, and have periods of volatility and range expansion due to larger active participant involvement. Bottom line, there has to be action. Without action, there is no opportunity. Meanwhile, trying to trade a stock that isn't playable only results in frustration and a lot of stops. More importantly, it distracts you from catching the moves on other playable stocks during their breaking moves, which only adds to your frustration levels.

A stock can be playable one day and then just chop in a small range for the next two days. Although the sector leaders will move with the SPY daily, the liquidity factor and trading range can shrink in dry climates. This can make them pretty unplayable, and continuing to press will only result in wasted energy, time, opportunity, and capital.

On any given day, it all boils down to picking the right playable stocks to trade that determines how your day goes. Stock selection is half the battle. Just like selecting the wet climates to trade, stocks also distinguish themselves as more playable than others. When I say "playable," I'm referring to individual "wetness" of the stock as it reacts well, follows through nicely, and jumps on triggers with good liquidity. It's got to have action. Playable stocks move. Nonplayable stocks don't. You can catch a quick, clean straight move for a +.40 scalp on 1,000 shares in 10 minutes versus sitting through a choppy .30 range for two hours to finally grab a +.20 scalp. Which trade is more efficient and less risky? That's what playable stocks are. However, this doesn't mean they stay playable all day. It means they have action, and your goal is to capture profits while the action is there.

There are two types of playable stocks; headliners and organic. The most action on any given day will usually be in the headliners, stocks gapping up big (gappers) or gapping down big (dumpers) as a result of news (earning reports/guidance/warnings, buyout rumors, FDA decisions, investigations, and so forth). These stocks draw the most attention, which draws the most participants that generate volatility, massive volume, momentum, and ultimately playability.

Organic stocks are less conspicuous. They require organically searching through individual chart patterns to catch them on strong breakouts or breakdowns. When they make a big move, they usually get discovered at the end of the move. Organic stocks should be tracked, stalked, and aged until they make their big moves. Every stock you get acclimated to is a potential organic play at some point. I'll show how to compile these and track them daily in the next chapter.

In this chapter, I will go over the various ways to find playable stocks every morning and throughout the day. This is where you make your money. The problem I have noticed with so many traders is they don't build up a solid foundation first and just move straight into unfamiliar grounds and pay the price. Before we get to the routines, let's build up the foundation thoroughly so that you won't be blindsided on the battlefield.

Stocks Are Battlegrounds and Participants Prey

You have the Katana and know how to use it effectively in any climate. What's next? Putting the weapon to work. Finding some prey. Eat what you kill, right?

In this thunder and tumbleweeds market landscape, opportunities can dissolve while you are focused elsewhere. With stocks tied to the SPY movement, every day is a case of the haves and have nots when it comes to which stocks get the action.

It's a misconception to assume every stock is playable every day. We've already discerned that when the overall market is in a wet climate, the momentum is greased and flows down from the SPY, which equates to more elasticity in terms of price movement, momentum, and liquidity. However, when the macro markets turn dry, the momentum and liquidity also dry up faster while it flows through fewer stocks.

Financial markets are a *minus sum game* where the majority will always lose in order for the minority to win. That shift between the majority losers and minority winners is fluid, changing, and dynamic. The algos/HFTs with their speed and access advantage will always remain at the top of the food chain as the apex predators. Therefore, playability boils down to what's left for the remaining participants. The prey is actually the participant that partakes in combat. *Stocks are the battleground. Participants are the prey, most of them.*

Referring back to the gunfight example mentioned earlier, it all boils down to having the most active participants in a stock that makes for opportunity. When the majority of the participants are crowded on one side of the trade, that's when the opportunity arises to take the other side and so forth. *The goal is finding those particular stocks that have the most active participants and using the Katana skillfully to strike under the cover of a wet climate.* It's interesting to note that algo/HFTs don't always win; they just have the bigger guns with unlimited ammo. With the addition of more algo/HFTs programs in the mix, the dynamics change as with the addition of more participants. More participants mean more prey and fewer chances of being singled out yourself as a target.

In a nutshell, stocks are the battleground where the participants partake in the minus sum game separating the predators from the prey. This is why finding the right stocks to monitor for play is critical to your success.

Playability: Internal and External Factors

The playability of a stock is factored on two levels: internal (you) and external (the stock). First, a stock that is playable for me, may not be playable for you based on my familiarity, experience, and skill level.

Internal Playability: Familiarity + Comfort Level

Internal playability refers to your own skill level and experience factor, which determines whether you are capable of trading any stock effectively as to avoid self-inflicted damage.

Failure to familiarize yourself with a stock leads to misallocations which could lead to panics responses. If you are aware that EBAY trades tightly in the 50s with a usual .20 to .30 oscillations in wet climates off the open, while it slows to .05 to .15 in dry climates, then you will know how to properly adjust your share allocations to optimize on the nominal range of movement. You would know to raise the size to 1,000 shares on perfect storms knowing that a .20 impulse spike is how it normally reacts so that you can take .15 out of it into the 1-minute high band mini pup, whereas it makes little sense to take only 100 shares for a limited .15 move. You may decide that a $15 profit is not good enough and ignore the 1-minute mini pup climax liquidity spike and end up stopped out when the liquidity and price drops afterwards. This mismatching of sizing leads to other problems like building the stigma of expecting more than what the stock will produce, which leads to ignoring the technical indicators in favor of trying to get a larger gain to justify the trade. When that liquidity dries up, you end up stopping out and taking a loss rather than the profit that was available. The typical newbie response is that you wanted more of a higher price move. Why? To capture a bigger profit, right? If you were familiar with how EBAY trades, then you should have taken larger shares to maximize the nominal movement and be properly aligned with the action. *When you let price expectations anchor your decisions rather than reacting fluidly to the actual price movements, you set yourself up for disaster.*

Internal Factor: Comfort Level

Referring back to the EBAY example, if you are not comfortable playing 1,000 shares to optimize the movement, then it addresses the other internal factor, which is comfort level. If you are only comfortable with playing 100 to 200 shares, then consider it the training period. Focus on the trade, not the money. This means continue to familiarize yourself with the stock's behavior during various climates as well as focusing on clean trades capturing the nominal scalp ranges. As you get consistent at spotting and reacting, then you give yourself the pay raise you deserve by gradually increasing your position size. The sizing has to be worked up gradually.

The Danger of Fixed Dollar Allocation

You can be right about the trade but still lose or feel like you lost because you under/overallocated your position size. Bear in mind, the conventional thinking of allocating based on a fixed dollar amount applied to the price is dangerously ineffective for intraday trading. For example, one may assume they will commit $20,000 capital to every trade. That value would equate to 4,000 shares of a $5 stock and 400 shares of a $50 stock. It assumes the $50 stock will have a larger trading range versus the cheaper stock. This is not always the case, especially with headliner stocks that gap/dump on earnings or news.

There is a nominal range of movement that adjusts every day. Sometimes the $5 stock will move more than the $50 stock at times, especially if the spreads are wider and/or liquidity is thinner, which means there will be more slippage involved. You can catch a +.30 move on the $50 stock ($150 profit) and then take a –$.10 stop on the $5 stock ($400 loss), wiping out earlier gains by having a static allocation method. Additionally, you may have been stopped out on a wiggle rather than a reversal because you didn't familiarize yourself with the rhythm of the cheaper stock. When you are unfamiliar, that triggers bad anxiety and panic especially when you are trading larger size. Trading 400 shares versus 4,000 shares is like night and day. It's like walking across a balance beam set on the ground versus one set 50 feet in the air. The walk is the same, but the risk is much higher, which makes you more susceptible to panic, because you are outside your comfort level. The comfort level is what it all boils down to. The familiarization process adds to creating a comfort zone. Share sizing is another process that has to be gradually worked up so as to not shock the system. Take that same balance beam and incrementally lift it one foot at a time to work up to the 50-foot level is the only way to grow your comfort zone properly. You may get away with it a few times, chasing momentum with large size, but unless you gradually work up your comfort level with the larger size, you are on borrowed time. Leverage cuts both ways.

Familiarization Process

Before any stock is individually playable, you have to be familiar with how the stock moves under varying wet and dry climates in terms of speed bid/ask movements and elasticity/rigidity of bumper levels. Acclimatize to the stock's behavior under various situations. This process should help you achieve familiarity. Remember that the more you observe in more conditions, the more you acclimatize. It takes time and repetition, but once you get there, it's like riding a bike. It sticks with you. Even better, you adjust quicker to other stocks with similar behaviors usually within the same sector or similar pricing.

1. Observe on charts, level 2 screen and time of sales, the speed of price movement, bid/ask spreads widening/tightening throughout the day; how the stock moves in the first 30 minutes off the open during the wet intraday climate, through the deadzone, and into the close. How does it react on heavy volume spikes and on light volume in terms of price movement, elasticity/rigidity of bumper levels, and spreads? How does it react to SPY movement during trending and chopping periods? How does it move with sector peers? How does it react on earnings? How fluid

are the price moves in wet and dry climates? Measure the nominal scalp range during 1-minute full oscillations in wet and dry climates.

2. Trade 100 shares to test out liquidity during the wet/dry, trending/chopping/oscillating periods. This is to familiarize yourself by direct contact to feel the fills, the speed of execution, and price movement. Of course, make sure that you are trading purposely on good setups and not just erroneously throwing orders out there. The 100 shares is just a standard low-risk amount that should not impact you emotionally as long as you remind yourself that this is just the familiarization process and training. Test out 1-minute 20 band bounces long and 1-minute 80 band crossovers down short. Test out perfect storms and observe how well they fade or follow through in wet and dry climates.

The process may seem time consuming and never ending since the universe of stocks is over 6,000 just on the NYSE and Nasdaq. Rest assured, the law of linearity applies with stock behavior as you will eventually discover that behavior tends to correlate strongest within sectors, price levels, and situations. This is why leaders pull the laggards. For example, retail stocks tend to trade very fast in wet climates and thick in dry climates. While the magnitude will vary, the overall rhythm within the sector is similar. ANF tends to move similar to LTD and ANN, while TGT and BBY tend to have similar rhythms as well. When prices are within the same range of $10 to $20, the rhythms tend to be identical. YUM and DRI tend to have similar rhythms. This applies until stocks get very disproportionate pricewise. As you get familiar with more stocks, you can start to follow 5 to 10 of them on a daily basis, your core stocks, which are interchangeable as they cycle through periods of volatility.

External Playability: Correlation + Catalyst

The external factors that impact playability are correlations to the market and sector along with a catalyst that spurs price movement generated by interest and active participants.

Catalyst

A stock needs a catalyst to spur interest and generate playable price action. This catalyst can be fundamental and/or technical. Fundamental catalysts are news, rumors, or event-based reactions that trigger large price gaps up or down, which generate elevated participants and volume.

Technical catalysts form without or prior to the news as the chart forms a range expansion via breakouts, breakdowns that trap one side into panicking.

When the SPY or QQQ makes a large enough gap up or down, this can have a gapping effect on stocks as well. However, the catalysts I am referring to are specific to the stock in the context of the SPY/QQQ indexes, not as a result of them. Technical catalysts tend to get magnified results when the market or sector as a whole forms a strong trending move in the same direction. Usually these movements are under the radar until after they hit peak transparency, which is when scanners pick them up and suck in late participants. These have to be stalked and tracked manually prior to the catalyst on your minder list. The next chapter will address how to stalk and age your prospects.

Sector Correlations

The market is all about correlations between sectors and within sectors. They are connected. When a stock makes headlines resulting in an excessive gap, it brings attention/interest not only to that stock but among its peers as well. This impacts market movement.

Correlations tend to change with time within sectors. The rule of thumb is that the leaders are usually the higher-priced stocks. The momentum flows down. The best website to check for sectors that I use is www.finviz.com. Click on the Groups link and click Industry for the current correlations. The Maps link is also very useful and current as it lists sector movement with component stocks. Eventually, you will gradually build up a first-hand account of active correlations within sectors. This opens up the opportunity to play peers when a particular stock is gapping or dumping extensively, as well as capture laggard movements with the portfolio trading by uncovering laggard correlations to swing. The best way to test correlation is to overlap the peer stock charts on top of each other or next to each other on the rifle charts. This is the visual proof that displays how these stocks correlate or correlate inversely. As I just said, when a stock is strongly correlated with its peers, this opens up multiple opportunities to play the peer stocks whenever one of them is making a strong move and even so far as to use the catalyst stock as a lead indicator.

The Two Types of Playable Stocks: Headliners and Corganic

Headliners: Gappers and Dumpers

A situation is an event created by abnormal, out of the ordinary factors triggering drastic and volatile price reactions. The equilibrium is shocked, resulting in the price gapping or dumping, sometimes after a trading halt is triggered. Trading halts can occur during excessive price movements during market hours via circuit breakers or due to a situation, usually initiated by the company. The abrupt surprise nature of trading halts magnifies the shock and tension multifold, further adding to the volatility and panic upon re-opening. This is one of the dangers of playing a stock that immediately collapses or spikes out of the blue drastically, absent news. Leave the interpretation, judgment, and speculation of the news to the other participants. Your sole objective is to game their reactions. Don't try to figure it out, let the others do the thinking. The only thing that matters is the price reaction. *This is not about how you would react to the news, it's about anticipating how others will react to the news.*

Most Significant News Situations

Here's a breakdown of the most significant news situations:

1. **Earnings-based:** For all public companies, during earnings season:
   a. Earnings surprise beats or misses
   b. Earnings raised or lowered guidance (warnings)
      i. Conference calls are usually scheduled right after an earnings release or the next morning. Make sure you are aware of the time of the call. In cases of dumpers, stocks tend to attempt some recovery going into the conference call, especially if the company actually beat estimates or raised guidance but still got a gap down (e.g., 1/22/2013—EAT beat guidance but dumped premarket to 31 and bounced to the 31.60s into the 10 A.M. conference call, which was bullish enough to rally it back to 33).
   c. Large cap retail stocks report store sales figures for every month during the first week of the next month.
2. **FDA decisions:** For biotechnology and pharmaceutical stocks. These events tend to implement a predecision stock halt, which should be expected.
   a. Advisory committee votes
      i. Approvals or denial majority votes tend to get more action oftentimes than the actual official FDA approvals, which tend to get a sell-the-news reaction (e.g., VVUS obesity drug Qnexa's positive advisory committee votes surged the stock higher ahead of the FDA decision to approve, which then caused it to sell-off).
   b. **FDA product rulings:** These always have a material impact on stock prices.

i. Approvals: Depending on how expected the approval was and whether it was priced in could result in a sell-the-news response or propel it higher.
ii. Denials, requests for more data, or postponing to later date: These usually gap down hard depending on the circumstances and the rebuttal from the company. As a rule of thumb, the cash per share value oftentimes tends to act as a floor and it's worth taking long if a stock gaps greater under the cash per share, especially if the company is vigilant about pushing for an approval.

3. **Clinical trial results**: For biotechnology and pharmaceuticals:
   a. Surpassed, passed, or failed to meet primary endpoints:
      i. Same applies to gapper/dumper rules but always check to see if the dumpers are pricing excessively below cash per share value, anything less than 50 percent is very worthy of playing for a bounce.
      ii. These can gap not only the company but also any partners and application specific peers in the sector (e.g., VVUS obesity pill events resonated with peers ARNA, OREX).
4. **Legal/Litigation/Regulatory Events:** For all public companies, notably technology companies.
   a. **Patent lawsuits:** These can drag on for years (e.g., RMBS, TIVO).
      i. Settlements, wins, losses, judgments: Depends on which side of the decision the company is at and terms of the settlement and appeals (e.g., MRVL nailed with $1 billion judgment tanked stock from 8.50s to 7s but recovered two months later).
      ii. Patent trolls are companies that acquire patents to pursue settlements through litigation (e.g., VHC). The caliber of the defendants and terms of settlements determine the magnitude of the gap.
   b. **Shareholder lawsuits:** These usually have little to no impact and are irrelevant in the long run since the O&A insurance tends to cover against these.
   c. **SEC investigations:** These will cause initial gaps down on the shock value; however, they tend to recover the losses after the initial panic is absorbed days to weeks later, depending on the size of the float and volume. Most companies issue a press release stating they will "work with regulators," or "defend vigorously" or claims have "no merit."
   d. **Department of Justice, FBI criminal investigations:** These carry much more impact and can take months to years to recover (e.g., WCG was raided by the FBI, which collapsed the stock from the 120s to

the 20s to the 9s in 2008! It took until 2012 for the stock to recover back to the 60s after charges were dropped). Anything criminal against an organization should be played extremely carefully.

5. **"Reviewing strategic alternatives":** For all public companies. When a company issues a press release of "review strategic alliances/alternatives to grow shareholder value," this drives up speculation of acquisition especially when company announces hiring specific investment bankers.
6. **Stock structure changes:** For all public companies.
   a. **Stock splits:** These still tend to get some gapping action in the announcement and into the split date (e.g., NKE, UA, LULU). Sustained momentum is more influenced by performance of the company.
   b. **Special dividends:** These tend to gap up initially but tend to sell back down. Usually the stock itself will gap down the amount of the special dividend, so it's a wash. The main reasons for the spikes are shorts covering since they would have to assume the responsibility of paying the dividend on the short positions on the ex-dividend date.
   c. **Spin-offs:** The mother company gets a gap up until the date of the spin-off and then proceeds to move in alignment with the newly issued company. If the IPO tanks, so does the mother stock (e.g., COMS collapsed on PALM IPO back in 2000. EMC rose when it spun off VMW.).
   d. **Conversion to REITs:** This happens with stocks that own their own real estate (e.g., PENN was a situation where the announcement of REIT spin-off representing the real estate of their casino properties caused a gap from 37 to 45s and grind to 50s. Very effective at squeezing the shorts!).
   e. **Convertible offerings:** These are usually the kiss of death for the share price as the institution(s) acquiring the debentures get a high yield coupled with a cheap (usually less than market price) conversion option to convert the note to stock. The institutions/funds tend to short the box by shorting the stock to lock the price differential between shorted price and conversion price. The shorting drives down the price as shareholders flee on fears of dilution upon conversion.
   f. **Secondary/shelf equity offerings:** These stocks tend to get a strong sustained price move higher with or without news. When they release the news of the secondary, it creates a sell-the-news reaction as late investors get duped into buying elevated prices in the open market while the secondary is likely priced lower but still higher due

to the recent stock pump. Stocks usually sell off on these headlines especially if the offering price is well below the current market price of the stock. Whether these stocks are able to return back to or above the pricing levels usually rests in the earnings moving forward. Each situation is different and should be addressed on a per situation basis. The purpose for the secondary offering and allocation of the proceeds make an impact; either the company receives the funds for working capital, strategic implementation or for insiders to unload shares directly without market impact as proceeds go to insiders (e.g., ZNGA secondary pricing by insiders at $12 screwed the buyers as stock eventually collapsed to $2. VVUS priced secondary at $24 to fund sales channels for Qnexa drug but collapsed ultimately to $11 on weak sales).

g. **Major index additions or replacement (rebalancing):** The major indexes like the Dow 30, Nasdaq 100, and S&P 500 are the most relevant additions or deletions. The additions tend to gap up initially but ultimately revert back towards where they were trading as they get more aligned and correlated to the index (e.g., UNH gapped on addition to S&P 500 and proceeded to give back the gap by the next day).
h. **Acquisitions:** Depending on the structure of the deal (cash vs. stock swap or combination) and market perception of the deal, acquisitions will impact the acquiring company shares positively or negatively. Don't bother to play the acquired company unless it is a pegged to the movement of the acquirer. Likely the arbitrageurs already have the spreads locked down; don't waste the effort.

7. **Activist hedge fund activity:** Celebrity activist hedge fund giants who issue public statements, interviews, and press conferences along with their stakes bring heavy attention to the stocks in particular. They get self-fulfilling prophecy effects as other funds and traders piggyback the trades. Names like David Einhorn who destroyed GMCR from 90s to under 20, Bill Ackman who tanked HLF from 40s to 20s, which then got squeezed by Dan Loeb back up to 40s. Loeb shook up the board of YHOO, taking the stock into 20s. Carl Icahn has often announced conditional tender offers that pump up the prices where he would liquidate as he walked away. This is getting more popular but as with everything, it can also backfire; Whitney Tilson got destroyed shorting NFLX up to $300 before it finally collapsed to under $50.
   a. **13D filings:** These are filed when up to 10 days after a fund or investor takes more than a 5 percent stake of any public company.

These filings tend to gap up stocks initially based on the caliber and reputation of the filer and most notably the purpose of the purchase.

8. **Insider activity:** Insider buying in the open market is bullish and tends to illicit knee-jerk stock bounces. The size of the purchases and who makes them impact the magnitude of the market reaction. Oftentimes, the purchase price levels act as bumpers in the open market. Insider selling is pretty common, and unless the quantity is significant, bears little impact on the stock price.
9. **New company and board of directors appointments:** New CEO, COO, and CFO appointments can be significant depending on their backgrounds and where they came from. If they are linked to a big bellwether company, then they will have a material impact on the stock price (e.g., JCP appoints new CEO, Ron Johnson, former president of AAPL retail sales resulted in a 20 to 30 percent price spike). Same applies for board members, notably members linked to private equity funds, which always opens the doors toward leveraged buyouts or mergers.
10. **Rumors:** They are everywhere. It's the ones that gain the most media attention that tend to impact price movement the most. Take rumors with a grain of salt, and play the momentum only. Throughout the years, the most credible source when it comes to rumors has been the *Wall Street Journal*. Significant rumors may include the sudden resignation of the CEO, takeover rumors, litigations, activist investor actions, acquisitions, spin-offs, stock splits, regulatory or criminal investigations, policy changes, and so on. These are out-of-the-ordinary events that trigger out-of-the-ordinary price reactions.
11. **Special company media events:** These events are used to launch new products or services without disclosing any further details to fuel speculation, driving up stock prices. AAPL really mastered this technique with Steve Jobs methodically building up huge speculation and expectations into the special events. Stocks tend to gap on the announcement and then rise into the event before a sell-the-news reaction triggers once the news and products are unveiled. The higher the gains up to the event, the larger the reversal reaction should initially be. It is important that you jot down dates of special events with bellwether companies (e.g., FB grinded from 20 to 31 ahead of its special event announced a few weeks in advance where they announced graph searches).
12. **Analyst upgrade/downgrades:** These have to be taken based on impact and whether they come on the tail end of another news item like earnings reports or any of the prior mentioned situations. It's important to see

how peers are reacting in the sector to see if the impact is isolated to the particular stock or takes the sector with it. Oftentimes, the sector stability can offset the downgrades and help to recover and vice versa.

Most headliners will fall into one or more of the aforementioned situations. Let everything sink in and just refer back anytime you need to qualify a situation. The purpose is to preacclimate yourself ahead of time to minimize the shock effect. Of course, nothing can substitute for experience. By having the situations clearly laid out ahead of time, your experience shouldn't be as harrowing (as mine was!).

Corganic Stocks: Core Vehicles and Post Headliners

As you get acclimated with more headliner situations and familiarized with more stocks, your universe of stocks will continue to grow. You should keep several minders lists of your favorite headliner stocks and stocks that continue to trade actively, which will be your core stocks. These are similar to my concept of basket/focus stocks from prior books. The difference is that core stocks are always changing due to the thunder and tumbleweeds landscape. It seems that even the most active generals go through their periods of playable wet climates and noncorrelating choppy dry climates more and more frequently. The old basket technique implied that you should stick to trading your main stocks through thick and thin. That was a different landscape where active stocks may go through a day or two of rigid price action before resuming elastic price fluidity. These days, active stocks can stick to a general rigid or bi-polar period for weeks to months at a time. Therefore, the focus on a key set of stocks still remains, but one has to be sensitive to the dryness and immediately switch over to more moist stocks. The focus has to be constantly tuned toward the playable periods of these stocks. Participants are fickle, and if the action tends to thin out for any duration, they will seek other battlefields. This happens at an unprecedented pace these days. Stocks like EBAY and SBUX will go through days of elasticity and then get rigid for weeks.

This doesn't mean every headliner should be a core stock. Remember that headliner stocks making excessive gapping or dumping are outlier situations. This period is the exception, not the rule. When a stock that trades an average of 100,000 shares a day spikes to 5,000,000 shares of volume on a 20 percent gapper or dumper day, it will eventually revert back to the prior volume level. The exception is newly discovered stocks that are getting increased institutional inflows with rising prices. These are the real headliner stocks that we want to add to our core list and continue to organically track. I will go over more of this in the next chapter where we stalk and age the food.

For now, consider stocks that continue to trade actively after their big headliner gap/dump as candidates to continue following as a core stock. Core stocks should correlate with the SPY and sector peer movement most of the time. The most important factor is that you have already cut your teeth and wet your toes playing these stocks, making you acclimatized to their behavior in extreme and nominal wet and dry climate situations. In a nutshell, you are experienced with the stock. This is what it all boils down to. Your core stocks have all been intimately experienced. Ultimately, many of these stocks will chop tighter ranges and should be put on the back burner in favor of current active stocks. Stocks, like people, lose interest. The high-quality core stocks tend to cycle this regularly, whereas one-shot wonders lose interest quickly and fade into oblivion. When the high-quality core stocks start to expand again, you should move them back into focus. As they get active again, you continue to gain experience through all situations and climates. Study them thoroughly first hand. Prioritize the active ones to manually screen charts for perfect storm setups.

Where to Find Playable Stocks: Sources for Ideas

Let's get into the actual scanning and filtering for playable stocks and sources that generate ideas for prospects.

Newsfeeds

I find gappers and dumpers on my CobraIQ trading platform under the Top Ten list of largest point gaps up and down for NYSE and Nasdaq. I also watch the CNBC ticker in the premarket to see what stocks are active and gapping/dumping premarket. Here are some more news sources that I recommend:

> www.benzinga.com (free) (pre/during/post-market/weekend ideas research)
>
> This site has great original market and stock specific analysis and articles. There's a lot of content on this site. The ideas flow fresh and freely. It never fails to impress me how their writers are able to present a fresh perspective from different angles ahead of the curve.

www.benzingapro.com (paid) (intraday newsfeed/analysis/idea generation tool)

This is a cream of the crop news feed for traders who want actionable news items. While Dow Jones newswire spits out everything, BenzingaPro filters to tradable stock-specific news items. The prescreening process saves traders time and resources and most importantly, helps to pinpoint where the action is taking place. These sources smoke the competition in terms of speed of reporting and depth of content. News is delivered via streaming news feed and audio squawk box.

Scanners and Screeners

A quick note about market scanners—these are to be used solely to generate ideas. They still require first-hand analysis through the pretrade process. Don't assume the stocks that show up always fall under the search criteria. Never impulse trade just because a stock pops up on the scanner. Ideas still have to be reviewed and verified. This sounds like common sense, but you'd be surprised how many people take the results on face value and dive into a trade headfirst. Scanners should only be used after you gain proficiency with the Katana. They can easily be a distraction and detrimental if you haven't built up a solid foundation of skills. They make good traders more effective and sloppy traders worse.

www.finviz.com (free/paid) (pre/during/post market/weekend research tool)

This site is great for the heat maps, the updating homepage has a ton of information, and the screener is pretty tight. The daily trend line charts are available with the paid subscription. I use this heavily on weekends for the technical pattern–based screener as well as fundamental screener. Here are some of my personal formulas for scans I use to find every filtered swing/portfolio trading ideas. These are just ideas that still need to be researched thoroughly through the four-level research process.

Favorite FinViz Day/Swing Trading Scans

I use these for swing trading ideas as well as corganic intraday trading if triggers are near, running through the Katana:

Inverse Head and Shoulders (Signal) + Average Volume over 400k – Bullish scan

Recent Insider Buying (Signal) + Average Volume over 400k – Bullish scan

Horizontal S/R (Signal) + Average Volume over 400k – Bull/Bear scan

Wedge (Signal) + Average Volume over 400k – Bull/Bear scan

Channel (Signal) + Average Volume over 400k – Bull/Bear scan
Head and Shoulders (Signal) + Average Volume over 400k – Bearish scan

Customized FinViz Swing/Portfolio Idea Scans

These are two customized scans I run weekly to generate the few ideas that may be compelling enough to stalk and age for swing/portfolio trading opportunities. The Cheap Undervalued scan requires Level 4 research and days to weeks worth of aging and tracking. The Excessive Overbought is a technical scan to generate short ideas.

Cheap Undervalued Fundamental Scan

These stocks are undervalued and cheap fundamentally. Make sure to screen them through the Katana and get a reversal daily candle.

Average Volume: Over 300k
Price/Cash: Low (<3)
Price/Free Cash Flow: Low (<15)
Sales Growth qtr over qtr: Positive (>0%)
P/B: Low (<1)

Excessive Overbought Potential Shorts Scan

These stocks are excessively overbought. Exhaustion short can be considered using the Katana and make sure you get a reversal daily candle. Just make sure the candidates are not merged or acquired companies.

Average Volume: Over 1 million
RSI : Overbought (80)
P/E: High (>50)

www.trade-ideas.com (paid) (intraday scanning for pre/during/post market ideas)

This is a good flexible scanner that can be programmed and comes with numerous canned scans. I always tend to find some good ideas from this scanner during the day. It's especially useful during dry climates to scavenge for pockets of action in the market. I love the flip option to invert bullish search to the bearish version.

Some of my favorite precanned scans are:

New Highs/Lows
Up Big Pre-Market (flip for down big pre-market)
Most 5-minute up candles (flip for down candles)—useful in finding pups, set volume above 500k
123 Continuation pattern—useful in finding mini pups, set volume above 500k

www.stockfetcher.com (paid) (evening scanning, weekend research)

This is a stock scanning website. You can preprogram your scan criteria to create personalized scans or use the prewired scans off the home page. I love how it will e-mail a list of stocks that trigger on your filters at the end of the day. It is pretty flexible, but there is a bit of a learning curve to use the custom filters, but they have a simple filter creator section where you just select your criteria, and the program will write the code for your filter. This is a great value and useful for evening and weekend research. For the first time ever, I am revealing my basic personal pup/mini pup scan formulas. The charts make it easy to spot the counter candle triggers. Just copy the formula into the custom filter window:

Pup Breakouts:

set{daily_diff, close - open}
show stocks where daily_diff has been above 0 for the last 3 days
show stocks where the 20 day slope of the close is above 0
and open has been increasing for 2 days
and close > 2
and average volume (45) > 200000
and closed above ma(5)
and stochastics (15,3) %k closed above stochastics (15,3) %d

Ascending Triangle Mini Pup:

close is above the upper ascending triangle (55,5)
and closed above ma(5)
and stochastics (15,3) %k crossed above stochastics (15,3) %d
and close > 2
and average volume (45) > 200000

Descending Triangle Mini Inverse Pup:

close is below the upper descending triangle (55,5)
and closed below ma(5)
and stochastics (15,3) %k crossed below stochastics (15,3) %d
and close > 2
and average volume (45) > 500000

Stock Research

These sites are good for quick fundamental research and investigating the sentiment, commentary, opinions, and analysis in depth.

http://finance.yahoo.com/ (free) (pre/during/post market/weekend research)

I still like to use Yahoo! Finance for quick stock research. The Financial Statistics link gives a great concise summary of the numbers. The Profile link gives a great summary of the company along with its website. I also check the Message Boards for the rare occasional post that actually contains some useful insight hidden between the rampant promotions, spams, cheerleading, and overall useless drivel. The Market Pulse link shows recent comments off StockTwits and Twitter.

www.slopeofhope.com (free) (evening/weekend research)

I like this site for ideas and commentary from its illustrious band of characters. I tend to get a few ideas a month, but I check it out for the entertainment value. Tim Knight is hilarious and a very sharp trader.

www.seekingalpha.com (free) (evening/weekend research)

This site has some pretty good content and opinion, but with so many contributors pitching services it's important not to overlook the motives behind the authors who contribute articles reflecting their views. Don't assume the articles are impartial. The consistency in management filtering articles from promotions can be lacking at times. The nice thing is they do tend to balance bull/bear articles on the biggest headliners in the news. Conference call transcripts are provided, which is the hidden gem for level 4 research.

www.zerohedge.com (free) (evening/weekend research)

This site is solely dedicated to the bearish point of view of the markets and economy. Tyler Durden is the Perez Hilton of world financial markets. There are some deep, brilliant minds on the site with well-thought-out articles, but the posted comments from its user base steal the show. They can be brutal in the sharpest-witted manner. They don't mince words on intent. I tend to check out the site more during market sell-offs as I'm sure a good chunk of their readers do as well. The entertainment value is off the scale.

www.stocktwits.com (free) (pre/during/post market opinions and secondhand analysis)

This site is a streaming version of Twitter for the financial markets, a social media themed improvement over the mIRC (internet relay) channels of old like #daytraders and #activetrader. Surprisingly the participants are well behaved with minimal moderation and limited commercial spam. There are some interesting characters on there. Like anything, you are only searching for ideas to run through your personal screen and filtering. Don't jump into anything headfirst.

Financial Television Channels

www.bloomberg.com (free) (pre/during/post market news)
www.cnbc.com (free)

I watch the CNBC ticker pre-market and post-market as they seem to have the most current data feed. For more serious commentary during the day, I prefer to switch to Bloomberg Television. After 15 years of watching CNBC, it can be pretty tough to stomach some of the personalities. I will switch between the two stations during economic reports and earnings releases. Overall, I prefer Bloomberg over CNBC.

While the financial information sources are ever expanding, the aforementioned sources are the most efficient places to generate a stream of fresh ideas and perpetuate good digging results. You have to consistently make the effort to hit those resources regularly. It's best to schedule these into a routine that works for you.

CHAPTER 8

Stalking Prey

As you continue to gather and compile stocks of interest, place them into a minder to monitor and track them. When a group of the corganics starts to pick up action, you want to select the most promising stocks to shift into stalking mode. These are the three stages of managing your growing collection of corganic stocks: monitoring, tracking, and stalking.

Monitoring involves passively observing your stocks' movements and behaviors to note anything that sticks out. Those that start to gain traction should be given more priority as you track them. When the tracking stocks get to the detonation stage, you switch to stalking mode. To get a better idea of the three stages, visualize the images:

> *Monitoring is passive observation from a distance.* Picture an owl perched high up in a tree observing the behavior and activities of the environment's inhabitants.
>
> *Tracking is more focused following for an imminent setup.* Picture a wolf following deer tracks extending back a mile from the prey, as it gradually closes the distance.
>
> *Stalking is aggressively pursuing an opening trigger for entry.* Picture a cheetah in furious pursuit of a singled-out gazelle in the open field.

Aging: Waiting for the Pattern to Form

When a corganic has a potential formation but hasn't reached a detonation trigger, it must be given time to age. This is what I call the aging process, to allow the volume to pick up and fermentation to slowly take place. It boils down to waiting, waiting for interest to build toward a boiling point. Either the stock has to digest new price ranges or needs to expand the price range as pressure builds toward a known bumper level. The trigger you are comfortable with just hasn't formed yet. The aging process takes place during the monitoring and tracking phase. When the stock is getting ripe for a move or has begun its move, it's time to stalk.

Stalking: Setting an Alerts Minder on Your Trading Platform

It's not humanly possible to spend an equal amount of intensity spread across one hundred or more stocks. This is where technology comes into play. Your minder list has corganic stocks, which you will continue to add to. When you start to get larger price gaps and volume rise, you should note them and move them into a tracking minder for closer observation. The ones that appear to be close to triggering a compelling setup like a perfect storm on the wider time frames, should go in an alerts minder with a visual and audio alarm set at a price level. Most platforms and even charting packages have a basic alerting function. I prefer to narrow down the stalking alerts minder to mostly perfect storm patterns.

When a stock is ready to break or is starting to make its move, I set the alert price in most cases beyond the coil resistance level using the +.20 rule on the breakout price (e.g., daily 5-period moving average is at 36.78 means I set the alert to trigger at 36.98) and –.20 below the breakdown bumper price level (e.g., daily 5-period moving average is at 36.78 would be set at 36.58). You can use however many ticks near or beyond the price trigger; the key is that you are comfortable with it and are aware of the premises for the trade. For lower-priced stocks under 10, I actually like to wait for pullback levels rather than chasing the +/–.20 coil break levels. Since the mini pups prioritize the 5-period moving average bumpers I like to use overlapping 5-period moving average bumpers when they exist on the daily, weekly, and/or monthly pup and mini pups. I prioritize 50- and 200-period moving averages that overlap with even more emphasis when they are trading within the range.

As Figure 8.1 illustrates, you can see the daily chart at the top with the weekly and monthly chart on OVTI and the stalking alert minder table.

FIGURE 8.1 Alerts for stalking minder.

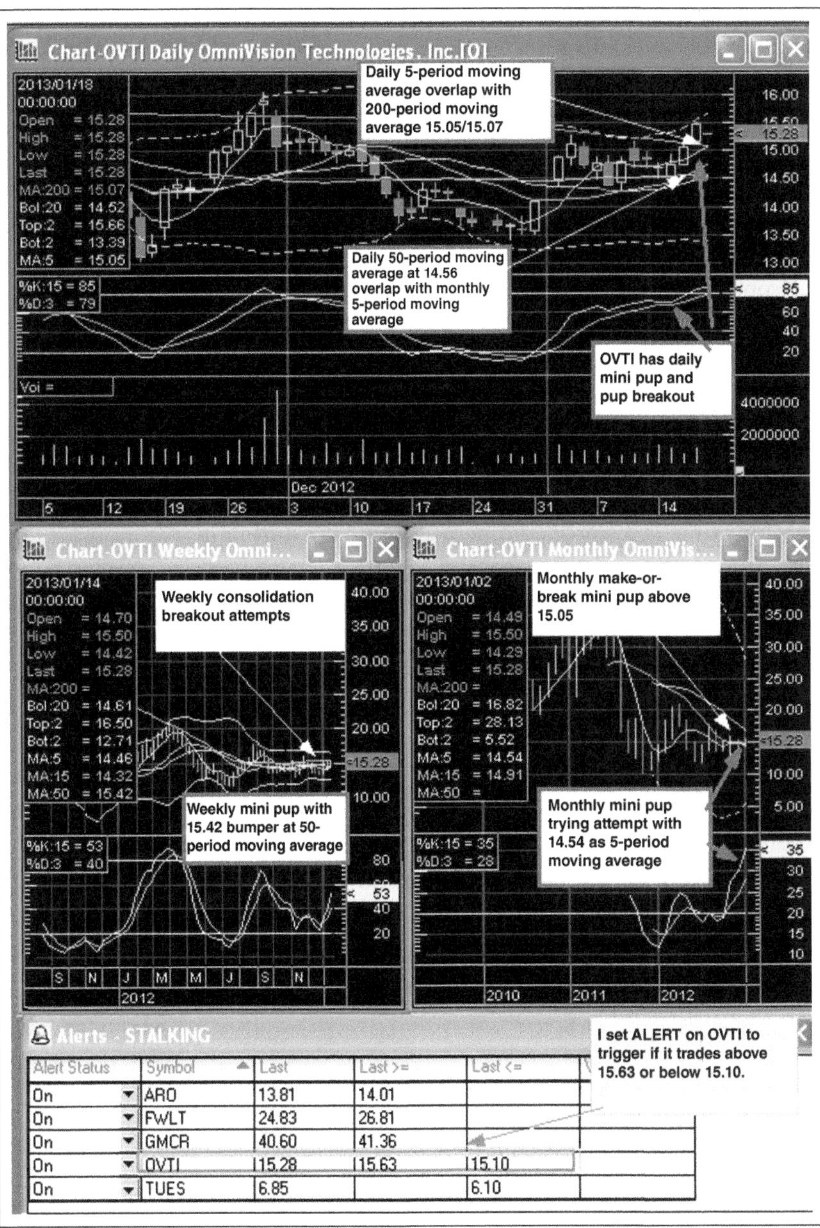

Alert Status	Symbol	Last	Last >=	Last <=
On	ARO	13.81	14.01	
On	FWLT	24.83	26.81	
On	GMCR	40.60	41.36	
On	OVTI	15.28	15.63	15.10
On	TUES	6.85		6.10

OVTI has a breakout on the daily with a pup and mini pup. The weekly and monthly have been in consolidations but stochastics are forming mini pups for a possible perfect storm breakout. The triggers would be either on pullbacks near the powerful overlapping daily 5/200-period ma under 15.10 or breakouts above stinky 5s level and weekly 50 bumper 15.42 +.20 coil resistance 15.62. So I set the alert prices above 15.63 or below 15.10 on pullback to alert me if those price envelopes get hit . . . then I unsheathe the Katana for a possible encounter. Set it and forget it, nice and easy! The key is to make sure the price envelopes are accurate AND you write down your setup premises somewhere so that you are prepared to react when it triggers! Repeat this process with each stock on your stalking alerts minder.

Make sure that you CLEARLY WRITE DOWN the setups and game plan (legibly) for each alert on the stalking minder and not rely solely on memory, so you are already prepared for the encounter when it triggers. It sounds like commonsense advice, but you'd be surprised how easy it is to overlook this.

Your time is a scarce commodity, especially during market hours. Don't bog yourself down with too many alert signals. Try to keep the stalking minder with audio alerts to no more than 15 to 20 max. Don't spread yourself too thin as that will start to dilute the efficiency of the process. Also, make sure to clean it often and delete stocks that are no longer worth pursuing. They still inhabit your corganic minder, so they won't be lost. Only the most compelling stocks at the moment should be on your alerts minder. Once they trigger, you still have to do a fast analysis as it correlates to intraday time frames to assess the proper entry triggers. The wider time frame perfect storms don't detonate until the intraday time frames align to allow for the unified move. The alerts are just that, an alert to consider a trade. This doesn't mean you need to jump in blindly headfirst. The next step is to implement the pretrade process as we head closer toward the encounter.

CHAPTER 9

The Encounter from Start to Finish

No matter how many thousands of trades you have executed, that first morning trade will always come with anxiety. It's a static factor. You never get used to it. The first trade sets the tone. While preparation will work to dilute some of the anxiety, it is always there. Too much anxiety can be debilitating, resulting in hesitation during the trigger moments and chasing the late stages to make up for it. The important thing is to acknowledge it will always be there. It will never go away. It is a part of the game. The best offset is preparation. Address the fear at its roots, meaning being thoroughly prepared as to the possible outcomes and most importantly having alternate prospects in place in the event the first set of trades fizzle out. This flexibility and resilience are what experienced pros have fostered and newbies need to train. Familiarity breeds confidence.

Anxiety: Bad versus Good

Bad anxiety stems from the insecurity that forms from the lack of solid morning preparation. You can't expect to just wing it anymore these days, hoping to pile into momentum blindly, and shoot from the hip as things pop up. This style worked in the good old days, but it falls dreadfully short in the thunder and tumbleweeds landscape. Being unprepared is the root cause of chasing terrible entries or impulse trades that backfire, chop, and headfake you into panic exits. This contaminates your mindset, focus, and spirit. Get smoked too many times, and desperation kicks in. From there, the tilt phase is not overly difficult to trigger. Blaming the markets is misguided. Lack of preparation leaves you with only a short-sighted, surface-level field of vision. It lacks the depth needed to make solid decisions because the depth of information is limited to the surface level. Surface-level information forms at the height of transparency. This is why unprepared traders usually end up chasing their entries and exits.

By following the routines outlined in Chapters 7 and 8, you should have your own morning ritual, outlined in Chapter 3, to generate a watch list of gapper/dumpers and organic prospects that you have been aging and stalking. Run the SPY and your watch list through F.A.S.T. chart analysis before 9:15 A.M. and you should be well prepared and armed with solid opportunities going into the opening bell.

You have done your homework and developed your watch list complete with noted bumpers levels awaiting the opening bell. You start to feel anxiety going into the open. This is the *good anxiety* that heightens your level of awareness and alertness and sensitizes you to spot pockets of nuances that may clue you ahead of transparency and the energy to react nimbly.

React, Don't Panic

Make the distinction between reaction and panic. Don't misconstrue panic as reaction. Panic is a psychological state you fall into, triggered by fear or greed, when you find yourself unprepared in an extreme situation that triggers an impulsive response. This response can range from chasing entries and exits, basically chasing rapidly depleting liquidity. The market systematically fuels itself on the panic of its participants. Panic is emotional, impulsive, and dangerous. It often takes you by surprise, because you weren't expecting it. *Reactions should be controlled, deliberate, swift, and prepared.* Preparation is the key word. Remember, you don't have to be right in every situation; you have to be prepared to react. Very rarely should a situation arise that you aren't prepared for, and in those instances, one simple rule applies: Don't put yourself in harm's way. This means not buying stocks ahead of an earnings report, unless you are hedged or holding in a portfolio with proper risk-allocated positions. *Good anxiety fuels decisive reactions. Bad anxiety magnifies panic.*

Distinguishing Trade Entry Stages: Early, Impact, Late

In the heat of the action, it's easy to overlook the stage of your entry until after you've taken a position and realized you entered late. The stage can typically be gauged by the 1-minute stochastics bands. On long positions, the early stage is the stochastics cross up 5–20 band level, but still under the 20 band. The impact stage occurs on the 20 band cross up and encompasses the 20–40 band area oftentimes with a mini pup. The late-stage is the 80 band or higher entry.

On short sells, the early stage is a stochastic cross down off the 95–80 band level but still above the 80 band. The impact stage occurs when the stochastics pierce the 80 band down at the 80–60 band area, often with a mini inverse pup. The late-stage occurs shorting under the 20 band.

The early and late-stages tend to provide the peak liquidity as they illustrate the optimal fear and greed points where either no one wants the shares (fewer than 20 bands) or everyone wants them (above 80 bands). The impact stage has the thinnest liquidity, which explains the rapid price movement as the algos/HFTs exploit their stealthy 30-millisecond advantage to swoop up all that liquidity causing traders to chase the impact stage only to get filled at the late-stage price peaks. On early stages, you can offset some risk by breaking up your entries into two or three orders, especially if you are taking a very early prestochastics cross entry or fishing bids. These precrosses should be reserved to wet climates, since they will have more liquidity and coil magnitude in the event you have to take a stop loss.

The climate always needs to be taken into consideration when assessing the entry stages of your trade. Wet climates tend to be more forgiving of late-stage entries, and in many cases the late-stage is where the large volume and climactic price moves take place. Dry climates are not forgiving and will oftentimes reverse quickly at the late-stages as liquidity and volume vaporize at the peaks. There are exceptions in dry climates where too many participants tried to get an early stage entry for a reversal only to end up getting trapped on an excessive grind. It's not possible to predict when this will happen in a dry climate, but that is the nature of dry climates. The exceptions to the rules can get extreme and more often than not when you are not in the trade or on the wrong side of it. This is the treacherous nature of dry climates.

General Rules for Entry Stages

The BEST 1-minute trigger entries occur at the impact stage with a mini pup (20–40 band cross up with mini pup or 80–60 band cross down with mini inverse pup).

Take *early stage entries* only when the wider time frames are providing additional overlapping bumper levels that can support your entry and/or if they are lined up to detonate a *perfect storm* on the 1-minute cross trigger. To minimize risk, early entry positions can be scaled in with two to three entries.

Don't take *late-stage entries* when there is no meat to the next bumper, especially if the entry is near or at the Bollinger Band bumper and volume is flat or falling, especially in dry climates.

Late-stage entries on the 1-minute chart should only be taken on rising volume and scalped or scaled out ahead of volume and liquidity drops.

Late-stage entries should mostly be taken during the wet climates with perfect storms, rising volume, expanding Bollinger Band with meat to the next price bumpers. At the very least, late-stage entries should only be taken on rising volume and exited before the stochastics peaks and turns. This is basically buying high and selling higher or shorting low and covering lower.

Late-stage entries can be taken on consolidation break perfect storms that form after extended consolidation/basing with constricted Bollinger Bands for at least two hours. These can happen on end of day dumpers that slip back below the 60-minute 5-period moving average with low band mini inverse pups. The breakout/breakdown should be accompanied with Bollinger Band expansion and rising volume. Since the basing took so long, the late-stage entry on the 1-minute chart is still an early-stage entry on the 5-minute chart where the consolidation break usually forms. Since the pullback is minimal, the risk is considered minimal, which allows for an extended late-stage grind.

HLF appears to be a late-stage entry (Figure 9.1) on the 1-minute chart as it nears the 80 band; the 5-minute has been on a consolidation that is ready to break out above 43.01, which is the 15-minute 5-period moving average with a pup breakout forming.

HLF produces the consolidation perfect storm breakout composed of the 60-minute mini pup, 15-minute pup, 5-minute consolidation breakout, and 1-minute mini pup that spikes HLF from 43.15 to 43.71 on heavy volume in a dry climate deadzone. Retail traders will notice the spike at 44.70 as it hits new highs on the ticker and hits the scanners . . . as they jump in to chase the momentum . . . and. . . .

HLF collapses fast from 44.70s to 44.10 on Figure 9.2 once the 1-minute stochastics crosses back down through the 80 band in a dry climate. The true late entry would be from chasing this one at the new highs above 43.66, and then getting chopped out in terror as the stock plunges back to the 15-minute 5-period moving average support at 44.10 in two minutes. The late-stage entry at 44.15 still had to be managed by scaling out into the momentum before the 1-minute stochastics peaks and slips the 80 band.

FIGURE 9.1 HLF late-stage entry on consolidation perfect storm breakout.

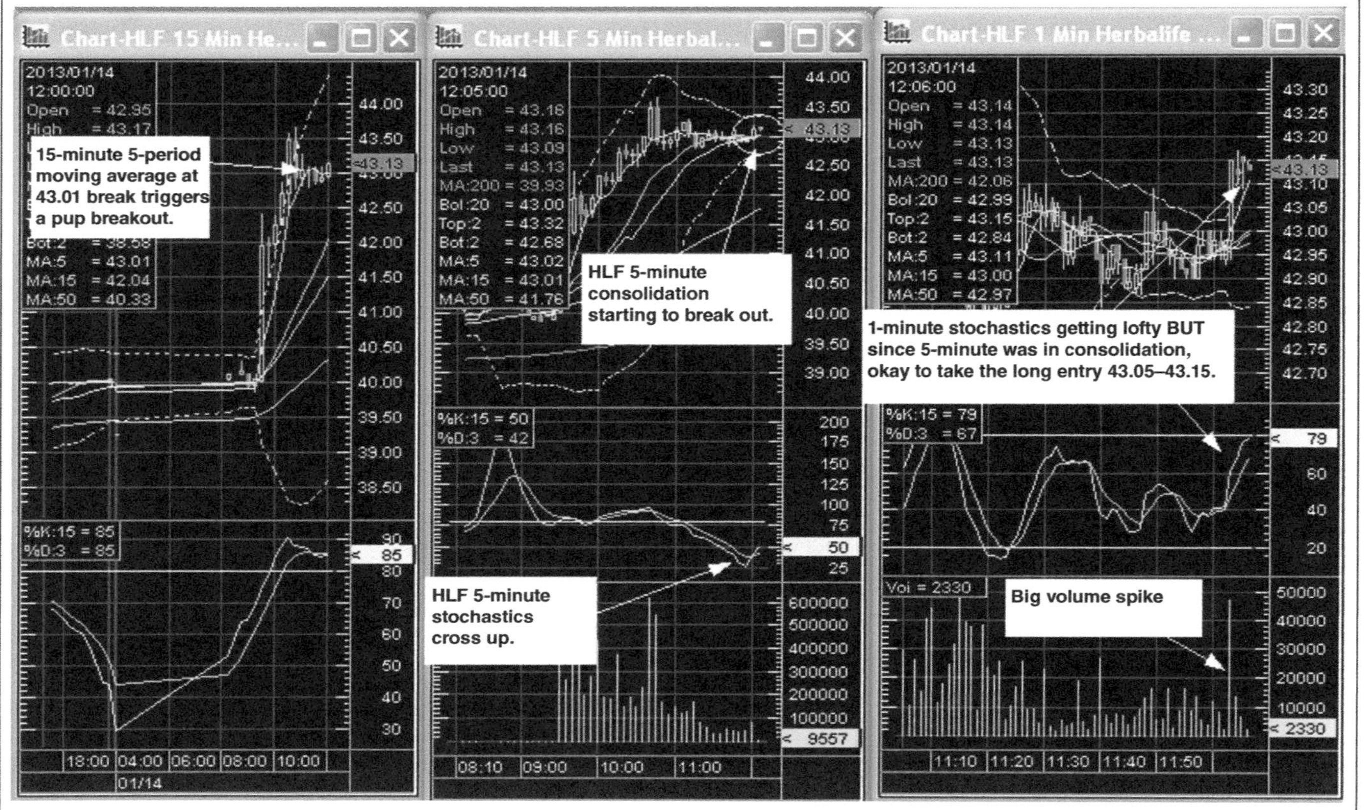

FIGURE 9.2 Shows the aftermath of the squeeze resulting in a rug pull.

COH sets up an end-of-day dumper rug pull setup (Figure 9.3) with the 60-minute inverse pup and mini inverse pup and the 5-minute mini inverse pup at 3:06 P.M. The 15-minute stochastics is still stalling and could either form a mini pup bounce or cross down, which sets up the perfect storm consolidation breakdown. We took COH short at 51.10 slightly early due to the 60-minute and 5-minute mini inverse pups knowing that 3:15 P.M. would be the moment of truth as the 15-minute stochastics should decide which way it goes. Our trail stop was just above the 5-minute 5-period moving average with wiggle to 51.26. The 51 level was support all day on COH, but sellers were getting more aggressive since the stock was not performing.

After the 3:15 P.M. candle closed (Figure 9.4), the 15-minute stochastics crossed down! The bulls tried to muster one last push as they tried to mini pup on the 1-minute. Keep in mind that we now have 3 lanes down with 2 mini inverse pups on the 60-minute and 5-minute charts with 15-minute stochastics aligned to the downside by crossing down. The 1-minute is the detonation trigger. As the bulls tried to lift COH, it resisted at the 5-minute 5-period moving average and then collapsed taking out the 51.04 counter candle to form another 5-minute mini inverse pup as the 1-minute stochastics cross down through the 5-period moving average forming a 1-minute inverse pup breakdown detonating a PERFECT STORM BREAKDOWN (60-min inverse pup and mini inverse pup + 5-min mini inv pup + 1-min inverse pup) as it collapsed in panic through the 51 area to lean down to the 15-minute lower Bollinger Bands near 50.76. We locked the panics out into the 50.80 overshoots, out + .30 on a very low-risk trade. Notice the preparation pretrade and being aware of the setup and most importantly watching the clock for that 15-minute candle close. Once the three larger time frames are aligned in direction, then the 1-minute is the FUSE that triggers upon the cross. Most traders will only catch COH in the 50.70s when it's too late to chase. With solid pretrade analysis, you will catch these ahead of the impact stage!

Scaling Requires per Share Pricing

One quick note: I mention scaling out in wet climates and scaling in during dry climates, but the scaling only works if your commission costs are minimal. While commission pricing continues to drop, the liquidity unfortunately is dropping as well in the markets. This is why it's very important to use a direct access broker with per share pricing when trading intraday. As I outlined in Chapter 4, scaling allows you to proportionately optimize

FIGURE 9.3 COH dumper stock about to get rug pulled.

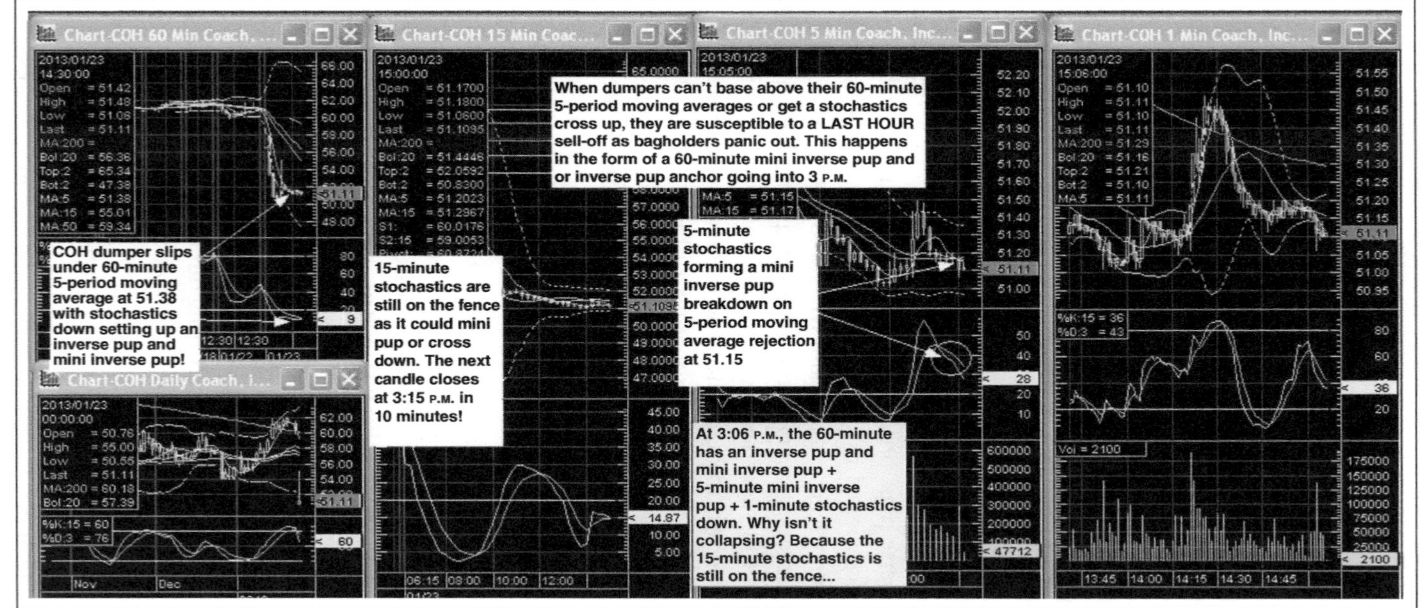

FIGURE 9.4 A dumper stock can't base firmly above its 60-minute 5-period moving average by the last hour; it is susceptible to an end of day sell-off.

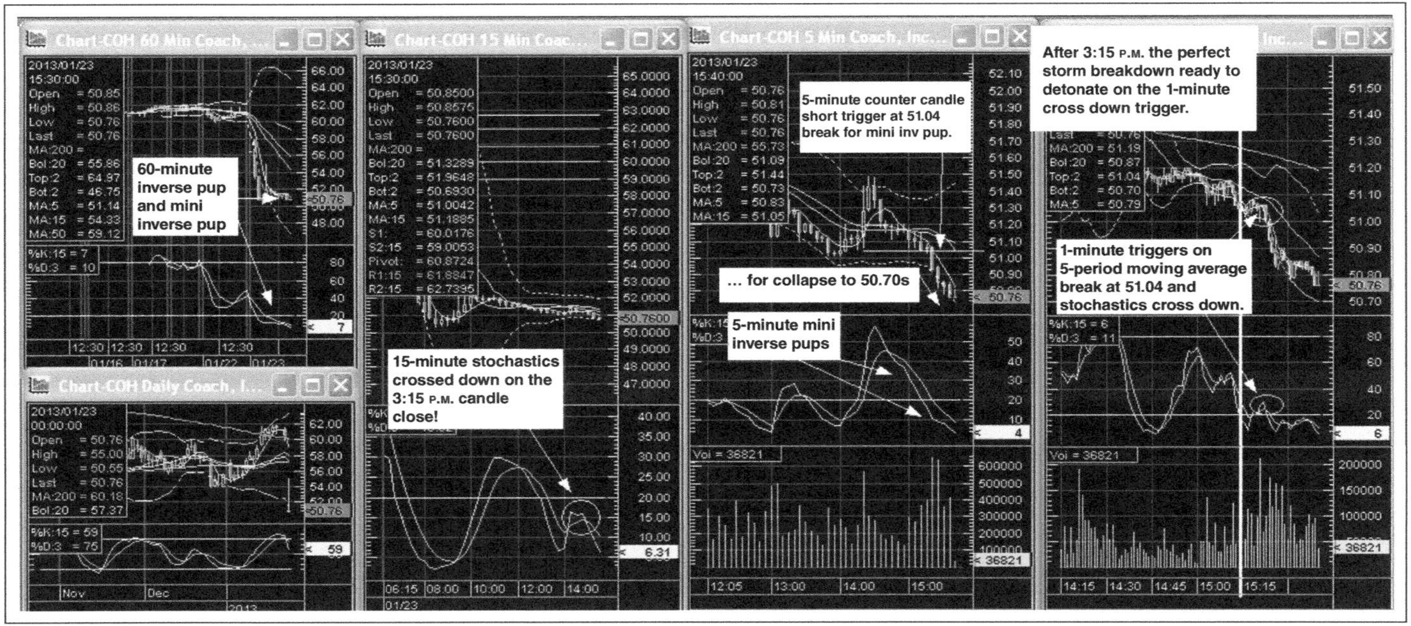

gains while minimizing risk. Flat fee pricing should be left for swing trading, unless the rate is very cheap and includes ECN pass throughs. Cobratrading.com is my preferred per share pricing direct access online broker. For swing trading, Venomtrading.com has an excellent flat rate per trade program.

The Complete Trade Sequence

While most of you may already have a routine when it comes to making a trade, I want to methodically go through each of the three parts (pretrade, execution, and management) that make up a trade from beginning to end. This is a good way to formalize the steps to take for optimum efficiency with your trading. Note that I call these processes for good reason. Refer back to the A + B = C equation in Chapter 1: *The goal of trading is to focus on optimizing the efficiency of the process components A + B and C will manifest itself as the by-product of profits.* As with most of the checklists and routines in this book, they may seem complicated or drawn out, but this is for the sake of thoroughness. This is the template that should flow automatically with time and experience. It also serves as a solid reference when you have to re-set yourself, which everyone does.

I chose to pursue depth over simplicity on purpose, documenting the checklist, steps, and routines. What may seem simple to me will seam vague to you. You can't simplify something without first acquiring the depth of knowledge to work with it. With time and experience, you will be able to streamline the processes to adapt to your essence. That has been the underlying goal throughout the book, to stimulate your focus on improving the efficiency of the process. I give you the depth to digest and metabolize into an efficient process specifically adapted for you. While you have to adapt to the market conditions, your trading system should be adapted to you, like an exoskeleton.

Pretrade Process: Information Gathering and Analysis

Prior to executing any trade, it's important to go through a quick pretrade information-gathering and analysis process to prevent impulse trading and tighten up your game plan so you are prepared to react to any situation once you are in position. Much of this checklist is already addressed during the SPY and watch list monitoring.

1. Monitor the SPY direction, trend, and key bumper levels.
2. Determine if stock is *fading or following* the SPY and/or peer leader:
   a. If stock is buy fading, then try to time longs with a 1-minute SPY bounce.
   b. If stock is sell fading, then try to time shorts with a 1-minute SPY slip.
3. Determine the trade setup pattern and the respective bumper support/resistance levels:
   a. Perfect storm patterns are recommended.
      i. Note the 5-period moving average and then overlapping bumpers.
   b. Slingshots: These are when two or more wider time frames (60-minute, daily, weekly, monthly) lower Bollinger Bands overlap as a resistance and get pierced. They create a slingshot bounce effect when coupled with two or more mini pups.
   c. End of day dumper rug pulls: These occur on dumper stocks that slip back under their 60-minute 5-period moving average with mini inverse pup stochastics. These set up a perfect storm breakdown in the last hour, which shakes out the bag holders in a panic oftentimes toward the lows or new lows.
   d. Make sure there is meat there to make trade worthwhile.
      i. If there is room to next bumpers on the 1-, 5-, 15-minute charts, then okay.
      ii. If stocks are trading AT three or more Bollinger Bands on falling or flat volume, then WAIT on the trade.
4. Determine the climate: wet or dry.
5. Gauge trade entry stage: early, impact, late.
6. Determine share allocation, based on climate and target bumper meat:
   a. Wet climates = more shares and scaling into liquidity for larger targets Dry climates = less shares and less scaling into liquidity for smaller targets
   b. Early stage entries can be scaled in two to three orders to average a better price level in wet climates.
7. Type in shares for execution and select routing:
   a. Have two order execution screens/modules, screens, or level 2 screens:
      i. One for Entry and one for Exit:
         1. Entry screen—type in shares and limit price a few ticks away from desired price to ensure a fill. To minimize commission costs, if market is not moving too fast, then select to route to the market makers. For quicker entries, then select ISLD, but be aware of the addition pass-through fees. If fishing

for very early scaled entries, then use ISLD or ARCA limit orders spaced apart incrementally. If desired position is over 2,000 shares, then use the reserve order option to show 100 to 200 shares on level 2 while having 1,000 to fill for each scale.

2. Exit screen—type in shares or increments of shares and select route. ISLD is preferred for rebates. ARCA is expensive but pays a better rebate. Check reserve shares to show 100 to 200 shares if scaling a larger position with 1,000 per scale.

8. Wait for price and indicators to trigger entry: Be patient.
   a. Counter candles, reversal candles, bumper price breaks.
   b. 1-minute stochastics cross.
      i. With mini pups or mini inverse pups are the highest caliber triggers.
      ii. Be aware of your entry stage; if late stage, be sure to exit quick.

Trade Execution Process: Entering the Position

1. Upon trigger, execute entry/entries into position.
2. Once your position is filled, cue up the share size to sell on Exit screen and cue up a sweeping stop limit price on the Entry screen, which should now be considered a stop screen. This price doesn't have to be exact. It should be several price levels beyond your stop level to assure a sweep order will get filled earlier. This is like an eject button to stop out of the position fast.
   a. Cue up full position size on Exit screen if scalping in dry climate.
   b. Cue up scaled size on Exit screen if scalping in wet climate.
      i. General % scaling runs: 50%, 25%, 25% or 75%, 25%.
      ii. If size is over 1,000 per scale then cue up the reserve order to display 100 to 300 shares, especially in dry climates.

Trade Management Process: Monitoring and Exiting the Position

1. Track any lead or peer stock along with the SPY for early transparency.
2. Monitor your stock movement:
   a. Track the time frames starting with the 1-minute on up for changes in setup premises.

   b. Gauge the next bumper levels especially stinky 2.50 and 5s ranges.
      i. Note any slope/hook reversals against you on the 5- and or 1-minute Bollinger Bands to suggest an early heads up to cut short the duration of trade.
      ii. Note any flagrant misticks as clues (as discussed in Chapter 3).
   c. Ask yourself, *If I wasn't in this trade, would I take a trade in the other direction?*
      i. No one knows better how weak a stock is than someone in a long position, or how strong a stock is than someone in a short position!
         1. This is firsthand information that you paid for. Use it as needed.
3. Adjust limit prices on Exit screen to execute exits as stock *moves with you, chops,* or *moves against you.*
   a. **With you** means the stock is following your premises and moving in your direction. This is ideally the reaction you want on most of your trades. Impact stage entries and late-stage entries should immediately move in your direction. Scalp/scale into the volume spikes prioritizing the 1-minute chart as it overshoots the Bollinger Band bumpers. Trail with the 1-minute 5-period moving average. After you scale out your first exit (50 to 75 percent), then continue to trail the 1-minute 5-period moving average and/or the 5-minute 5-period moving average. Final exits should be on breaks of the 5-period moving average(s) and stochastics 80 band slips.
      i. Offensive pare scale to add to your position on stalls/wiggles ahead of another 1-minute mini pup, if the nominal upside is minimized but the pattern is a particularly strong perfect storm composed of 5 or more lanes with an additional 1-minute mini pup. This should only be used in rising volume wet climates.
   b. **Chop** means stock is not reacting much as it holds a small range. This tends to happen during early-stage entries. Refer back to your premises, especially if a boss chart is still active in your direction. Gauge the SPY to make sure it's not making a move against your direction. Give it some time into the next candle close on the boss chart, but be vigilant about spotting early fades. From here, it will either move with you or reverse against you. Prioritize the boss chart here and track the candle closes as they will update the 5-period moving averages, which will spur a reaction. Don't hesitate to take an early precautionary stop loss or scale down if the 1-minute stochastics fade and cross against you.
   c. **Against you** means the stock has climaxed and is attempting a reversal. This tends to happen on early- and late-stage entries. If you are early,

then refer to your overlapping bumper supports, but don't hesitate to stop out if it's a slow grind. If you are late, refer back to the overlapping bumper supports and consider either a stop or defensive sprawl scale.

i. **Stop out**—if it's a slow grind move against you, especially if you are on the wrong side of a perfect storm, then stop out. If the wider time frames are also against you, then stop out. Don't take chances in a dry climate. Once you are stopped out, continue to watch for a possible re-entry if indeed the 1-minute was the only culprit and re-enter on the 1-minute cross back in your original direction or a reversal trade if the 1-minute was the precursor to a muscling fade that reverses the wider time frame. *Remember, you can only reverse a trade after you stop out. Reversal trades should be limited to wet climates only!* These climates should still have enough momentum to switch with liquidity, if you are nimble enough to stop out in time. Do not reverse trades in dry climates as the thin liquidity assures you will chase the reversal at peaks, only to get stopped out again. *If you take a reversal trade, then go back to the trade execution process, step 1.*

ii. **Defensive sprawl scale**—*This technique is only for disciplined and experienced traders who are nimble enough to react and will not freeze. Refer to the "Essence of Stops" and "STOPS and SPRAWLS" sections in Chapter 4 for additional details. It is not an excuse to avoid taking a stop.* If the stock reverses in a panic too fast to stop out, liquidity has dried up. Make sure wider time frame premises are still intact, but the 1-minute stochastics is moving against you in a wet climate. Consider adding at key multiple overlap bumper levels as close to the 1-minute stochastics reversal as possible. Gauge the SPY as well to time the adds with SPY coils in your direction. The bumper levels get even more significant as the time frames get wider. *Remember that your goal is only to average your cost of shares at key supports for the 1-minute reversal back in your direction so you can scalp/scale out on reversions to resistance bumpers, usually the 5-period moving averages on the 1-minute and/or 5-minute chart.* This is damage control, so don't get fixated on getting back to even. You need to start scaling out at the 5-period moving average bumper into the pockets of liquidity. Stay vigilant about unloading your shares. Once the 5-period moving average tests, it will likely stall to either break it and form a 1-minute mini pup, turning the 5-period moving average into your support/stop level, or reject back through the 5-period moving average against you for the 1-minute to form a pup against you when the stochastics crosses against you. Remember to scale that first 5-period moving average bumper test to be safe, especially in a dry market. *Once you exit out of the defensive sprawl, take the information gathered to consider a possible re-entry or reversal trade, only in wet climates. Revert back to step 1 of the trade execution process for re-entry or reversal trades.*

iii. **Double-hedge sword sequence:** If your stock is buy fading while another watchlist stock is sell fading, and the SPY is forming a downdraft, you can execute this trade provided they are opposing perfect storms (i.e., perfect storm breakout vs. perfect storm breakout). Time the entries and exit in conjunction with the SPY. If the SPY sells off to a coil support level, then cover the perfect storm breakdown. If SPY breaks out to a resistance bumper, then sell the perfect storm breakout into the liquidity surge. The goal is to scale down the positions on both sides during the SPY oscillations. Both sides should eventually revert back to alignment with the SPY. The advantage of the perfect storms is the extra protection surge of price movement, volume, and momentum on both sides of the divergence, which allows for stronger pockets of liquidity to exit into.

4. **Closure:** Take a break per completed trade sequence to clear head, pace properly, and avoid the imminent dry climate. Use a screen capture program like Hypersnap to capture your chart screens on stressful trades for the post trade analysis.

It's best to have TWO of the level 2 order modules/screens (Figure 9.5) up for any stock you are trading, Use one for entries and the other for exits. Once you are entered into a position, you can use the Entry screen as a stop screen, where you have your stop limit price cued in several levels beyond to sweep the liquidity in one swoop without having to cancel and re-enter the order. Use the Exit screen to focus on scaling out into liquidity.

Figure 9.6 demonstrates how double-hedge sword sequence trades should only be considered once you've become experienced playing perfect storm breakouts and breakdowns thoroughly. Work the divergence while it exists and get out into the spikes on both legs. These are detailed in Chapter 5, "The Perfect Storm Pattern Trade."

Figure 9.7 illustrates how valuable the wider time frames weekly and monthly can be when trading dumpers. COH gapped down 9pt on earnings making our watchlist as a dumper du jour. We spotted the special situation of a double overlap on the daily and weekly lower Bollinger Bands at 51.28.

FIGURE 9.5 A level 2 order entry screen with time of sales.

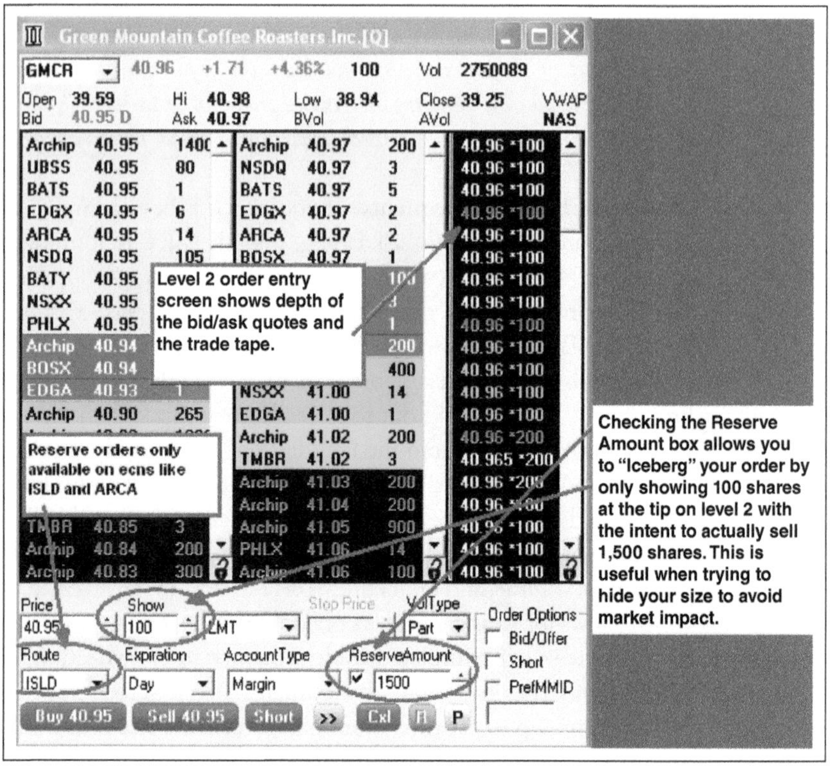

Source: Cobratrading.com. All Rights Reserved.

This makes it very significant as a resistance but even more so as a potential slingshot bounce trade. We took longs at 51.30 as it formed a 5- and 1-minute dual mini pup that spiked up hard to trim out 51.70s on its way to 52 in less than 5 minutes! The spike was dramatic due to the slingshot through not only a powerful daily lower Bollinger Band but also an even more powerful weekly lower Bollinger Band. The wider time frame Bollinger Bands, the stronger the impact of the slingshot.

Identifying Maladies in Your Trading

These trading situations can each be the loose thread that completely unravels your mindset if not identified and handled accordingly. The following are common maladies and their respective remedies. Familiarize yourself

FIGURE 9.6 Double-hedge sword sequence trades.

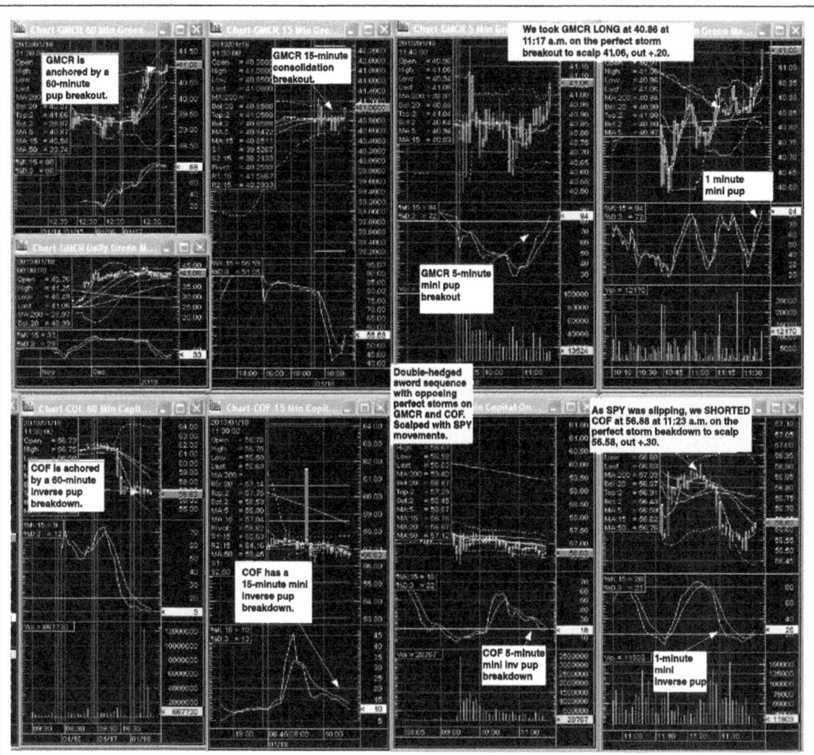

with these so you can apply the remedies properly in the post trade sequence analysis process.

Malady: Taking Profits Too Soon

"I made a profit but the stock continued to move a lot higher! "

In this situation, the trade continues to move beyond your exits (Figure 9.8). You may have played this trade reasonably well as you sold into the liquidity on the 1-minute high band exits ahead of a resistance bumper. In most cases, you optimized a nominal gain, but in this particular case, the trade continued to squeeze beyond the resistance bumpers for an *exceptional price move.*

FIGURE 9.7 Value of wider time frames weekly and monthly when trading dumpers.

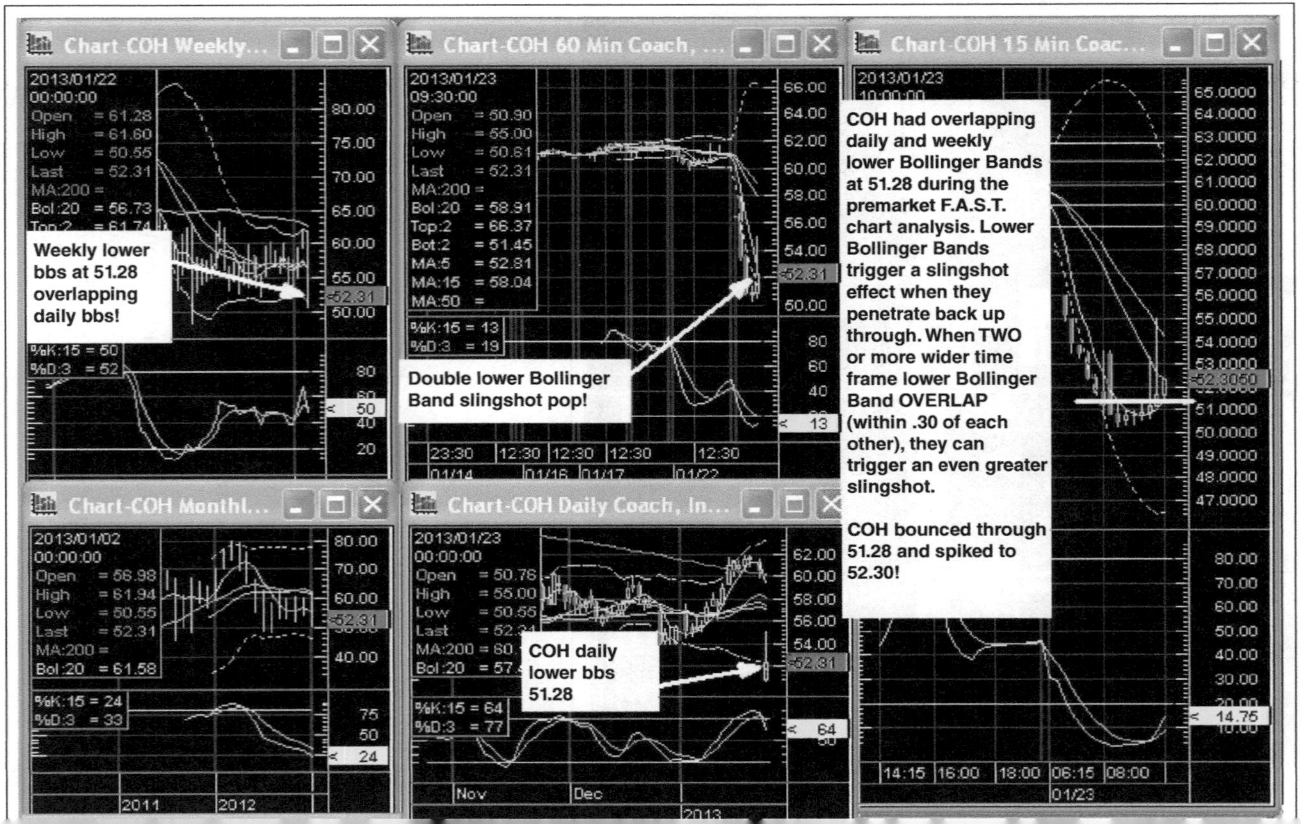

FIGURE 9.8 Our STX trade continued higher after we took profits.

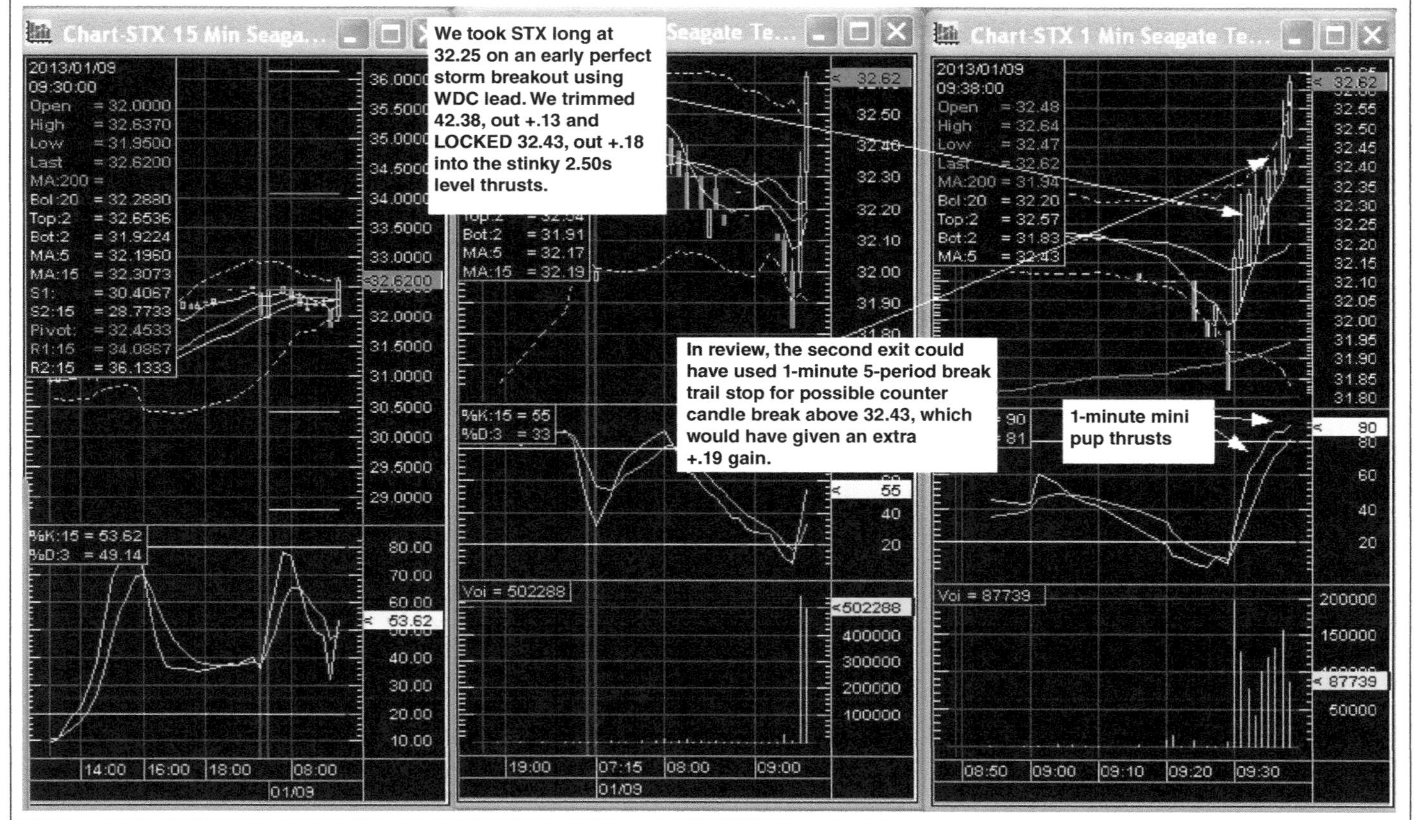

Keep in mind that this is an exception, not the rule. As long as you understand that it's an exception, you won't beat yourself up for an otherwise well-managed trade. Yet, it still tends to sting seeing the price move double or triple your exit without the expected wiggle.

Remedy: A good way to manage the potential exceptional moves is to *scale and trail* with the 1-minute 5-period moving average versus the counter candle. First off, take your nominal exit on most of your position, leaving a minimal position of one third to one fourth the original size toward the next bumper level trailing the 1-minute 5-period moving average specifically when there is a clear counter candle. The result will either be a profit stop on the 1-minute 5-period moving average break on candle close or a break of the counter candle toward the next bumper.

If you took the profit too early, ask yourself first why you exited the position and if you were too tight or too sloppy? Was there something that you honestly could have taken as a clue to stay in the trade longer? Could you have trailed a wider time frame 5-period moving average support?

Malady: Entering Trade Too Early

"I stepped in too early and got stopped right before it moved in my direction!"

In this situation, you followed the SPY and spotted an excessive fader and decided to step in earlier on the 1-minute confirmed SPY bounce. Your stock upticks initially, then stalls and sells off even more when the SPY pauses as demonstrated on SBUX in Figure 9.9. As the SPY bounces, your stock continues to fade until you throw in the towel with a stop loss notably because the SPY is reaching a key resistance bumper. Just as you stop out, the stock finally bounces back to where you entered! This drives you nuts as you kick yourself for stopping out too soon before the bounce.

Funny how easy it is to interpret the ailment based on the outcome after the fact. If you stopped out and the stock collapsed much lower, you wouldn't be as upset about taking the stop but still peeved that you stayed in the trade too long and stopped out *late*. If the stock bounces after your stop out, then you kick yourself for not holding on long enough to allow the inevitable bounce and stopped out too *early*.

It's easy for the mind to play these tricks as the market has a tendency to trick the mind into simplifying and curve fitting the ailments based on the outcome. This minimizes what the trader had to work with in the heat of the action and overly takes for granted the hindsightedness of that line of thinking.

FIGURE 9.9 An anomaly sell fade situation with SBUX as it blatantly sell fades the SPY when stacking the charts for comparison.

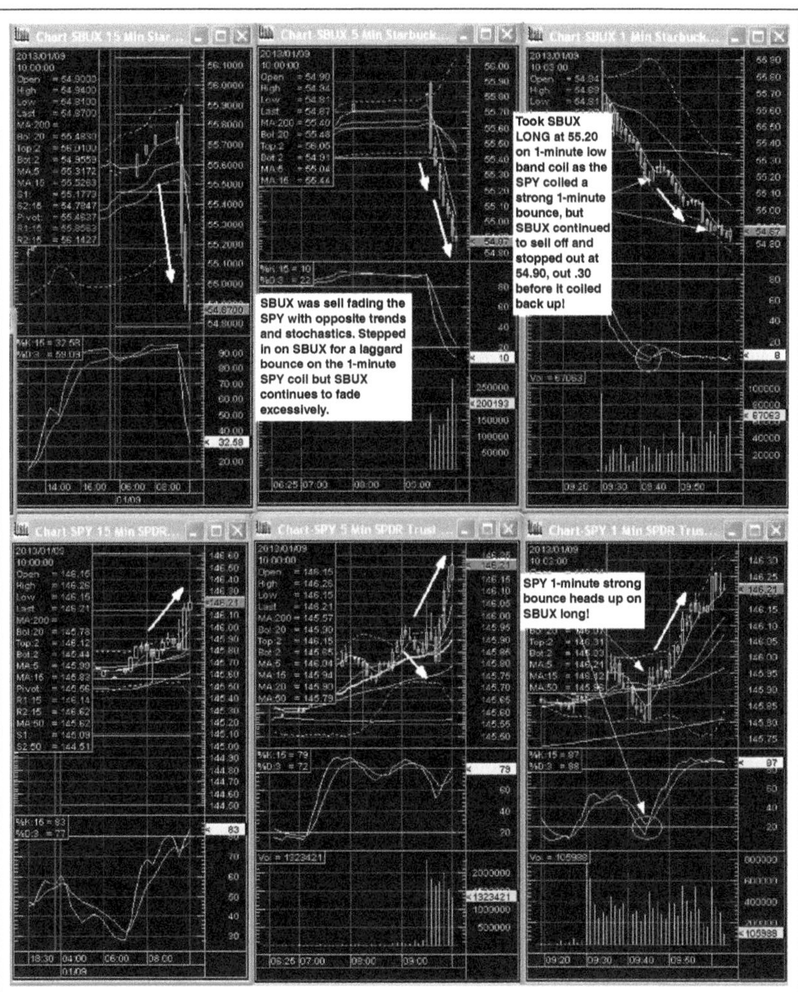

Remedy: First off, you have to identify the situation correctly. When the 5-minute chart exceeds seven consecutive trending candles, this should be qualified as an *excessive grind*. The excessive grind is addressed in Chapter 4 in detail. This is an exception situation, but one that could be very costly if misplayed. It's the exceptions that lead to blowouts and erode the spirit. The play on an excessive grind is to time a solid reversal for reversion trade. This is a situation where the SPY is rising while your stock is excessively falling or vice versa. To play a *reversal for reversion trade*, you have to wait for the following confirmation signals before stepping into the trade:

1. Wait for a 1-minute stochastics cross up.
2. Wait for a reversal candle on the 1- or 5-minute chart.
3. Measure the 5-minute lower Bollinger Band bumper.
4. Measure the meat from the 5-minute lower Bollinger Band bumper to the 5-period moving average and the next bumpers. Make sure there is meat. Measure the 1-minute and the 5-minute counter candle break price trigger (body high price break).
5. Enter on the 1-minute counter candle break with the 20 band stochastics bounce, even better if the 1-minute has a mini pup.
6. Scalp/scale out into the bumpers on the 1-minute and 5-minute charts while trailing the 5-period moving average on the 5- and/or 1-minute chart.

In the SBUX trade illustrated in Figure 9.10, the optimum approach for this play was to follow the above checklist for an entry long on the counter

FIGURE 9.10 SBUX exhaustion long after excessive grind down.

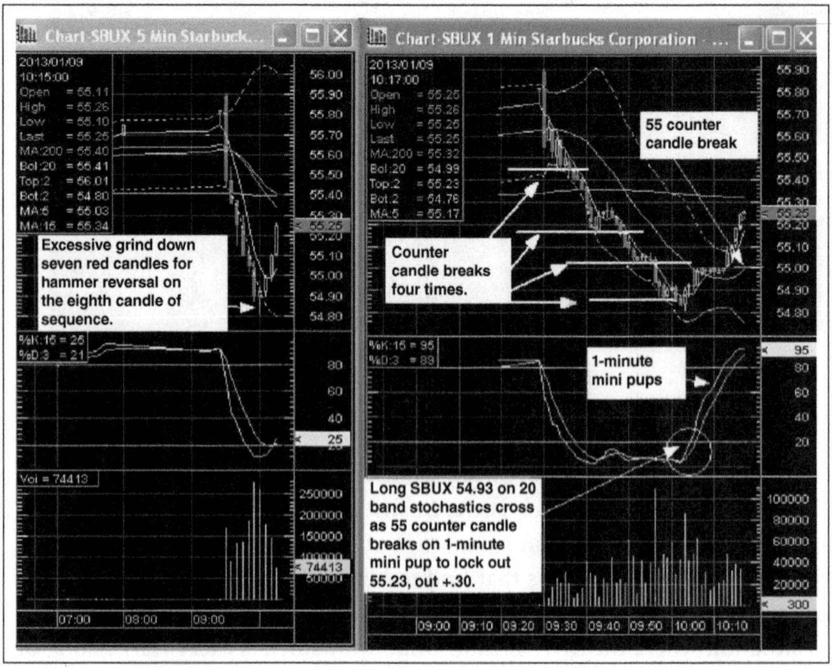

candle break at 54.93 as the one-minute formed a mini pup to the 5-period moving average where it formed another mini pup where it squeezed hard to scalp out 55.23 ahead of the 55.30 coil resistance. You could have taken an initial scale out at 55 and then trailed the 1-minute 5-period moving average break for the counter candle break at 55.02 on the second portion to lock into the 55.20s.

The initial entry at 55.23 on a 1-minute low band stochastics cross was a good entry in most cases; however, it was an early entry without the 20 band cross confirmation and most importantly, lacked a counter candle stress test. The stop out signal was the break of the 55.18 counter candle body low as that triggered a 1-minute inverse pup breakdown, for a –.05 to – .10 precautionary stop. The 1-minute inverse pup indicates a sell-off toward the 54.90 lower Bollinger Band and coil support. Remember that stops are just a pause in your trading to buy time to see if the premises are still intact. Keep in mind that you always have the ability to step back into the trade after taking a precautionary stop.

The reason why the stop should have been taken is because the trend was unflinchingly indisputably down, not up. Don't be so stuck in the short-term reversal attempt that you forget the overall trend is down and the long entry is counter to the trend!

Since the SPY was grinding higher, the other option for the more advanced traders would be a defensive sprawl scale to buy more shares at the 55.93 to 55.85 range to average your price closer to 55.08. This is not something to implement if you are just trying to avoid taking a stop or can't take a stop. This is not recommended for newbies because it can backfire if the SPY sells off or volume picks up on SBUX to the downside. Be very straightforward with yourself and know that if you aren't one that can take stops, then do not implement the DSS because it can compound your losses if you freeze.

Malady: Giving Back Morning Profits

"Market is just chopping me! Made some profits off the open but giving it back now and getting chopped. Everything I touch backfires on me!"

Figure 9.11 is an example of ignoring the climate as it alters from wet during the market open to dry after 11 A.M. EST. As the climate erodes, you should be slowing down your activity or adapting to a more risk-averse mode, but by continuing to trade wet you start to spiral out of control as the losses build. This is like a bad computer virus that infects your mindset as you struggle harder. You are getting frustrated from stops and getting sick from giving back the house money you made earlier. You continue to press

FIGURE 9.11 Dry climate.

trades but keep getting stopped out oftentimes just before the move you were looking for. You try to make up for losses by increasing your size. You score a few winners but can't walk away. You figure a larger allocation should pay off since you are only looking for the smallest moves, but incidentally, you still find yourself getting headfaked and wiggled out of trades. You can't leave your seat anymore and push the envelope of risk by taking even larger shares. Your modest gains in the morning have now turned into large losses with a good chunk from commissions as you find yourself paying less and less attention to the charts and more to the level 2 screen. If you fall into this scenario, it means you are on active tilt and need to immediately get up and walk away.

Remedy: It is urgent that you are able to step outside of yourself and acknowledge that you are quickly heading down a nasty path toward the abyss also known as *going on tilt.* You must take steps to rectify this

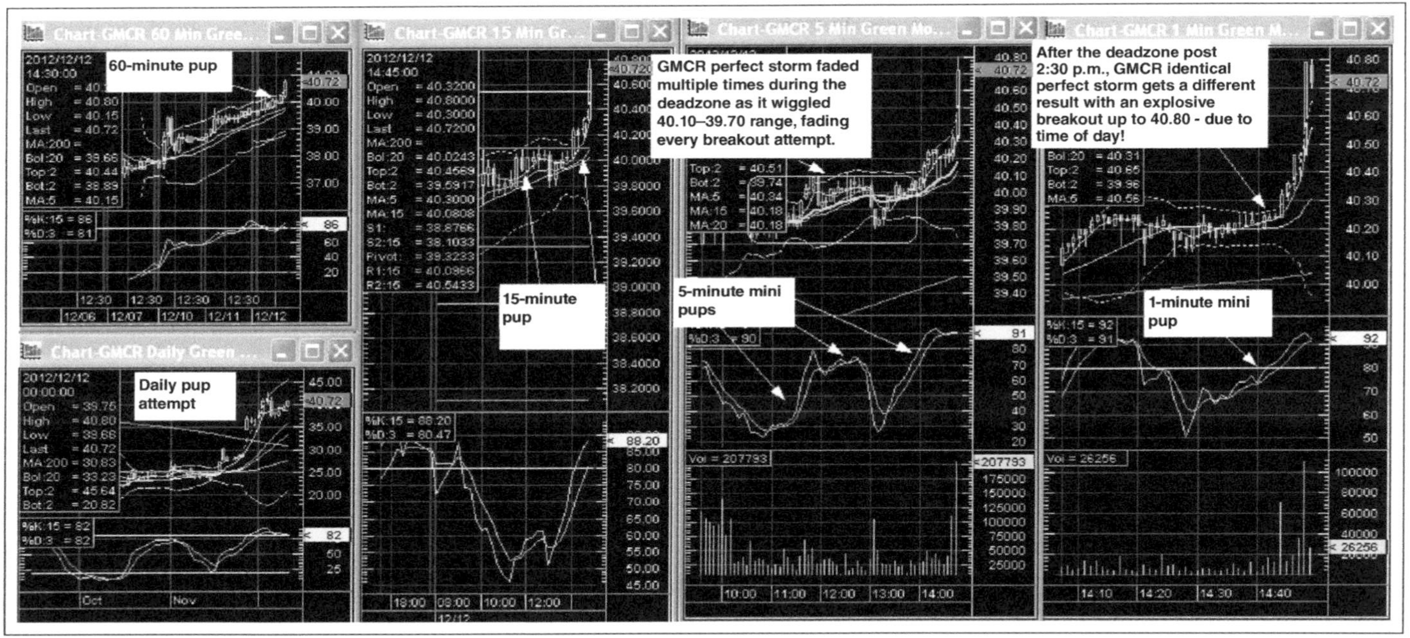

FIGURE 9.12 The contrast of trading GMCR on the identical setup during the dry deadzone climate and the wet post deadzone climate

situation immediately. First and foremost, you must stop trading. It's easier said than done when you are in that highly emotional state where desperation, frustration, and hope are in a three-way rain dance. You are in a dry climate stuck in quicksand and struggling too hard to get out. Quit trading immediately and refer to *The Three Steps for Proper Re-Setting* outlined in Chapter 4.

Malady: Failing to Identify Current Trading Climate

"I'm getting chopped out constantly on my trades. Stock will move up a little but then sell off and stop me right out."

Remedy: Check your 1-minute stochastics entries and make sure you are not chasing 1-minute high bands (above 80) on longs or 1-minute low bands (under 20) on shorts in a dry climate. Wet climates tend to get extended momentum at the 80/20 stochastics bands, whereas dry climates tend to peak quicker beyond those levels and thus exits need to be taken faster. Also make sure there is 'meat' on your entry. Make sure that you are not chasing an entry that is trading near or at an upper Bollinger Band on longs or lower Bollinger Bands on shorts. Most importantly, assess the climate, macro and micro. Chances are you are trading a dry climate that is chopping the 5-minute 5-period moving average on almost every single candle. This is not, nor should it be, a tradable-period. Don't try to fit a square peg into a round hole. Bottom line, quit trading until the wet climate returns. If the macro climate is wet, then it could return later in the day. If the macro climate is dry, then come back in the morning.

Malady: Trading in a Dry Market Climate

"I played a perfect storm breakout this morning for nice profits but got chopped out twice on the same setup in the midday. Then it took off when I finally decided not to play it again! I feel like a sucker, the market chopped me twice and then broke out when I wasn't in!"

Remedy: Can you say *climate*? Once again, this goes right back to defining and identifying wet and dry micro climates. Wet climates form off the open and then revert to dry climates by late morning and early afternoon. A pattern that worked out great in the morning wet climate will often just chop around in the dry climate. The clue will be the rising volume that usually shows up in the last 90 minutes of the day (after the deadzone). Pace yourself to push in the morning wet climate and pull in your trading activity during the mid-day dry climate and slowly push accordingly in the final 90 minutes of the day.

Post-Trade Sequence Analysis

Let's put everything together. It's a good idea to evaluate each trade sequence when things slow down during the day, notably, the ones that may be bothering you. The screen snapshot is incredibly useful when taken at the time of the exits as it captures all the bumper values at the time of the trade and prevents too much hindsight goggle distorting the picture. Keep a folder on your desktop specifically for these screenshots. This is the BEST tool you can use to maintain and sharpen your trading edge.

Everyone makes trades they regret. Whether they took profits too soon or stuck around too long in a losing position. The important aspect is the takeaway from the trade (not just the profit or losses). The money lost on the trade can be transformed into tuition only if properly analyzed and lessons are taken away.

First off, if you are feeling upset about a trade, there is an obvious issue that needs to be addressed to alleviate the stress. It's important to address them with a clear head and early on while they're fresh. Allowing them to linger and fester will gradually build up the interference until disaster exposes the infestation down the road. It's critical to nip the problem in the bud and not let it fester into a mutation. Let's call them maladies. The maladies stem from two types of misplayed actions;

Took entry and/or exit **too soon**.
Took entry and/or exit **too late**.

For example, you took a long on XYZ *too soon* and stopped out when it continued to sell off lower. You took a short on XYZ *too late*, and it bounced against you and stopped you out. You get the picture. The above statements are generalizations but when addressing your maladies, it's important to avoid generalizing and simplifying; otherwise, you will blur the distinction between a well-managed trade and a mismanaged one, which will erode your filtering and selectively edge. It's like a blade that doesn't get sharpened after use. It starts to get dull and ineffective. Think of the post trade sequence analysis as sharpening and maintaining the blade. This will help keep your edge sharp.

Reconstruct the Trade and Conditions Accurately

To assess the trade, break down the following factors first either formally or in the narrative. The narrative is the important portion as you are replaying the action as you remember it. Feel free to include all the feelings you felt afterwards, let it all out.

Climate: (Wet/Dry)
Fade: (None/Buy or sell fade to SPY)
Setup Pattern: (Perfect storm? Dual mini pups? Exhaustion short? etc.)
Allocation: (Number of shares)
Trigger: (1-minute crossover, mini pup, counter candle?)
Entry Stage/Type: (Early, Impact, Late)/Full (single order) or Scaled (multiple orders)
Exit Stage/Type: (Early, Impact [right near the top or bottom], Late)/Full (one exit on all shares) or Scaled (multiple exits)
Anomaly/Normal: Were the conditions to the trade an anomaly (excessive) or normal?

Summary

Provide a first-person narrative of your trade and the thinking before your actions. Make sure to look at the charts at the time of the trade. For this reason, it is a good idea to use a screen capture program like Hypersnap or just MS Paint. Try to note the details of why you took the position and why you took the exits. Mention your fill entries and note any catalysts, fades, nuances, and so forth in a narrative fashion, and BE SPECIFIC. Treat this like a police report where you have to give a detailed account of what happened from your perspective. When you actually write a narrative, it really pinpoints the details and oftentimes brings out nuances you may have noticed but didn't react on. If you have a screenshot, you can actually write your narrative on the screenshot either on paper or on the image. I personally like to write it right on the image and print them out later. This takes some effort but . . . what did we say about putting in the extra effort? The law of reciprocity will make sure you get paid off!

Example: "Took XYZ long on the perfect storm breakout 800 shares on the 1-minute mini pup trigger at 27.72 at the 80 band around 11:35 A.M. SPY took a 1-minute coil on the 5-minute pup. Trimmed out 27.92 on 500 shares, out +.20. The 1-minute peaked at the 5-minute upper Bollinger Bands and slipped 1-minute 80 band cross down through the 5-minute 5-period ma at 27.80 as volume was declining. Waited for 1-minute oscillation all the way down to the 20 band and stopped out the 300 shares at 27.52, out –.20 on the rest. Stupid stupid stupid for sticking around too long!! Because it bounced off 27.50 back to 27.70 after I got shaken out. GRR!! The 15-minute held the 5-period moving average with the mini pup, this was the BOSS chart."

Maladies: What is the actual problem that is causing you the stress? What should you have done based on the information at the time of the trade? Did you actually manage it well and are just upset because you hate taking a loss on remaining shares when you had the chance to scalp the profit.

Example: "I should have taken my profits on the full 800 shares at the 1-minute high band mini pups into the liquidity since it was a known resistance and dry climate! The SPY also had peaked out and sold off even before the 1-minute peaked on XYZ. I noticed the 1-minute upper Bollinger Band hooked DOWN— and ignored it—d'oh! I should have at least stopped out on the rest of the profits when the 1-minute broke the 5-period moving average at 27.75 as volume was slipping. Next time, I will just scalp it out in the dry climate and not sit through the tumbleweeds as volume evaporates going into deadzone! Macro market dry climate and intraday dry climate was the key to selling it all. Will do next time!!"

Remedies: This is where you write down your takeaways based on the information and summary. BE SPECIFIC.

Example: "Next time, I will scalp out the full position in the dry climate or at least sell 600 out on the first batch with a tight trail stop on the 1-minute 5-period ma break. If the upper 1-minute Bollinger Band hooks down with declining volume, then I will dump it all. I can always re-enter if need be. I had no interest in riding the 15-minute chart since the upper Bollinger Bands were around 28.05 anyways. No reason to give back profits in a dry climate. Got it! Breathe . . . move on!"

Does this sound familiar? It's the same trade assessment you would normally do prior to making the trade. It's important not to make unfair apples to oranges comparisons. In many cases, you will find that you did take the most efficient actions at the time of the trade. It's important to also place yourself back in the eye of the storm, which shouldn't be hard to do if it's something that is really bothering you as you subconsciously replay the trade numerous times. The screenshot taken at the time of the trade is most helpful. I can't stress this enough. It keeps the analysis accurate without having to rely on memory or after too much time has lapsed which makes the hindsight goggles even stickier.

The purpose of the replay is to gauge if there were any clues at the time of the trade that would have allowed you to take more efficient actions. Trying to apply hindsight analysis based on how the trade played out five minutes after your exit is futile. Try to take yourself back to the minute that you executed the trade(s) or at the point where you should have executed the trade. This is like doing a system restore on a Windows-based PC. You want to take yourself back to the identical conditions leading up to and during the trade in order to apply a solid analysis.

CHAPTER 10

Portfolio Trading: The Skillset of the Evolved Hybrid Market Predator

The greatest mistake you can make in life is to be continually fearing you will make one.

—Elbert Hubbard

Way of the Trade has guided you so far toward the path we stand in front of now. Educating yourself on the philosophies and history of current market landscape dynamics and how they came to be in Chapters 1 and 2. Use Chapter 3 to construct your morning ritual to prepare for the trading day. Use Chapter 4 to learn the Katana. Educate and train yourself on the nuances and applications of the perfect storm pattern in Chapter 5. Use Chapter 6 to apply the four-level research to evaluate stock candidates. Use the information from Chapter 7 to screen, qualify, and filter for prospects. Use Chapter 8 to track and stalk the most viable candidates. Chapter 9 goes through all the steps to prepare and manage your trades and the proper application of the Katana. Now we approach the ultimate destiny. All roads (and chapters) lead to this destination.

Portfolio trading employs the integration of all three skillsets working in unison to attain the cumulative effect. The strengths of one offset the deficiencies of another and vice versa throughout the alternating situations you will encounter. It's like a vampire, werewolf, and witch all merged into one, a hybrid predator. Your armor is triple-layered with the protection and your Katana is triple reinforced to effectively handle any encounter.

Market-Calibrated Portfolio Creation and Management

Think of your portfolio as a palette that includes trading stocks and positions stocks. The portfolio is not the traditional sense of the word referring only to positions, but is all-inclusive of the trades you make. Professionals also refer to this as a book. You want to grow and harvest your book. Make sure that you have daytrading margin and at least a level 3 options approval to write covered calls and options spread trades. In the past, I advocated a separation of daytrading and position accounts. You can still do this if you haven't acclimated to a swing trading temperament. It's important that you don't treat position trades like day trades. Position trades are premeditated and planned. It may take some time to acclimate to both temperaments. Once you are acclimated, it is preferred that you merge them into a single account for convenience and accessibility as well as consolidation of data and software fees. If you feel more comfortable with separated accounts, then it is okay to keep them separated as long as you have simultaneous access to both.

We are constantly on the lookout for playable stocks not only on an intraday basis but also for swing and core position considerations. In order to efficiently construct a portfolio, we first have to determine general allocations of capital for daytrading and positions (swings and longer-term core) and adjust them with terrain changes. In dry macro market climates, the flat terrain tends to favor more position trades. In wet macro market climates, the additional volatility of the terrain tends to favor more intraday trading. This isn't an absolute, but more of a general guideline to place your emphasis. It is also very helpful when trying to diagnose periods of weak performance. Oftentimes you may find yourself with losing long positions in a bull market. As it turns out, the terrain may be the issue as the wet climate creates better intraday volatility that results in a net decline in the positions and exposure to gaps down.

Then we have to assess the general market trend to determine the direction of the macro market headwinds. Naturally a bullish uptrending market favors more long positions and vice versa on bearish downtrending markets. All the materials from the prior chapters apply in the portfolio construction and management process. Be sure to refer back to prior chapters as reference to each step. Let's get started.

General Capital Allocation

General capital allocation is split between intraday trading and position trading. If you have consolidated your trading capital into one account, then determine what percent you will be using for the daytrading versus position trading. Keep in mind that daytrading gives you 4-to-1 leverage intraday and 2-to-1 overnight for positions. As a rule, we want to keep margin usage limited to intraday. Position trades should rarely dip into margin. That is to ensure we don't run the risk of a margin call since these trades always run the risk of a gap working against us. Just because you've allocated it, doesn't mean you have to use it. Always leave a buffer of capital (ammo) available, and only tap margin on the shortest duration of exposure intraday if needed. As they say, it's better to have a gun and not need it than need it and not have one. In trading terms, that gun is actually ammo, known as buying power. With a single consolidated account, you must always be aware of your buying power throughout the day and make sure that you don't take overnights beyond the 2-to-1 threshold. This can be an easy oversight during especially volatile sessions. With daytrading, the emphasis is on closure of exposure. If a daytrade goes overnight, it should be consciously converted to position trade allocation and rules.

If you have two separate accounts apportioned to daytrading and position trading, then you've already determined the allocation split of total capital. Despite the conventional notion of daytrading being risky and position trading being passive and lower risk, the reality is the opposite. The essence of well-managed intraday trading is shaped around rapid closure of positions to eliminate exposure risk while simultaneously trying to lock in profits or minimize losses. Closure is the elimination of risk by zeroing out exposure.

Due to the risk-averse nature of intraday trading, we want to allocate a higher allocation of total capital to that side initially. The ratio will adjust as opportunities, market conditions, and climates change. Of course, your account size will determine this as well. The PDT (pattern day trading) rules require a minimum of $25,000 to be able to actively trade; otherwise it limits activity to no more than four round trips (buy and sell of complete position) in a week. I personally think this outdated rule hurts traders more than it helps. It inadvertently pushes those who fall under the 25k rule to pursue riskier leveraged financial products like options, futures, currencies, and commodities where the participants are more well-armed and unified. It forces traders to take overnight positions, which inherently elevate risk by extending the holding period leaving the positions susceptible to adverse price gaps. I would hope the regulators come to their senses and adjust this reckless rule. It is another factor behind the ever-declining volumes in the markets as it only hurts the retail traders. For this reason as well, it helps to consolidate to one account so that neither account risks the threat of PDT violation. As for starting capital, I would stress at least $50k of risk capital. The greater your bankroll, the more buffer you will have.

Activity Allocation = General Capital Allocation

Ideally, you want to keep an initial 2-to-1 daytrading-to-position-trading ratio. This is a capital and activity allocation. If you find your time constrained for intraday trading activities, then *you must allocate a more realistic ratio that is proportionate to your availability.* As I said, this is the initial allocation, but it will adjust in time to your schedule and market conditions. You may only be available for the first hour of the day, and then you want to adjust to a 30/70 split. You will be using margin for daytrading. The key takeaway is to have the additional buying power available when needed. This keeps the door open to execute defensive/offensive sprawl and double hedge sword sequence trades without being forced to liquidate positions.

Risk Averse Nature of Intraday Trading

Daytrading places more emphasis on probability factors over the conventional risk-reward theory. Higher probability and well managed execution are the primary considerations. For example, if there is a 80 percent probability of a stock moving from 36.15 to 36.40 overlap bumper resistance based on a tightening perfect storm triggered by a 1-minute lower band mini pup with rising 15 and 5-minute period moving averages at 35.80 and 35.60 as the SPY bounces, it tells me that my potential upside is + .25 reward versus –.50 risk to the downside. That is a 2-to-1 risk-to-reward ratio, which would make conventional thinkers squirm as it goes against the preferred 1-to-3 risk-to-reward ratio they have been taught to believe in. What they don't take into account is probability. If all things equal on the probability side, then it would be a dumb trade. However, we know that perfect storms are the highest of probability. The 80 percent probability arms us with a greater chance of hitting the upside before hitting the downside as long as we implement closure and time our exits before liquidity dries up. Also consider that if we shorten the upside price, we proportionally raise the probability. The probability moves higher as the reward moves lower. We can offset the reward drop by increasing the position size with more leverage. However, that would increase our allocation exposure. We can offset that portion of risk by shortening our duration of holding time. As the stock price rises, we offset risk by scaling out the position into the liquidity in an upside-down pyramid scale allocation by trimming out the most down to smaller shares. The risk drops proportionally as the price reward rises until we close out the position completely. Therefore, it would be more risk averse to take 2,000 shares at 36.15 and start to scale out at 36.25 and higher, than to take 500 shares and scalp it out at 36.38. This takes into consideration the other reality that we are not the only participants watching that 36.40 bumper resistance. We have to assume others will try to step in front as well. By lowering our initial exit area, we sacrifice price appreciation in exchange for higher probability and liquidity. We offset this by raising our size and cutting our duration of exposure to balance things out. As the stock pops to 36.42, we scaled out 36.25 for +.10 on 1,500 shares and locked 36.38 for +.23 on 500 shares, grabbing a +$265 profit versus a +$115 profit. Ironically, the latter takes on more risk due to the longer duration of holding period, which exposes the position to possibilities of a rogue sell-off and more slippage before bumper price hits. *The heavier leveraged trade was less risky reaping more reward than the lower leveraged "safer" play.* Less risk reaped over twice the reward than the "safer" play. Of course the stock could bounce to 36.42, reject, and collapse back down to 35.70. The likelihood of this is higher if the 60-minute chart is showing an inverse pup and mini inverse pup and the 5- and 15-minute stochastics are already at lofty high bands above 90. *An experienced, skilled trader will not wait for this to happen.*

Her Majesty, Queen Leverage

Leverage must be respected and graciously catered to. She is the queen. Assume any less and it is off to the gallows. She will uphold a reciprocal relationship as long as you diligently uphold your end. The purpose of using higher leverage (calling on the queen) is to cut the price target and duration of time in the trade without diminishing the net profit potential. You must uphold your end of the deal but executing closure sooner NOT later. To do any less is a slap in the face; not doing so is a recipe for disaster. Her vengeance is swift, ruthless, and merciless. She is the number one cause of blow-ups, tilts, and account blowouts.

Unfortunately, this is the common pitfall with newbies and even experienced traders. They aren't taught or have not gained the required respect for Her Majesty. She can be your greatest ally in battle or your worst nemesis. If you acknowledge and diligently honor her rules, then she will aid you in your time of need. This means don't overuse here, don't misuse her, and don't break the agreement. Mock her at your own peril. As in life and trading, treat the ladies with respect, honor, and reciprocity—or face the abyss . . . no joke.

Application of Well-Managed Allocation Management

As I illustrated the dynamic nature of risk-to-reward ratios, I hope you realized a key point. Every action you take will have an effect on the ratio. Not only is risk to reward dynamic, but can be altered. This may be a new concept to many traders. Yes, you can deliberately alter the risk to reward ratio, as it pertains to you! You are in control, as long as you understand the flow. Following are the rules that apply to effectively controlling your risk-to-reward ratio on every trade, scalp, or swing:

Lower Expected Price Target = Raises Probability
Raised Probability = Raise Leverage (Higher Shares)
Raised Leverage = Quicker Closer (Faster Exits)
Raise Expected Price Target = Lowers Probability
Lowered Probability = Lower Leverage (Less Shares)
Lower Leverage = Longer Closer (Slower Exits)

This is a trade management application. It assumes the trade in consideration is a high-probability trade. It doesn't measure the probability of the setup. That has to be shored up in the pretrade sequence. This may seem like common sense. It makes sense but is not practiced commonly. For you, it should be. Incorporate this into the structure of every managed trade, and your consistency will improve.

truTV: "Not Reality. Actuality"

A well-managed daytrade runs circles around the conventional notion of the 3-to-1 reward to risk. The market rarely gives those types of opportunities, and when they arise, they don't sit around waiting for people to jump in. The algo/HFTs are all over them. The risk to reward is always dynamic, not static. It is theory until proven. The job of a trader is to balance the theory with reality and game the actuality. It's like the truTV slogan, "Not reality. Actuality." That sums up well-managed trading in a nutshell.

Constructing the Portfolio

This task is not as daunting as it may seem. In fact, if you have been progressing through the book, you should already have minder lists full of corganic stocks and headliners. You should have a stalking minder of stocks with alerts/

alarms set for price triggers complete with notes on each individual setup. Right? If not, then get to work compiling those lists. If so, then continue.

Portfolio trading is not a new frontier that you are traversing, but an amalgamation of the existing territory you have already treaded. If you followed the flow of this book, you have inadvertently begun constructing your portfolio. Our definition of portfolio encompasses your accumulating universe of playable stocks.

What defines portfolio trading is the *active balancing* of the deficient areas according to the initial general capital allocations. If we allocated a 2-to-1 daytrading-to-position-trading allocation and currently have no position trades, then we must either change our allocation ratio or actively seek out position trades. This is what distinguishes portfolio trading from just straight daytrading or swing trading. We have to maintain the balance according to our predetermined general capital allocation. If nothing currently looks appealing for a position trade, this is not a problem as long as you have actively put in the efforts to scan, search, and filter through at least the level 2 research process on candidates to get to a stalking point. *Don't ever force yourself to curve fit an inadequate position trade just for the sake of appeasing the ratio with a position.* This is not the point. It's the motive behind the expended effort that matters the most, not the position. This means that you MUST allocate your time and effort on a 2-to-1 ratio for daytrades and position trades. Therefore you must allocate your time proportionately, or change the ratio.

It means that the stalking minder should always contain position candidates with alert triggers. Get in the habit of feeding and replenishing the stalking minder on a daily basis. Update, adjust, or remove candidates that are no longer viable.

The macro market assessment is something that you perform premarket with a SPY analysis. The holding period on position trades will vary accordingly with the wider time frame boss chart premises.

General Macro Market Analysis and Allocation Assessment

This is part of the morning ritual as outlined in Chapter 3. The only additional factors to consider are running the same FAST chart analysis on the QQQ and DIA. The QQQ analysis helps if you are especially heavy in technology stocks. The DIA analysis helps if you are especially heavy on transports, financials, and consumer products, or Dow Jones components. You also gain a larger bird's eye perspective to gauge any divergence amongst the indexes.

Granted these are price weighted, so the biggest priced components will have the heaviest impact, especially with the DIA, which can corrupt the picture. The SPY is naturally the top preference due to its sample size of 500 stocks as opposed to just 100 for the QQQ and 30 for the DIA.

1. Run a FAST SPY (QQQ and DIA are optional) chart analysis on the daily, weekly, and monthly charts.
   a. Determine general trend, notable setups, and bumpers: Mini pups or pups? Perfect storms? Include bumpers.
   b. Determine general market climate: wet or dry?
   c. When market headwinds are in a general longer time frame upswing, then longs should be allocated more over shorts. The opposite applies during general market downdrafts where shorts should receive a higher allocation over long positions. This depends on your comfort level with holding short positions. If you want to play conservatively, then make it a habit to at least trim the allocations on longs during downdrafts as opposed to taking direct shorts, especially if you are trading in an IRA (which doesn't allow for shorts). You can substitute put contracts or opt to hedge with short positions through leveraged inverse sector exchange traded funds (ETFs).
2. Adjust position trading allocations as needed. This applies to the percent per trade of what has already been allocated to position trading split of general capital (i.e., if the split has allocated \$30k of capital to position trades, then the maximum capital you can use for a single position will be \$9.3k or 30 percent). This is just the initial allocation as we look to trim that down ultimately to a less than 10 percent portion if it turns out to be a core position, following the Queen's rules of leverage. *More details on this under Position Trade Considerations just ahead.*

Qualifying the Three Types of Trade Considerations

There are three types of trades you will be making in your portfolio: intraday trades, swing trades, and core positions. Each of these types of trades plays to its respective skillsets of daytrading, swing trading, and investing. The differentiating factors are setup, capital allocation, duration of holding period, and price range variance. Each type of trade has its own set of rules and conditions, which I will review. One thing to keep in mind, trades can start as one type and convert into another type of trade. As long as this transition is deliberate, premeditated, and well managed, there are no issues. As you will see with core positions, I like to actually step in with a swing allocation, or even a daytrading allocation, and start to scale it down to a core position. Meanwhile, the extra profits attained during the daytrading portion give us a good buffer of profits to make the core hold easier.

However, be very honest with yourself in that you don't allow a bad daytrade to turn into an even worse swing trade simply because you couldn't bring yourself to take the stop loss. This is a no-no. When in doubt, get out!

Daytrading Considerations

Daytrading or intraday trading is most effective with an abundance of participants. This can be gauged by the heavy volume, volatility, momentum, price movement follow-through, and fast action. It may seem a daunting task to look for all those qualities prior to the trade. I'll make it easy. It's called a wet climate. You will find it consistently off the market open every trading day from 9:30 to 10:15 A.M. (some mornings may extend the action to 11 A.M.) and in the last 30 to 90 minutes of the day. However, keep in mind that the day is long in the tooth, making the price levels very rigid. Unless volume picks up tremendously or the SPY makes a very strong move, expect smaller price movement. Be aware that the end of the day is not the market open!

Allocations are determined by the probability of the setup and your entry stage. Perfect storms carry the highest probability. The defining factor of daytrading is the closure of positions intraday. You don't take positions overnight on daytrades. Does this mean never ever take overnights? Not quite. If a trade looks compelling going into the close (e.g., wider time frame perfect storm finally triggers as the 60-minute stochastics finally crosses up in the last hour), then you will have to convert it into a swing trade position. This means you have to make sure you are adjusted to the position trade allocation rules. *These will be covered in the Position Trade Considerations coming up.*

Intraday Trade Profiles

There are two kinds of daytrades you will be making during the intraday session. While they are both closed out before the end of the day, the similarities end there. Scalps involve precision entry and exits with the highest concentration of shares, which require the shortest holding period. Range trades are similar to swing trading but on an intraday time frame where the trade is closed out before the market close. Daytrades can start off as a scalp entry and then scaled down as profits are taken to a smaller position that you may wish to range trade for a longer holding period intraday. This allows traders to control their risk in proper alignment with probability.

SCALP Trade

Type of trade:	**SCALP**
Leverage per trade:	50 to 100 percent of daytrading portion of portfolio allocation
Setups:	Perfect storms, dual pup/mini pups, exhaustion/countertrend, reversion, oscillations, slingshots/rug pulls
Position duration:	1 to 20 minutes
Priority charts:	15-minute, 5-minute, 1-minute
Research level:	Level 1–2
Risk factors:	Algo/HFTs, liquidity vaporization, dry climates

These are highest share positions taken for the shortest duration of holding time. Scalps seek to capture a direct move with the most minimal of wiggles. Scalps are usually taken on a single entry unless you are working an early-stage entry where you are scaling into a position, or executing a defensive sprawl scaling trade, offensive sprawl sequence, or double hedged sword sequence. These will require more leverage, which naturally means less holding time. As a rule, limit the scaled entries to a maximum of three to four. Leverage is called upon the most in this type of trade. Be vigilant in taking stops when the patterns aren't reacting. Stops buy that precious time needed to grasp a little more transparency to consider re-entry or reversal. Exits are usually scaled out in one to three pieces contingent on market climate and stage of entry. Dry climates with late entries should be avoided. Stick to the wet climates every morning. The first 30 minutes of the market open tend to offer the richest opportunities. The last 90 minutes of the day are a coin toss, depending on the overall market climate. Earnings seasons tend to give better action, especially when gapper/dumpers spend all day setting up a perfect storm in the direction of the gap in the last hour.

Case Study: RIMM Short Scalp on Perfect Storm Breakdowns

On 1/28/2013, as Figure 10.1 illustrates, RIMM collapsed from 17.60s to 16.20s before making a spike back to 17 where it rejected and started a choppy erosion. The 60-minute mini inverse pup had a green counter candle at 16.65. The 5-minute mini pup tightening attempt started to fail while the 1-minute stochastics formed a series of stair-step mini inverse pups.

FIGURE 10.1 RIMM short scalp.

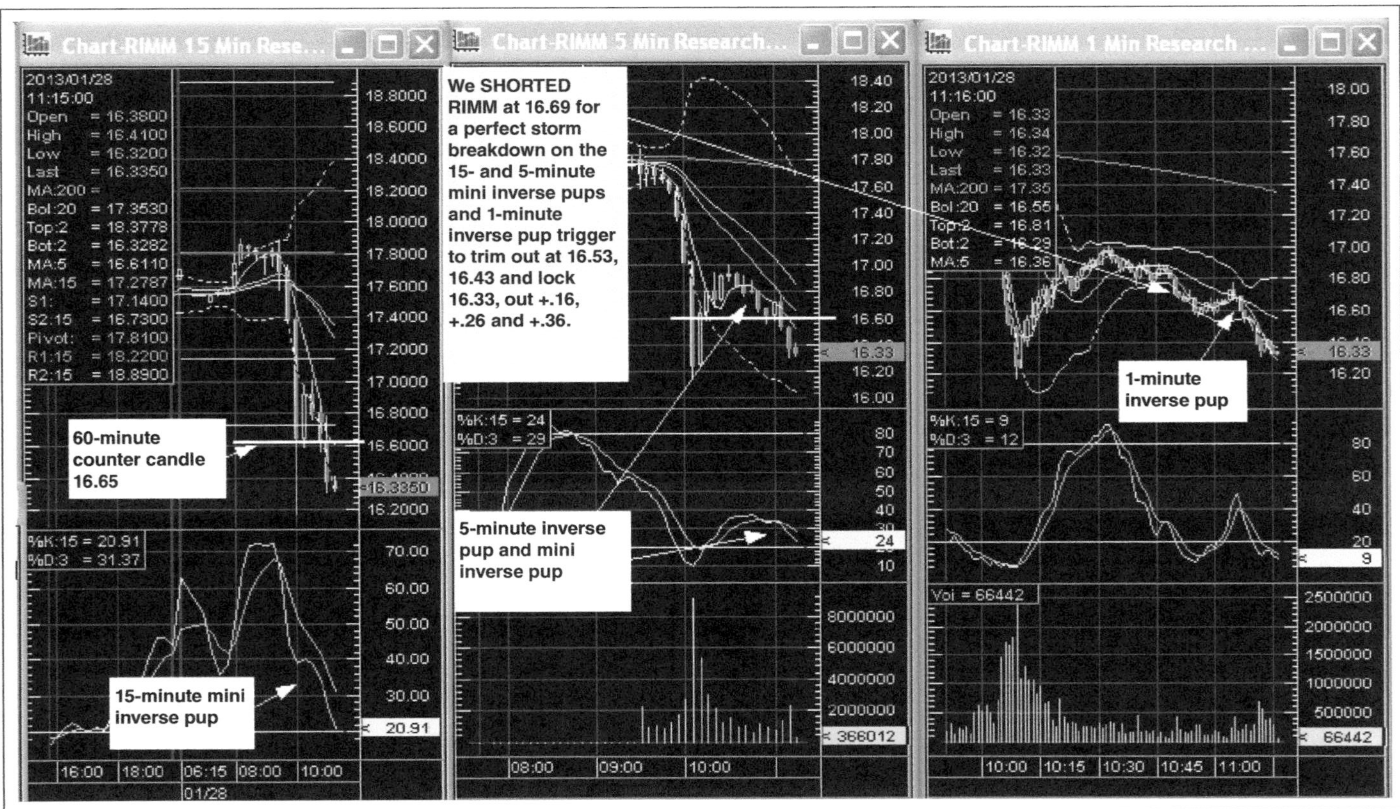

We used the 1-minute mini inverse pup trigger for entry signal to short RIMM at 16.69 for a perfect storm breakdown on a 15-minute mini inverse pup, 5-minute inverse pup, and 1-minute mini inverse pup to scale out scalp exits at 16.53, 16.43, and closed it completely at 16.43, out +.36. The macro market was in a choppy dry climate, but RIMM had set up a very compelling perfect storm breakdown which in turn generated the volume giving it a wet climate.

Case Study: RIMM Long Scalp on Perfect Storm Breakout

On 1/30/2013, as Figure 10.2 illustrates, RIMM set up a 60-minute mini pup going into the market open. The 15-minute stochastics crossed back up as well. We took RIMM long at 16.12 on the 1-minute counter candle break above 16.08 for a perfect storm breakout to scale out scalps at 16.25, out +.12 and locked 16.32, out +.20 in a 3-minute trade. This scalp was made off the wet climate market open, which supplied plenty of liquidity and momentum. As dry climate sets in, a +.20 price move could take several hours to achieve.

RANGE Trade

Type of trade:	**RANGE**
Leverage:	25 to 50 percent of daytrading portion of portfolio allocation
Setups:	Perfect storms, dual pup/mini pups, exhaustion/countertrend, reversion, oscillations
Position duration:	30 minutes to hours
Priority charts:	60-minute, 15-minute, 5-minute
Research level:	Levels 1–2
Risk factors:	Algo/HFTs, liquidity vaporization, dry climates

Range trades are the equivalent of an intraday swing trade. The position is still closed out same day. These trades are taken with 25 to 50 percent of the allocation for a scalp trade. Many times, range trades are the remaining shares of a scalp trade that has been scaled down. These trades are taken due to a dominant trend based on the 60-minute and 15-minute charts with the 5-minute chart in alignment. Range trades weather the 1-minute downdrafts while focusing on the wider intraday time frames for an accurate trend reading. The 60-minute chart tends to work as the anchor. Oftentimes, wider time frame perfect storms continue to grind after the scalp and you may opt to ride it out longer.

FIGURE 10.2 RIMM long scalp.

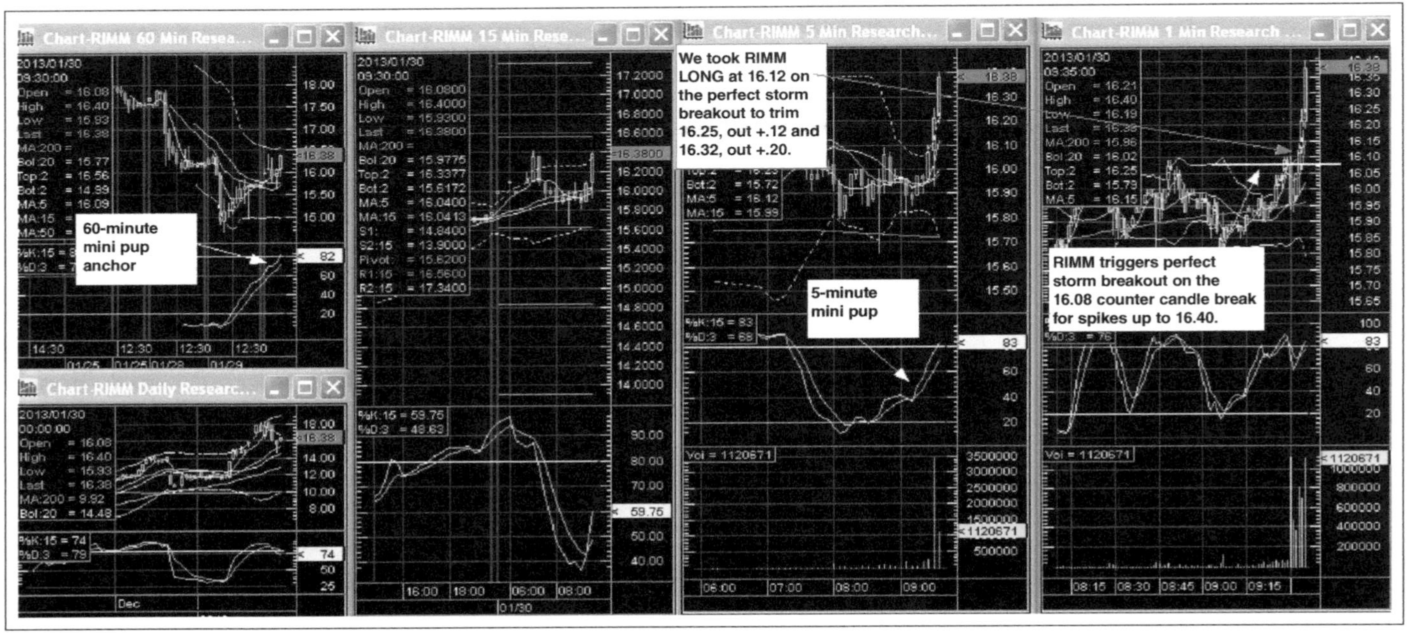

Stocks that traditionally trade under 500,000 shares a day may carry wider bid ask spreads representing the thinner liquidity, which will often require a shift to the swing trader skillset. The key distinction is the smaller share allocation and longer holding time. These may also be premeditated and taken as a range trade from the initial entry. These can convert to a position trade if taken overnight. Make sure to adjust to the position trade allocation when doing this.

Case Study: MGAM Range Trade Long on Breakout

1/30/2013—MGAM is traditionally a thin volume stock. Figure 10.3 shows that the morning after the earnings report price reaction, MGAM had a strong beat and raised guidance causing a gap up. MGAM shook out lots of the early impulse buyers as it sold off from 16.50s to 15.50s stinky 5s level before coiling back through the 60-minute 5-period moving average at 16.10. The bid/ask spreads were as wide as .20! We let it solidify a base above 16.10 to solidify a 60-minute mini pup breakout anchor. The 15-minute chart shorted a pup breakout and a mini pup above 16.20. The 5-minute chart showed a mini pup as well. This was a perfect storm forming. We took MGAM long at 16.34 around 10:30 A.M. It initially spiked up to 16.70 on the 1-minute mini pup and then fell down to 16.15 to shake out weak hands. *This is why it is so important to be familiar with the stock you are trading.* We continued to hold with more priority set on the 60-minute, 15-minute, and 5-minute charts. As the 1-minute stochastics crossed back up MGAM resumed its perfect storm breakout. We used the liquidity spikes to scale out at 16.75, 17.10, and final shares at 17.35 into momentum for +.41, +.75, and +1.01 profits. We anticipated the 17.50 de facto resistance level and closed out the trade ahead of it. While this trade didn't take hours to play out, we did manage it based on the wider time frames, which kept us in the trade on the wiggles to 16.15s before the big steady bounce and perfect storm breakout resumption.

Position Trade Profiles

These trades carry the added risk of exposure to price gap and headline risk with the longer holding period as a trade-off for larger price range moves. Ideally, you are aiming for a positive gap in your favor based on the wider time frame charts. Swing trades holding times can vary from overnight to several weeks. Core positions may be held for weeks to months. Equal emphasis is placed on the fundamentals as with the technicals.

FIGURE 10.3 MGAM ranged long trade.

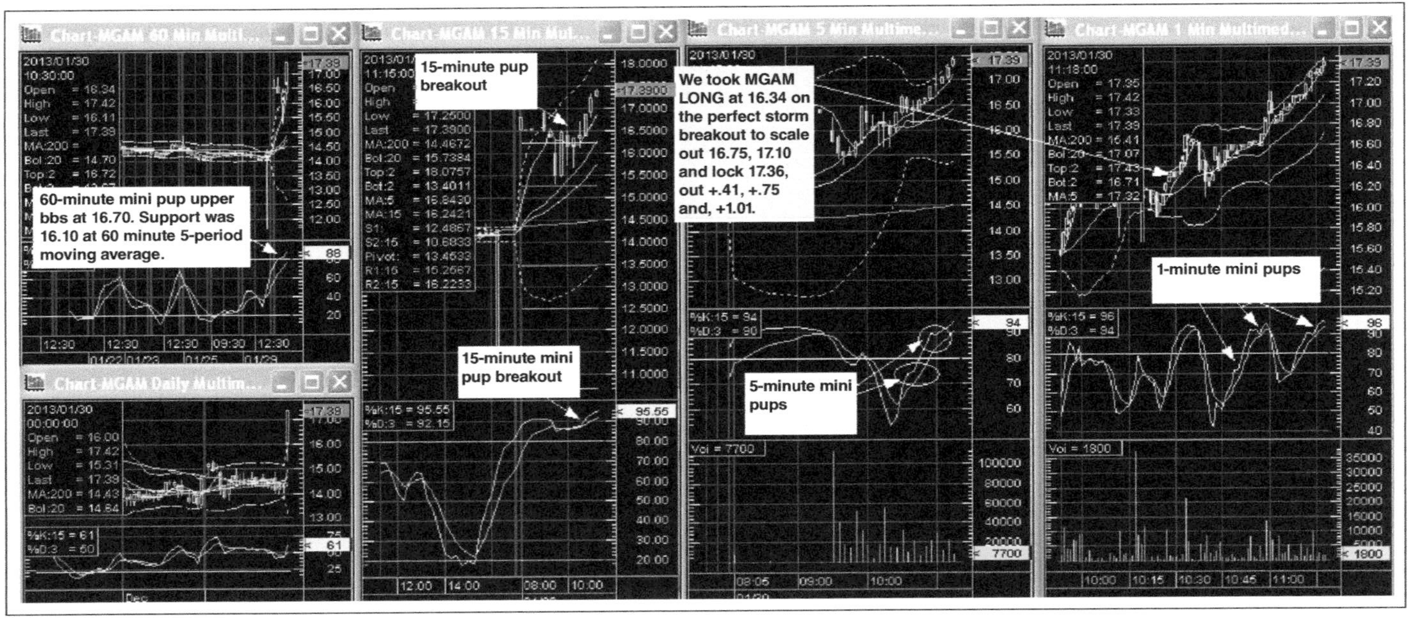

Intraday traders have to condition themselves to be more patient and passive with overnight holds. Initial positions as small as 10 to 50 shares should be taken for several days to condition the buildup comfort levels gradually with holding positions.

Adjusting Position Allocation Percentages

Based on general market trend and climate, you should adjust your allocation percentages per position. Max percent of position capital per trade should rarely exceed 30 percent for a single position. These are percentages of the position trade allocation determined from the total capital earlier. If you have a $90k total portfolio account and allocate 2 to 1, daytrades ($60k) to position trades ($30k) general allocation, then the 30 percent maximum position allocation would be around $9k per single position. In regard to headline event risk, this pertains to whether the markets are focused on any particular headline event risk or focusing on itself. Earnings periods tend to shift market focus back to components whereas the gap between earnings seasons is where the market tends to get attention deficit disorder and latch onto headline event risks like the European debt crisis, Greek defaulting, and so forth. You can gauge this by monitoring Bloomberg TV and CNBC if they continually keep focusing on specific headlines or events. Here's a breakdown of recommended allocation percentages within the position trade portion of your portfolio.

> *30 percent = Most wet climate with perfect storm macro market headwinds aligned with highest probability perfect storm set-up to specific stock: Strong correlation with SPY: Minimal headline event risk.*
> *20 percent = Wet climate with trend intact: Good correlation with SPY: Flat headline event risk.*
> *10 percent = Dry climate with trend/consolidation in mid to upper range: Weak correlation with SPY: Rising headline event risk.*
> *5 percent = Extremely dry climate with thin liquidity and/or abundance of gap risk: No correlation with SPY: Overwhelming headline event risk.*

If you are new to position trading, then cut all the above percentages by 50 percent or more until you gradually build your threshold to handle the wider price swings that come with the holds. Don't slack on the filters, just cut down the exposure so you can focus on the trade without the presence of fear from carrying overnight positions.

SWING Trade

Type of trade:	**SWING**
Leverage per trade:	10 to 30 percent portion of position trade portfolio allocation
Setups:	Daily perfect storms, breakouts/breakdowns, exhaustion/countertrend, trend reversals
Position duration:	1 day to weeks
Priority charts:	Weekly, daily, 60-minute
Research level:	Levels 1–3
Risk factors:	Gap risk, headline/event risk

These are positions taken with the intent of holding at several days to weeks based on the wider time frame patterns tempered with fundamentals. Overnight gap plays fall under these allocations and rules as well. As the pattern plays out we look to scale out usually upwards of three exits. The initial exit should be at least 50 to 70 percent of the position. On those swing trades that are still valid technically and fundamentally, we can opt to convert the remaining shares into a core position. These positions can also be taken with options to increase leverage without the capital restraint. It's very important to remember that directional options take on erosion so keep duration times limited to one to five days maximum on these types of trades. Sell sooner rather than later.

Case Study: UA Jan 45 Call Options Swing Trade

The footwear sector was very strong on 12/17/2012 as NKE, LULU, CROX, FL, FINL were all showing strength on their daily charts in uptrends near their upper Bollinger Bands. There was one stock that was completely fading the sector momentum, Under Armor (NYSE Symbol: UA). We stalked this one intraday and determined a swing trade was definitely in the cards. We allocated 10 percent due to the overextended nature of the markets on dry climate thinner liquidity.

As illustrated in Figure 10.4, we took long 8 UA Jan 45 call options at 3.60 as UA was trading in the 47.30s as the daily was trying to form a hammer, and the 60-minute stochastics were finally crossing up through the 20 band with 15-minute mini pups. UA was still trading under its daily lower Bollinger Bands at 48.10. *The premise was for a laggard bounce triggered by a daily hammer and slingshot bounce upon piercing the daily lower Bollinger Bands back up.* UA proceeded to chop around 47.50 to 47.80s into the close.

The next morning UA gapped above the 48.10 daily lower Bollinger Bands as the 60-minute, 15-minute, and 5-minute all triggered mini pups off

FIGURE 10.4 UA long call options swing trade.

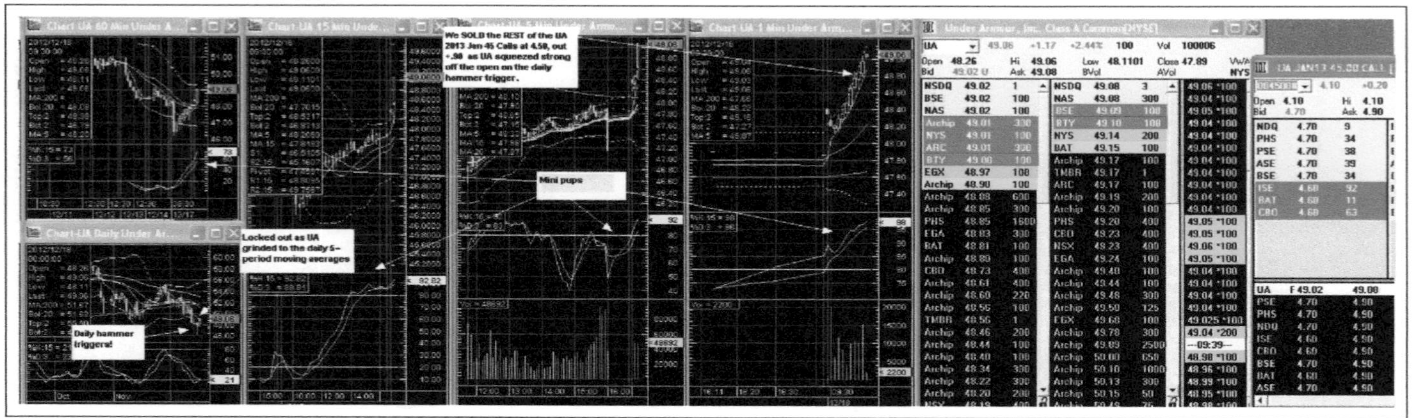

the open. This is called a . . . tightening perfect storm! UA proceeded to blast higher off the open toward the daily 5-period moving average bumper at 49. Since this was an exhaustion slingshot trade, we proceeded to sell the position at 4.50, out +.90 gain for a +$720 profit (+24 percent gain). UA proceeded to trade upward to 50 that day as the options went as high as 6.20! We took profits quickly into the liquidity because of the dry macro market climate. This was proven to be prudent as UA proceeded to sell off again back down to 46s and the UA Jan 45 calls fell back under the 3.20s!

CORE Trade

Type of trade:	**CORE**
Leverage per trade:	3 to 10 percent portion of position trade portfolio allocation
Setups:	Perfect storms, undervalued/sector laggard, turn-around/restructuring, undiscovered hot market theme, takeover/spin-off candidate
Position duration:	Weeks to months
Priority charts:	Weekly, daily, 60-minute
Research level:	Level 4
Risk factors:	Gap risk, headline/event risk

These are position trades that are held from weeks to months with the lightest capital allocation. They often start off as a swing trade (10 to 30 percent allocation) and as profits get scaled out at 7 to 20 percent gains, they convert into a core position (3 to 10 percent allocation) with a nice solid buffer of profits. The compelling nature of the fundamentals tempered with the chart technicals convinces us to hold longer term. In doing so, we want to pay most attention to the weekly and monthly charts. Although you are checking on the price action on a day-to-day basis, this is mostly a passive trade that you will react on when stops get triggered. The stops will be based on price and/or fundamentals.

Case Study: APP Swing Trade to Core Long-Term Position Trade

We stalked APP for several weeks. The level 4 research process revealed American Apparel (NYSE symbol: APP) was a turnaround/recovery story after receiving financing from Soros. This stock had traded as high as 17s in 2008 and proceeded to collapse as low as .50 amid CEO scandals and backlash from an immigration raid that saw 30 percent of its workforce get deported. Incidentally, the company revenues still remained steady in the $520 to $550 range despite heavy losses.

The debt service was debilitating with 16 percent interest rates on $130 million in debt. The CEO, Dov Charney, had been personally sued over 20 different times on various sexual harassment allegations. Yet the brand American Apparel still continued to survive. They have a vertically integrated supply chain that can take an idea to product in 48 hours as opposed to weeks. They have the largest textile factory in the United States located in Los Angeles. The most compelling fundamental aspect was the amazing improvement in same-store sales numbers. As competitors URBN, ARO, GPS, and ANF were seeing single digit to negative monthly sss (sale store sales) numbers, APP was seeing 10 to 20 percent improvements! That is SEXY!

CEO Charney bought 1.1 million shares in the open market in the .80 to1.00 range. We decided to allocate an initial 20 percent in an APP position. Support sat firmly at the .80 price level. APP was the cheapest well-known retailer costwise and had been left for dead, understandably so, as the monthly chart had been in a downtrend for four years! Therefore, when the monthly stochastics finally crossed up through the 20 band, not too many eyeballs were watching it. The beauty of this situation was the perfect storm breakout forming with daily, weekly, and monthly mini pups.

On 7/1/2012, as illustrated in Figure 10.5, we entered APP long for 6,500 shares at .92. It proceeded to chop on super light volume for over a month in the .83 to .96 range. APP released earnings afterhours on 8/11/2012, with a nice beat and raised forecasts. This spiked up APP on volume and liquidity the next morning allowing us to sell 80 percent of the initial swing trade which was 5,200 shares at 1.07 for a +.15 gain and +$780 profit. We still held 1,300 shares long from .92 as a core position with a nice profit buffer for protection. APP reported a stunning +24 percent same-store sales increase on 9/12/2012 that propelled the stock up to 1.50. We couldn't pass up the opportunity to trim out another 50 percent selling 650 shares at 1.47, out +.55 gain, for another $357.50 profit for a *total gross profit of +$1,137.50 with a remaining 650-share core position from .92 moving forward.* The original capital allocated to the trade was $5,980 (20 percent allocation of $30k position trading portion of portfolio), and we had cashed out a +19 percent return on capital with a remaining 650 share core long position.

FIGURE 10.5 APP core swing trade.

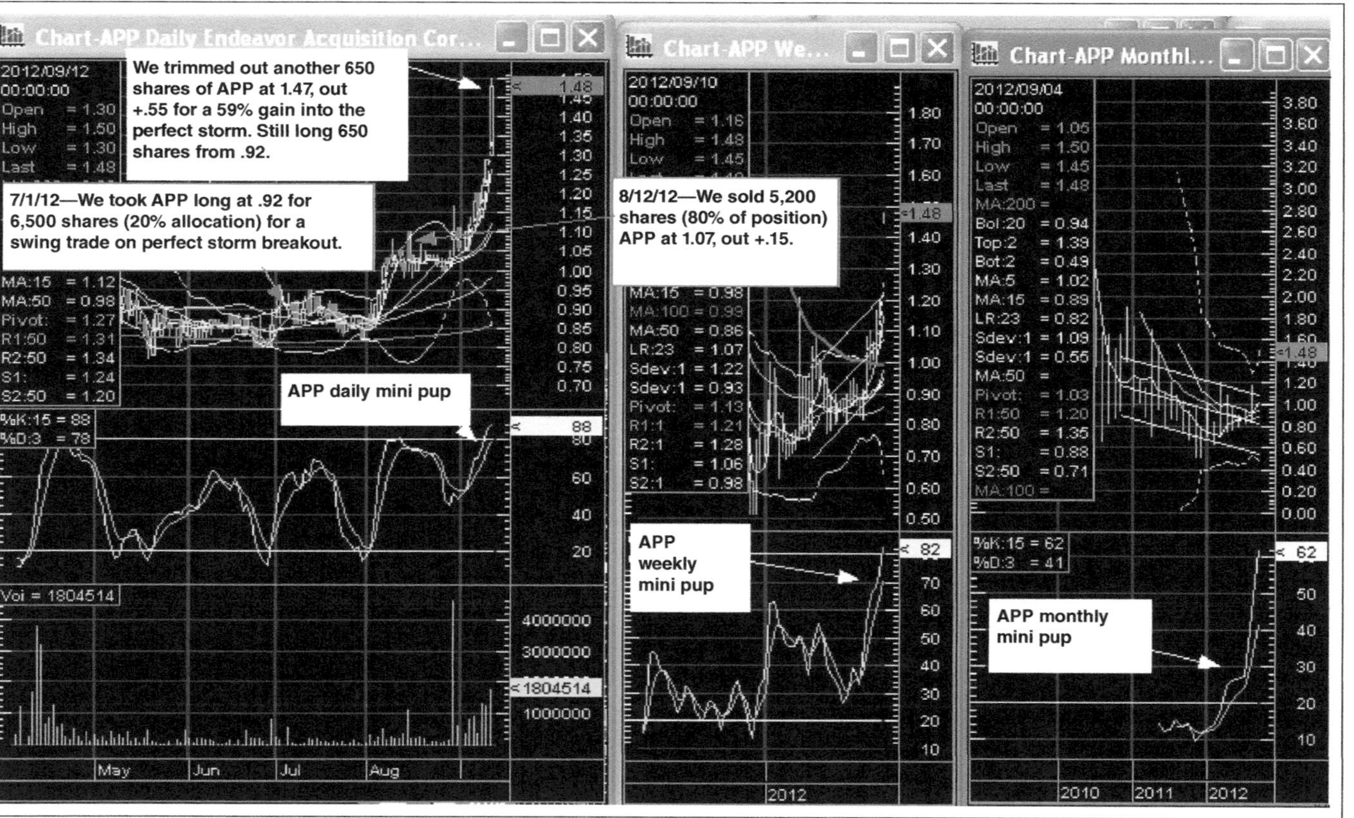

Courtesy of Undergroundswingtrades.com.

Active Portfolio Management

Integrate all the knowledge from the preceding chapters from morning ritual, to the four-level research process, to scanning, monitoring, tracking, and stalking prospects, to trade execution management filtering for highest probability setup perfect storms, and all the variations, to managing entries, scaling, defensive sprawl scales to offensive pare scales, double-hedged sword sequence to pacing your activity in alignment with market climate and the seamless shifting between skill sets. You've learned to address maladies and apply remedies to re-set the template to ensure a measured steady improvement as you nurture your transformation to hybrid market predator.

Intraday trading is structured around the morning ritual preparation. This sets the tone moving forward into the trading day as you work the watch list, scan for opportunities with news feeds throughout the day, carefully pacing and navigating through the alternating climates. These are the most focus-intensive trades where daily income should be generated. Be careful to manage the frequency of trades in this thunder and tumbleweeds landscape run by the algo/HFT apex predators. Stick to the wet climates where there is liquidity and more participants.

Swing trades will be derived mostly from nightly scans and weekend research. Sometimes you will find swing trades from remnants of intraday watch list or trades. Ideas can literally pop up anywhere and anytime randomly. Since idea generation is crucial, we don't want to rely solely on random chance. This is why it's important that you continue to keep manual notes of stocks that you are monitoring during the day that are perhaps constantly bouncing off a certain price level or rejecting off a certain price level. These are the organic seeds that will bear fruit as you continue to track them on paper. When a swing position is initiated, it should be monitored in regular intervals intraday.

Core positions should be checked once a day. You can have a core position minder to set an alert when a price range is tested with an upper price range and lower price range. This is especially helpful when working with limited screen real estate or a large amount of core positions (over 10). These will be less actively traded and should be evaluated when certain price thresholds get tested. A core alert minder with price envelopes is the best way to assure passive yet proactive attention is given as needed.

Options Strategies

Options utilize leverage but cap your losses. There are tons of strategies out there. Since my focus is always on the directional focus of the underlying instrument, I tend to utilize directional options trades. Statistics will say these are the worst odds in the game as most of these options expire worthless, but the reality is that if you have very tight filters with super high probability setups, then the direction options can't be beat as far as leverage and reward to risk. I usually hit the direction options with daily pup/mini pup–based perfect storm trades whether they are breakouts or breakdowns. I treat these like swing trades but limit the holding periods between one to five days. When perfect storms trigger, the volume spikes and implied volatility premiums along with it offset some of the time (theta) erosion. However, that is only for a limited duration of time, therefore it's best to lock these out sooner rather than later. Here are my criteria for directional options trades:

Directional Options Trade Profile

Setup:*Perfect storm breakout or breakdown* with monthly, weekly, daily, and 60-minute chart alignment, or any three of the time frames; 60-minute chart stochastics must be aligned in the direction of the perfect storm (i.e., perfect storm breakout means 60-minute stochastics should be crossed up.). A low band cross up is preferable unless there is a mini pup above the 80 band.

Slingshot bounces: Slingshots are taken for a bounce on an oversold and sector lagging stock trading under a daily and/or weekly, monthly lower Bollinger Bands without news or several days after news. Intraday charts should have a perfect storm setup with the 5-/15-/60-minute if possible. Daily hammers and doji candles are preferred. Peer sector stocks trading strong and candidate stock usually correlates with the peer stocks.

Rug pull drops: These form after excessive run ups with stock trading above the daily and or weekly, monthly upper Bollinger Bands. Shooting stars and dojis mark a good line in the sand. Intraday charts should form perfect storm breakdowns upon entry with the 60-minute, 15-minute, and 5-minute.

Options criteria: Expiration one to three months out regular monthly options.

Tight spreads no more than .10 spread.

In the money by one strike price with a greater than –50 delta.

Duration: Overnight to five days maximum.

Allocation: 50 percent of current swing trade equity allocation for options. Since options are more leveraged, if your current equity allocation is 20 percent, then trim the options down to 10 percent capital allocation. Very important! If there is a catalyst in the post-market or premarket that causes the stock to gap big, you can always collar the gain or loss by taking the opposite position with the stock by getting delta to zero (delta neutral). In order to do this, you must have the capital available to take an opposite position in the stock.

Targets: Since these are countertrend exhaustion trades, target the next bumper on the daily and 60-minute charts. Usually they will be the 5-period moving average on the daily charts and/or Bollinger Bands on the 60-minute charts. Scale out in 50 to 70 percent initial exit, then trail with intraday trends to scale out the rest of the 30 percent or split into 20 percent, then 10 percent.

Delta Neutral Hedging

Since a lot of action can happen during the post/premarket session when the options markets are closed, it's important to utilize delta neutral hedging to box in profits from eroding or box losses from getting larger. Options carry positive delta on longs and negative delta on shorts. When the delta is zero, then you are delta neutral, which means you are completely hedged. Of course, with the slippage from spreads and other factors like theta and vega, there is no absolute perfect hedge, but it's as close as you can get.

If you are long 5 XYZ Mar 30 calls at 3 while the stock is trading at 33 with a +1 delta, that means you are carrying +500 delta. Stocks carry a +1 delta per share on longs and –1 delta on shorts. Let's say XYZ reports news post-market that shoots the stock up to 35 in the post-market. Normally, you would have to wait for the options market to open the next morning at 9:32 A.M. EST. Meanwhile, you bear the risk of overnight and premarket profit taking without you. Perhaps the S&P 500 futures (macro market) is gapping down –10 points. In this case, you want to hedge your profit. The way to do this is to go delta neutral on the position. Since you have 5 call contracts with +500 delta, you will need to offset that by SHORTING 500 XYZ shares at 35 which buys you –500 delta to negate the +500 from the call contracts and go delta neutral. This protects your +2 point profit gain into the market open allowing you time to close out both legs at your discretion.

Covered Calls: Creating Your Own Dividend

Swing trades and especially core positions can be used to collect your own dividend by writing covered calls. These should be written utilizing the weekly and monthly resistance and support bumpers. Depending on the liquidity and spreads of the options for your stock, you should consider writing calls if there is liquidity and then spreads are not more than .20 between the bid and ask. Otherwise, there is just too much slippage involved. Factor in commission costs as well. If the premiums barely cover the commissions, then the point is moot. The best time to write these covered calls is when prices spike on your stock with heavy relative volume due to a catalyst. Many times, rather than selling the position, you can opt to write at the money strike price calls or if the stock is looking overbought at or above the weekly and or monthly lower Bollinger Bands, then write in the money strike calls for one to two expirations out preferably prior to the earnings report date. Make sure there is a good premium, or else the point is moot again.

Keep in mind, writing covered calls will often require you to hold the position through expiration to capture all the premiums. This rings especially true if the spreads are wide (.20 or more). Therefore, these should be limited to swing/core positions that you are committed to holding and feel strong enough about to tie up the capital.

Bullish Call Debit Spreads

You will need options level 3 permissions for this, so check with your broker. Debit spreads allow you to take a controlled directional position for a cheaper price by simultaneously buying in-the-money calls and selling out-of-the money calls one or two strike prices higher in the same month. The further out the strike price, the more your upside as well as your downside will be. If the underlying stock price exceeds the highest call strike sold, then you reach maximum profit if you hold into expiration. I like to close these out when the stock price gets a full strike above the highest strike price the call was sold to avoid the chance of assignment. Your downside is limited to the cost of the net debit, which is triggered if the stock falls under your call purchase strike price by expiration. Most broker platforms have modules to perform these trades. Be aware that you should expect at least four transaction fees especially if you close out ahead of expiration.

Bearish Call Debit Spreads

The bearish call debit spread is done by buying out-of-the-money calls and selling in-the-money calls one or two strikes below. Further strikes below increase your maximum profit as well as losses. Maximum loss level is hit if the stock exceeds the higher strike price, and maximum profit is hit when the stock drops below the lower strike price. The same mechanics of transaction costs and management apply. Check with your broker for the options module that will execute this and also calculate your maximum profit, breakeven, and loss level amounts.

Portfolio Trading Schedule of Activity

We've covered the key aspects of the portfolio trading. Here is a more streamlined breakdown of what is required as a portfolio trader. Acclimatize to this schedule and then work on your own to optimize the process to comply with your schedule. As with anything in trading, keep it fluid and flexible within your comfort zone.

Daily

1. Proceed with morning ritual routine to gather morning watch list: While this places emphasis on intraday trading, you will find portfolio position candidates tend to also present themselves down the road.
2. Review and update your stalking minder list. Add or remove stocks that are no longer relevant. Adjust alert prices as needed.
3. Day trade during wet climates (first 90 minutes and last 90 minutes).
4. Take notes for any overlapping bumper rejections or basing.
5. Screen newsfeeds and intraday scanners for potential setups.
6. Conduct research levels 1–3 on any prospects.
7. Manage swing and core trades in portfolio, set alerts for price levels on core positions.
8. Evening, scan and screen for new candidates to add to watch list for next morning or minders to track.
9. Conduct level 3–4 research as needed in the evening.

Weekends

1. Run macro market analysis on SPY, QQQ, DIA.
2. Evaluate open swing and core positions.

3. Update, adjust stalking minder with price level alerts.
4. Create weekly watch list corganic stock setups for Monday morning.
5. Levels 1–4 research process on watch lists and swing candidates.

Harnessing Your Hybrid Evolution

As you get more comfortable with the position trade portion of your portfolio, you can start to allocate more capital to that portion as you build up core positions. Remember that you have to do this gradually and nurture your propensity for passively managing these trades. The best way to nurture this is to start off with scalps that are scaled into range trades. If the swing trades behave robustly, then they can be scaled down into a core position. Continue to repeat this, and your comfort level will grow quickly. Most importantly, your ability to shift from the scalping mindset to a swing mindset will become more fluid with practice. *It is this area of fluid and seamless transitioning between skill sets that defines the portfolio trader. When you've grown comfortable during the transitions, then you know you are truly evolving as a hybrid market predator. Congrats!*

CHAPTER 11

Conclusion: Cultivating Your Personal Evolution

There is never time in the future in which we will work out our salvation. The challenge is in the moment; the time is always now.

—James A. Baldwin

So here we are, at the end. Congratulations and kudos for making it this far. I hope that you will continue to utilize this manifesto, *Way of the Trade*, as a constant reference and travel companion to accompany your own personal journey toward trading excellence. In this chapter, I address some final thoughts to further prepare you for the road ahead.

Acknowledging the Spirit

While one's trades can be documented and analyzed, no one else knows the resonating effects to the trader: his emotions, his anxiety, his state of mind, his frame of reference, his will to continue, and so forth. These are invisible to outsiders. Yet these internal components pull the strings.

While traders tend to focus on improving their methods, as well as the psychological aspect of trading and physical wellbeing to enhance their mindset, the deeper ingrained component that drives one back into the markets or any challenge is the third component, spirit. Spirit is the underlying component that drives one to continue forward in the face of adversity to triumph against insurmountable odds. Spirit fuels one's evolution.

Ignorance is not what drives someone to get back up and continue forward again only to get knocked down for the umpteenth time so he can get back up and continue forward again, rinse and repeat. It's his spirit. Spirit tends to be synonymous with different labels like will, heart, tenacity, and resolve. Spirit encompasses all of those descriptions.

Conventional thinking is a mixture of ignorance, complacency, and convenience. Obviously, you and I are not of the conventional thinking humanoid crowd. After making it this far in the book, you should know a little something about process. Conventional thinking ignores the impact of context (background factors) that can make the *same process* wildly successful in a particular context and consistently flop in another context. The challenge often lies not in fixing the process, but in determining in which context the process applies most effectively. Does this sound familiar? Landscape, climate, terrain . . . and if you're truly brilliant, then you actually factor in the environment as inclusive of the process, thereby allowing you to focus on optimizing the process to generate the by-product, A + B = C (A + B being the process). Even if you do feel pretty ignorant, what drives you to continue? Not ignorance, but spirit.

We're not referring to religious or supernatural ghost hunter interpretations of spirit. The spirit we're dealing with is intangible on a literal level, yet so intricately woven into our very nature that it often defines our character. Spirit is the driver that pushes us to pursue a course of action to the very end. Spirit is the force behind anything we are passionate about. With something so significant, it only makes sense that we understand how to nurture this powerful driving force that resides inside every one of us. As with anything so powerful, we must acknowledge, respect, and reciprocate. There's that law of reciprocity again!

Elements That Affect One's Spirit

Everyone can identify with the various elements that impact one's spirit either positively or negatively. This is a list of elements off the top of my head in no particular order. You will find that many of the elements overlap. Feel free to add on to the list.

Positive Elements That Impact Spirit

Enlightenment
Insight
Foresight

Propensity
Discovery
Faith in one's ability
Structure
Humility
Reinforcement
Victory
Growth
Evolution
Interaction with family and friends
Positive reinforcement
Respect
Loyalty
Confidence
Decency
Targets
Passion
Goals
Depth
Layers
Purpose
Focus
Unity
Balance
Security
Resolution
Healing
Compassion
Control
Contrast
Endurance
Purity
Rewards
Confirmation
Preparation
Warmth
Recognition
Acceptance
Awareness
Affirmation

Acclaim
Guidance
Acknowledgement
Salvation
Positivity
Advancement
Fortification

Negative Elements That Impact Spirit

Complacency
Lack of challenge
Beating oneself up
Fatigue
Boredom
Avarice
Gluttony
Arrogance
Negative reinforcement (especially self-administered)
Being minimized
Emptiness
Abandonment
Indifference
Lack of structure
Paranoia
Evil
Lack of direction
Lack of purpose
Inconsistency
Limbo
Isolation
Abandonment
Ambiguity
Punishment
Contempt
Mistrust
Humiliation
Rejection
Cold
Abuse
Guilt

Shame
Misdirection
Disorientation
Depletion
Squandering
Distraction
Scorn
Discourtesy
Aimlessness
Insincerity
Vilification
Indignity
Contamination
Persecution
Belittlement
Nagging
Strain
Violence
Distortion
Burden
Damnation
Negativity
Degradation
Erosion

Just as every little piece of information around you is converted into cognitions that subconsciously shape your attitudes, beliefs, and behaviors, the aforementioned elements all make subtle and sometimes not so subtle impacts on your spirit. The magnitude of each element may have more or less of an affect personally on you depending on your background and past experiences. That's for you to define.

Broken Spirits' Blowout

When one's spirit is depleted, significantly weakened, or broken, one is susceptible to going on tilt and blowing out one's account in desperation and frustration. It's the spirit that is crying out for help. Trading should never get to that point, but it can and often does. Challenge is welcomed. Misery is not. It is urgent that you consciously evaluate your spirit condition along with your trading for a complete assessment. From there, you can work to re-set and redirect your templates back on the correct path.

Blowing out your account, getting margin called, and having to close out the account is debilitating, initially because one has no choice but to accept defeat and acknowledge failure. Conventional wisdom leaves it at that end. For those who still have the will to continue, reality whispers a different story. George Soros blew out his final account just before he started the Quantum fund in his forties, which went on to legendary status in the hedge fund world averaging up to 30 percent annually for over three decades.

The upside of blowing out an account is the tension relief, clarity, and concession of defeat, and the chance to take a much-needed break. The shackles are finally released. There is a cleansing effect afterwards that may feel as though you had pressed the re-set button. We've gone over the healing and re-set process in Chapter 4, without having to get to the blowout stage. Make sure to review the re-setting process.

Nourish Your Spirit

Spirit can be measured during challenging situations. The irony of spirit is that it becomes most transparent during times of struggle and conflict. Spirit intensifies in challenging situations. A healthy spirit rises to the challenge. A weak spirit avoids challenge while harboring an insurmountable feeling of emptiness. This is a sign of malnourishment.

As with anything related to human nature, a template is created with or without your permission that serves as the prewiring makeup of the component. As we went over re-setting habits by actively and consciously repairing the misaligned, ingrained behavioral templates, the same dynamics apply with the spirit.

Due to the subconscious, involuntary, and elusive nature of spirit, you can't sit it down and talk to it. What you have to do is play the role of a dietician or traffic cop and expose yourself to more of the positive list and consciously avoid the negative list.

Nourish you spirit with the positive list while screening out as much of the negative list as possible. Absolute elimination of the negatives isn't possible unless you never leave the house (like me). Identification and awareness is half the battle toward eventually building immunity and a firewall to as much of the negative list as possible. You will notice most of the elements in the positive list are the opposite of the elements on the negative list. That's called contrast. Awareness of this simple distinction grants you access to the garbage disposal switch to automatically flip on when needed. Treat the positive list as the diet to nourish spirit while making a conscious effort to minimize too much exposure to the negative elements.

Continuing Your Progress

Guidance is a helpful component not only for your spirit but continued evolution. I have several services along with partners that can help further propel your progress and improvement. Most importantly, the Katana continues to improve with each encounter as new modifications or configurations to the system are developed. To stay on the cutting edge, advance your education, profit from trade alerts and see the methods in action, feel free to try my services:

> www.UndergroundTrader.com for intraday analysis of scalp and range trades. I am logged into my chat room all day to provide market analysis, education, and trade alerts. The trader training is a cumulative section that encompasses all seminars and chart archives for over a decade. A special two-week free trial is available to purchasers of *Way of the Trade*; click book referral in the trial application. This site caters to active intra-day traders.
>
> www.Markety.com/product/perfect-storm for scalp trades in the first 90-minute. This is the Morning Profit Maker service on Marketfy.com. I provide a morning watch list in the chat room every morning along with market analysis and precision trade alerts with complete allocation, entry, and exit signals. My charts are displayed in real time on a live video stream. Educational content is updated in daily blog, weekly video seminars, and study halls. This service applies to active morning traders who want to generate a consistent morning income stream before heading off to their jobs or businesses.
>
> www.UndergroundSwingTrades.com for swing and core portfolio trades. This is a high-premium swing, core, and portfolio trade newsletter service. I do all the scanning, filtering, tracking, and stalking for candidates to include in our portfolio. Allocation ratios are given along with precise entry and exit signals with nightly updates and real-time e-mail/pager alerts. This service is for self-directed investors, swing traders, and busy professionals who are willing to pay a premium for having my team handle the small stuff. Auto-trading options are available. Call 1-888-233-1431 for setup and pricing details.

I hope I have aided you in flipping on the power switch unleashing megawatts of blissful enlightenment. I thank you for allowing me into your psyche. It's been my pleasure and honor to serve and reciprocate. For many of you, it may take more time for saturation to form—keep chipping away. If anything, I hope to have implanted the seed that you will nurture to grow and harvest your own personal by-product. Everyone has a destiny waiting to be uncovered. Keep digging to reach it. Awaken, embrace, embellish, and immerse yourself in enlightenment. Focus on the process, and the by-product will come to you . . . this is the *Way of the Trade.*

Appendix A
My Trading Tools and Anatomy of Pattern Trades

Suri Duddella
www.surinotes.com

There are hundreds of trading methods or strategies for traders to pursue in the trading world. They could be auto trading strategies to discretionary methods encompassing a wide variety of time frames such as short term for scalp traders, medium term for swing traders, or long term for investors. Trading styles could be technical or fundamental trading. In each of these styles, there are hundreds of other trading ideas like momentum trading, patterns trading, breakout trading, trading on the key fundamentals, or anticipation of news exits.

Any trading system or methodology must be appropriate and fit the trader's personality. A trader also must choose trading instruments of her choice (Forex, commodities, stocks, etc.) and test (backward and forward) a variety of systems to fit her trading plan and trading goals.

In this section, I will discuss my thinking behind the pattern trading process and how I approach trading. I trade harmonic/geometric chart pattern setups like ABCs and Gartleys/Butterflys with market context both in automated and discretionary process using the TradeStation platform. I trade E-mini futures intraday and trade stocks/options using end-of-day (EOD) and weekly charts from a swing trading (short to medium term) perspective. I will discuss a few of my trading tools and trade setups and my psychological and emotional preparation for the trading process.

Why Pattern Trading?

Pattern Recognition

Pattern recognition is the basic and primary ability any trader develops in technical analysis. It may be a basic development, but the perfection of pattern recognition takes extensive practice and repetitive exposure. The expert recognition of patterns helps traders to quantify and react to the changing market environment. Chart patterns are categorized into *continuous* and *reversal* patterns, and these categories are further classified as *simple* and *complex* patterns. The complex patterns consist of collections of simple patterns. The knowledge of this classification of pattern recognition and its properties gives traders greater potential to react and adapt to a wider range of trading conditions.

Pattern Formations

Market prices always exhibit trend, consolidation, and retrend behavior. They rarely reverse their trends and transitional phases to turn from a previous trend on a single bar. During this transitional phase, they experience trading ranges and price fluctuations. This ranging action defines identifiable price patterns. These consolidation phases occasionally favor prevailing trends prior to their formation and continue their direction. These are called *continuation* patterns, and a few examples of these patterns are *Symmetric Triangle*, *Flags*, and *Cup and Handle*. Some phases result in reversing the prior trend and continue in reversal conditions. These are called *reversal* patterns. A few examples of reversal patterns include *Head and Shoulders*, *Double Bottoms*, and *Broadening* patterns.

Harmonic Chart Pattern Auto-Detection Tools

The primary theory behind harmonic patterns is that price/time movements adhere to Fibonacci ratio relationships in markets. Fibonacci ratio analysis works well with any markets and on any time-frame charts. The basic idea of using these ratios is to identify key turning points, retracements, and extensions along with a series of swing high and swing low points. The derived projections and retracements using these swing points (highs and lows) will give key price levels for targets or stops.

The following is a layout of my trading plan and how I make my trading decisions. All these ideas are well tested in real time and end-of-day analysis in auto/discretionary trading styles for the past 16-plus years of my full-time trading. These methods fit my personality.

Intraday Futures Trading Plan

1. Trade pattern–based setups (entry, stops, targets) only, and never trade support tools like MAs, pivot levels.
2. Market structure and key market levels (MAs, pivots) and support and resistance levels must be part of the pattern.
3. Market internals direction and current pattern trade direction must be the same, using the Combined Market Internals indicator.
4. For intraday trades, the time to complete each bar (bartime) for the instrument must be within reasonable levels.
5. Current volatility (VLTY) must be tradable.
6. Entry, exit, and targets must be within my trading plan. Never trade micro chart patterns or scalp counter-trend chart patterns. Check for confluence of target levels or zones with other key support/resistance levels.
7. Time of the day or time to complete my trade must be within my trading plan: "Do not initiate a new trade in the last 30 minutes to close or some major news like FOMC news is imminent in the next 60 minutes."
8. Must adhere with strict discipline for my entry and exit rules and money management rules.
9. If at any point during the trade, my trade decision is violated or becomes wrong, exit the trade regardless of profit or loss.
10. Never add to a losing trade.

The following is a brief discussion of tools I use in my trading:

1. Auto chart pattern detection tools (like ABCs, Gartleys, Butterflys, double bottoms/tops, channel breakouts, etc.)
2. Support tools like market structure identifications, pivots (floor, Globex, Fibonacci zone), and Fibonacci bands
3. Market internals indicator (for intraday trading only)—combined market internals (CMI)
4. Follow single trend detection indicator (kTrend or SuperBars)
5. Market volatility (VLTY)
6. BarTime indicator

Auto Chart Pattern Detection Tools

Most traders struggle to find valid patterns as they try to find them with the naked eye. There may be a few patterns that are possible to detect with the naked eye, but many times this type of detection process is very limited to one chart and one time-frame and could be error prone. Hence, automatic detection of chart patterns with the right rule set is necessary.

I have written many chart pattern detection tools in the TradeStation platform and use few patterns in my trading. One of the key patterns I detect is called the ABC chart pattern, as shown in Figure A.1. The ABC pattern is the simplest but most unique and universal pattern in trading. ABC chart patterns are also embedded in many other chart patterns like Gartleys, Butterflys, Head and Shoulders, Double Top/Bottoms, Elliott Waves, Dragons, and so on.

The basic ABC pattern was first described in H.M. Gartley's book, *Profits in the Stock Market* (1935). This pattern is shaped like a lightning bolt and signals a trend, a retracement, and the resumption of the trend. This pattern is also called the ABC Wave or 1-2-3 pattern by technical analysts. The ABC patterns forecast key market turning points and profit targets for traders. ABC patterns pinpoint important pivot levels with high and low prices, and identify key trading zones.

The key process in identifying an ABC is correctly finding the A, B, and C pivot points in a chart without any delays. These key price swings (A, B, C)

FIGURE A.1 Developing ABC Bullish Pattern

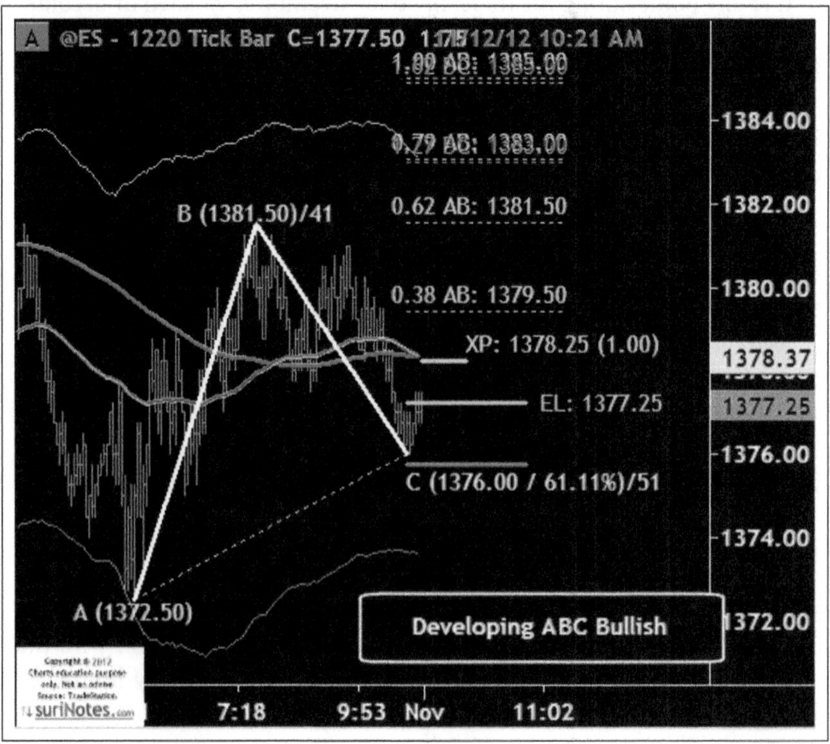

are found using various auto-detection algorithms, and for its correction waves. Once A, B, and C pivots are identified, an auto-levels algorithm generates the entry, stop, and target levels.

The C pivot in ABC patterns is determined by the Fibonacci retracement of (38.2 to 61.8 percent) of AB swing. The projection from the C level is measured using fib-ratios of AB and BC swings. A radar screen component finds ABCs for multiple instruments and multiple time-frames.

Fibonacci Bands

Fibonacci Bands are derived from Fibonacci ratios expansion from a fixed moving average. These bands help traders find key areas of support and resistance. Fibonacci Bands are computed by adding a Fibonacci ratio distance (up and down) from a key dynamically adjusted moving average. The Fibonacci ratios of true-range are added to the fixed moving average to compute Fibonacci Bands (see Figure A.2).

FIGURE A.2 Fibonacci Bands and SuperBars

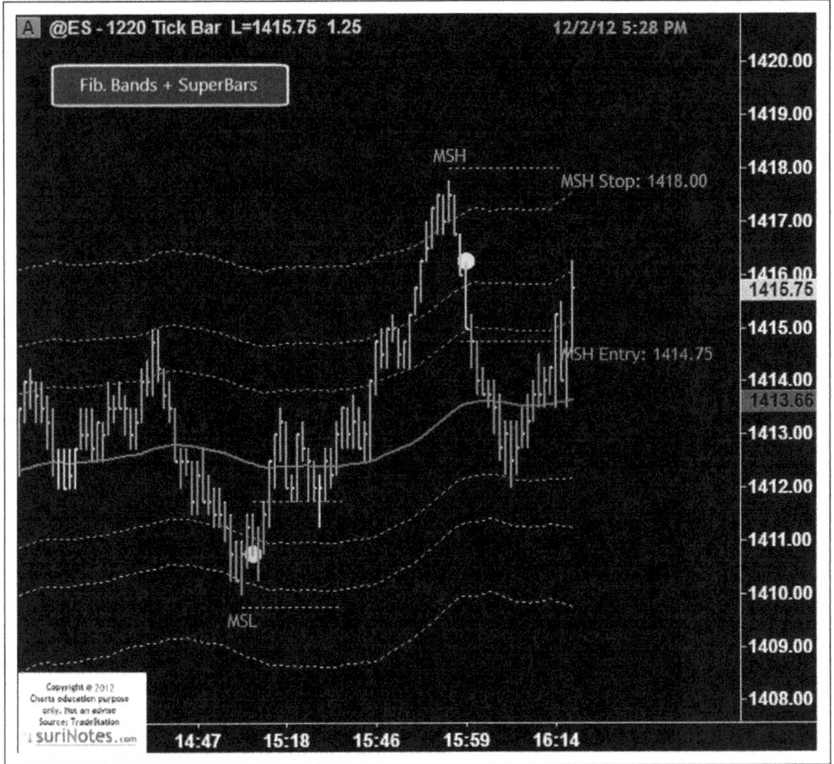

Pivots (Floor Trader, Globex, and Fibonacci Zone Pivots)

Traders believe the market direction can be divulged by pivot levels. They buy or sell these pivot levels and exit at either the first or second resistance levels. They also have the option to sell the pivot level and cover at the first or second support levels. Floor pivot trading is an effective way to find support and resistance levels, and is widely used by many traders. Prices around pivot levels signal choppy or trend market modes. In bullish markets, when prices consolidate around the pivot levels, prices tend to pick the prior trend direction and trade higher. Pivot trading is very crucial, and most traders utilize daily pivots for trading. However, weekly and monthly pivots are equally important when swing trading. Some traders compute the midpoints between the pivot and support or resistance levels and plot them on their charts.

A confluence of pivots increases the chance of potential support/resistance compared to a single pivot level. Often there will be many confluences between daily and weekly pivots on a chart, and these levels could be significant for traders. Pivots are very efficient for both day and swing trading. Pivot trading is quite profitable using these support/resistance levels in the direction of the trend along with good money management techniques.

I compute floor pivots, Globex pivots (overnight pivots), and Fibonacci zone pivots using the prior day's range and plot them on the current trading chart. For my trading, I use these price levels and confluence zones as critical areas of support and resistance for my pattern trading.

Combined Market Internals Indicator (CMI)

Market internals use market breadth indicators and work as leading indicators. The key aspect is to find a group of market breadth indicators and combine them to form a single Combined Market Internals (CMI) indicator and follow its direction. The CMI indicator shows a Combined Market Trend of Internals of $ADV, $DECL, $TICK, $TRIN, $ESINX, XLF, and SPY in real time. The CMI shows the underlying trend in a histogram. CMI Ribbon shows the detail of internal trends (see Figure A.3).

I look for CMI direction in 3-minute and 5-minute charts to assist my pattern trade for entry. Any bullish pattern setup must match the CMI direction (in GREEN) at entry point and vice versa for bearish setups. CMI also assists me in finding divergences.

FIGURE A.3 Combined Market Internals (CMI 5m)

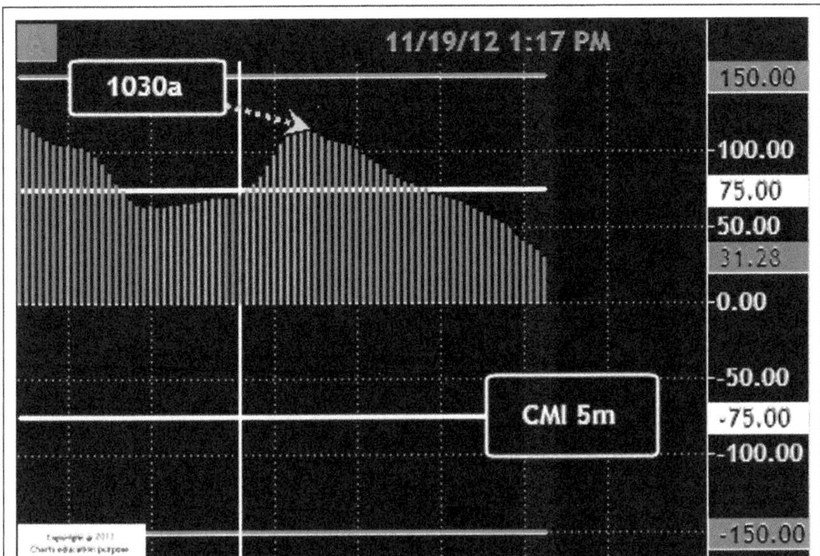

Market Volatility Indicator (VLTY)

Market volatility (VLTY) provides a way to gauge the current instrument volatility in its time frame. It is plotted in a subgraph as the percentile rank. When VLTY range is below 50, it may be suggesting a decent VLTY range to trade. I plot VLTY on the ES intraday chart to compute volatility zones. If VLTY is trading above 50, it may be signaling a higher volatile period, and any NEW trades should be avoided. Trading above 50 up to 100 is considered a RISKY zone, and I usually avoid taking new trades. Above 100 is considered to be extreme volatile and extreme risky trades and I'll exit all trades (see Figure A.4).

BarTime Indicator

BarTime is used for tick- and volume-based charts. Short-term traders get chopped in the nontrending or slow-moving markets, even though they may be right with their setup and direction. The purpose of this indicator is to detect slow and choppy trading times. BarTimer computes and shows how much time each of the 1220 tick bar is taking. I have a threshold setup of 150 seconds per bar (you

FIGURE A.4 BarTime and Volatility (VLTY) for the Trading Instrument

can set it to any value). When each bar is printing beyond this threshold (150 sec.), the market may be entering into slow market, and trades may be chopped and unsafe. I also employ another 5-period average of this timer to see if the average is below or above my threshold to protect me from nontrending zones.

Trade 1: November 20, 2012

I am a big believer in the confluence of various price levels forming support and resistance zones. Confluence zones from multiple patterns or trade setups act as key areas for price-action. Trading solely with these price levels may not be the best choice, but using these confluence zones with pattern setups may result in profitable trades. Here I show how I anticipate these confluence price zones and trade the ABC chart pattern with market context.

First Clues

Most ABC patterns I trade have decent AB swings (at least 5 @ES points) followed by at least 50 percent retracement (closer to 62 percent would be better). On November 20th, I started watching an ABC pattern evolve right from the open from 1,378.25 to 1,386. Around 10.30 A.M., the AB swing started to retrace into form to show a developing ABC. My first inclination into trading this pattern is to wait for 50 to 62 percent range retracement and a close over EL (entry level) for me to enter the trade. From 11 A.M., @ ES started to trade sideways and showed the first sign of completion of the pattern as it traded above 200-SMA and mid Fibonacci Band. Once price closed above mid Fibonacci band and the entry level (EL), the ABC pattern is complete and tradable.

Now monitoring the market context elements, price is trading above mid Fibonacci Band, and VLTY is comfortably less than 50 (normal). BarTime is showing about 60 to 90 seconds for ES 1220 Tick (my trade chart). CMI is also green signaling potential ABC bullish setup.

Trade Entry

I entered a long position around 11.20 A.M. at 1,383, with the initial stop set at 1,381 (below C from Figure A.5). There are a few more price levels to note: At my trade entry time (Figure A.7), price is already trading above the floor pivot (1,379.5) and point of control (1,378.5). This price-action adds strength to my trade. My ABC stop 1,381 is also below 200-SMA. If price violates the 200-SMA, my bullish trade could be wrong.

Now, looking at targets, I compute ABC measured move projections from C level as targets (62 percent AB to 79 percent AB). Here I look for these projected targets' confluence with other pivots, Mas, or any other support or resistance levels. From Fibonacci zone pivots (FZPs), the first FZP resistance zone is at 1,386.5 to 1,388. My second target is set at 1,389 (just before 100 percent AB level) (see Figure A.6).

My confidence in this trade was pretty high, as I have traded many ABC patterns with strong confluence levels and strong support levels.

FIGURE A.5 Trade 1: Developing ABC Bullish Pattern above 200-SMA Level

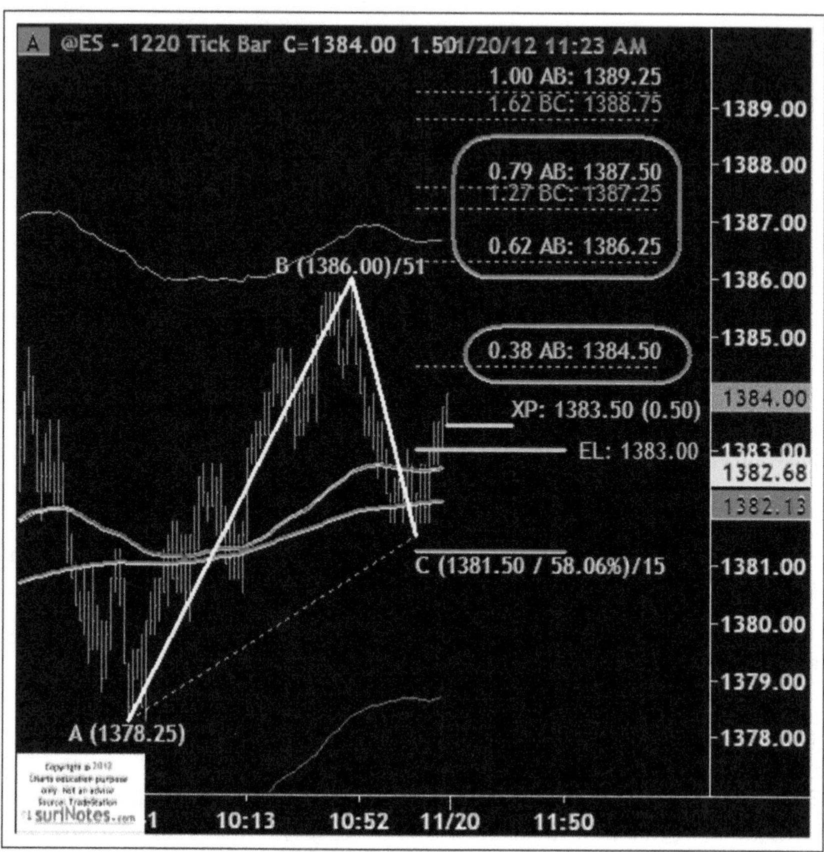

Exits

Around 11.50 A.M., about 30 minutes after trade entry, ABC long trade from 1,383 level reached its first target: 1,386.5. I exited half of my position at 1,386.5 (3.5 pts profit), and then I waited for my next target 1,389 and raised stop from 1,381 to 1,385 (see Figure A.8 for Trade 1). Price went up to 1,387.5 (79 percent AB), but my next target (1,389) was never reached. Fibonacci zone pivots resistance zone is located from 1,386.5 to 1,388 and confluence with ABC 79 percent AB level (Figure A.9 for Trade 1). I had doubts about the second target 1,389. Using trail stop at 1,385, I exited my

FIGURE A.6 Trade 1: ABC Bullish Pattern with Entry, Stop, and Targets

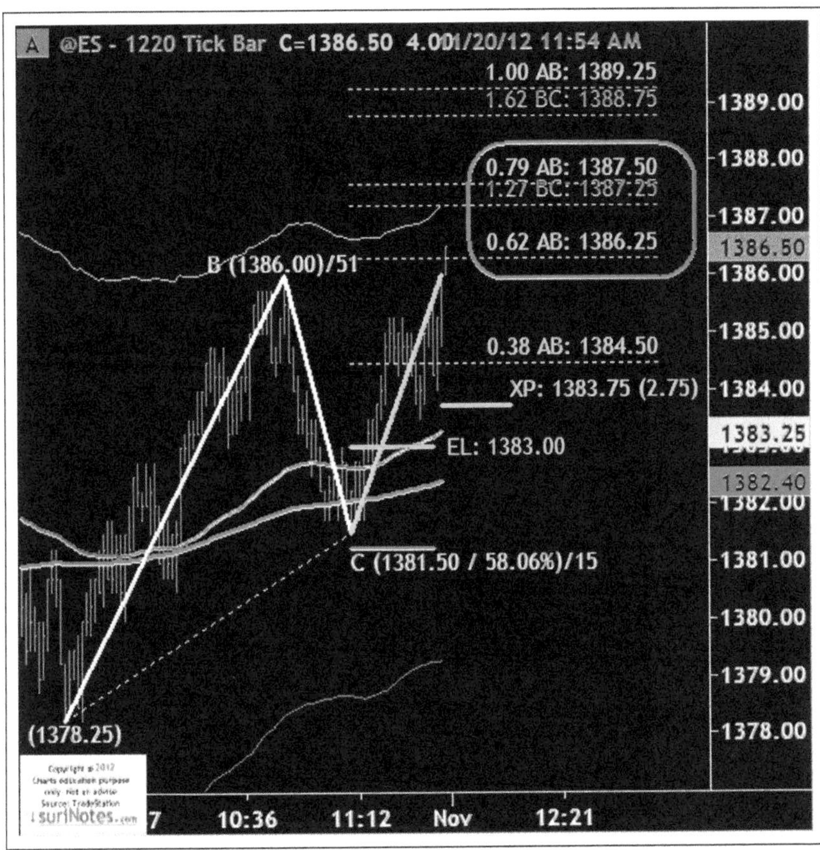

second set of contracts and closed my long trade at 1,385 (2 pts profit) illustrated by Figure A.10 for Trade 1.

Trade 2: November 12, 2012

Market wisdom constantly teaches us that "TREND IS YOUR FRIEND" and never ignore trends or never trade counter-trend setups. Traders look for plenty of trend indicators to find trends. In pattern trading, it is most important to trade patterns with the trend for any trading success.

FIGURE A.7 Trade 1: All Pivots, BarTime, and Volatility Chart

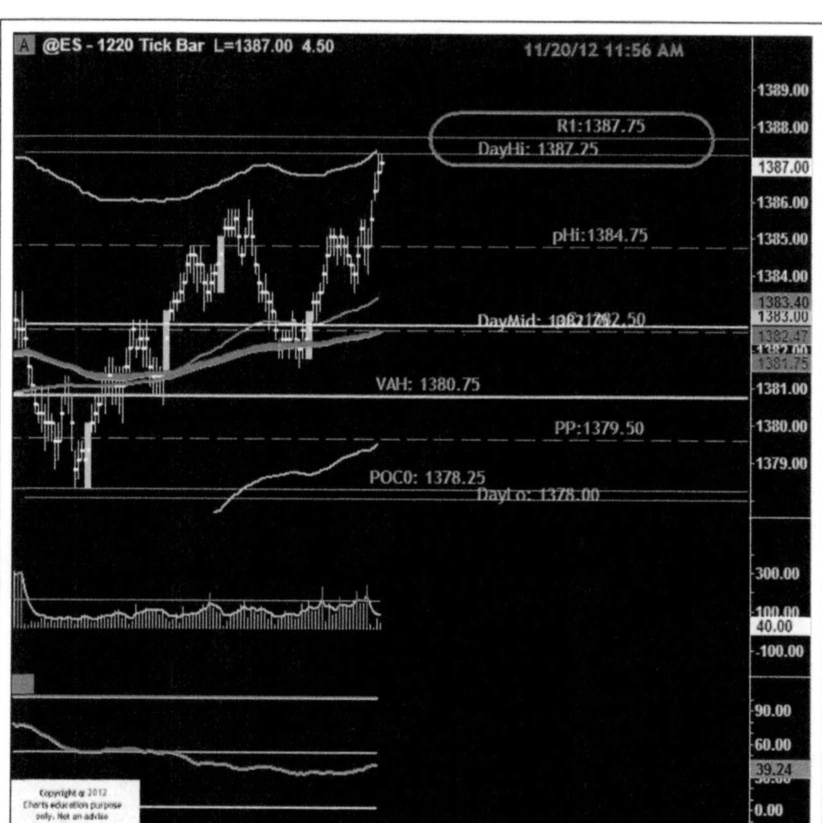

My primary trading methodology is to trade a few geometric patterns (ABCs, Gartleys, DB/DTs, Dragons, H&S/Inv. HS, Breakouts/Breakdowns in the direction of trend with market context). One of the aspects of my trading is to wait for trend confirmation through the SuperBars indicator before entering into any pattern trade. Patience and discipline pay off big if you wait for trend confirmations before entering into a trade.

First Clues

On November 12th, 2012, S&P E-minis presented a case for clear trend confirmation into ABC pattern setups.

FIGURE A.8 Trade 1: ABC Bullish Pattern with Target Ranges

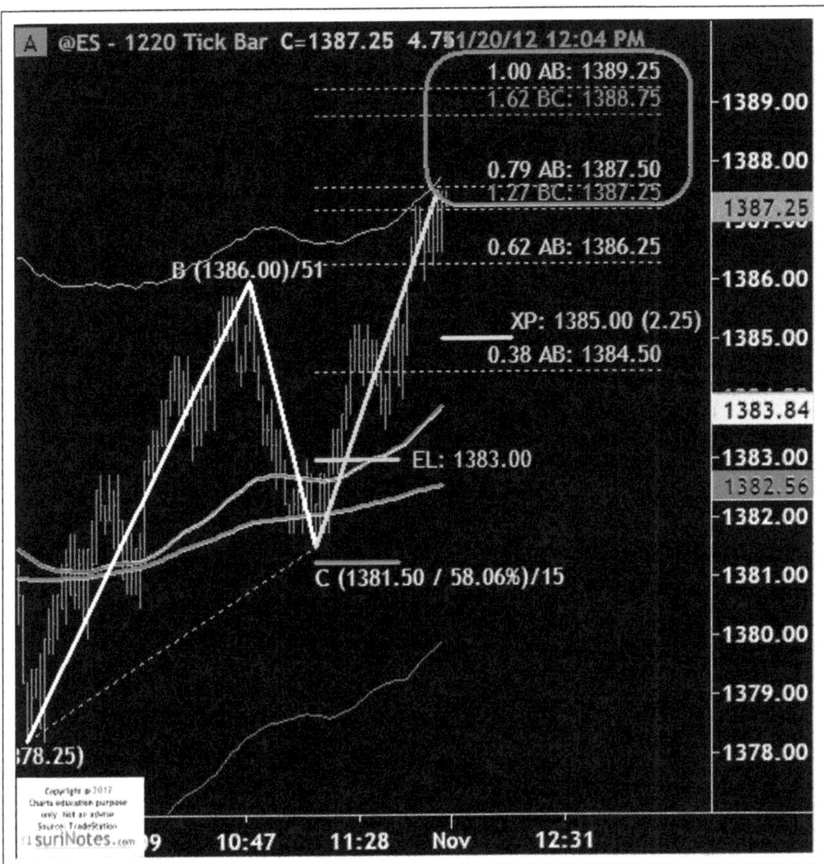

Around 10 A.M., I started watching an ABC bullish pattern set up (Figure A.11) with entry level (EL) above 1,377.5 with a stop at 1,376. I was also watching my trend indicator SuperBars (Figure A.12). To my surprise, SuperBars (trend-based paint bars) were still showing continuation of bearish trend (RED) and never changed to bullish mode (GREEN). This signals to me that the down leg (BC) in the ABC pattern is not quite complete and price may retrace further. I hesitated a bit and removed my bid to buy at 1,377.5. ES tried to break above 200-SMA and started drifting lower below 200-SMA with bearish SuperBar trend (red). Once price closed below the ABC stop level with bearish SuperBars, I was certain further correction into ABC leg is possible and it may be forming a potential double bottom setup (Figure A.12).

FIGURE A.9 Trade 1: Fibonacci Zone Pivots and ABC Bullish Pattern Showing Confluence

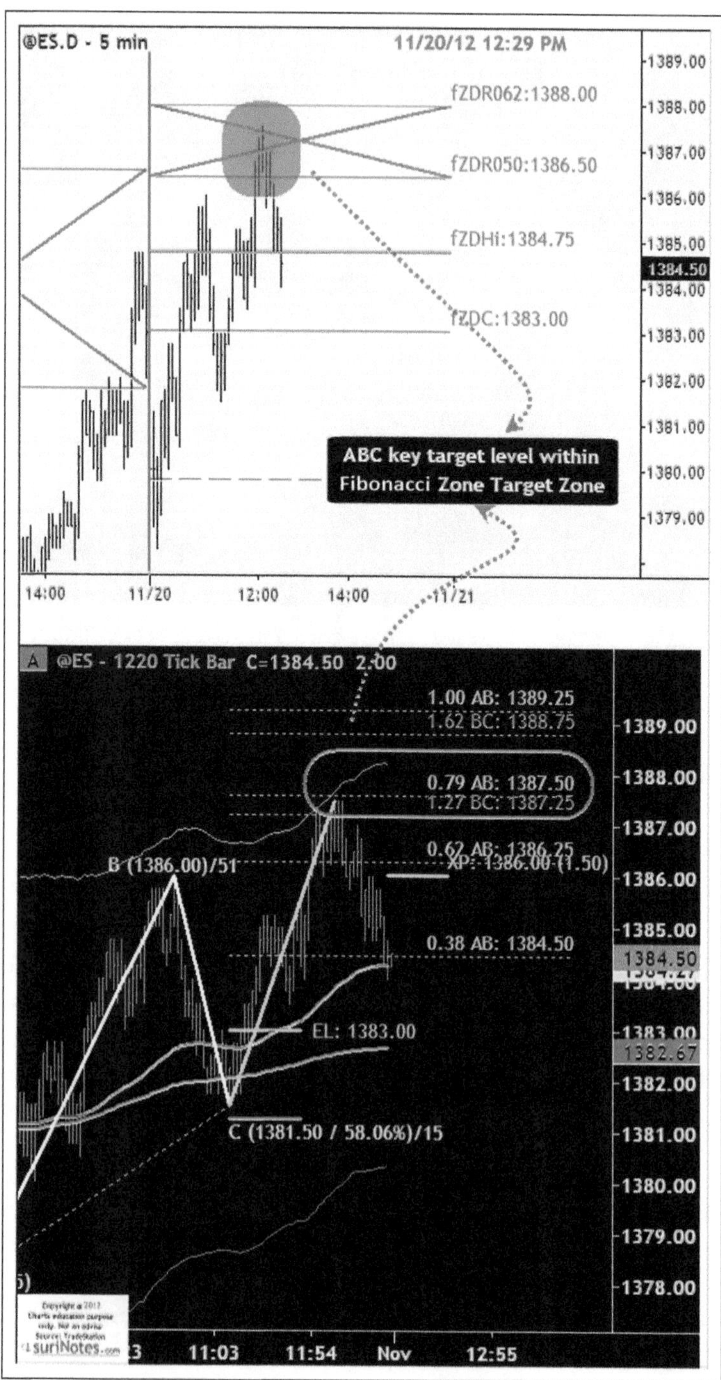

FIGURE A.10 Trade 1: Trade Chart Showing Entry and Exits

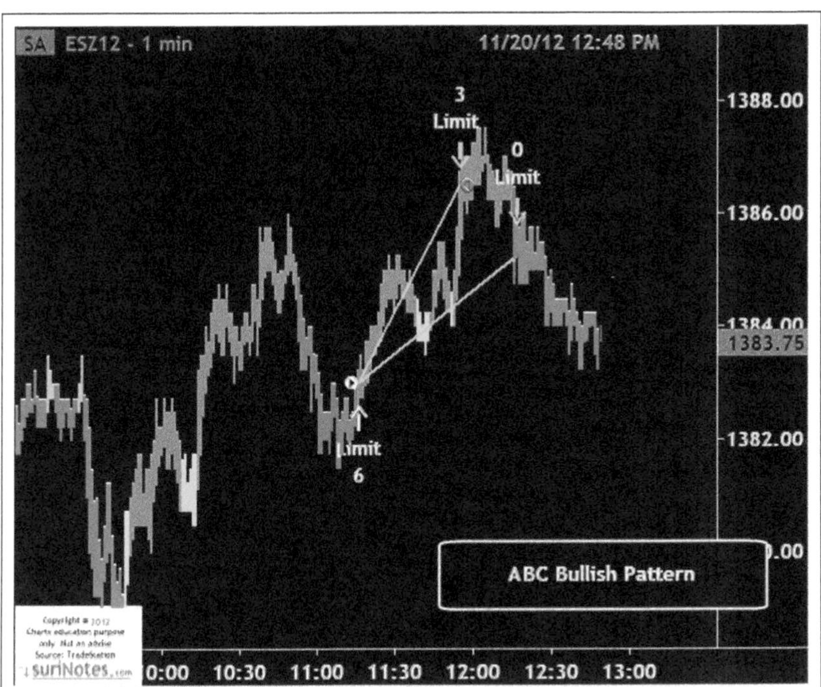

Trade Entry

I waited for another 90 minutes for ES to complete its double bottom setup (still in ABC with C at 94 percent). Around 11:30 A.M. I started seeing GREEN SuperBars signaling a potential reversal and completion of double bottom and ABC bullish trade setup. I entered a long trade into ABC pattern at 1,374.5 with a stop at 1,372.5 (below C) shown in Figure A.13, Trade 2. Targets were placed at 1,374.5 (+2), 1,376.5 (+4), and 1,378 (+5.5). Stop was set at –2 points at 1,372.5.

Trade Exits

Within 90 minutes all my targets were hit (Figure A.14, Trade 2) as I trailed the stops (Figure A.15, Trade 2). Patience and discipline do pay off and have great merit in trading.

FIGURE A.11 Trade 2: Developing ABC Bullish Pattern

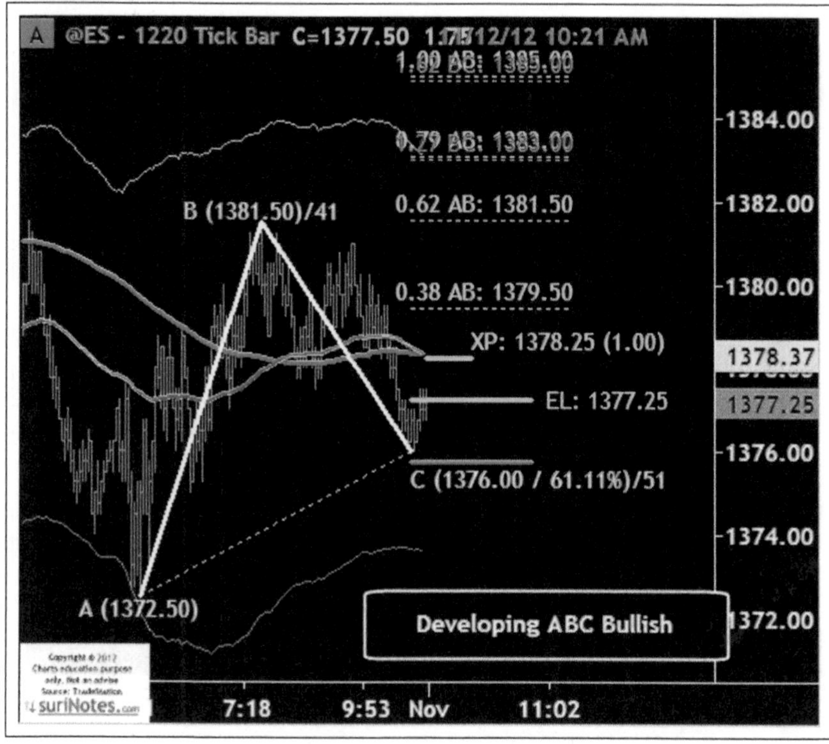

FIGURE A.12 Trade 2: ABC Pattern with SuperBars and Double Bottom Formation

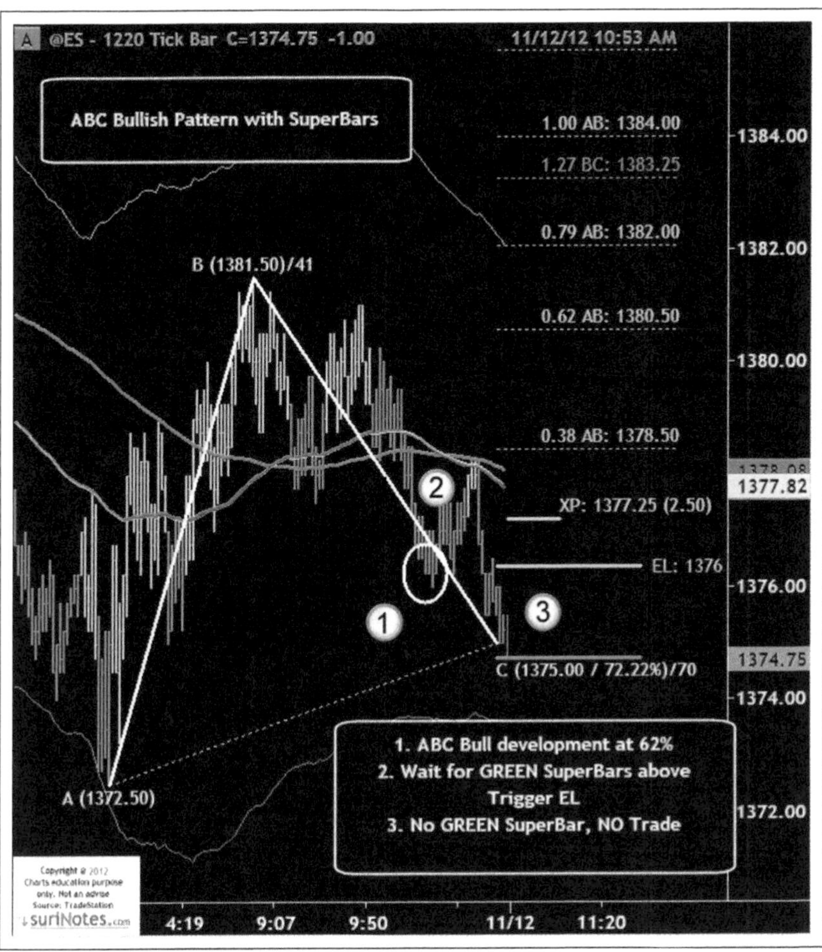

FIGURE A.13 Trade 2: ABC/Double Bottom Trade Entry with Stop and Targets

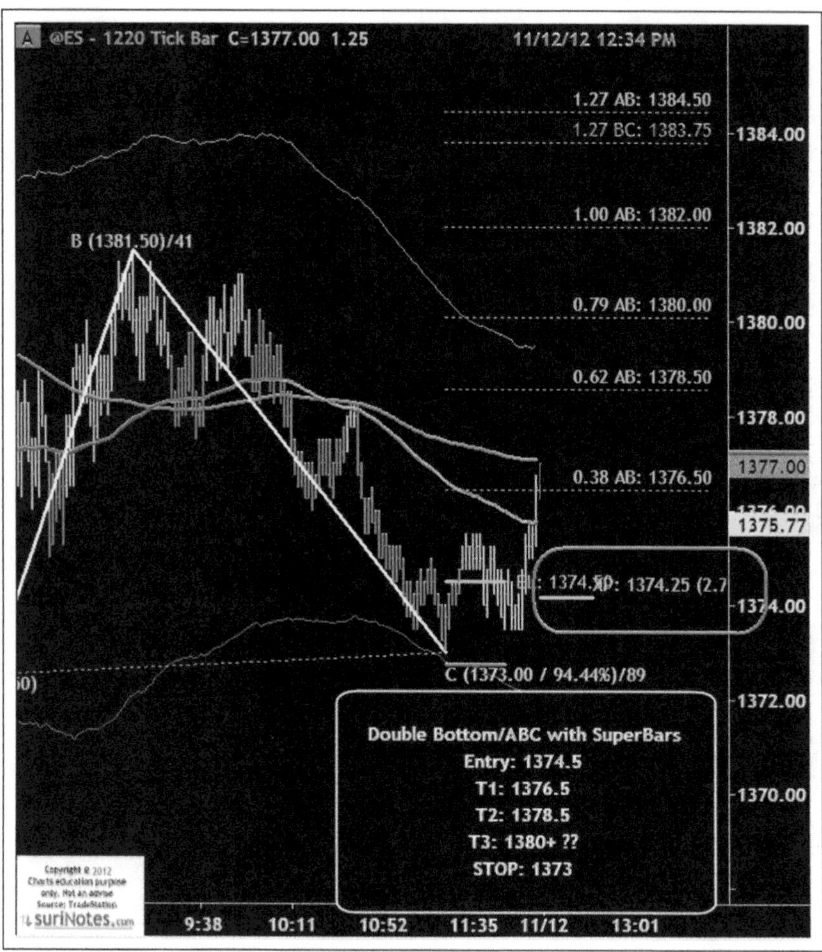

FIGURE A.14 Trade 2: Trade Entry, Targets

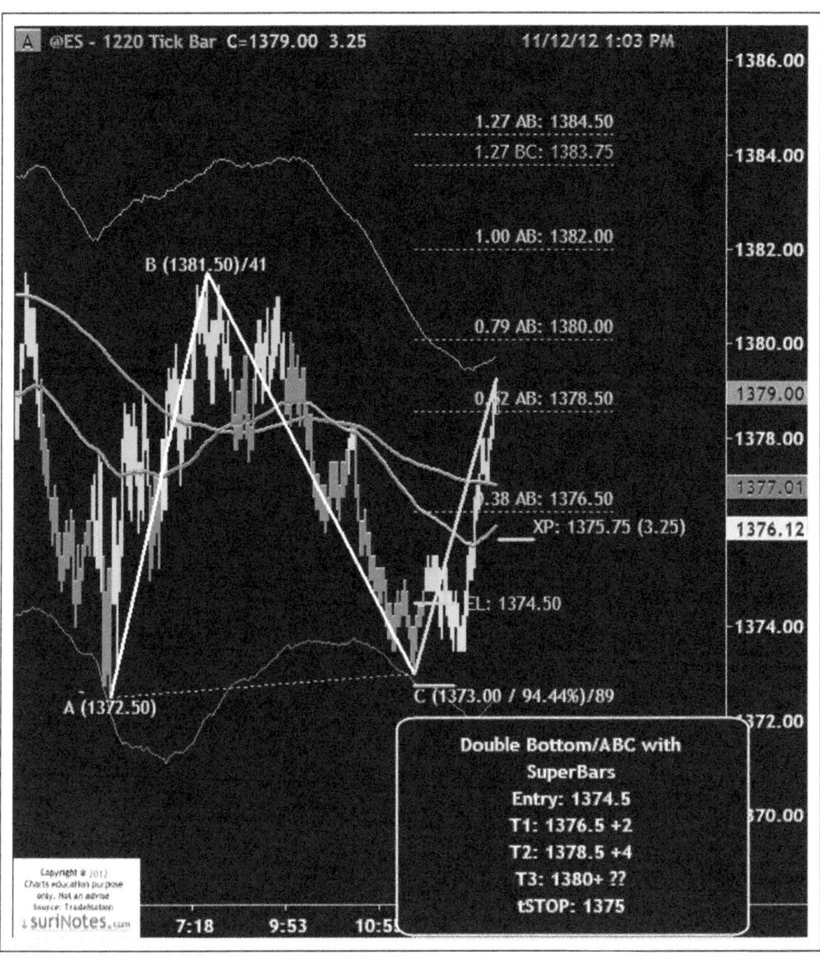

FIGURE A.15 Trade 2: Trade Chart with Entry and Exits

About the Video

This book is accompanied by a 70-minute online video course. To access this content, go to www.wiley.com/go/wayoftrade and follow the instructions on the page. Your unique access code is located on the back of the card provided at the back of the book. If you purchased an e-book, you can find instructions for verifying your purchase and obtaining an access code at the end of the book.

The *Way of the Trade* video provides a simple and concise overview of many of the key concepts found in the book, complete with animation, additional detailed charts, and a trade sequence example. The video should be used in conjunction with the book as a reference to further galvanize your understanding of key topics. Each video scene takes on several concepts covered in the book in a simple and straightforward approach so the reader can effectively speed up their progress in the development of their skill sets, integration of the methods, and their application in the markets.

Video	**Text Chapter and Topic**
Video 1: Thunder and Tumbleweeds	Chapter 1, "Enter the Thunder and Tumbleweeds Market Landscape"
Video 2: The Market Trading Climates	Chapter 1, "Defining Market Landscapes, Climates, and Terrains"
Video 3: The 5 Invisible Laws of the Market	Chapter 1, "The Five Laws of the Marketplace"
Video 4: The Katana	Chapter 4
Video 5: Pup and Mini Pup	Chapter 4, "The Two Most Important Price Patterns: Pups and Mini Pups"
Video 6: Perfect Storms	Chapter 5
Video 7: The Morning Ritual	Chapter 3, "The Morning Ritual"
Video 8: The Market Trading Day	Chapter 3, "Step-by-Step Ritual Routine by Time"
Video 9: Engagement Trade Sequence	Chapter 9, "The Complete Trade Sequence"
Video 10: Example Trade Sequence	Chapter 9, "Trade Sequence"
Video 11: Portfolio Trading	Chapter 10
Video 12: Manifest Your Evolution	Chapter 12, "Broken Spirits' Blowout"

About the Author

Jea Yu is a co-founder of Undergroundtrader.com, the premiere virtual trading desk and trader education site, which has served over 10,000 traders, fund managers, and investors worldwide since 1998. His brainchild was voted *Forbes* Best of the Web for four consecutive years under the active trader category. Mr. Yu has published three bestsellers through Wiley Trading and McGraw-Hill: *Trading Full Circle* (2010; German translation 2011), *Undergroundtrader.com Guide to Electronic Trading* (2001), and *Secrets of the Undergroundtrader* (2003), as well as four popular trading videos entitled "Swing Trading Secrets," "Short Term Profit Hunter," "Level 2 Trading Warfare," and "Beating the Bear" published through Wiley Trading and Traders Library. He has been a featured speaker all over the country at various expos and seminars and has enjoyed a standing-room-only reception in the largest convention halls from New York to Las Vegas. He is also a featured speaker for the prestigious International Speakers Bureau. Mr. Yu's energetic presentation style, along with his obvious mastery of the materials being covered makes him an audience favorite. He has been quoted and featured in *USA Today*, the *Wall Street Journal*, *Traders Magazine*, and the *Financial Times*. Mr. Yu has been a contributing writer for Benzinga.com, TradingMarkets.com, Trade2Win.com, and *Active Trader Magazine*, with over 60 articles to his credit.

With over 15 years of market experience through bull mania and bear manic markets, Mr. Yu has developed a complete proprietary synergistic trading and investment methodology that incorporates multiple technical filters added to converging time frames to produce a foreshadowing element to market trends. By always having a finger on the pulse of the markets and shifting with the market paradigms, Mr. Yu has stayed on the cutting edge of strategy development. Mr. Yu's philosophy of the markets can be summed up in the following statements: "The name of the game is to find transparency before it becomes too transparent. The goal is to capture the profits before the window of opportunity shuts. When full transparency has hit the markets, the window of opportunity has closed."

Mr. Yu has a BA in liberal arts from of the University of Maryland.

Index

A

B